Surfing the World

Chris Nelson and Demi Taylor

66 99

A wave does not occupy a space. It can be waiting, hidden
on a point, at the foot of a cliff, on a specific tide or swell
direction. It may not be easy to access but the result can

Contents

Surfing the World

USA and Hawaii

Central America and the Caribbean

South America

Europe

Africa

Indian Ocean

Australia and New Zealand

The Pacific

Directory

About the book

It's 1962 and head-high waves are peeling from the outside section at Malibu through to the beach. The line-up is clogged, choked with new Velzies and Hobies, fresh from the factory. After Gidget, everyone wants a piece of the beach action. Just up the coast, in the seclusion of the Hollister Ranch, a surfer is swivelling and dropping down the face of a wave, carving an arcing bottom turn, rail buried deep, long curved fin straining under the torque. The most progressive waverider on the coastline, George Greenough, shuns the chaos of the 'best wave' in California for the glorious isolation of these kelp-filled line-ups. To him this is perfection.

We can all point to a moment when we thought we rode/found/saw that special wave. But is there such a thing as the *best* wave in the world? How easy is it to draw up a list of the top ten waves on the planet? Who would be qualified to draw up such a list? So many personal preferences go into deciding whether a break is good or not: its size, consistency, whether it is a left or a right, a coral reef or a rivermouth sandbank, tropical or cold water, barrelling or walling, busy or quiet, long or short, sharky or safe, in a stunning setting or on an urban beachfront, a voyage away or right on your doorstep… the list is endless.

So how did we come up with our top 80 waves? This book contains the collective views of a cross section of surfers from across the globe. We polled waveriders from all countries, from all generations, from groms to legends, big wave chargers to aerialists, from WCT rippers to local legends, from magazine editors to top surf photographers, and from surf travellers to ASP bigwigs. The criteria they used to draw up their list was completely down to them. What did they consider worthy of being in the list of the world's best waves? "That's a good starting point," said Randy Rarick at the end of his list. "It is actually better to pick categories, as trying to decide on the 10 best is like saying, what are the best women? Easier, if you say, what are the best blondes, or what are the best brunettes?"

"My list is in favour of rights," said legendary photographer John Callahan, "as most surfers are regular footers, and there are few places that require a wetsuit, as most surfers fantasize about warm water destinations. Also no Chopes or Peahi or Pipeline or Waimea, as those waves are beyond the ability level of the average to good surfers and are for experts only." Some are waves that define an era or a year. After all, if you've had uncrowded Lennox or Kirra at a time when surfing was at its most exciting and revolutionary, at a time when the world was changing, how do you compare that to a session at Cloudbreak or the crowded Superbank? "I've left out a few secrets," said Bob McTavish. "Also, all the places I named were great in the uncrowded eras. Now there are obviously better, less crowded waves in places like Indo, etc."

The last decade has seen the World Championship Tour shift from the beaches and crowds to what is now dubbed the 'dream tour': waves that by any criteria are among the best on the planet. "We all dreamed of pro surfing as it is today: amazing waves, big prize money, generous sponsors, surfing for life… we just hoped it would happen for us," said pro surfing pioneer Ian Cairns of his list. "In the end it is very cool that it is happening today for Kelly, Andy, Mick and Bruce, and maybe it will happen for my boys as well."

This is not a surf guide and it isn't meant to be *the* definitive list. It is the condensed perspective of the wider surf community. It is designed to give you a taste of the amazing waves that are out there, where they fit into surf history in terms of time and space, who are the people associated with these breaks and what their significance is today. We have also included 'Surfers' tales' as snapshots of surf culture that relate to the world of waveriding. We have Shaun Tomson on J-Bay, John Callahan on discovering Cloud 9, Zach Wormhoudt on what it's like to wipe out on a Mavericks' bomb and Tubesteak's insight into a day at Malibu Beach. Other 'Surfers' tales' are designed to give surfers' organizations a voice, including **Surfaid**, **Surfrider** and **Save The Waves**.

For each break featured in *Surfing the World* there is a board recommendation. For this we worked with 2006 SIMA Board Builder of the Year, **Surftech**. We wanted to liaise with shapers across the globe to find the best boards for each spot, and **Surftech**, through their extensive network of leading shapers and their huge range of boards, offer this opportunity. Duke Brouwer coordinated the selection of boards for each break, with input from the **Surftech** shapers, demonstrating the huge depth of knowledge and expertise that the brand has. For our swell and weather predictions we worked with top meteorologist Vic DeJesus at **Wavewatch**, one of the world's leading global swell prediction websites. Vic, who is also the official forecaster for *Surfer* and *Surfing* magazines, applied his experience and knowledge of global weather patterns and swell generation to each region of the globe to provide an accurate summary of when and where the surf comes from, pinpointing the best seasons to go. At each break we also worked with local legends and chargers to discover what makes their wave so special, how the breaks got their monikers and defining moments in a spot's history. Thanks to everyone for their input.

There are no secret spots on this list, although there are many great waves out there that deserve to be considered among the best. *Surfing the World* is meant to spark debate and to inspire. Draw up a list of your own top 10 and then get out there and ride them. This is the golden age of the surf trip. Your dream wave is a lot closer than you think.

About the authors

Chris grew up surfing the frigid reefs of the northeast of England, before spending 10 years interviewing surfing's heroes and anti-heroes as the editor of *Asylum* and *Freeride* – two of the UK's most influential boardsports magazines. Demi has travel in her blood – her childhood spanned four continents, she caught her first wave in '92 and has been hooked ever since. Before becoming a freelance photo-journalist, she managed the UK communications for the world's largest surf brand.

Having dreamt up the idea for *Surfing Europe* on a long road trip north, they packed in their desk jobs, packed up their van and undertook a year of 'intensive' on-the-road research – surfing, exploring and documenting the whole of Europe's Atlantic coastline. The resulting book, published by Footprint in the summer of 2004, has been critically acclaimed and hailed as the ultimate guide to surfing and travelling the continent. The pair contribute to surf media across the globe as well as national magazines and newspapers on surf and travel issues. As well as the ground-breaking *Surfing Europe*, they have authored *Surfing Britain* and *How to be a Surfer*. They currently live in Cornwall overlooking the sea. www.halfnelson.co.uk.

GREG MARTIN/FINDYOURWAVE.CO.UK

Acknowledgements

In making this a global project we have had input from surfers around the world. We'd like to say a thank you to all those who contributed their time, thoughts, tales, images, recollections as well as cast votes in the search for the world's best 80 waves. A big thank you goes to Duke Brouwer of **Surftech** for coordinating the 80 board recommendations and hitting those big, bad deadlines, as well as Vic DeJesus of **Wavewatch** for consistently being on it. Special appreciation goes to John Callahan, Garth Robinson and Willy Uribe who, as their surf travel exploits show, are always willing to go that extra mile. Many thanks also to Phil Grace, Shaun Tomson, Terry Fitzgerald, Keala Kennelly, Ian Cairns, Zach Wormhoudt, Sean Davey, David Pu'u, Bob McTavish, Marcus Sanders of *Surfline*, Jimmy O'Keefe, Buzzy Kerbox, Mick Lowe, Joel Fitzgerald, Andrew Shield, Gary Stellern,

Nev Hyman, Franck Lacaze at *TripSurf*, Mitch Varnes, CJ Hobgood, Damien Hobgood, Tubesteak, Chris Mauro of Surfer Magazine, Chris Cote of *TWS*, Óscar Tramontana Figallo and Roberto Mezza of *Olas Peru*, Mark Hartman, Shea Lopez, Bruce Savage, Dion Ahern, Rudy Palmboom, Ross Lindsay, Peter Neely of *Indo Surf & Lingo*, Jason Childs, Paul Gill, Chris Griffiths, Al MacKinnon, Jordy Smith, Luellen Smith, Tony Canadas, John McCarthy, Sam Lamiroy, Zed Layson, Jamie Scott, Michel Velasco, Orlando Pereira, Greg Gordon of crsurf.com, Jack English at **Surf Images**, Geoff Ragatz, Didier Piter, Neridah Falconer, Luciano Ferrero of *Fluir*, Alfredo Escobar of *Marejada*, Paul Kennedy, John Severson, Randy Rarick, Robert August, Javier Amezaga of *Tres60*, Ben Bourgeois, Cory Scott, Don Balch, Kyoko Nakayama, Darrick Doerner, Tom Cozad, Phil Myers, Tom Morey, Kalani Robb, Dan Malloy, Patrick Beven, Thierry Organoff, Tiago Pires, Garrett McNamara, Fred Robin, Tom Korber, Sean Holmes, Laurent Miramon, Chris Millet at Kiwi Surfer, Will Bendix at *Zigzag*, Stef Fournet, Maria de la Luz Cornejo at *Surfeando*, Lars Jacobsen of *Surfers Magazine*, Joe Moran at Pit Pilot, Richie Hopson, Mike Fordham at Huck, Greg Martin, Nick Lavery, Mickey Smith, Antonia Atha, Sarah Bentley, João Valente of *Surf Portugal*, Alex Dick-Read at *The Surfer's Path*, Christian Guevara at *Pukas*, Steve Wilkings, Hilton Dawe, Ben Selway, Alex Laurel, Kristen Pelou, Mario Dillanes Valverde and Wendy Rall at *Planeta Surf*, Andy Morrell, Karen Wilson, Gerry Degan, Tim McKenna, Amber Gourlay, Wayne Arthur, Peter MacGreggor, Sophie and Ian Coutanche, Alan van Gysen, Darren Robinson, Basilio Ruy, Thiago Machado, Philippe Chevodian and Tony Butt. We'd also like to thank Lou Niles at **SurfAid International**, William Henry at **Save the Waves**, Jim Moriarty and Matt McClain at **Surfrider Foundation International**, Giselle Firme at **Surfrider Brazil**, Joshua Berry at **Proplaya** and Andy Cummins at **SAS** for their contributions to the book and the work they continue to do on behalf of surfers worldwide.

Special thanks to Joe Traynor and Damian Tate for technical support, Bron, Maisie, Bryony and Sarah for moral support and Claire King for being a wonder brah!

Huge appreciation goes to Footprint on our third project together. They epitomize the real spirit of surf and travel – they've had their van stolen in Sydney, crashed motorbikes in Nam, caught dengue fever in Venezuela, been robbed by banditos in Costa Rica, arrested in Laos and shot in a hold-up in Mexico, all in the name of research. Special thanks go to the tireless Alan 'Silver Murpher' Murphy, for fearlessly charging this Teahupoo-like project from beginning to end, plus Angus Dawson, Rob Lunn, Sarah Sorensen, Pat Dawson, Andy Riddle, Debbie Wylde and the rest of the Footprint crew.

Sean Tully, Ventura sunrise.

DAVID PU'U

DAVID PU'U

Malibu Ranch, California, 1926. For nearly 20 years, the landowner, May Rindge, has been battling to prevent the new Pacific Coast Highway crossing her property. But the battle is all but lost. Sunlight glares off the sea and wakes are visible far out, heading towards the point. Squinting, a gnarled *ranchero* tries to decide whether they are cruising sea lions or whether his ageing eyes are playing tricks on him. He turns and spurs his horse back inland with a flurry of dust. The sea gives him the creeps.

Tom Blake and friend Sam Reid are making the long paddle out to Malibu Point. "In those days, cowboys with rifles still rode the Malibu Ranch," recalls Sam. "The gate at Las Flores Canyon had 'Forbidden – No Trespassing' on it. We paddled the mile out to the beautiful white crescent-shaped beach. It didn't have a footprint in the sand." Three-foot high sets are rolling down the point as the two arrive in the line-up. They turn to see a man on horseback disappear over a ridge. Blake paddles into a wave and pops to his feet, trimming his 10-ft redwood board out on the face. Part of the magic of riding a virgin spot is that the future is unwritten. Within a year the wave may be gone, destroyed by a new breakwater or accident of nature, or it may go on to become a defining wave of a generation. Blake is the first man to surf Malibu and, in doing so, he has discovered a place that will become not just a waveriding location, but a seminal focal point for the embryonic counter-culture during America's post-war years.

During the 1950s, surf travel really meant just two things – going to the Hawaiian islands from California, or going to California from the islands. Just pushing up the coast to discover Rincon was seen as an adventure. By the time *The Endless Summer* reached cinema screens across the world in the mid-sixties, the elements were about to combine and bring about a surf travel revolution. Boards were about to get smaller, air travel was about to become more widespread and affordable, just as the surf media was about to start unveiling exotic new waves in exotic new locations. Once surfers saw images of Mike Hynson and Robert August standing on the fringes of Cape St Francis, and heard Bruce Brown's voice-over telling them through the cinema speakers that these crazy waves were breaking "day after day", there was no going back. By the end of the decade, surfers were on the road.

"In 1970 I'd been in London and I was heading south through Europe to the Canaries. I'd made it as far as Madrid but I started to run out of money and thought I'd head home, so I just turned left." Sitting on the beach in Hossegor in the blazing sun, Aussie shaper Phil Grace alludes to an epic voyage, casually dropped into the conversation with that classic

PAUL KENNEDY

Australian understatement. "I just kept on going until I hit Singapore. Yeah, it was a great trip, overland through Persia. You know you could go from Istanbul to Delhi for US$26. I'd like to do that again someday, maybe." Phil is lost in thought for a while, maybe recalling an incident on the Afghan border or the moment he crossed the Euphrates in Iraq. A trip like this would be all but impossible these days. And not just because of the political tensions and closed borders. How many surfers today would set out on a surf trip and then just change direction, cross three continents to a completely different destination out of contact for weeks or months, without email or a laptop? But in the seventies, a whole generation was fired up on the new notion of travel. Flights were becoming cheaper and the world was suddenly a big place, ready to be explored. And, if you couldn't afford the air fare, there were always other ways. "The first time I went to Bali, all the flights over there were booked up," says Phil; "so we drove from Melbourne to Darwin and then took the crossing to Timor."

In 1972, Bob Laverty set off from Bali for the jungles of Java armed only with a map, a moped and a mate – Aussie surfer Bill Boyum. They rode the moped till they could ride no more, then they hiked along soft sand and through clawing bush until they awoke to find they had discovered the perfect wave, G-Land. They then surfed the grinding coral point with no leashes until their water and provisions ran out and they were forced to leave. By 1975, Kevin Lovett, John Giesel and Peter Troy were trekking through mosquito-infested Nias to discover the epic waves of Lagundri Bay. After Troy left to carry on his Indo exploration, the two Aussies camped on the point, enduring the harsh conditions in return for the flawless waves that rolled through. Then came Kevin Naughton and Craig Peterson's *Surfer Magazine*-sponsored dispatches from across the globe. The discoveries were coming thick and fast, and the new destinations that seemed to open up only fuelled a frenzy of ticket buying.

GREG MARTIN/FINDYOURWAVE.CO.UK

Above: Bali sunrise and stoke's already high.
Left: Tom Harper, backlit Britain.
Opposite page: Your definition of perfection depends on your perspective.

Surfers' Top 10

⊙ Bob McTavish

"I've left out a few secrets. Also, all the places I named were great in the uncrowded eras. Now there are obviously better and less crowded waves in Indo, etc."

1 Lennox Head, Aus
2 Ti-tree Bay, Noosa, Aus
3 Sunset Beach, Hawaii
4 National Park, Noosa, Aus
5 The Pass, Byron, Aus
6 The Boxes, central coast, Aus
7 Angourie, Aus
8 Snapper, Aus
9 Laniakea, Oahu, Hawaii
10 The Bommie, Byron, Aus

"I moved to Lennox Head in 1967 because it had warm water and took big swells, needed for the new short boards. I decided it was a great place to raise a family, so lived there for over 30 years. Still surf it regularly." **Bob McTavish**

⊙ Buzzy Kerbox

"Here are my top ten paddle-surfing not tow-surfing spots."

1 Maalaea, Hawaii
2 Backdoor Pipeline, Hawaii
3 Honolua Bay, Hawaii
4 Hanalei Bay, Hawaii
5 Pipeline, Hawaii
6 Kirra, Aus
7 Burleigh Heads, Aus
8 J-Bay, South Africa
9 Lances Right, Mentawais
10 Velzyland

"The Stubbies contest used to be held at Burleigh. So I surfed there many times from the late '70s to early '80s. What I like about Burleigh Heads is it's a long hollow right, allowing for deep and long tube-riding. Rabbit always had it wired. I have great memories of man-on-man heats with Shaun, Mark Richards, Michael Ho, Larry Bertlemann, Rabbit and young Tom Carroll. It was one of the best stops on the world tour back then because it was always somewhere

Below: "Velzeyland, where I learned to ride the tube." Buzzy Kerbox.

JS CALLAHAN/TROPICALPIX

you really got to show what you could do with a long hollow wave. I had a heat there with Michael Ho in like '79 that I will always remember as one of my best heats ever. There were 6-to 8-ft sets and we both got great long rides in a duel that we were separated by a mere half a point in my favour. Michael seemed to be in the right place for the first one of the set, then I would get the next one that was always a bit bigger and longer. If you asked Michael about that heat today he is still mad I beat him in that one." **Buzzy Kerbox**

⊙ Damien Hobgood

1 Monster Hole, FL
2 J-Bay, South Africa
3 Snapper, Aus
4 Teahupoo, Tahiti
5 No Kandui, Indo
6 Macaronis, Indo
7 Hossegor, France
8 Sebastian Inlet, FL
9 Deserts, Indo
10 North Point, Aus

⊙ Ben Bourgeois

1 Wrightsville Beach, North Carolina
2 Lance's Right, Indo
3 The Superbank, Aus
4 Tavarua, Fiji
5 The Caribbean
6 West coast Aus
7 Rincon, USA
8 J-Bay, South Africa
9 G-land, Indo
10 Newfoundland, Canada

"Wrightsville Beach, North Carolina – you gotta love your home break." **Ben Bourgeois**

⊙ Amber Gourlay

1 Secret spot, South Western Aus
2 Turtles, north Western Aus
3 Bingin, Indo
4 Macaronis, Indo
5 Lefties/Karate's, South Western Aus
6 Bawa, Indo
7 Asu, Indo
8 Nias, Indo
9 J-Bay, South Africa
10 Snapper, Gold Coast, Aus

⊙ Garrett McNamara

1 Jaws, Hawaii
2 Teahupoo, Tahiti
3 Honolua Bay, Hawaii
4 Pipeline, Hawaii
5 Backdoor, Hawaii
6 G-Land, Indo
7 Desert Point, Indo
8 Fiji
9 Tamai on Morea
10 Sunset Beach, USA

🌀 Joel Fitzgerald

1 North Narrabeen, Sydney, Aus
2 Mavericks, USA
3 Kirra, Aus
4 J-Bay, South Africa
5 G-Land, Indo
6 Deserts, Indo
7 Margaret's, Western Aus
8 Whale beach, Sydney, Aus
9 Teahupo'o, Tahiti
10 Cape St Francis, South Africa
11 The Bath Tub!

"If you got an extra six layers of skin and an extra lung, and the heart of a lion then Mav's is for you. I guess there is surf on the Moon because that what it feels like when you are out at Mav's. Scared the shit out of me first time I paddled out. The shore break is 15 to 20 ft and if you make that you can creep out to the line-up! By the time you get out you are beat! One wipe out and you can kiss your ass goodnight. Place is a freak of nature! Like Teahupo'o but with giant sharks instead of jet skis." **Joel Fitzgerald**

"The Bath Tub – Because it is safe and you can dream about all the perfect waves in the world and feel like a king. Put the spa on and you got jets to add the sensation of a filthy pit." **Joel Fitzgerald**

🌀 Michel Velasco

1 Riffles, Mentawais
2 Macaronis, Mentawais
3 J-Bay, South Africa
4 El Brusco, Cantabria
5 Santa Marina, Cantabria
6 Mundaka, Basque Country
7 La Santa Left, Lanzarote
8 Supertubos, Portugal
9 Hossegor, France
10 Coxos, Portugal

"El Brusco (Cantabria): this is my favourite beach break. It has two main peaks that give powerful rights and lefts. It's not a long wave, so you have to make good use of the beginning of the wave to get a hollow tube and after this start doing turns, airs, etc." **Michel Velasco**

🌀 Neridah Falconer

1 Scotts Head Point, Aus
2 Angourie Point, Aus
3 Honolua Bay, Maui
4 Restaurants, Tavarua, Fiji
5 Cloudbreak, Tavarua, Fiji
6 Hossegor, France
7 Winki pop, Victoria, Aus
8 G-Land, Indo
9 J-Bay, South Africa
10 Tamrin Bay, Mauritius

"Hossegor beach breaks, France. I just love surfing their beachies – consistent, powerful. I love their long summer days as well. The only place I miss not travelling to each year not being on tour. A very special place in my heart!" **Neridah Falconer**

🌀 Randy Rarick

1 Sunset Beach, Hawaii
2 Pipeline, Hawaii
3 Number 3's, Waikiki
4 Honolua Bay, Maui
5 J-Bay
6 Rag's Rights, Mentawais
7 G-Land
8 St Leu, Réunion
9 Europa
10 Malibu, CA

🌀 Robert August

"These waves can accommodate ALL surfers and can also produce lifetime memories!"

1 Cape St Francis (40 years ago)
2 Malibu, CA
3 Chicama, Peru
4 Lower Trestles, CA
5 Witches Rock, Costa Rica
6 San Onofre, CA
7 Playa Negra, Costa Rica
8 San Miguel, Mexico
9 Noosa Head, Aus
10 Huntington, Beach Pier

🌀 Terry Fitzgerald

"Eeewwwwwuuuuuuu... nah, too hard, the reason is simple... a lot of places I haven't visited for years, even decades, and places change, radically, over time. Perhaps a better way to answer is to list the top 10 places I love to surf(ed) in no particular order."

North Narrabeen more moods than a harem, perfect one day, unsurfable the next. But, you can ride waves there more than 80% of the time.
Jeffrey's anyplace where you can peg a three-minute ride three times rates.
Bells fat, funky, big, bad and loveable.
Winkipop Lowers is a cold water speed line where your board can be totally edged and still not have enough to blow the section.
Honolua from the back, peel off, roll-out around the bowl, pull up and duck!
Sunset west is best, fade, fade fade, run to the bottom and lean into speed, pull up, pull up and peel off, with your eyelids peeled back...
Fiti/Fare shhhhhh!
Burleigh Cove I don't know if it even works any more. I'm sure it does, before dawn, when no one is looking and the water is a shade of green rarely seen.
Namotu not perfect, sometimes it will grind, across the pass... an island in the sun.
Monobe River/Barra/Laniekea/Hanalei/Cave Rock/Bali can all tie for tenth... and all the others I have forgotten... like that right in the Mentawais, or Periscopes... oh yes, Periscopes... in the morning sun, at dead high tide...

Terry Fitzgerald is currently... surfing Narrabeen, shaping a few boards now and again (for therapy) and is working on his tan... at HB.

12 But the follow-up tales for many of these great surf exploration epics often involved a lot of time spent not surfing. The travel was as much a part of the experience as the waveriding. Whether it was overland marathons by rickety bus, journeys through towering mountain ranges, haggling in the souks of Marrakech or trekking across the barren Namib deserts, surf travel meant surfing and travelling. Time away from the sea wasn't seen as time wasted, it was all part of the journey, all part of the experience. This cultural interaction defines the difference between a traveller and a tourist. In today's era of surf camps, boat trips, swell prediction, budget airlines and instant access, have we lost the art of surf travel? Have we become mere surf tourists? Or are we doing as previous generations did, by embracing the advances that new technologies offer?

Although the pioneering seventies are looked back on as the golden age of adventure and discovery, there are new world-class surf spots being uncovered every year. What is undeniable about today is that *this* truly is the golden age of the surf 'trip'. Each year more and more surfers are travelling than ever before, some to waves that just a few years ago were out there on the cutting edge. Many surfers boast a list of stamps in their passports that would shame a touring professional, as even the most distant locations are now within reach of virtually every proficient waverider in your local line-up.

But it's not just the destinations that are changing; the waves we choose to surf are changing too. What was once considered unrideable may now be considered a classic. Take Burleigh or J-Bay. "I have surfed Jeffrey's Bay many times since that (first) day in 1968 and many things have changed," says ex-world champ Shaun Tomson. "Back then we were, in fact, riding only the very tail end. We would sit out in the line-up and watch these grinding tubes wind down for about a mile before they would get to us. We all called the spot south of us Indicators, and we all thought it was too fast and too dangerous to surf." Suddenly spots like Teahupoo are no longer just the realm of the world's top few chargers, while the elite have evolved to a point where they are pulling into warped beasts barrelling over semi-exposed rock slabs. Tow surfing has redefined what is considered big or too big to surf to such a point that Jaws sees crowds in the line-up every time it breaks. "When I first started surfing the central coast had good waves. In the mid seventies Indo was great too," says shaping legend Dick van Straalen. "But as our equipment changes, we ride waves that we thought were not rideable. Good waves for me are warm water sorts and good friends to enjoy them with."

Surfing has always had a predisposition built into its genetic make-up. It is a throwback to its Polynesian roots, passing on a trait to every new generation of waveriders. We are drawn towards the warmth, like a glacier grinding down a valley, pulled inexorably away from the freezing latitudes to the comfortable heat of the lush green that lies below, always waiting. Surfers have for decades migrated towards the sun and empty line-ups of the tropics: the original lure of 'The Islands'; the cross-border smash and grab to Baja; the adrenalin rush of exploring Central America; the European road to Morocco, and the Aussie dash to Indo. But now, with boats swarming around Macaronis and surf camps springing up on One Palm Point, there is a change taking place. It only took a few to start with, brave souls fighting the pull of the tide, but the rewards they reaped have changed the way we look at surfing.

There have always been those who have gone against the flow, like salmon swimming upstream: those early pioneers of the waves of Canada, Ireland, Scotland and Norway. The recent advances in wetsuit technology have helped this change in surfing's polarity, and have seen water time in places such as Vancouver Island stretch like neoprene from the glorious summer into one, unending season – if you don't mind surfing in the snow.

'The Search' for perfect waves used to be based around the template of 'warm water' and 'uncrowded'. Today surf travel has become more of a 'Google' with infinitely variable search criteria entered, and no hard and fast rules on what constitutes the best waves. "The best waves change as your mood changes, as your boards change, as you get older," says Dick van Straalen. "Like music, you need variety, which is the spice of life." The search will never end, as the very essence of what we are searching for changes. Like the moods of the sea. After all, in surfing nothing is set in stone. By its very definition, surfing is built on fluid foundations. Suddenly the globe looks a very different place.

Below left: Mary Osborne, cross stepping in the Seychelles.
Below right: Accommodation options range from 5 star to seeing the stars.
Opposite page: Empty perfection, Hawaii.

DAVID PU'U

PAUL KENNEDY

Surfers' tales
Save the Waves

Will Henry, executive director, Save the Waves coalition

Surf spots are valuable. To a surfer this may seem an obvious statement, but to the general public it is a fact that is frequently and widely ignored. I should know: in 2003 I watched my favourite surf spot disappear under tons of concrete blocks. What made matters all the more aggravating was that there is a widely held view that the project that buried this beautiful wave did absolutely nothing for anyone other than the contractors who built it. And why? Because it made some people rich, and the government saw no value in the surf spot that it replaced.

This was the fate of Jardim do Mar, Madeira, which was discovered by the surfing world in the mid 1990s and was considered by many to be the best big wave spot in all of Europe. A decade later it was destroyed by a government that, in our opinion, was more concerned with short-term economic gain than the long-term happiness of its local population. The culprit was a seaside promenade and seawall, sponsored by the European Union's development fund, that would bury half the spot under new concrete. The local surfers, aided by a young **Save the Waves Coalition**, tried to fight the project with everything they had. In the end they failed, victims of what many considered to be politically motivated slander and a general misconception of the sport they represented.

This was not the first wave in the world to be destroyed nor will it be the last. We all can name great surf spots that were buried by industrial progress – Killer Dana, Petacalco, La Barre, to name a few – and the forces that bury them are still at work. The main problem in most of these cases is an ignorance of the socio-economic value that surf spots represent, and a general misunderstanding of the sport itself. As surfers we know how important a quality spot is, and how many people walk away stoked after every good session. But how do we place a value on that? Not to mention what a quality wave can do to a local tourism economy. One only has to look at Puerto Escondido, Kuta Beach or the entire country of Costa Rica to see how surf can make tourism explode.

Most people do not understand the unique geologic circumstances that make a quality wave break. During our work in Madeira, many people would ask why we couldn't just surf somewhere else on the island. They didn't recognize what made the point in Jardim do Mar so special to surfers. Waves were breaking everywhere on the island, and they had no idea what the difference was between a close-out and a perfect point break, so why couldn't we just paddle out

somewhere else? We realized that this ignorance of the mechanisms of our sport could lead to more widespread surf spot destruction.

In today's world, surfing has never seen such widespread acceptance and success, and the surf industry is larger than ever. The surf apparel industry now boasts sales in excess of US$7 billion annually, surf camps have sprung up in every ocean, and surf tourism is at an all-time high. So why do we continue to lose our precious spots? The problem is that most governments do not recognize the high benefits that a good wave brings to a local population.

Save the Waves Coalition is a non-profit organization that fights to preserve the world's surfing resources, and educates the public about their value. We are partners with the **Surfrider Foundation** and many other conservation organizations, and operate on an international level to protect the rights of surfers and to make sure that we all have plenty of places to surf in the future.

Save the Waves formed in 2001 and has, to date, prevented the destruction of many surf spots worldwide. We have run successful campaigns in Ireland, Madeira, Chile and Peru, to name a few. We are committed to our work and to making maximum difference on minimal monetary investment. Beginning in 2006 we are sponsoring a market research study to show the world how important surfing is to the world's tourism economies. We have also produced a film, released in 2006, to further emphasize the point that surf spots are never to be destroyed, and that they should be protected like any other natural treasure.

In order to maintain our vigilance over the world's waves, we need your support. For more information about current endangered waves and how you might be able to help, please visit our website at www.savethewaves.org.

SEAN DAVEY

Editors' essential selection

GREENLAND

Lars Jacobsen, Surfers

1. Noosa Heads, Australia
2. Sultans, Maldives
3. Mundaka, Spain
4. Snapper Rocks, Australia
5. Teahupoo, Tahiti
6. Mentawai, Indo
7. Uluwatu, Indo
8. Pipeline, Hawaii
9. Hossegor, France
10. Nörre Vorupör, North Denmark

Franck Lacaze, Trip Surf

1. La Graviere
2. G-Land
3. Supertubes
4. Ta'apuna
5. Mundaka
6. Thurso East
7. La Pointe des Ancres
8. Coxos
9. Black Rock
10. Les Sables d'Or

John Severson, Surfer Magazine

Sunset Beach
Honolua Bay
Makaha
Maalaea
Grajagen
Ala Moana
Number Threes
Hanalei
Cottons Point
Rincon

Chris Mauro, Surfer Magazine

1. Jeffrey's Bay
2. Hazards Canyon
3. Boulders, Vancouver Island
4. Merimbula
5. Skunk Point, Channel Islands
6. Winchester Bay
7. Sunset Beach, Hawaii
8. Queens, South Shore, Hawaii
9. Buchi Purero
10. El Capitan

Joe Moran, Pit Pilot

1. Restaurants, Fiji
2. Porthleven, Cornwall
3. Newport Beach, CA
4. G-Land, Indo
5. Haleiwa, Hawaii
6. North Fistral, Cornwall
7. Soupbowl, Barbados
8. North Point, West Oz
9. Supertubes, Portugal
10. Thurso East, Scotland
11. The Superbank

João Valente, Surf Portugal

1. G-Land
2. Padang Padang
3. Ponta Pequeña (Madeira)
4. Ribeira da Janela (Madeira)
5. Lance's Left
6. Lance's Right (HT's)
7. Jocho's (North Shore)
8. Pipeline
9. Sunset Beach
10. Haleiwa

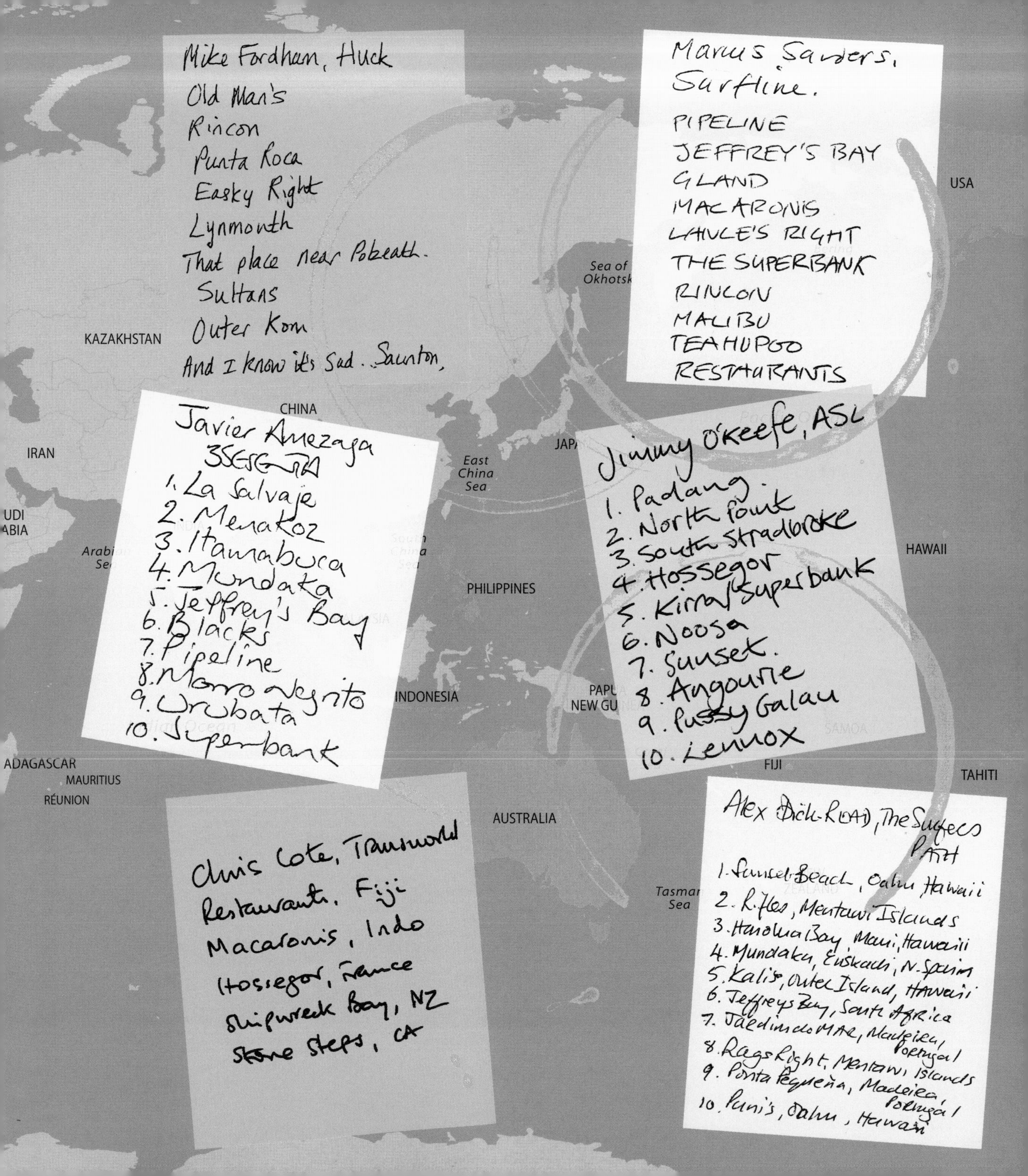

Mike Fordham, Huck
Old Man's
Rincon
Punta Roca
Easky Right
Lynmouth
That place near Polzeath.
Sultans
Outer Kom
And I know it's sad.. Saunton,
Marcus Sanders, Surfline.
PIPELINE
JEFFREY'S BAY
G-LAND
MACARONIS
LANCE'S RIGHT
THE SUPERBANK
RINCON
MALIBU
TEAHUPOO
RESTAURANTS
Javier Amezaga
3SESENTA
1. La Salvaje
2. Menakoz
3. Itamabuca
4. Mundaka
5. Jeffrey's Bay
6. Blacks
7. Pipeline
8. Morro Negrito
9. Urubata
10. Superbank
Jimmy O'Keefe, ASL
1. Padang.
2. North Point
3. South Stradbroke
4. Hossegor
5. Kirra/Superbank
6. Noosa
7. Sunset.
8. Angourie
9. Pussy Galau
10. Lennox
Chris Cote, Transworld
Restaurants, Fiji
Macaronis, Indo
Hossegor, France
Shipwreck Bay, NZ
Stone Steps, CA
Alex Dick-Read, The Surfer's Path
1. Sunset Beach, Oahu, Hawaii
2. Rifles, Mentawai Islands
3. Honolua Bay, Maui, Hawaii
4. Mundaka, Euskadi, N. Spain
5. Kalis, Outer Island, Hawaii
6. Jeffreys Bay, South Africa
7. Jardim do Mar, Madeira, Portugal
8. Rags Right, Mentawai Islands
9. Ponta Pequena, Madeira, Portugal
10. Puni's, Oahu, Hawaii
KAZAKHSTAN
CHINA
IRAN
East China Sea
USA
HAWAII
PHILIPPINES
INDONESIA
MAURITIUS
RÉUNION
AUSTRALIA
FIJI
TAHITI

16 **Waves and swell by Vic DeJesus**   WAVEWATCH

The uneven heating of the Earth's surface means that the atmosphere is in constant motion, with air moving vertically and horizontally, arranging into areas of high and low pressure. Air naturally travels from high pressure to lower pressure, but this does not occur in straight lines. The force of the Earth's spin, known as the Coriolis effect, combines with additional forces inducing a circular motion to the air. In the northern hemisphere air rotates counter-clockwise around low-pressure systems and clockwise around high-pressure systems. In the southern hemisphere this force is reversed with clockwise flow around low pressure and counter-clockwise around high-pressure areas.

The atmosphere and the oceans are also in a constant state of interaction. As winds persist, they transfer energy to the oceans through friction. This combines with three key elements to produce large waves. First, the winds are necessary. Stronger winds are associated with larger waves. The duration of these winds is also important. The longer the winds are sustained, the more time waves have to increase in size. Finally, the fetch, which is the overall area covered by a given wind, must be sufficiently large.

Large waves can build almost anywhere, but it is groundswell that surfers desire most. As large waves build, they travel outwards tangentially from the generation area where they begin to decay. Eventually, as periods lengthen out, these swells organize themselves into groups called wave trains where they begin to conserve energy. Once this occurs, energy loss is more gradual, allowing swells to travel thousands of miles before breaking on a beach or reef – hopefully near you.

The storms associated with large swells are directly related to the season. The most powerful and largest storms are fuelled by the variation in temperature between the equator and the poles. This temperature gradient is strongest during the winter months of a given hemisphere. During the summer months, select areas on the globe receive swell from tropical cyclones. Cyclones require warmer, calmer, more uniform atmospheric conditions as well as the warmer water temperatures, that characterize the tropical summer months.

Global warming

Reefs are dying, islands are disappearing under the waters of the Pacific, record numbers of hurricanes and typhoons are sweeping through the warmer regions of the world, while extremes in weather are causing landslides and flooding of coastal areas. These are some of the most obvious ways in which global warming is affecting surfers. But what is global warming? Global warming literally means a rise in the temperature of the Earth's atmosphere. The planet, surrounded by the gaseous atmosphere, is constantly warmed by radiation from the sun's rays. This solar energy enters the atmosphere, but much escapes back out to space. This layer of gases acts like a blanket, trapping some of the heat and keeping the planet warm. If more of these gases are added to the blanket, it is less easy for heat to escape. These so called 'greenhouse gases' include carbon dioxide, methane, nitrous oxide, ozone and CFC's (found in some aerosols).

Carbon Dioxide (CO_2) is absorbed by all plant life and converted into organic matter (leaves and wood), with oxygen produced as a by-product. However, huge swathes of our woodlands and jungles are

JACK ENGLISH/SURF IMAGES

AL MACKINNON

unrelated to global warming, yet the effects on the environment is clear in terms of weather disruption, wind patterns and the displacement of the Humbolt Current, home to a rich marine environment thriving in the cold waters off South America. This in turn impacts on fish stocks, local economies and communities.

In a joint statement by 11 national science academies to world leaders, it was estimated that "By 2100 temperatures will increase between 1.4° and 5.8°C above 1990 levels." So what can we do about it? 2005 saw the signing of the Kyoto Protocol as 35 industrial counties, including member states of the EU, agreed to cut their carbon dioxide emissions and set targets for the maximum pollution that countries can produce, in order to limit the amount of greenhouse gases we pump into the atmosphere. Kyoto is a good start. But not everyone understands that this is a global problem that relies on everyone taking a global interest, so some countries failed to sign the agreement. According to **Friends of the Earth**, with just 5% of the population, the USA accounts for a staggering 25% of all the world's carbon emissions. The USA, the world's biggest polluter, did not sign up. Nor did Australia. In order to safeguard the planet, we need to lobby our governments to ensure that the real facts, backed up by science are getting through, and that they are representing our wishes and really acting in our best interests, not just in the 'national' interest. On a personal basis we can all try to manage our own carbon emissions. Look at things like not leaving appliances on standby, turning the thermostat down by 1°C, recycling, using energy-saving bulbs, considering the number of miles our food and other consumables have travelled to reach us. We can try using our cars less and our fuel more efficiently, flying less, as well as looking at offsetting are carbon emissions for those irresistible trips away. There are now various organizations springing up that can help you do this, although this is obviously not a quick-fix solution. According to climatecare.org, a tree can absorb around half a tonne of carbon dioxide over its lifetime. But it's not just about planting trees, many organizations also offer climate-friendly technology as well.

being destroyed on a daily basis. The cutting down of rainforests has a two-fold effect on the levels of greenhouse gases. The loss of carbon fixing plants means less CO_2 is absorbed from the atmosphere each year. Also, many rainforests are cleared by 'slash and burn' tactics. Here the organic material is burnt, releasing the carbon back into the atmosphere as carbon dioxide. Large quantities of CO_2 are also released into the atmosphere by burning coal, oil, gas and other fossil fuels (so called as they are the fossilized remains of plants). This unlocks carbon that has remained trapped below ground for millions of years and happens every time you turn the key in your car, board an aircraft or even switch on a light.

The earth is getting hotter. Between 2005 and 2006, Canada experienced its warmest winter on record, with temperature rises between 3.9° and 8°C. This increase in global temperatures causes sea levels to rise. Warmer water expands and this increased volume is added to by melt water from shrinking glaciers and sea ice. We've seen the obvious effects of the rising water levels in the islands of Tuvalu in the Pacific. This archipelago is slowly being submerged, creating a whole population of environmental refugees. With increasing global temperatures, weather patterns and natural cycles become disrupted. This results in increasing numbers of, and more intense hurricanes, tropical storms and coastal floods. 2005 saw the worst storm season ever experienced by the USA. Other areas are affected by extreme heat and severe drought. According to Greenpeace, 2003 was the hottest summer in Europe for 500 years, resulting in a death toll of more than 15,000. Ocean currents will become disrupted if these temperature rises continue. Many scientists believe that the Gulf Stream, which warms northern Europe, is slowing down. To understand what a temperature rise of just 2° can do, just look at the effects El Niño years have on the planet. The change in ocean currents associated with these years is a natural occurrence,

Board manufacturers are going through a period of change. The collapse of the blank manufacturer Clark Foam really opened the door to both shapers and consumers, highlighting the array of new possibilities on offer in terms of materials and manufacturing techniques. An industry that has been less than kind to the environment is rethinking and redefining itself. In doing so, it is creating boards that are less toxic, ensuring that we can surf with a clear conscience. As people who enjoy and utilize all facets of the environment, we need to take the lead. "We ourselves have become a force of nature," says leading naturalist David Attenborough. "We are changing the climate and what happens next really is up to us."

For more information on how global warming is affecting us, check out **Greenpeace**, www.greenpeace.org, and **Friends of the Earth**, www.foe.org.

Above: Cold water locations have become the new frontiers in surf travel.
Opposite page: Bron Heusenstamm – air travel in South Africa.

Surfers' tales
Surfrider Foundation Jim Moriarty, Executive Director, Surfrider Foundation

No one gets up in the morning and wants to pick up trash on the beach, test ocean water or fight to save something. People would rather get up in the morning and take a walk on the beach, go surfing or hang out with their friends.

A group of people do, however, spend their time doing beach clean-ups, orchestrating an environmental campaign or raising money to buy supplies for a beach programme. They do this because they were pushed over the line that separates inaction and action.

Surfrider Foundation is made up of people willing to act to protect something they hold dear: oceans, waves and beaches. We're not some abstract group in some far-off land. We're local. We live where you live. We're people who work to protect our favourite spot or the beach we love going to on summer weekends. We're made up of tens of thousands of emissaries all over the globe who refuse to accept the destruction of our oceans, waves and beaches. We're people who think the environment the next generation will have should be like the one we had, and we're willing to spend our time, energy and money to make that happen.

Who is **Surfrider Foundation**? If you read the above and see yourself as such a person then **Surfrider Foundation** is you – beach enthusiasts, surfers, soccer moms, boys, girls and seniors.

"75% of Americans will live within 80 miles of the coast by 2025"
Source: Pew Oceans Commissions Report

This isn't an 'American phenomenon', it's happening all over the globe. People are moving to the coast because they want some part of their lives to be interacting with oceans, waves and beaches.

"By 2030, one half of the buildings in the US will have been built after 2000"
Source: Brookings Institute

This second statistic makes logical sense following the first. A lot of people are moving to coastal regions and so there will be (and is) a whole lot of building and construction along the coastlines of the world.

DAVID PU'U

Surfrider Foundation Top 10 surfing beaches Matt McClain

10 New Smyrna Inlet, FL → New Smyrna typifies the laid-back sort of beach town most vacationers dream about. It captures both northeast and southeast swell directions. Most of the action takes place adjacent to the Inlet's jetty.

✖ **The Bad** – Local surfers can be grumpy at times.
☻ **The Rad** – The on-beach parking puts you mere steps from the action.

9 San Onofre, CA → With its grass shacks, broad sandy beach, gentle surf and the ever-present smell of barbeques, San Onofre State Beach is quintessential California surfing at its best.

✖ **The Bad** – On a weekend, the park fills up to capacity quickly. Make sure to get there early or be prepared to wait... and wait... and wait.
☻ **The Rad** – No one has ever had a bad day at San Onofre. Ever.

8 Cape Hatteras, NC → North Carolina's Outer Banks have long been a hotbed of eastern surfing. Located on a prominent peninsula towards the middle-to-southern end of the Outer Banks, Cape Hattaras picks up swells from nearly every direction.

✖ **The Bad** – Cold in the winter.
☻ **The Rad** – Warm in the summer.

7 Rincon, CA → Unquestionably the best point break in the United States. So close to perfection are the long and incredibly well shaped right-hand point waves, the spot is nicknamed 'The Queen of the Coast.'

✖ **The Bad** – Steer clear of this spot for a good few days after a rainstorm, when run-off from the nearby rivermouth lowers the water quality to unhealthy levels.
☻ **The Rad** – Proximity to Santa Barbara's restaurants and cosy B&Bs, make Rincon a stellar weekend surf getaway with a loved one.

6 Sunset Beach, HI → Sunset Beach on Oahu's North Shore has long been the ultimate proving grounds for surfers.

✖ **The Bad** – Strong rip currents even make swimming a risky venture when the surf is up.
☻ **The Rad** – Head to nearby Ehukai Beach Park for a less risky surfing experience.

5 Steamer Lane, CA → Home to a number of surfing's elite, including Shawn Baron, Jason Collins and Flea Virostko.

✖ **The Bad** – Just getting to the surf may prove nearly as treacherous as the waves themselves. Less experienced surfers may want to paddle out at Cowells, inside the cove.

☻ **The Rad** – Santa Cruz's Surfing Museum, located on the bluff right above the break.

4 Sebastian Inlet, FL → Notoriously more fickle than New Smyrna Inlet, but unquestionably the most sought-after wave along the Atlantic Seaboard. The reason? When it's working, Sebastian Inlet is a machine.

✖ **The Bad** – Keep an ever-watchful eye out for the man in the grey suit (sharks!).
☻ **The Rad** – With the amount of photographers on the beach, a good wave just might get you into the magazines.

3 Maria's, PR → Located near the coastal town of Rincon on the northwest corner of Puerto Rico, Maria's could possibly be America's best-kept surfing secret.

✖ **The Bad** – Watch your feet. If the reef doesn't get you, the urchins will!
☻ **The Rad** – The restaurant/bar on the beach above the break serves the world's best shrimp tacos.

2 Malibu, CA → Perhaps no other wave in the world has played as pivotal a role in shaping surfing's culture. 'The Bu' is still considered to be one of the country's premier surf breaks.

✖ **The Bad** – Ultra-crowded. Be prepared to paddle-battle for waves.
☻ **The Rad** – "Hey, was that David Duchoveny who just dropped in on Tom Hanks?"

1 Pipeline, HI → If there is one consummate surfing wave, this must be it. Each winter, professional surfers from around the world make a pilgrimage to the North Shore of Oahu to surf Pipeline.

✖ **The Bad** – Unless your first name is Kelly and your last name is Slater, don't even think about paddling out.
☻ **The Rad** – Make your way to the North Shore in November and watch the world's best surfers take on the world's best wave in the annual Pipe Masters contest.

The Surfrider Foundation is a grassroots nonprofit environmental organization dedicated to protecting and preserving our world's oceans, waves and beaches. Founded in 1984 by a handful of visionary surfers, the Surfrider Foundation now maintains over 50,000 members and 64 chapters throughout the United States and Puerto Rico, as well as international affiliates in Australia, Europe, Japan and Brazil. For more information visit us online at www.surfrider.org.

Surfers' tales

Mickey Dora – Da Cat that walked by himself Chris Nelson

It is a time when all animals are wild. The dog is wild, the horse is wild and man and woman are wild. One by one, the animals are tricked into becoming the servants of man. All but one. There is one animal that is too wise, too wired to be tricked. Too clever to lose his freedom. "I am the cat that walks by himself and all places are alike to me."

The first thing I notice is a wave of nausea. Peripheral vision bleaches from total blackness through a spectrum of pain until a piercing harsh white fills my field of view. As my brain is slowly becoming accustomed to the blinding light, a beaverskin hat enters stage left and blocks out the sun, allowing me to focus on the face peering down at me. The huge fur hat is balanced by a grey beard. Tanned, aged skin is wrinkled in the glare and his young eyes are edged with concern. "You OK?" he says kneeling. "Missed my fucking landing," I reply, as I prop myself up on my elbows. Dora unclips and sits down. "Take your time." In the three days we'd been in the Alps, there had been a lot of silences, interspersed by a collage of stories and thoughts. "You know I like golf? They got me to play a round with Kelly Slater. Afterwards he gave me a brand new set of Callaways. When they'd gone, I threw them in the lake." Another enigmatic story tossed into the staggeringly beautiful Alpine valley below. A challenge – interpret it as you will. If you get it, good. If you don't – I don't give a damn.

Mickey Dora died on 3 January 2002. His death sent shock waves through line-ups around the world. He was surfing's greatest enigma. Fact. It is one of the few certainties of Mickey's life. Even in a lifestyle where many of society's fringe characters took refuge, Dora was unique. There was no label you could hang on him, no box that he would fit neatly into. He wasn't a tortured soul burnt out by drugs, he wasn't the arrogant bad boy fuelled by alcohol and success. Dora was amorphous. Dora was a mirage. Ask 10 people who knew him and you'll get 10 different opinions on what Dora was about. Like Chinese whispers, stories have mutated and changed as they have been passed on through surfing folklore. Fact and fiction blurred. "I never saw him surf in Nazi regalia like they say, but I remember him playing tennis in a Nazi uniform once…"

A grainy, 16-mm image fires up on the screen, scratches and hairs dancing around the bleached oceanscape. A young Dora appears on a waist-high wave, lays down a drop knee turn and sidesteps up to the nose. The line-up is peppered with myriad boards. Dora takes two steps

back, sideslips the board around a kook paddling out. Two surfers drop in on him. He grabs the shorts of the first one and yanks him backwards off the board. The other he dispatches with a single shove. Dora wasn't just the best surfer at Malibu, Dora was the landlord. "I remember once he pulled me off a wave," says surf filmmaker Ira Opper. "Those icy fingers grabbed me from behind and yanked me off my board. I have to say I have never dropped in on a surfer since for fear of those icy fingers." Mickey grew up surfing empty Malibu. To anyone else the place was overrun – to him the place was over. As Dora put it, "I'm not aggressive, I'm vicious. The way I see it, if I catch a wave, it's mine."

Miklos Szandor Dora II was born in Budapest, Hungary in 1935. His stepfather was Gard Chapin, a renowned surfer of the '30s and '40s. Chapin died under mysterious circumstances, which Dora always claimed had sinister undertones. Gard was renowned for his arrogance and attitude, something that Dora took to a new level. The burgeoning Malibu scene was an insatiable cyclone, sucking people into the surfing world and Mickey was the supercharged epicentre around which it revolved. Dora dominated the line-ups with an aggression that was legendary and a grace that was unique. Mickey was more than the dominant surfer, he was the guy everyone wanted to hang with, the one all the girls wanted to date. But Dora wasn't interested in being the top of the social tree. As the fame of a choking Malibu hit its peak, Dora was already sick of it. To Dora, these people, these parasites, were killing his spot.

One of Dora's few friends from that era was John Millius, legendary filmmaker, writer of *Apocalypse Now* and director of *Big Wednesday*. He recalls, "Mickey was comfortable with the beatniks of the '50s Malibu era, but when surfing became really popular it brought in a whole new crowd of people who he considered bordered on Neanderthal. There were only a few of us who he considered were up to talking to. He was extremely well read. We spent months discussing the Kennedy assassination when it happened. We discussed the Vietnam War, not like people did in a later era. Mickey was asking 'Why are we really going to war? Who's making money off this?' Conspiracies, you know, years before its time."

Bang. "Sold!" One bottle of Cognac. Just another lot. Just another auction. This time it's not another poor victim of the harsh Reagan economic climate. Going under the hammer are the accumulated belongings of one Miklos Dora – Da Cat, Mickey Mouse, the Black

Knight: small time scam artist and living legend. Next lot: a wooden snuff box; a Nepalese shield; a silk sleeping bag; a leather SS trenchcoat; a tailor-made tuxedo. But this is no ordinary auction crowd. The cognac is immediately popped open by its new owner, who mutters a toast under his breath, takes a long hit and hands it to the left. The next raises the bottle, nods his head, drinks and passes it on. New lot: two rolls of exposed cinefilm. Bang. Sold. One bid. An open pact. Personal stuff will be bought and sent back to Mickey. A guy that most of them have never met, never known. What was it that inspired men to drive out to this auction house, to look in awe at the belongings on display? What makes men want to own just a small piece of a guy who would have looked them in the face and told them to "Fuck off back to the Valley"?

Derek Hynd waxes lyrical over the image of a surfer making a stuttering take off at J-Bay. He trims along the feathering wave, lost in time, transfixed in the moment. One truly magical wave in the classic soul surfing film *Litmus*. Is this as much as the new generation of surfers know about Mickey Dora? Surfing's first superstar and first anti-hero; the guy who dropped his shorts as a 'Fuck You' salute to the judges in his last surf contest. The first voice to cry out against the rampant commercialization of modern surfing, while at the same time holding out his hand for the paycheck. Greg Noll may have been christened Da Bull for his big wave charging, but Dora was Da Cat. A name awarded for his grace and style on the water. But the moniker was more apt than anyone knew at the time. Like a cat, Dora was a loner. Sometimes friendly, often charming, occasionally vulnerable, introverted, defensive, wary of new faces. He could disappear and establish a new territory. People were drawn to Da Cat – to the legend, the enigma. Even though he had been known to bite the hand that fed him, there were always board sponsors waiting to add the aura of Dora to their rider list. He was quick to engage the services of his attorney if he felt his image had been used without his strict authorization, yet was happy to take paid bit parts in the Hollywood teen surf flicks that were murdering the scene. But to the average surfer, it appeared that Dora never sold out. His faults were generally overlooked as he railed against what he saw as big business making a buck off the back of the ordinary surfer. He loved to say 'Thank God for a few free waves.' But with Dora, the free waves were probably courtesy of some other sucker's dollars.

There it was, first-hand. The stuff of legends. Dora the consummate scammer. At the counter in the board hire shop, Mickey leant forward and quietly asked to see the manager. I watched him produce a stack of business cards from his pocket, snap one off the top like a poker dealer and hand it over. "I'm Harry Hodge, head of Quiksilver. I'd like to borrow some equipment for the afternoon." The manager looked down at the card, up at Dora. "Certainly Mr Hodge, come this way." It wasn't the scam that was amazing. It was the grace with which it was carried out. It was pure Da Cat style.

"Don't I know you?" asks the French surfer. "I don't think so," replies the American. The local pushes the point. "What's your name?" "Mickey – Mickey Dorado." Maybe the choice of name was just a spur of the moment thing or maybe he liked the link with another legend. Eldorado, mythical city of gold. Dora's life had been the antithesis of the late '50s/early '60s American work ethos. At a time when careers were all important and surfing was seen as a passing fad, many had already left the beach to move inland, get jobs and pay taxes. The Dora ethos was live now, surf now and use whatever means at your disposal to support your lifestyle. To Mickey, rules were there to be bent or broken. Not surprisingly, the authorities were not of the same opinion. Just because some bum was the most famous surfer on the planet, it didn't mean he could break laws, fuck with the system. Suddenly Mickey was on the run in Europe. The line-ups were not crowded, the lifestyle was good and, in Guéthary, he found a wave that reminded him of Sunset Beach on the North Shore of Hawaii. The burgeoning French surf community was in awe of this legend in their midst. Maybe this was a place he could call home, a place he could escape the crowds, escape his past.

If there's one thing a surfer knows, it's that the world is a place of balance – nose to tail. Swells follow flat spells. A perfect barrel followed by a thumping close-out. And Dora's close-out was due – big time. Dora fell into the hands of the establishment in September 1981 and Da Cat was caged. Grand lifestyle, grand image, grand travels followed by grand larceny. Hauled back from France by the FBI, belongings auctioned off to pay his debts. No endless search in a concrete cell. For many that would have been the end of the story. Released, drift back into obscurity, occasional sighting at a 7/11. Not for Dora this fate. A spell in Ireland's emerald waves, followed by a retreat to J-Bay where he lived on the legendary right point, before it too blew up. But it was to Guéthary that he finally 'retired'.

But Da Cat couldn't change his spots. Former *Tracks* editor and Quiksilver luminary Phil Jarratt was a close friend. "We took Mickey to the Noosa Longboard comp I organize every year in Oz. We flew

him over, paid for his hotel, everything. When we dropped him off at the hotel I said 'Listen Mickey, there's gonna be a phone in your room. I don't want you making long-distance calls on it unless you pay for them, you understand?' Well, after the contest we check Mickey out and the manager says that in addition there are a number of long-distance phone calls to be paid for. Mickey says in a shocked voice, 'I never made any calls from my room!' The manager patiently explained that every night Mickey would come down into the lobby and use the phone there. Mickey says, 'But I never used the phone in my room!'"

We're sitting on the bench overlooking the bay in Guéthary, the Mickey Dora Memorial Bench. Parliamentia is breaking at about 8 ft and there are about 30 guys in. This bench always makes me smile. It was dedicated to Mickey just after his death. Speeches were made by the mayor of the village and various surf industry luminaries about what a great character Mickey was. But, truth be told, if all surfers were like Dora, the global surf industry would never have made a cent. "You remember the story of Mickey's gems," asks Nick Gammon, artist and resident of this small Basque village. "The jewels he supposedly gathered when he was in southern Africa years ago?" It's one of the most famous Dora

legends. He appropriates a wealth of gems in Namibia and South Africa, hides them in the hubcap of an old VW kombi and buries it. Not just the hubcap, the whole damn van. He continues: "Well a friend of mine was helping to sort through Mickey's stuff after he died, and they claim they found polaroids of these jewels sitting in an old hubcap. Mickey's fortune is out there somewhere," he says with a laugh.

Following on from his success with *Big Wednesday*, director John Millius wrote *Apocalypse Now*, the classic Vietnam war film-noir in which Brando's Colonel Kurtz character draws in Martin Sheen to hear his final

thoughts on the world, his philosophy on life and its cruelty. For Dora there was to be no 'Heart of Darkness' epiphany. No last 'Confessions of Mickey Dora' articles or words from the wise. Mickey didn't want to tell his story, or sell his story. As Millius himself said, "When the day came to an end, he walked away from the beach. One thing Mickey taught me as an ethos was that at the end of the day, you just walk away."

That was Dora. That was the Cat that walked by himself.

USA and Hawaii

Dan Malloy, Supertubes, Ventura, CA.

DAVID PUU

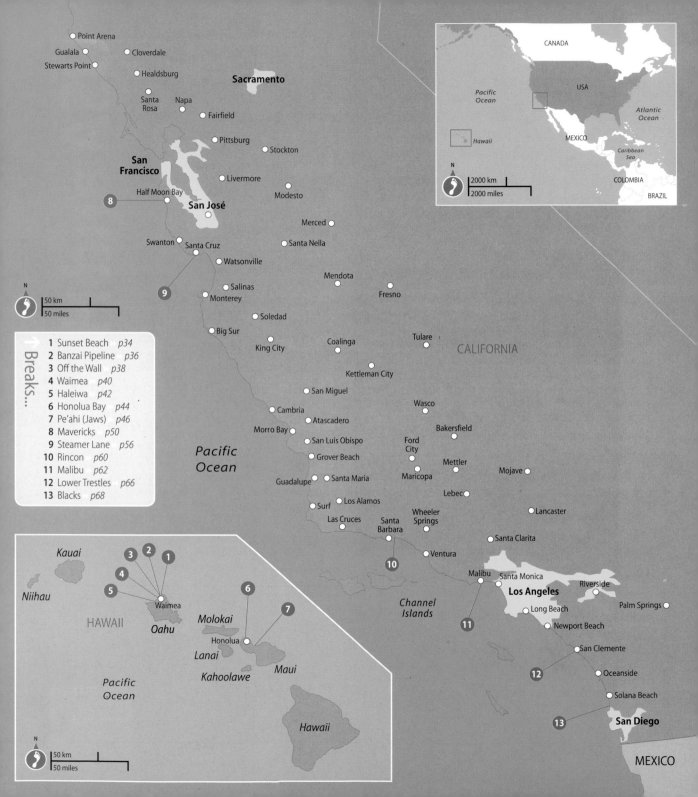

Point Arena
Gualala
Stewarts Point
Cloverdale
Healdsburg
Sacramento
Santa Rosa
Napa
Fairfield
Pittsburg
Stockton
San Francisco
Livermore
Modesto
Half Moon Bay
8
San José
Merced
Swanton
Santa Cruz
Santa Nella
9
Watsonville
Mendota
Salinas
Monterey
Fresno
Soledad
Big Sur
Tulare
CALIFORNIA
King City
Coalinga
Kettleman City
San Miguel
Wasco
Cambria
Atascadero
Bakersfield
Morro Bay
San Luis Obispo
Ford City
Mettler
Grover Beach
Maricopa
Mojave
Pacific Ocean
Guadalupe
Santa Maria
Lebec
Surf
Los Alamos
Lancaster
Las Cruces
Wheeler Springs
Santa Barbara
Santa Clarita
10
Ventura
Malibu
Santa Monica
Channel Islands
Los Angeles
Riverside
Long Beach
Palm Springs
11
Newport Beach
San Clemente
12
Oceanside
Solana Beach
13
San Diego

MEXICO

N
50 km
50 miles

Kauai
3 **2** **1**
4
Niihau
5
Molokai
6
Waimea
HAWAII
Oahu
Lanai
7
Honolulu
Kahoolawe
Maui
Pacific Ocean
Hawaii

N
50 km
50 miles

CANADA
Pacific Ocean
USA
Atlantic Ocean
MEXICO
Caribbean Sea
Hawaii
N
2000 km
2000 miles
COLOMBIA
BRAZIL

Surfers have always been a misunderstood bunch. Nowhere is this more apparent than Hawaii, the spiritual home of surfing. Shortly after Captain Cook 'discovered' the islands in 1778 (and was killed there on Valentine's Day the following year), the missionaries arrived. For centuries the 'Sport of Kings' had played a central role in Hawaiian culture but the missionaries feared the liberalism of the surfer and soon put paid to this. At the start of the 20th century surfing re-emerged in the islands and began to gain a foothold on the US mainland. Hawaiian customs and waves provided a reference point for the booming surf culture of 1950s California, as well as a place for the top surfers to test themselves on the most feared and respected waves on the planet. The boom in surf culture created a new generation of misunderstood rebels without a cause – Dora, Tubesteak and crew – only this time, instead of missionaries, Hollywood turned up and simply added fuel to the fire of the surf revolution, in full Technicolour. And while youth culture was born, the surfing counterculture was submerged under the sheer weight of numbers.

From the pioneering influences of Duke Kahanamoku and Tom Blake through to the modern-day dual between Kelly Slater and Andy Irons, there has been a somewhat symbiotic relationship between the islands and the mainland. While big wave surfing was redefined on the North Shore of Oahu at breaks such as Sunset and Waimea, performance surfing and boardriding equipment was refined on the reeling Californian point breaks of Malibu and Rincon.

The North Shore of Oahu is home to the most concentrated stretch of world-class breaks anywhere on the planet. On Maui, the limits of big wave riding are pushed every time a new swell hits the legendary reef at Pe'ahi. For years it was thought that these monstrous waves were limited to the islands but now such mainland spots as Ghost Trees, Nelscott Reef and Mavericks rival their Hawaiian kin.

Modern surfing may have sprouted and flourished in the Golden State, but today it thrives the length and breadth of the US, from the chilly, green fringes of Washington State through to the unlikely shores of Texas and Louisiana. Professional surfers from Florida have lifted the world title while neoprene-clad New Yorkers can enjoy some early morning barrels against the stunning urban skyline. Surfing has quickly grown from misunderstood to multi-million dollar, becoming a truly 'All American' lifestyle. But surfing in the US has as many layers as an onion and lurking beneath the surface there are still the punks and the rebels who give the lifestyle its cutting edge. Money and subversion: Dora would approve.

Surfing USA and Hawaii

Although surfing was brought to the mainland from 'The Islands' by the likes of George Freeth and Duke Kahanamoku at the start of the 20th century, the 'Sport of Kings' only really exploded in the hothouse environment of the 1950s. It became more than just a sport; it was suddenly one of America's first real countercultures. Surfers were rebels. By eschewing the prevailing work ethic and establishing a beach culture they went against all the social mores of the time. Surfing became a broad church and has continued to grow through many incarnations to the point where it is now woven into the very fabric of US coastal life. "I lived in San Diego for 15 months, and the whole experience of working, living and surfing in California is amazing," says European surfer Nick Lavery. "It is so much part of life, and so civilized it's like being part of a yachting club! But don't get me wrong – I love it. Seeing three generations of a family out surfing together is great and with all the crowds, I never once sensed any violence or bad vibes in the water."

Pros & cons
USA

Pros

Incredibly long and diverse coastline.

Amazing geography with an endless assortment of points, sandy beaches, classic rivermouths and hollow reefs.

Great transport links.

World's biggest surf culture.

Excellent standard of surfing.

Cons

Many breaks are very crowded with a high standard of surfing.

Certain areas are very urban with pollution problems.

Less crowded areas like Oregon and Washington have BIG sharks.

Black Ball Beaches? What is that about?

Pros & cons
Hawaii

Pros

Spiritual home of surfing.

Stunningly beautiful landscape, ocean and culture.

Some of the most famous and powerful waves on the planet.

Every big swell becomes a part of surf history.

The world's best surfers in one place for 10 weeks.

Cons

Very localized line-ups.

Dangerous and crowded waves.

No real potential to explore new spots.

Expensive.

The world's best surfers in one place for 10 weeks.

Opposite page: Sean Tully, Thornehill Broome Beach, right on Coast Highway 1, north of Malibu.

Surfing in the US has now split into many sub-groups. The recent explosion in retro boards is just part of the continuing evolution and metamorphosis of the surfing lifestyle, from those who see it as an artistic expression through to those who see it purely as a sport. In a country of 291 million people, Kelly Slater is a household name and Laird Hamilton fronts an American Express campaign, following in the footsteps of NFL heroes and Hollywood stars. Who would have guessed that surf brands would float on the world stock market or even be owned by global giants like Nike? But outside this mainstream flow, there are eddies of calm where surfing flourishes quietly in the clear waters off forest-fringed beaches with only 4WD access. While US surfers used to look at California and Florida as the only places to be, suddenly there is a whole coastline of surfing opportunities out there.

Tradition has it that to establish yourself as a top-flight surfer, you have to tackle the intimidating and highly competitive North Shore of Oahu. Growing up in Florida, former WCT high-flyer Shea Lopez would dream of tackling the island waves. "I remember watching surf movies with my dad when I was little, that was always the part that I was most into. Pipeline and Gerry Lopez – nastiest wave in the world and Gerry just toying with it." Everyone remembers their first – Hawaiian surf experience that is. To enter Hawaii is to enter the spiritual home of surfing, a land that has produced so many legends: The Duke, Tom Blake, Jeff Hakman, Gerry Lopez, Reno Abellira, Buttons, Eddie Aikau,

the Ho brothers, Sunny Garcia. This is a pretty daunting prospect, for any surfer – from hitting the warm air on exiting the plane to hitting the warm water, and praying you won't end in hot water. "I think being a good barrel-rider is essential to proving yourself as an elite surfer," says women's WCT surfer Keala Kennelly. "I remember my first time at Pipeline when I was 12. It was small but I was still sitting on the shoulder in awe." "The first time I saw Pipeline I was scared," says European pro Patrick Bevan. "It was the biggest thing I'd ever seen. I surfed with Kelly Slater and the other guys. That night I went to the shop to get some food and I saw all the guys again in the supermarket. I was like 'Oh, wow – this is the North Shore.' It's pretty small and everybody's there."

To those who grow up on the islands, there is a strong sense of tradition and waveriding history. But being home to such an awesome array of breaks is a double-edged sword. It brings the waves but it also brings surfers from across the globe to ride them. "I like being in Hawaii," says top international surfer Kalani Robb. "I'm lucky that it's my home because if it hadn't been I would have found a way to get to live here."

Position

North America is home to 49 of the 50 United States of America. The 'lower 48' lie neatly between Mexico to the south and Canada to the

30 north (which, make no mistake, is definitely not part of the USA). Number 49, Alaska, is the biggest state and was bought from the Russians in 1867 for 2 cents an acre. It lies to the northwest of Canada and separates the Bering Strait from the North Pacific. Continental USA is bounded by the Pacific to the west and the Gulf of Mexico to the south while the eastern seaboard is fringed by the North Atlantic. Head 3800 km to the southwest into the middle of the Pacific and you come to the tropical, volcanic archipelago of Hawaii – the land of 'Aloha' and state number 50. Formerly a British colony, the United States of America is the fourth largest country in the world.

Culture

Modern American culture has spread throughout the world in the guises of music, film, literature, fashion and art. Pioneers of consumerism, US businesses are global brand leaders in many fields. The surf culture of the '50s and '60s combined the burgeoning youth culture of California with a strong dose of Hawaiian inspiration, and now the American 'can do' ethic has transformed beachfront boardie traders into multi-million dollar worldwide phenomena, complete with huge rosters of team riders and internationally covered contests. The US has a real love of any kind of sport or competitive activity, be it baseball, American football, basketball, ice hockey or even spelling. Self-belief and optimism are important characteristics of the American psyche and when this combines with the nation's seriously competitive streak, anything is possible – even some kid from Florida taking down seven world titles.

Climates and seasons

Located in the northern hemisphere, the seasons in the US and Hawaii are the same as Europe but opposite to Australia: spring – March to May; summer – June to August; autumn – September to November; winter – December to February.

Mainland US covers a vast area so while the majority enjoys a temperate climate, there are also arid, semi-arid and even tropical regions. On the northwest coast, temperatures in Seattle range from just 4°C in January, with heavy rainfall of 130 mm, to 18°C in July with rain easing to just 18 mm. San Francisco is a lot milder with temperature ranging from around 10°C in January to an average of 15°C in July, while January sees up to 100 mm of rain and May to August has negligible downpours. On the east coast, Florida has a tropical climate, ranging from around 21°C in January to 25°C in July. January is the peak of the 'dry' season with 50 mm rain while June to October is the wettest time with more than 160 mm falling each month. To the north, New York City has a consistent year-round rainfall of around 100 mm per month and average temperatures from a freezing 0°C in January to 25°C in July.

SEAN DAVEY

◉ WAVEWATCH	Dec-Feb Winter	Mar-May Spring	Jun-Aug Summer	Sep-Nov Autumn
USA WEST COAST				
Wave size/direction	WNW 7-9'	NW 4-6'	SW/NW 3-4'	NW/SSW 5-7'
Wind force/direction	SE F2	W F3	W F3	W F2
Surfable days	20-25	15-20	15-20	20-25
Water/air temp	12/10°C	13/13°C	14/19°C	12/12°C

USA EAST COAST
This is centred on the Outer Banks, NC. This is the most consistent sizeable spot and represents a decent average of directions and weather, although swell is just above average.

Wave size/direction	ENE 3-4'	E 2-3'	ESE 1-2'	SE 3-4'
Wind force/direction	N F3	SW F2	SW F2	NE F3
Surfable days	10-15	5-10	0-5	10-15
Water/air temp	8/4°C	11/21°C	21/27°C	14/10°C

HAWAII				
Wave size/direction	NE 8-10'	NW 6-8'	SSW 2-3'	S/NW 4-6'
Wind force/direction	E F3	E F4	ENE F4	E F4
Surfable days	20-25	15-20	15-20	20-25
Water/air temp	24/24°C	25/26°C	26/26°C	26/27°C

Above: Dave Wassel, Off the Wall.
Opposite page: Dane Gudauskas hits the lip in California.

Wavewatch report by Vic DeJesus

West coast USA The west coast sees swell year round from a variety of sources and directions. Powerful north Pacific storms generate large groundswells that slam breaks from the Pacific northwest to southern California during the northern hemisphere's winter. This occurs at its peak from late autumn (fall) to early spring. The southern hemisphere serves as the primary groundswell producer from late spring to mid fall. Coastal windswells are common in the spring as are tropical cyclone swells in late summer to early fall. The fall months, from late September to early November, are generally the best months to catch the west coast going off, when the north Pacific activity increases along with late-season southern hemisphere swells and even tropical cyclone swells. During these months conditions are ideal with many days of offshore winds, which bring dry and warm weather. Springtime is usually very windy and the peak winter months often see poor conditions as many of the swell-generating systems impact on the coast.

East coast USA The east coast of the United States receives most of its recognition during the Atlantic Basin hurricane season. This reaches a peak during the late summer and early fall months of August and September when conditions are usually most favourable. The ideal set-up involves a trough of low pressure in the proximity of the east coast steering the storms northeastward and allowing swell to hit the entire coast. Unfortunately, these storms often devastate areas in the southeast and along the Gulf Coast. Typically, summer months are flat with small high-pressure swells allowing for periods of small surf. Late fall to spring sees mainly locally generated windswells associated with fronts and north-easterlies. Often these take favourable tracks into the Atlantic sending in solid groundswells with good conditions as winds turn offshore behind the trailing cold front.

Hawaii The Hawaiian Islands rest in the middle of the Pacific Ocean with 360° of open swell window. Hawaii gets hit by a variety of swell year round, although it's world famous for the consistent and extra-large north Pacific swells from November to February. During these peak winter months, massive low pressures generate huge swells that slam directly into exposed breaks, occasionally doubling or tripling in size, and 30 to 50-ft face heights are not uncommon. Many

DAVID PU'U

SEAN DAVEY

solid swells also hit the area during the fall and spring months as winter begins and ends respectively. South swell season characterizes the summer months of May to September. South-facing shores receive reasonably consistent swell from Antarctic storms passing New Zealand. Swell is much smaller during these months but overhead swells are frequent. Towards late summer, the occasional stray tropical cyclone brings periods of punchy swell.

Geography and breaks

The USA is the fourth largest country in the world, covering around 3,800,000 sq miles (6,080,000 sq km). The Californian coastline is dominated by the San Andreas Fault, where the Pacific and North American tectonic plates come together producing a huge amount of friction. This leads to the formation of the coastal ranges, a spine of mountains that run up the western seaboard of the North American continent. Occasional releases of energy take place in the form of earthquakes. The Californian coastline is predominantly rocky with an abundance of large and small bays interspersed by headlands and with large tracts of urbanized land. Along a large part of the coast access is generally excellent. However, once into Oregon and Washington, the scenery becomes lush and green and there are many forest-fringed beaches and point breaks.

The USA's Atlantic coastline is regarded as less consistent and with fewer quality spots than the Pacific. The gradually sloping continental shelf takes some of the sting out of groundswells and the weather patterns of the Atlantic don't help. There are, however, some excellent beach breaks along this coastline, from the Long Island peninsula south to the hot lowlands of Florida, and the east

coast has produced a series of world champion surfers including Freida Zamba, Kelly Slater, Lisa Anderson and CJ Hobgood.

Hawaii is a lush, green tropical island chain that is volcanic in nature; the islands are the visible tips of huge volcanoes both live and extinct. The fact that they rise from the depths of the Pacific Ocean is the reason why the waves have such power. The lack of a continental shelf means there is little to drain away the power of swells before they unload on the islands' many reefs. Fan-shaped lava outflows can produce outer reefs which may act as excellent foils for huge swells.

Health and safety

There are no specific immunizations required for travel to the US and it is a fairly safe destination in terms of potential health issues such as infectious diseases. As with most major urbanized countries, crime is an issue here but it's not all guns and gangs. Use common sense as you would anywhere else; ie, ask about potential no-go areas, be aware of your surroundings – especially at night – and don't stash your car key in your wheel arch when surfing. In Hawaii car break-ins are unfortunately prevalent so don't leave any valuables in your car, even if they are out of sight.

Sharks aside, the only other real health risks come from scorpions (if you're here to surf and don't stray into the desert, chances are you won't see one), snakes, spiders, ticks and mosquitoes. Ticks are small blood-sucking parasites that lurk in grasslands, forest and brush and can be carriers of Lyme disease (usually in late spring/summer). If you've been trekking in secluded areas of long grass, check for ticks. Mosquitoes are mostly an annoyance but can also carry the potentially life-threatening West Nile Virus. From August to November insect repellents and other measures (long trousers, long sleeves etc) are advised especially after dusk and in particular to protect against the *culex* mosquito.

Above left: Surfing in the shadow of the Golden Gate Bridge.
Above right: Don't let the warm afternoon lighting fool you – Pipeline is home to one of the most fiercely regulated line-ups and is still the benchmark against which most surfers are judged.

Surfing and the environment

Founded in the US in 1984, the Surfrider Foundation is a grassroots, non-profit, environmental organization that works to protect the oceans, waves and beaches. Here Executive Director Jim Moriarty highlights their key environmental campaigns.

 Our mission statement includes the core phrase 'protect oceans, waves and beaches' and everything we do can be pointed back to support that phrase. We have environmental programmes that span testing of ocean water all over the United States to providing 'Beachology' curriculum for kids in school.

However, the core of our organization is our campaigns. With over 60 chapters and over 50,000 members in the United States we have representation in most coastal regions. In every one of these regions there are coastal challenges. In fact at any given time we are tracking over 100 such campaigns. We segment these into the following four categories:

Beach access   These are campaigns dealing with areas where beach access has been restricted. Currently there are Beach Access campaigns in Asbury, Long Island, Monterey, Florida, Malibu, Pismo, Rincon and Washington.

Beach preservation   When the actual beach itself is challenged or may cease to exist as it was, we become involved in Beach Preservation campaigns. We have such campaigns in Monterey, Santa Cruz, Elberon, Elwha, Goleta, Port Angeles, Jersey Shore, Long Beach-NY, Maui, Ventura and Pebble Beach.

Special places   These are areas that are especially noteworthy and deserving of extraordinary preservation efforts. We have such campaigns in Gaviota Coast, Oregon, Monterey, Rincon, Trestles and Washington.

Water quality   When the ocean water itself becomes chronically poor we engage in Water Quality campaigns. Examples of these can be found in Morro Bay, National, Santa Barbara, Huntington Beach, Florida, Newport Beach, Gray's Harbor, Oregon, Ventura, Malibu and Long Beach-CA.

Help protect your local waves and beaches, join us at www.surfrider.org.

Surfing resources

The US has a wealth of surf media ranging from the printed through to the expanding number of web-based sites. *Surfer Magazine* (www.surfermag.com) kicked everything off back in 1961 when John Severson launched the magazine as a quarterly. It now has 12 issues a year. Its rival *Surfing* (www.surfingthemag.com) launched as *International Surfing Magazine* in 1964, dropped the International part

" "

I remember watching surf movies with my dad when I was little, that was always the part that I was most into. Pipeline and Gerry Lopez – nastiest wave in the world and Gerry just toying with it.

Ex-WCT high-flyer Shea Lopez

10 years later, and is now a stablemate at Primedia. Other major titles include *Transworld Surf* (www.transworldsurf.com), which publishes 12 issues a year and also the bi-monthly *Surfers Journal* (www.surfersjournal.com). There is also *Water* (www.waterzine.com), *Eastern Surf Magazine* (www.easternsurf.com), *Longboard Magazine* (www.longboardmagazine.com), *SG Magazine* for girls and Hawaii-based *Freesurf* (www.freesurfmagazine.com).

There has also been a resurgence of the surf web media after a slightly premature start. The following two sites are excellent platforms for up-to-the-minute news and features from around the globe: *Wavewatch* (www.wavewatch.com) provides a free surf forecast service as well as news and editorial; and *Surfline* (www.surfline.com) provides a surf travel, news, editorial and forecasting site.

USA & Hawaii Surfing

Sunset Beach

◈ Location:	Sunset Beach, North Shore, Oahu
◔ Break type:	Right-hand reef break
◕ Conditions:	All swells
◔ Size:	6-15 ft
◷ Length:	50-300 m
◔ Tide:	All tides
◔ Swell direction:	West through to north
◔ Wind:	Light easterly trade winds
◔ Bottom:	Reef
◔ Ability level:	Expert
◔ Best months:	Oct-Feb
◔ Access:	Off the beach at the edge of Val's Reef
◔ Hazards:	Heavy inside section, shifting peaks

Wide open spaces, roaming shifting peaks and inside hell barrels – Sunset Beach is a complex beast that few surfers ever really master. While many spots have day-to-day mood swings that come with tide and swell direction, here is a spot that changes its personality from wave to wave. This is a vast expanse of ocean where surfers spread out, eyes fixed on the approaching mountains of water – judging, guessing where that feathering peak is going and whether they are in its path. From the earliest days on the North Shore, this break has held an esteemed place at the head of surfing's high table. "The absolute true test of skill for any surfer is how he carves," says former world champion and legendary North Shore performer Shaun Tomson. "The big wall at Sunset quickly reveals how good or bad you really are."

Head out onto the Kam Highway, west past Pipe, and you will come to the curving shore and sandy point at Sunset Beach. Magical 7'6" to 8'6" pintails are waxed in a careful and considered way by owners lost in concentration. It's just a slow walk to the edge of Val's Reef and the launch over the white water into the channel to access this huge gladiatorial arena. Once in the rip the vast open break appears to the right with the hollow, grinding Inside Bowl section spinning towards you and the huge, mountain-like peaks rearing up way out the back. This is not a place for the faint-hearted and most first timers are happy just to make it back to the shore safe and sound. "My very first surf in Hawaii was way back in late 1990," says women's WCT veteran Neridah Falconer. "Sunset was 10-12 ft plus, I paddled out and sat in the channel just shitting myself and dodging the clean-up sets. It was the first time I had really seen such power and watching people actually ride down mountains. It was really beyond anything I expected to see on my very first day in Hawaii. I kissed the sand that day when I reached the beach."

Legend has it that the modern era of surfing Sunset began back in 1939 and the roll call of those who have dominated since has become a 'Who's Who' of the most respected surfers on the planet. Jeff Hakman's win at the inaugural Duke Kahanamoku Invitational started what would become the world's most prestigious contest, in its many guises, and helped him on his way to becoming the first Sunset legend.

Although Sunset looks deceptively easy from the safety of the beach, it is generally considered the world's most difficult wave. The wide channel and helpful rip make access to the line-up a relatively simple

Below: Tom Curren faces the other face of Sunset – the notorious inside section.
Opposite page: Terry Fitzgerald fades into the pocket of a Sunset Peak.

Sunset Beach Board
7'5" Brewer Sunset
Shaper: Dick Brewer
7'5" x 18¼" x 2⁵⁄₁₆"
Designed with North Shore charger, Myles Padaca, the 7'5" Sunset is the right board for those big thick peaks at Sunset Beach.
Single to double concave.
Futures fins.
ⓘ Boards by **Surftech** www.surftech.com info@surftech.com

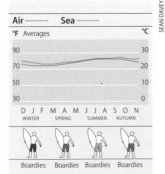

Air —— Sea ——
°F Averages °C

90 — 30
70 — 20
50 — 10
30 — 0

D J F M A M J J A S O N
WINTER SPRING SUMMER AUTUMN

Boardies Boardies Boardies Boardies

matter, but almost everything else is much more complicated. The take-off zone is vast. Jeff Hakman explains: "Things move around a lot, depending on the size and direction of the swell. It's not like Pipeline, where there's one definite take-off spot." The line-up has three distinct peaks depending on the swell direction – the West Peak, the Northwest Peak and the North Peak. But sets can swing in and hit different peaks, making the choice of take-off spot a matter of experience, local knowledge or just plain luck. "Sunset is extremely challenging and technically demanding and requires an introspective approach," says legend Shaun Tomson. "The line-up is very deceptive and it's difficult to find that perfect take-off spot. The swells zigzag towards you in a very unusual way, rearing up on the outside reefs, then backing down, moving to the right and then veering left until they finally jack up onto the reef." If through skill (or chance) you find yourself in the slot and paddling into a perfect 12-ft peak, you have to force yourself over the ledge of a moving mountain of water carrying all the raw energy and power of an uninterrupted open ocean swell. "You are sitting about a half a mile out directly in the path of fierce offshore trade winds," explains Shaun. "That makes the take-off very risky and often blind, with eyes filled with stinging spray. The wave is powerful, large, expansive and unpredictable and on a 12-15 ft north swell with a heaving, sucking inside section it's the most demanding wave that one can paddle into.

The drop is steep, the wall is long and fast allowing for creative radical surfing, and the inside section offers one of the world's most heart-stopping tubes." And it is the grinding Inside Bowl section that is the speeding, barrelling pay-off. This isn't a wave for second thoughts. "You can't halfway commit, you gotta put yourself right in the guts of it," confirms Jeff. Sunset may no longer be the epicentre of surfing, but the sun hasn't set on this legendary spot as standards are pushed to new boundaries by a new breed of high-performance chargers such as Marcus Hickman. But if you want to know how to really surf it just ask one of the best, the Sultan of Speed, Terry Fitzgerald: "West is best, fade, fade, fade, run to the bottom and lean into speed, pull up, pull up and peel off, with your eyelids peeled back...."

Locals and legends

George Downing, Peter Cole, Paul Strauch, Jeff Hakman, Barry Kanaiapuni, Owl Chapman, Terry Fitzgerald, Michael Ho, Sunny Garcia, Myles Padaca, Pancho Sullivan, Fred Patacchi, Marcus Hickman.

Nearby breaks Across the channel from Sunset is **Kammieland** reef, best in small swells. **Rocky Point** is a centre for progressive surfing on the North Shore and a popular spot with travelling pros. Further to the east are the awesome barrels of **Banzai Pipeline**. West of Sunset is the shifty reef break of **Backyards** with its unpredictable lefts and rights.

Banzai Pipeline

📍 **Location:**	West of Ehukai Beach Park, North Shore, Oahu, Hawaii
Break type:	Reef break
Conditions:	All swells
Size:	4-15 ft +
Length:	50-100 m
Tide:	All, best at mid
Swell direction:	Westerly or northwesterly
Wind:	Light easterlies
Bottom:	Lava reef
Ability level:	Advanced
Best months:	Oct-Mar
Access:	To right of break in channel
Hazards:	Shallow reef, powerful waves, aggressive, very localized line-up

There is nowhere like Pipeline. It's not just the danger rating that makes this spot so special. This is the complete wave. It has the history, reputation, location, pedigree, credibility and kudos. Although countless waves have been discovered since Pipeline was first ridden by a reluctant Phil Edwards back in 1961, no wave has managed to surpass this Hawaiian giant as the ultimate reference point for world-class surfers.

There is also no small amount of lore surrounding Pipe. Legend has it that 1960s filmmaker Bruce Brown persuaded the best surfer in the word, Phil Edwards, to surf this virgin, shallow, hollow wave that broke amazingly close to Ehukai Beach. Edwards caught one wave,

saw the reef as he skimmed along the glassy surface and came straight back in, relieved that his cinematic role had been completed. Mike Diffenderfer is said to have seen a sewer pipe being laid on the Kam Highway just behind the break, with a sign warning 'Danger – Pipeline'. With the similarities in physical appearance, the long, hollow break was thus named.

Edwards had shown that the wave was surfable; now came the challengers. Early line-ups included Tom Chamberlain, Jock Sutherland, Butch van Artsdalen, Fred Hemmings, Jeff Hakman and a young Gerry Lopez. Although many longboarders survived, the shortboard revolution brought with it a new performance era headed by 'Mr Pipeline', Gerry Lopez. His stylish and relaxed deep tube-riding reverberated around the world and images of his poised, backlit stance on his trademark red Lightning Bolt became *the* pin-up for surfers. Pipeline was now established as the greatest test in world surfing and through the '70s the influx of overseas talent saw Shaun Tomson, Mark Richards, Ian Cairns and Rabbit Bartholomew taking up the gauntlet. The Pipeline Masters has traditionally been the final event of the ASP world championship tour. It is still the most coveted trophy on the tour and has seen many a world title resolved in dramatic fashion. Highlights include Slater and Machado's trading of perfect waves in the 1995 semi-final followed by a high five in the channel, and the 2003 final with Andy Irons coming from behind in the ratings to snatch the world title from Kelly Slater.

Classic Pipe conditions occur when a clean westerly swell is channelled between the outer reefs of Log Cabins and third reef Pipe, in towards first or second reef. Here the wave feathers, peaks and fires down the shallow lava reef producing huge, hollow (predominantly left-hand) barrels that spit into the sandy channel. As the swell size increases, the line-up shifts further outside from first reef, to second reef and, in huge swells, third reef. The pack that occupies Pipe is one of the most fiercely competitive anywhere in the world. In good swells the hierarchy is strictly enforced – partly due to the high quality of the waves and the sheer number of surfers wanting to make a name for themselves in front of the assembled photographers and partly due to sheer danger. Surfers have lost their lives at Pipe on even the smallest of days and when the power and size cranks up, so does the risk factor. In December 2005, internationally celebrated big wave charger

Left: Pipeline aerial view.
Opposite page: Still the benchmark for performance surfing.

and Teahupoo local Malik Joyeux tragically died in medium sized 6-8 ft surf at Pipeline. In a northwest swell, in the right conditions, Pipeline will produce a right-hand 'Backdoor' wave. In the early days these super-hollow, grinding barrels would go unridden. Then, in the mid-seventies, the influx of talented surfers pushed standards to new heights within weeks. Today 'Backdoor' produces some of the best tube-riding displays on the planet. However, while the left offers an exit into the channel, a surfer exiting a 'Backdoor' barrel can be treated to the sight of a set of waves closing out on the shallow reef in front of them. This is where wave choice and local knowledge become invaluable.

"Pipe is the birthplace of barrel-riding," explains New Zealand pro Dion Ahern. "For the last 30 years it has been responsible for making or breaking the careers of many pros. Underwater caves, close-outs and extreme crowds still cannot deny Pipeline its right as the proving ground for riding big barrels." World title contender Keala Kennelly agrees: "The drop is super steep and you have to know how to ride the barrel. I think being a good barrel-rider is essential to proving yourself as an elite surfer." If you can make it here, you can make it anywhere.

Locals and legends
Butch van Artsdalen, Jeff Hakman, Gerry Lopez, Shaun Tomson, Ian Cairns, Rabbit, Tom Carroll, Gary Elkerton, Michael Ho, Rainos Hayes, Derek Ho, Liam McNamara, Johnny Boy Gomes, Sunny Garcia, Tamayo Perry, Pancho Sullivan, Kelly Slater, Andy Irons, Jamie O'Brien, Kalani Chapman, Makua Rothman.

Nearby breaks This is a 7-mile stretch of pure quality: to the south are Off the Wall, Rockpile and Log Cabins, to the north is the popular reef **Rocky Point**. At the head of the Northshore table sits V-land, or **Velzyland**, the hollow, barrelling, local right named after pioneering shaper Dale Velzy.

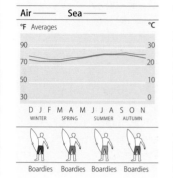

Pipeline Board		
6'10" Minami M-1		
Shaper: Glen Minami		
6'10" x 18⅜" x 3⅜"		

For the steep elevator drops and gapping tubes of the legendary Banzai Pipeline, you'll need the 6'10" Minami M-1.

Extra rocker and a tight round pintail to drive you through the deepest pits you can handle!

FCS fins.

(i) Boards by **Surftech**
www.surftech.com info@surftech.com

Air		Sea	
°F	Averages		°C
90			30
70			20
50			10
30			0
D J F	M A M	J J A	S O N
WINTER	SPRING	SUMMER	AUTUMN
Boardies	Boardies	Boardies	Boardies

SEAN DAVEY

Off the Wall

Location:	West of Backdoor, North Shore, Oahu, Hawaii
Break type:	Right-hand reef break
Conditions:	Small to medium swells
Size:	4-6 ft
Length:	50 m
Tide:	Mid tide
Swell direction:	Northwesterly
Wind:	Southeasterly
Bottom:	Rock reef with sand
Ability level:	Intermediate to advanced
Best months:	Nov-Mar
Access:	Paddle off the beach
Hazards:	Rocks, crowds

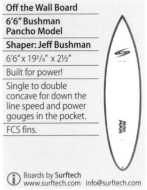

Off the Wall Board
6'6" Bushman Pancho Model
Shaper: Jeff Bushman
6'6" x 19³/₈" x 2½"
Built for power!
Single to double concave for down the line speed and power gouges in the pocket.
FCS fins.

Boards by Surftech
www.surftech.com info@surftech.com

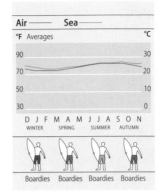

Air ——	Sea	
°F Averages		°C
90		30
70		20
50		10
30		0

D J F M A M J J A S O N
WINTER SPRING SUMMER AUTUMN

Boardies Boardies Boardies Boardies

Grab your coffee and head through the access from Ke Nui Road onto Ehukai Beach. Leaning on the wall, the whitewater in front of you is picking up the light from the first rays of sun as it climbs above the horizon. The coffee tastes good. To your right, a set unloads on the reef at Pipe, sending a reeling right through Backdoor. There is already a heavy crowd out. But sitting directly in front of your vantage point is the wave you've come to check – Off the Wall. It's 4-6 ft and perfect. And it's easy to see why it's such a popular wave with surfers and photographers. The name comes from the wall you're leaning against, rather than any physical characteristics, and if you hurry, you just might catch a few before the crowds descend…

Off the Wall has been much maligned over the years. In the days before Backdoor was ridden, it had no official name and was just referred to as Pipeline Rights and considered a poor cousin of its neighbour, Banzai Pipeline. During the explosion of numbers and the expansion of visiting professionals, it was given the somewhat derisory moniker of 'Kodak Reef,' alluding to the number of eager young pros who would frequent the wave, keen to get those Hawaiian pictures for their portfolio. Today's 'Hawaii' issues of the top surf mags always feature those choice cuts from the best Off the Wall sessions, providing some classic 6-ft foot barrels or feathering walls with slashing fins out off-the-tops.

The reef at Off the Wall is separated from Backdoor by a narrow channel just visible in the clear, shallow waters. On a clean northwesterly swell a wedging right comes onto the flat lava reef, producing anything from a nice, bashable wall to a crystalline tuberide or a semi-close-out. Optimum swell size is 4-6 ft but it can also work in bigger swells. On those special days perfect oval barrels will spin along the reef offering classic tube-riding conditions. There is also the left that can break towards Backdoor. Although Off the Wall may be a great place to catch some less intense waves or pull into some close-out barrels for those watershots, it pays not to underestimate the power here. This is still the North Shore and people can and do get hurt. In 2004, Australian pro Heath Walker hit the reef after a heavy close-out, resulting in Walker having to be airlifted to hospital with a broken collarbone and rib and a punctured lung.

Right: Cory Lopez takes some time out from the crowds next door at Pipe.
Opposite page: Matt Archbold – the innermost limits of Off the Wall.

SEAN DAVEY

The line-up is just as competitive here as any major North Shore spot with overflow surfers from Pipe, Ehukai locals and the whole spectrum of the world's top pros. "At Off the Wall you can't really link a bunch of turns but you can get going really fast and do anything your mind can come up with," says Cheyne Magnusson in *Surfer Magazine*. "It's probably the most popular spot with surfers because there are so many photographers there." During the winter this stretch of beach houses the entire top 44 and OTW is always there to tempt. "Pipe is a real challenge," says former world champion CJ Hobgood. "I kinda like 'Off the Wall' a bit more now."

Locals and legends
Mike Hynson, BK, Jeff Hakman, Owl Chapman, Herbie Fletcher, Tiger Espere, Jamie O'Brien, Kalani Chapman, Makua Rothman.

Nearby breaks The stretch of sand between Keiki and Rocky Point boasts what is probably one of the most concentrated collection of classic surf spots on the planet. These include **Log Cabins**, **Rock Pile**, **Off the Wall**, **Backdoor**, **Banzai Pipeline**, **Gums**, **Pupukea**, **Gas Chambers** and **Rocky Point**, which, as Kalani Robb explains, is a good spot for busting out your full repertoire of manoeuvres: "For hot-dogging and doing tricks then Rocky Point is my favourite." Pipe, to the northwest, is probably the most famous surf spot but to the southeast lies **Rockpile**, a wave named after the pile of basalt boulders that mark out the break. Rockpile is located just in front of Lifeguard Tower 27 and the North Shore lifeguard headquarters.

Waimea

Location:	North Shore, Oahu, Hawaii
Break type:	Right-hand reef
Conditions:	Big swells
Size:	12-30 ft
Length:	50 m +
Tide:	All tides
Swell direction:	Northwesterly
Wind:	Light easterlies
Bottom:	Lava reef
Ability level:	Intermediate
Best months:	Nov-Mar
Access:	Through shore break
Hazards:	Heavy waves, hold downs, crowds

SEAN DAVEY

From feared to revered, Waimea has endured a rollercoaster ride of a reputation. As the haunt of evil spirits and the pinnacle of big wave riding, Waimea became *the* place for every visitor to prove their manhood. It wasn't long before the spotlight moved and today some consider it a jaded heavyweight. What isn't in doubt, however, is that Waimea is a truly beautiful spot with a proud tradition. And, when the really big swells roll through, the car parks are jammed as nature puts on a remarkable spectacle – one with potentially serious consequences for anyone who paddles out to become a willing participant.

Waimea Bay lies at the mouth of the Waimea Falls Valley. During the summer it's a family beach offering safe swimming and the occasional

small waves. Come winter, however, the scene is very different. 'The Bay' lies directly in the path of huge northwesterly swells that roll unimpeded for thousands of miles across the Pacific until they slam into the lava ledge that sits off the point. This has always been hallowed ground for Hawaiians. At the top of the valley lies a sacred site or *heiau* – for years the early North Shore pioneers would pass by only to look in wonder at the huge rollers breaking. Then, in 1943, two surfers, Woody Brown and Dickie Cross, were caught out in the line-up at Sunset as the swell suddenly jumped massively. They tried to paddle southwest towards safety but were caught by a big set at Waimea. Cross drowned and Brown barely escaped with his life. This only served to heighten the apprehension many felt about this spot.

In November 1957, a group of surfers, including Pat Curren, Mike Diffenderfer, Mike Stange and Fred Van Dyke, stopped to check the surf as they had done many times previously. This time, egged on by ringleader Greg Noll, they took the plunge. The surf was bigger than they thought and the equipment they rode was completely unsuited to the job. "We thought it was maybe 12 ft," recalled Curren later. "We got a big surprise when we got out there. I don't think anybody made a wave." But the ice had been broken. With refinements in board design and a better understanding of the wave, this group spearheaded the art of big wave charging at its new spiritual home.

Although Waimea was a mountain of a wave, coming out of deep water onto a rock shelf, it usually produced little more than an exhilarating drop, followed by a short run out onto the mushy

Waimea Bay Board

9'6" Brewer Doerner Gun

Shaper: Dick Brewer

9'6" x 20½" x 3⅜"

Dick Brewer designed this board with Darrick Doerner for the biggest waves Waimea has to offer.

Plenty of flotation, just enough rocker, this board will go as steep and deep as you dare go!

Futures fins.

Boards by Surftech
www.surftech.com   info@surftech.com

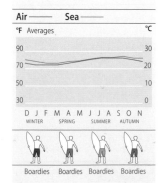

Air ——— Sea ———

°F	Averages			°C
90				30
70				20
50				10
30				0

D J F	M A M	J J A	S O N
WINTER	SPRING	SUMMER	AUTUMN
Boardies	Boardies	Boardies	Boardies

Above: Big wave hellman Garrett McNamara drops in on Waimea.
Opposite page: Gazing down on the spiritual home of big wave riding.

shoulder. Lacking the peeling walls of Sunset, it had its critics. Former world champion Shaun Tomson says, "Only on extremely rare occasions it might offer a wall and an opportunity for more than one manoeuvre. Most of the time it's a mad scramble on take-off and an elevator drop and a hard turn for the shoulder. Some people have compared surfing Waimea to climbing Mount Everest. I disagree. I compare riding Waimea to falling off Everest, not climbing it." However, over the next couple of decades the waves at the Bay remained the domain of a dedicated crew of big wave chargers who pushed the boundaries on their huge rhino-chasers.

In 1986 a big wave event was set up in honour of the late, great Hawaiian waterman, Eddie Aikau. There is an annual waiting period for the paddle-in contest that is only held when the surf tops 20 ft, as event director George Downing said, "the Bay calls the day" – which isn't every year. The line-up is only open to a select list of 24 invitees and 'The Eddie' has become one of surfing's most prestigious events. Just to be invited to compete is seen as a great honour and the event was won in its inaugural year by Eddie's brother, Clyde. Subsequent winners include Keone Downing, Noah Johnson, Ross Clarke-Jones, Kelly Slater and Bruce Irons.

Over the past decade, with the discovery of other big wave spots around the globe, Waimea has lost the number one position. At times it is invaded by hordes of surfers who will go out on huge boards in swells that previous generations would consider too small, just to say that they've surfed Waimea. Many of the old crew now avoid the spot except on the biggest days. But that in itself says something of the reputation and history that this spot carries. And when the big days dawn and the ground shakes, Waimea is still a life and death wave.

Locals and legends
Pat Curren, Mike Diffenderfer, Mike Stange, Fred Van Dyke, Greg Noll, Ricky Grigg, José Angel, Eddie and Clyde Aikau, Reno Abellira, Mark Foo, Ken Bradshaw, Darrick Doerner, Brock Little, Ross Clarke-Jones.

Nearby breaks To the northwest lie the right-hand reef **Log Cabins** and big wave sister spot **Outside Log Cabins** – famously towed into by Ken Bradshaw. On a condition black day in 1998, christened 'Biggest Wednesday', 45-year-old Bradshaw towed into an 80-ft face – arguably the biggest wave ever ridden. To the south lie **Chuns** and **Jockos** reefs, a less intense right and a long, consistent left respectively.

SEAN DAVEY

Haleiwa

Location:	Ali'i Beach Park, North Shore, Oahu, Hawaii
Break type:	Right-hand reef break
Conditions:	All swells
Size:	3-12 ft
Length:	Up to 100 m
Tide:	Mid tide
Swell direction:	Northwesterly
Wind:	Southerly
Bottom:	Rock reef
Ability level:	Intermediate to advanced
Best months:	Nov-Mar
Access:	Paddle off beach
Hazards:	Nasty rips, rocks, crowds, close-out inside section

Three-times world champion Tom Curren is acknowledged as the most fluid and stylish surfer in the world. Sitting in the line-up at Haleiwa on a November afternoon in 1992, he knows that counts for little. This is the North Shore, the domain of the power surfer, and Curren has never won an event here. He looks around at the other three finalists of the Wyland Galleries Pro: former world champions Tom Carroll and Martin Potter plus Johnny Boy Gomes, one of Hawaii's fiercest and most talented competitors. Time is tight – Curren needs a solid score. The swell is a solid 8 ft and the chunky waves are cloudy and choppy; big, open faces reel right toward the notorious inside Toilet Bowl section. The clock is ticking as a set peaks out on the fringes of the reef. Someone at Ali'i Beach Park stands and points. Curren is dropping down the face, laying down a smooth, drawn-out bottom turn, the rail of his white, stickerless Maurice Cole pintail is buried deep in the face. He has a point to prove. Big, open carves and solid, liquid turns – he knows the contest title will be his. This moment, frozen in time on celluloid, has become one of the defining moments in surfing. In 1992, the style master finally nailed that elusive Hawaiian event, his white board free from sponsor logos. Was it a statement about the art of surfing versus commercialization? The debate still rages on. It did, however, establish the Haleiwa event as a contest where big things happened – a very local wave on a world stage.

The North Shore starts here. The bridge at the edge of Haleiwa is the gateway to surfing's greatest collection of classics within one stretch of sand. This beach is home to a tight-knit surfing community that has produced many generations of North Shore chargers and the waves were the nursery for the likes of George Downing, Gerry Lopez and Fred Patacchia. But that's not to say that Haleiwa is an easy wave or a lesser North Shore break. This reef is a heavyweight and can be punishing.

In big swells up to 12 ft, waves peak over 250 m offshore and reeling right-handers roll along the reef. These provide big, chunky walls that eventually unload into the 'Toilet Bowl' – the inside close-out section. The reef likes a northwesterly direction when, at 6 ft, it can produce fast, clean barrels. In smaller swells with a lot of northerly, a walling left

SEAN DAVEY

Right: The rip carries you straight to the peak at Haleiwa, while out back breaks the notorious big wave spot Avalanch.
Opposite page: Bonga Perkins making deceptively easy work of his home break.

SEAN DAVEY

can peel towards the harbour. But a word of warning: if you do make your way out into this experienced and competitive line-up, beware of the infamous Haleiwa rip. Water draining back out to sea produces a nasty conveyor belt current heading straight towards the peak. Don't get sucked too deep into the pit or you may find yourself scrabbling to get out of the way as a set unloads on your head. As local surfer Jason Shibata puts it, "Once the sets start coming in, you better hope that you don't get caught, 'cause once the sets start to roll in, it's over!"

Time in the water certainly pays off here. As legendary pro surfer Ian Cairns says, "It got to be that I expected to make the finals at Sunset, Waimea or Haleiwa and felt like I would probably win. I was confident because of the amount of water time I spent getting to know each of the waves… time at each of the breaks all added up to strong results." Haleiwa hosts the annual OP Pro, one of the three events in the much-vaunted Vans Triple Crown. It has become established as one the most exciting contest venues in the world, but when the marquees pack up and the judges move on, the wave goes back to being the home of the North Shore's biggest surfing community and a hot bed for new talent.

Locals and legends

George Downing, Woody Brown, Wally Froiseth, Uncle Earl, Henry Preece, Kerry Terukina, Allan Wicklund, Marvin, Leonard and Kawika Foster, Kanoa Dahlin, Bonga Perkins, Fred Patacchia, Jason Shibata, Sean Moody, Joel Centeio, Zen Yoshifuku.

Nearby breaks Puaena Point is a fun right that breaks to the west of Ali'i, into the boat channel and is popular with less experienced surfers. Sleeping out the back **Avalanche** is a huge reef that comes to life in massive swells. Paddle surfed for the past four decades, it has recently become a popular tow surf spot.

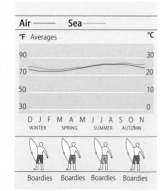

Haleiwa Board

6'10" Rawson Hyper Skate

Shaper: Pat Rawson

6'10" x 18¾" x 2½"

Designed for all around in the 6' to 8'+ range.

Fast and drivey through turns and cutbacks with enough stability to hold in the steep sections.

Futures FTP1 fins.

ⓘ Boards by Surftech
www.surftech.com info@surftech.com

Air —— Sea ——		
°F Averages		°C
90		30
70		20
50		10
30		0

D J F M A M J J A S O N
WINTER   SPRING   SUMMER   AUTUMN

| Boardies | Boardies | Boardies | Boardies |

Honolua Bay

◈ **Location:**	Honolua Bay, Northwest Maui, Hawaii
◐ **Break type:**	Right-hand reef break
☁ **Conditions:**	Big swells
◷ **Size:**	3-10 ft
⬖ **Length:**	up to 200 m
≋ **Tide:**	Mid tide
⊚ **Swell direction:**	Northeasterly
◔ **Wind:**	Southerly
⬡ **Bottom:**	Rock reef
◉ **Ability level:**	Intermediate to advanced
⬗ **Best months:**	Nov-Mar
⬚ **Access:**	Paddle off the ramp
⊖ **Hazards:**	Rocks, crowds

"Mark Richards, on the wave of the day at Honolua Bay." The voice of Jan Michael Vincent appears over the image of MR with his famous 'Wounded Seagull' stance, dropping down the face of a feathering wall. The wave reels across the bay, Richards pumps and tucks briefly under the lip, almost knock-kneed. The wave speeds slightly, then slows as MR works the perfect wall through to the inside where he kicks out. One of the opening sequences of one of surfing's pivotal movies, *Free Ride*, showed the true potential of one of surfing's hottest stars, riding one of surfing's most coveted waves. By the time these images hit the screens across the US, Honolua Bay had been home ground for some of the world's top surfers and most cutting-edge shapers for over a decade.

Standing on the clifftop, looking down over this beautiful bay, the whole scene looks like a surfer's dream. After the chaos and carnage of the North Shore, Honolua Bay was a surfing nirvana to the great surfers of the exploding shortboard era. Running below the surface of the glassy ocean on the eastern side of the bay is a long, flat reef, just waiting to capture the long distance, lined pacific swells and translate them into reeling, point wave perfection. However, although the bay points out into the North Pacific, the world-class waves here are surprisingly fickle. The northwesterly swells that turn on Oahu's 'big hitters' are cut out by the island of Molokai. Honolua Bay relies on a big northeasterly swell sneaking through. A 20-ft wave on the north shore will translate into an 8 to 10-ft wave here. But in the *quid pro quo* of surfing's checks and balances, Honolua benefits from the shelter it provides in the prevailing trade winds that blow during the winter surf season.

It took a certain level of skill and commitment to surf here in the pre-leash era. Blow the take-off on the outside section, known as 'Coconuts', and not only would you be faced with a long swim in, your board would end up either trashed on the rocks or stuffed in the cave. Guys like Buddy Boy Kaohi, Les Potts, Herbie Fletcher, Albert Jenks and Mark Martinson would savour the quiet line-ups, the high board toll keeping all but the experienced out of the line-up. Jeff Hakman would surf session after session without falling off, whereas Jock Sutherland would charge the barrelling right-hander on both his forehand and backhand. In 1967, Bob

Below: Honolua Bay – it's all about barrels.
Opposite page: In the pre-leash era, boards were regularly decimated on the rocks here but Jeff Hakman could surf session after session without even falling off.

Honolua Bay Board
6'3" JC SD-3
Shaper: John Carper
6'3" x 18.15" x 2.2"

Shane Dorian's favourite board because it's versatile!

Whether you're surfing the Point, The Cave or even Keiki Bowls, this board with its round pintail, single to double concave and finely tuned rails is right for Honolua.

Futures JC1 fins.

ⓘ Boards by **Surftech**
www.surftech.com info@surftech.com

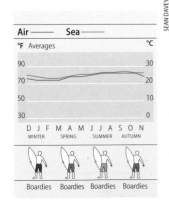

Air ——— Sea ———
°F Averages   °C
90   30
70   20
50   10
30   0
  D J F M A M J J A S O N
  WINTER SPRING SUMMER AUTUMN

Boardies | Boardies | Boardies | Boardies

SEAN DAVEY

McTavish and Nat Young came through to surf at Honolua Bay on their new V-bottomed shortboards with George Greenough charging on his Velo. They put the boards into the critical part of the wave, impressing those who looked on. MacTavish loved it. "The wave can bowl from the take-off," he says. "Get a good wave here and it will tube and speed down the line." Then came leashes and with them, the hordes.

Today, Honolua Bay is more popular than ever. Access is easy with improved road systems and, with Internet wave predictions, those precious northeasterly swells can be anticipated well in advance. Recently it has become the site for the annual Billabong Maui Pro where the women's world champion is crowned. But the spot has lost none of its allure over the years. And with a bit of luck, it's still possible to score the occasional magic session. "I surfed at Honolua Bay last Easter," says Mundaka charger Nick Lavery. "I was impressed how clean the water was, the reef is perfectly shaped and flat, and the wave just zips along. I had clean 4 to 6-ft surf with only six guys – until another 40 joined us after work! I got out at that stage. The Hawaiians are amazing people, and really friendly to lone *haole*."

Locals and legends

Paul Strauch, Herbie Fletcher, Buddy Boy Kaohi, Les Potts, Herbie Fletcher, Albert Jenks, Mark Martinson, Jeff Hakman, Jock Sutherland, Bill Fury, Greg Tucker, Barry Kanaiapuni, Reno Abellira, Buzzy Kerbox, Laird Hamilton, Dave Kalama.

Nearby breaks To the south is the town of Lahaina which is open to summer swells and has a couple of fairly consistent breaks including the **Harbour**, a peak with decent rights, and the **Breakwall** which can deliver some good barrels – just watch out for urchins. If you're searching for speed then carry on south to **Ma'alaea** – reputedly home to the fastest (makeable) wave in the world. Groomed by the breakwall here, this capricious right-hander needs just the right kind of big southerly swell to get going, but when it does, it is the stuff of legend.

SEAN DAVEY

Pe'ahi (Jaws)

◈ **Location:**	Pe'ahi, North Coast, Maui, Hawaii
◔ **Break type:**	A-frame reef
◓ **Conditions:**	Big to huge swells
◉ **Size:**	15-70 ft
◖ **Length:**	Up to 400 m
◑ **Tide:**	All tides
◉ **Swell direction:**	Northwesterly through to northeasterly
◔ **Wind:**	Light southerly
◉ **Bottom:**	Rock
◐ **Ability level:**	Expert
◉ **Best months:**	Nov-Mar
◉ **Access:**	Jet ski only
◉ **Hazards:**	Huge waves, massive hold downs

Throughout surfing history there have been breaks that have had to wait – either for surfing technology to catch up, or for surfers to make the mental leap needed to take the next step. The speeding barrels of Kirra and Burleigh needed the shortboard revolution to supply the vehicles to ride them; the huge peaks of Mavericks needed surfers to acknowledge that, yes, these waves could and should actually be ridden. Pe'ahi (or Jaws as it is also known) was a wave that needed both a mental and a technological leap. Lucky then that the wave sits off the northern coast of Maui – home to a unique collective of watermen who have pushed the boundaries of waveriding for decades and were more than eager to take up the challenge.

Pe'ahi had been studied from the clifftops for years. Surfers sat, like hunters studying their prey through binoculars, wondering – was it possible? Guys like Dave Kalama cruised the line-up on windsurfers. Then, back in the early nineties, the story broke. The leap had been made: a quantum leap in imagination, faith and physics. These bigger waves travel at higher speeds and are therefore impossible to paddle into. A team of watermen, including Buzzy Kerbox, Darrick Doerner and Laird Hamilton, had come up with the concept of towing each other into waves. Today, tow surfing with jet skis occurs across every continent at countless spots, but back in the early nineties this was mind-blowing stuff. This collective of Maui surfers had the foresight to take influences from outside surfing and apply them to the basic problem of catching these huge waves. Pe'ahi was their testing ground.

"Pe'ahi is the gathering place for all waves," says pioneer, Darrick Doerner. "Naturally a big wave spot will attract or should attract the most experienced watermen in the world. It was once a place where only kings (or *Aliis*) were allowed. If you survived, you were regarded as a true all-around waterman. On a scale from one to ten, it is a ten. It is truly the most awesome wave in the world."

Violent storms in the frigid Alaskan waters push massive, open ocean swells south towards the north shore of Maui. Pe'ahi is blessed with a gigantic, deep, fan-shaped lava reef, which provides the perfect foil for such huge swells. The waves here don't even form until the swell hits 15 ft. In 25-ft swells there are 60-ft faces, breaking so far out that they are cross-chopped by wind. The speed at which the waves travel and the resulting up-draft would simply blow paddle surfers off the top. A wave here peaks into a huge A- frame and reels along the reef, producing a massive, barrelling left and right that wall for up to 400 m. This is no Waimea drop and sprint to the shoulder; it is a 40 mph charge across a corrugated face that just keeps on reeling.

Tow teams waiting on the shoulder see the sets approaching as mere lines. They have to pick a wave and line-up far out from the reef – like planes coming in to land. This is a wave where the rider is tied to the skill of the tow-surf partner. Take the wrong wave, get pulled too deep, and the consequences can be severe. At Pe'ahi, surfing is a team sport.

Stand-out moments happen here every session. From just surviving the wave, the top teams are now laying down power manoeuvres, huge

Below: In Maui, sometimes you can see monsters from the pineapple fields.
Opposite page: Mike Parsons, more than just a wave – this is an Odyssey.

CORY SCOTT

DAVID PUU

carves and even tube rides. In 2002 Garret McNamara scored what many people are calling the biggest barrel ever ridden, in 2004 Rush Randle towed Pete Cabrinha into a 70-ft left and into the record books, while virtually every wave ridden by Laird Hamilton redefines what can be done out there. But what is it like to wipe-out here? Darrick puts it simply: "When you go down, and you will, it will be the most devastating experience of your life."

Bizarrely, at a spot once thought unrideable, the spectre of overcrowding is rearing its head. Just as tow surfing allowed the most talented watermen access to this spot, it has also paved the way for others who may be less proficient. This worries the likes of Laird and the Pe'ahi pioneers. "The risks surfing Pe'ahi are, for obvious reasons, extreme," says Darrick. "My advice to a visitor is do not go there unless you have 25 years of surfing big and powerful waves and you know your limits. There are so many risks that this is not a place to begin to learn from life-threatening mistakes."

Locals and legends

Laird Hamilton, Dave Kalama, Darrick Doerner, Mike Waltze, Buzzy Kerbox, Rush Randle, Pete Cabrinha, Garrett McNamara, Shane Dorian, Dan Moore.

Pe'ahi (Jaws) Board

6'3" Brewer Tow Board

Shaper: Dick Brewer

6'3" x 15½" x 1½"

Flat deck, tapered rails, extremely responsive, deep single concave for for maximum speed after you let go of the rope.

Developed and tested with legendary Laird Hamilton, specifically for the giant waves at Jaws.

Custom G10 fins.

(i) Boards by Surftech
www.surftech.com info@surftech.com

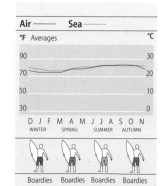

Air —— Sea ——		
°F Averages		°C
90		30
70		20
50		10
30		0

D J F   M A M   J J A S   O N
WINTER   SPRING   SUMMER   AUTUMN

Boardies Boardies Boardies Boardies

Nearby breaks If you need a little warm-up session before testing your mettle at Jaws, the north shore of Maui does offer up a few less intense surf experiences. Remember, however, that this area is extremely popular with windsurfers, for good reason. On a still day, **Hookipa** has a decent right point to the east and a reef to the west. Further west the peaks at **Paia** offer a more gentle beach break solution.

NATHAN FLETCHER_

SOME PEOPLE N

WHAT TRULY HORRIBLE

Mavericks

Location:	Half Moon Bay, south of San Francisco, California
Break type:	A-frame reef
Conditions:	Big to huge swells
Size:	15 ft +
Length:	50-200 m
Tide:	All tides
Swell direction:	Northwesterly through to westerly
Wind:	Light easterly
Bottom:	Rock reef
Ability level:	Elite
Best months:	Sep-Apr
Access:	Out from the rocks south in the rip, then turn north around Mushroom Rock
Hazards:	Sharks, spine-snapping waves, endless cold hold downs, rocks...

The world's great waves don't usually just appear from nowhere, unless there has been some great interference from humans. Usually they break in glorious isolation before being stumbled upon by a passing surfer and rolling onto the world stage. Surfers are the worst at keeping secrets. Word always seems to leak out somehow. One of the truly amazing things about Mavericks is that, in 1975, when Jeff Clark tried to tell people about this wave he had discovered, no one would believe him. So he carried on surfing the spot – by himself – for nearly 15 years.

Today Mavericks is universally accepted as the premier big wave spot to paddle into. A whole generation has dined out on pictures of hell drops and sickening wipe-outs at this cold water cauldron of

Below left: The pack jostles for position in front of Pillar Point, Half Moon Bay.
Opposite page: Ken 'Skindog' Collins screams down another Mavs mountain.

mountainous water and jagged rocks. But 15 years ago the wave riding landscape was very different. No one believed that anywhere outside the Hawaiian Islands could lay down a legitimate challenge for the big wave crown. Although the line-up today is relatively crowded, there are very few surfers who genuinely relish this environment. This is a truly life-threatening wave – one that claimed the life of renowned big wave rider Mark Foo in 1994 – and it takes a certain skill and a certain mindset to take it on.

Mavericks breaks in the chilly waters off the northern reaches of Central California in front of Pillar Point, Half Moon Bay. Huge swells come out of deep water and onto the submerged rocky ledge that lies a few hundred yards in front of a line of treacherous rocks that protect the lagoon. Feeling the reef, the wave rises into an A-frame peak, siphoning more water in, before the lip throws over and forms huge walls that reel away to the left and right. Just getting into the line-up is a mission. Surfers launch off the point behind the rockline and paddle south, fringing the lagoon and taking advantage of the rip. The rounded Mushroom Rock is the point to turn and head out to the line-up, forcing through the inside waves – which can be 6-10 ft – and heading out into deep water. From here it is a long paddle to the looming peaks and the flotilla of boards and jet skis. Then things get even scarier.

Taking off at Mavs you have to put yourself under the lip and be totally committed. The last place to be is suspended at the top as the wave throws out. As Billabong XXL winner and Santa Cruz local, Zach Wormhoudt explains, to catch waves here, it's all or nothing:

TONY CANADAS

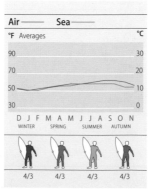

Mavericks Board
10" Clarke Gun
Shaper: Jeff Clarke
10' x 20" x 3½"
Nobody has ridden more waves at Mavericks than Jeff Clarke.
Jeff designed this 10' Gun specifically for the ledging mountains that roll through Mavericks every winter.
FCS GAM fins.

(i) Boards by Surftech
www.surftech.com   info@surftech.com

Air ———	Sea ———	
°F Averages		°C
90		30
70		20
50		10
30		0

D J F	M A M	J J A	S O N
WINTER	SPRING	SUMMER	AUTUMN
4/3	4/3	4/3	4/3

TONY CANADAS

"If you want to sit conservatively and make sure you're not going to get clobbered by a set, you're never going to catch a wave. To be in position to catch and ride waves out there, you have to pretty much commit to the whole situation and end up in a position where you might get caught by a set wave – which is the worst-case scenario."

The classic Mavericks shot shows surfers dropping down the face and bottom turning, but there is more to this wave than just the drop. Once the surfer hits the bottom and leans into the turn, Mavericks can deliver a huge, walling ride that races and, on occasion, actually grows in size as it speeds across the inside fingers of the reef towards Mushroom Rock. Many surfers kick out half way through, but it is possible to ride Mavs for over 200 m, though the inside section can be punishing.

Although most surfers take the right, the left is also surfable, though it is an even deadlier proposition. The take-off is steeper and the wave is gnarlier. "It's pretty hard to paddle into," says Zach. "The way the waves come across the reef it makes the drops that much ledgier. It's really steep and a shorter wave. The problem with the left is you tend to get pretty worked if you don't make it. With the left, if you fall on either the drop, or on the inside part, and there's more waves coming, it's almost guaranteed you're going through the rocks."

If you surf Mavs regularly you can guarantee the worst wipe-outs of your life. "The very best guys still have to contend with their wipe-outs," states Zach. "If you're wiping out on the big waves, sooner or later you're going to have one that's really bad. You might fall on a 20-ft wave and one time it might be not so punishing, and the next time it might be to the point that you're right at the brink." Imagine falling down the face of a 20-ft wave, landing with a slap in the trough before a mountain of water lands on top, driving you deep into the cold depths; so deep that the pain from the pressure in your ears can't distract you from the fact that you are being pulled down into a swirling cauldron of water, and, 30 ft above, the tip of your board is tomb-stoning like a fishing float. When you open your eyes it's pitch black, and impossible to see which way is up. If you're lucky, the wave will release you as your lungs reach bursting point in time to surface before the next wave unloads on you. If you are unlucky you may be washed through the huge rocks and into the lagoon. "Sometimes I watch someone take a wipe-out and I'm like 'Wow, what would make these guys come back after that? That was just brutal.' They're right back there again," says Zach. "That's the thing, you've got to get back in the saddle."

Locals and legends
Jeff Clark, Richard Schmidt, Vince Collier, Bud Miller, Vince Broglio, Nacho Lopez, Shawn Barron, Marcel Soros, Anthony Ruffo, Peter Mel, Darryl Virostko, Zach Wormoudt, Josh Loya, Jake Wormhoudt.

Nearby breaks On smaller days there is an inside section out at Mavs known as **Phlegm Balls**, the site of a recent great white shark attack. Just to the north of Pillar point is a left point called **Ross' Cove**. The left is pretty chunky and breaks into the bay round the headland from Mavs.

Surfers' tales
In deep water

TONY CANADAS

"I had a wipe-out yesterday. It was probably one of the worst ones of my whole life. For some reason it wasn't that it was violent or that it hurt me, it pushed me so deep that both my ears were popping, and there was all this tension on my leg and my leash. I have a quick release leash but there was so much tension that I couldn't reach down to my leg. I opened my eyes at one point to try to orientate myself and it was just pitch black. It just seemed like forever. I was just like 'well, I'm doing OK just holding my breath but if the next wave is bigger, I'm going to be in trouble'. It was definitely the longest hold down of my life. I had a guy call me today who was doing water patrol rescue, and he said 'I can't believe that. That was the most crazy thing I've ever seen in my life.'"

Zach Wormhoudt is one of the most respected big wave surfers in the world. But the Billabong XXL Biggest Paddle-In Award winner of the 2003-04 season isn't one for hyperbole. The way he talks about big wave surfing is very honest and matter-of-fact. At times he laughs and says things like, "The shark thing is kind of a bummer. It's bad enough with the rocks, and the cold water, and how big the waves are and how hard it is to surf… the shark thing is just an unnecessary evil we don't really need." None of the usual clichés such as 'sharks are just another factor you have to live with'.

Thirty-six-year-old Zach came up through the hothouse, cold water environment of Steamer Lane, Santa Cruz. His peers are guys such as Darryl 'Flea' Virostko, Josh Loya, Jason 'Ratboy' Collins and Ken 'Skindog' Collins. Steamer Lane is one of the best point breaks in

the US but it is also one of the most competitive. The surfers here have been at the cutting edge for decades, in both small and big waves. Middle Peak at the Lane is where Zach got his first taste of big wave surfing and the hook was set. "I remember biking down to the Lane and seeing this guy, Nacho Lopez, he was surfing Middle Peak. This is before Mavericks was known to us and I was just sitting on the cliff and going 'That is just the coolest thing. I can't believe guys do that. One day I'm going to get a board and go and sit on the shoulder and watch.'"

Santa Cruz had a tradition for producing big wave chargers. "Vince Collier and Richard Schmidt, they were the big wave icons, not only for the Santa Cruz guys, but for the whole of California. They were the guys who had gone over to Hawaii and ridden huge waves and done it here in the Santa Cruz area." It was through the grapevine that Zach and his friends learned of this new surf spot breaking up the coast. "I was about 17 or 18 and heard of it through word of mouth. We were in the pre-Internet era so it wasn't like you could just go online and see some photos. Once we heard about it I ordered boards to surf it almost immediately, and this was like a year and a half before I surfed it. I wasn't sure how I was going to surf it. I'm the sort of guy that the fact that I'm out there surfing it now I still kind of like have to pinch myself. I just dreamed of checking it out from the cliff and maybe one day paddling out and watching it out from the shoulder. I just figured I'd do what I needed to do to learn how to ride this board. A couple of my friends had been going up there for maybe a season before that – guys like Darryl Virostko, Josh Loya and Vince Collier." That first trip with Josh and Flea saw Zach in the Mavericks line-up. It was a sink or swim moment, literally. "I got like four or five waves and I was instantly hooked."

The Mavericks line-up is no place for the faint-hearted. "Besides just trying to surf it and make the wave, there's all the other stuff to contend with. There's a level of anxiousness, sometimes it's nervousness and other times it's just being super-alert and ready. It doesn't always translate to fear, not always, if things are going right. You can see it in people's eyes. Sometimes there are people out there and they're just twitchy and you can tell they're more scared than anything. If you're having a good day out there the fear is not even a factor and you're just focused on doing what you need to do to not get caught by set waves and to actually make the drop."

Big wave surfing can have that old 'Greg Noll turn up and charge reputation' with the wider public. But the reality is that many of today's big wave riders utilize everything from concerted fitness regimes to modern sports psychology techniques. It all starts the night before a big day. "I try to keep my confidence as high as possible, not really worry about it and then it's just another night. It's got to that point now that there's nothing more you can do to prepare yourself by the night before, physically. Mentally I try to visualize surfing Mavericks successfully so I picture waves that are really gnarly big waves, and I'll picture myself making something that's difficult to make and I'll visualize it again and again and again. Mainly the drop, but all parts of the ride. I think that there's huge value in that. It's pretty much tested and proven that there's a lot to visualization. Jay Moriarty was someone who did that, and he and I talked about it a lot. Doing that as opposed to focusing on 'what if I wipe-out?' You kinda have to have a game plan in case you wipe-out. For most people that plan is don't panic! However, you can pull that off. I train a lot for surfing out there, but I try to focus on successful riding and having everything go my way. Sometimes if I'm watching and I see a guy's just about to get pitched, I just won't even watch it. Because I just don't want that in my mindset. Block that out. Like I said, sooner or later you either have a wipe-out, or you see a wipe-out that makes you not want to come back. You can see one that's ugly enough to go 'forget this.' There's nothing you can do once you start wiping out, you're pretty much at the mercy of the wave. It's going to do whatever it wants with you. The thing to do is just to get back out there and get another wave so you don't have to think about that any more. A really bad wipe-out can either chip away at your confidence or it can make you feel somewhat invincible. Which is probably not a good idea – because you're not, obviously. It can pump you up or it can just as easily send you to the hospital. The sport is so weird – I can't believe what people do, to tell you the truth. All the things people are doing – making it and not making it – and coming back for more."

As well as paddle-in, Zach has also been tow surfing huge waves off the Californian and Oregon coastline. With his brother Jake, he won the inaugural Nelscott Reef event, beating many of the world's most famous tow teams. In tow surfing there is a lot invested in the relationship between the driver and the surfer, but if you're towing with you're brother there must be an extra vested interest because of the family bond. "The dynamic in terms of being partners with someone is a twist to the sport of surfing because in one sense it's a cheat because you have somebody there watching out for you. If you fall off and are in a dangerous situation, there is someone whose mission is to save you, and they've got good equipment to do it. But at the same time the hardest part is, each wave has the potential to have an awesome outcome or a horrific outcome. It's hard when it's your brother, or any tow partner you're working with, you're tied to the result of their ride. If you put them in deep and they make it you get a pat on the back from people at the end of the day. But in the worst-case situation, if someone dies, which hopefully never will, whoever it is will have to live with that. So it's scary, you tow him into a wave and you're like 'Turn, turn, turn!' and he's fading closer and closer to the pit and you want them to make it so bad. It's a pretty interesting dynamic." But this must add tension to an already charged line-up? "Every tow team has their arguments between each other. We call it 'Domestic Battles'. When you're being towed in you have to give up many decisions you would usually take yourself – which wave you go for, where you'd be – you have to give those over to somebody else. You see people just screaming at each other; they're good friends, but every tow team has their moments. The successful tow teams are the ones that can have their arguments and then set them aside."

So is Mavericks at the apex of big wave surfing? "I kind of think it is. I've surfed Waimea, Todos Santos and I've tow surfed up at Nelscott Reef. It's so gnarly, the wave. I have a lot of good friends who film up there for a living and they're always telling me 'Dude, the wave's just so gnarly. I can't believe it.' And I say, yeah but you've been filming it for 15 years, quit saying it and they say, 'But it's true. I can't believe it. How loud it is. It's going right through the rocks, every wave.' Every time you go out there it's totally breathtaking how heavy a wave it is. There's that sense with it."

Zach's company designs the world's leading concrete skate parks, built across the US and around the globe. Check out the awesome website for past and up and coming projects at www.skateparks.com.

Opposite page: Zach Wormhoudt.
Next page: Zach making the drop at Mavs. [TONY CANADAS]

> **"It's bad enough with the rocks, and the cold water, and how big the waves are and how hard it is to surf... the shark thing is just an unnecessary evil.**

Zach Wormhoudt

Steamer Lane

- ◈ **Location:** Lighthouse Point, Santa Cruz, California
- ◔ **Break type:** Point break
- ◍ **Conditions:** All swells
- ◉ **Size:** 3-12 ft
- ◔ **Length:** 50-100 m
- ◒ **Tide:** All tides, best at mid
- ◎ **Swell direction:** All southerly swells, big westerly to northwesterly swells
- ◎ **Wind:** Northwesterly to easterly
- ◉ **Bottom:** Rock and kelp
- ◉ **Ability level:** Intermediate to advanced
- ◎ **Best months:** Year round
- ◉ **Access:** Cliff paths
- ◉ **Hazards:** Crowds, rocks

Steamer Lane Board
6'8" JC Peter Mel Machine
Shaper: John Carper
6'8" x 19½" x 2.4"

Designed for Santa Cruz charger Peter Mel, blends medium rocker and single to double concave to get into waves early and drive hard down the line.

Plenty of volume for big Middle Peak.

FCS G5 fins.

ⓘ Boards by **Surftech**
www.surftech.com info@surftech.com

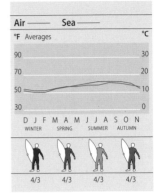

Air —— Sea ——
°F Averages °C

D J F	M A M	J J A	S O N
WINTER	SPRING	SUMMER	AUTUMN
4/3	4/3	4/3	4/3

Steamer Lane is more than just a wave, it's a selection of 'rights' of passage – a proving ground. The four waves of 'The Lane' are some of the most crowded and competitive in the whole of California but that doesn't seem to deter new contenders from stepping up to the plate. It's also one of the most consistent spots on the whole coastline. Pointing due south, Steamers fires when those big northwesterly storms roll in, producing offshore winds and tapering lines when most of the coastline is blown out. It also picks up anything else on offer, as local big-wave charger, Zach Wormhoudt, explains: "Steamer Lane will break on any swell direction. In the summer when the south swells are running it will break, even when southern California – which is notorious for south swells – is pretty small, we still pick up south swells that they don't even get. Steamer Lane breaks all year round and it breaks pretty big."

Steamer Lane is at the heart of the Santa Cruz surf scene, one of the most progressive and innovative in the world. Legend has it that the break took its name from the steam ships that would round the point as they sailed into Monterey Bay. It was here that the likes of Ricky Grigg and Peter Cole honed their big wave riding skills in the 1950s before heading for the warmer waters of Point Makaha and Hawaii. In the late fifties Jack O'Neill moved back to Santa Cruz where he opened a surf shop and began experimenting with wetsuit design. Both the surfing

wetsuit and the resultant multi-national surfing giant, O'Neill were spawned and refined in these chilly central Californian waters. Fifteen years ago the general consensus was that big wave surfing happened in Hawaii, and Hawaii alone. Today, a whole bus-load of the world's best big wave watermen live in this central Californian city. Times are always a-changing but Santa Cruz somehow manages to stay at the cutting edge.

The city has a population of 56,000 and occupies 12 sq miles in the northern part of Monterey Bay, 74 miles south of San Francisco. Sitting at the heart of the city's coastline, Steamer Lane is an 'amphitheatre of dreams', the cliffs acting as the perfect viewing platform for the voyeuristic onlookers to watch – entranced as the bobbing mass of black neoprene below jostles for waves in the marble-green water. To the casual passer-by, The Lane is a place to catch a few waves. To those who have more than a passing acquaintance, it is a series of breaks, each

JACK ENGLISH/SURF IMAGES

Right: Steamer Lane local Adam Replogle throws a back-lit rooster tail.
Opposite page: Driving down the lane.

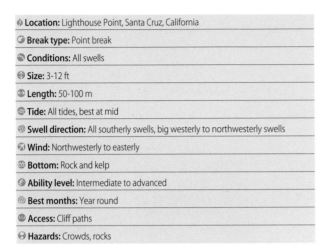

with there own characteristics and moods depending on the subtle shifts in tide, swell and winds. Furthest on the outside sits **The Point**, a high performance, highly crowded combat zone where surfers literally pick waves off the end of Lighthouse Point. The take-off is small and crammed with super-hot locals. The wave walls up begging to be spanked and that is what happens time after time. Huge, tail-out slashes, reverse airs and 360° aerials are all commonplace here, and the critical crowd are waiting to pass judgment on your first manoeuvre. Don't expect to paddle out and dazzle the locals. This is one of the most progressive spots on the surfing planet.

Middle Peak is a left and right that breaks inside the point but further over into the bay. On small days it has some fun rides but as the swell picks up, the wave keeps on building and moving out along the reef until double-overhead peaks are rearing up in front of a jostling pack of wave-hungry locals. On medium days the longboarders love the peeling walls but when the swell jumps and the wave breaks on second reef, a more serious challenge is on offer. Many locals cut their big wave riding teeth here. Sitting between the Point and Middle Peak is **The Slot**. Here waves run through the cove and may either close-out, allowing for that big inside aerial or floater, or connect through to the inside break, **Indicator**, a walling right waiting for the days when bigger swells roll down The Lane. "The way it works as a point break, the waves taper all the way until they reach Cal's beach,

which is a renowned beginners spot," says Zach. "You can literally learn how to surf at Cal's – which almost all the guys who surf Mavericks from Santa Cruz did – and then just incrementally work your way up the point to Middle Peak."

The popularity of Steamer Lane increases every year as more and more surfers venture out into the already crowded water, and while this is a source of frustration to many locals, they can see why. "There's way better waves than The Lane in this area," says Ken 'Skindog' Collins, "But it's not really the wave that draws people here. It's the proving grounds. Just like the North Shore, if you're any good in Santa Cruz you gotta show you can push it with the big boys." And that means showing you can push it at Steamer Lane.

Locals and legends
Jack O'Neill, Robbie Waldemar, Kevin Reed, Vince Collier, Steve Colton, Richard Schmidt, Anthony Ruffo, Jason 'Ratboy' Collins, Adam 'Rodent' Replogle, Peter Mel, Ken 'Skindog' Collins, Darryl 'Flea' Virostko, Shawn 'Barney' Barron, Josh Loya, Noi Kaulukakui, Anthony Tashnick.

Nearby breaks Just to the south of Steamer Lane is **Cowell's Beach** or Cal's. This is a long, gradual, mellow beach break popular with beginners in the summer and longboarders year round. The vibe here is pretty mellow but it can be super crowded. To the north, **Mitchell's Cove** is a fickle but classic right-hand point break that can throw up some epic sessions in big, clean swells.

JARRAD HOWSE

JARRAD HOWSE TEAM O'NEILL

O'NEILL
oneilleurope.com

Rincon

Location:	South of Santa Barbara, Highway 101, California
Break type:	Right-hand point
Conditions:	Medium to big swells
Size:	3-15 ft
Length:	50-150 m
Tide:	All, favouring low
Swell direction:	North to west
Wind:	Northeasterly
Bottom:	Cobblestone
Ability level:	Intermediate to advanced
Best months:	Nov-Mar
Access:	Off the point
Hazards:	Crowds

DAVID PUU

While Malibu brings to mind images of summer-fun peelers set against the strains of jangly surf guitar, Rincon del Mar conjures up a deeper, darker, more complex collage of scenes. Although both are truly world-class waves, they are yin and yang, operating in a seasonal dichotomy and have inspired a whole ocean's worth of analogies from surfers across the world (moon/sun, night/day, king/queen, dark/light). Simply put, Rincon is the colder cousin to Malibu's warm water waves. While Malibu rocks out to the summer southwesterly swells, it takes the brooding northwesterly and westerly swells that roll in with the cold winter months for Rincon to come to life.

Sitting off Highway 101, Rincon straddles the county line between Santa Barbara to the north and Ventura to the south. As the growing band of Californian watermen of the postwar era pushed north in search of new breaks, they came across this classic point. And when the first big winter swells hit in the early1950s, *Surfer Magazine* founder John Severson was on hand to capture huge Rincon on film for the first time. Soon the full Malibu crew – Dora, Edwards, et al – were testing themselves in the brooding winter swells that followed.

Rincon became the proving ground for the young George Greenough and his various waveriding vehicles. It was here that Greenough and Australian shaper Bob McTavish traded waves, with McTavish riding

the first 'shortboard' to be put through its paces on the American mainland. He shaped the board at Tom Morey's factory and Rincon provided the surf to analyse it. "We had pumping Rincon for weeks," says Bob. "George was on his 4'8" spoon and me on my 8-ft lightweight dream board. We were the only two guys in California on shortboards." The physical characteristics of the wave at Rincon helped hone the trademark – and much-imitated – bottom turn, fluid style and flowing turns of another reluctant icon. Like Greenough, three-time world champion Tom Curren was brought up on a diet of high-calorie Rincon and ultra-progressive boards, this time care of local global shaper Al Merrick.

Often referred to as the 'perfect point', due to the way the walls relentlessly roll along the cobblestone point, it creates a perfect surfing canvas. "So close to perfection are the long and incredibly well shaped right-hand point waves, the spot is nicknamed 'The Queen of

Rincon Board
6'3" Channel Islands Flyer II
Shaper: Al Merrick
6'3" x 18¾" x 2⅜"
One of the most versatile shortboards on earth, made for the long lined up waves of Rincon.
Works best in waves from knee high to a few feet overhead.
Single to double concave.
FCS fins.
ⓘ Boards by Surftech www.surftech.com info@surftech.com

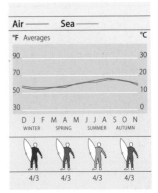

Air ——	Sea ——	
°F Averages		°C
90		30
70		20
50		10
30		0
D J F M A M J J A S O N		
WINTER	SPRING SUMMER	AUTUMN
4/3	4/3 4/3	4/3

Above right: If Malibu is the day, Rincon is the dark night.
Opposite page: Large northwest ground swell wraps around the boulder point.

the Coast,'" expands Surfrider Foundation's Matt McClain. Many agree that it is not a difficult wave to surf and sitting in the line-up it's easy to imagine what a year of uncrowded Rincon could do for your surfing.

Although it is possible to connect waves from the outside through to the inside, Rincon usually has three recognizable sections. The Indicator is the outside section and, although a great wave, is the easiest section of the break. In a good swell it can be possible to take off here and connect through to the inside. Second Point or Rivermouth is the middle section and a somewhat unpredictable beast. It can be a hollow, grinding racetrack where the super-fast section can shut down or it can open up and allow a sprint through the speeding barrel. It may be worth trying if the Cove is clogged but it can be polluted by run-off from Rincon Creek.

The Cove, the inside section, is the real gem. The wave winds its way down the point and fires through this section offering a fast, walling freight train or a barrelling dream, depending on the swell direction and sandbank. The take-off point here will be a jostling pack of waveriders, all knowing that just one wave here could be the wave of their lives. "You can't compare anything to the Cove when it's on," says local surfer Joe Curren. "Get a six footer here and you feel like you're as good as Slater." A set wave here can be a slalom run through surfers on the inside and those hovering on the shoulder waiting for the slightest mistake but it is also a thing of outstanding beauty – the sight of that ruler-topped, tapering wall reeling ahead as you drop down the face. "Subtract the 200 guys, and Rincon is one of the best waves in the world," eulogizes *Surfline*'s Marcus Sanders. "The outside carving speed section, the speedy, bulbous, throwing section through the rivermouth, and the way the lip line angles perfectly down the point. Plus, it's long as shit." What more do you want?

Locals and legends
The Malibu crew – Dora and co, plus George Greenough, Tom Curren, Shaun Tomson, Joe Curren, Ryan Moore, Clyde Beatty, Al Merrick, Aaron Ernst.

Nearby breaks Heading north on Highway 101 you come to the town of **Carpinteria** and a mile of fun beach breaks. South of Rincon are several other right-handers including **Little Rincon** – the queen's smaller, less perfect little sister point break. Further south still is **Pitas Point**, another right which, on its day, can open up into some decent little barrels.

USA & Hawaii Rincon

DAVID PU'U

Malibu

Location:	Surfrider Beach State Park, Pacific Coast HW, west of Santa Monica, CA
Break type:	Right-hand point
Conditions:	All swells
Size:	2-8 ft
Length:	50-200 m
Tide:	All (best mid)
Swell direction:	Southwesterly to northwesterly
Wind:	Northeasterly
Bottom:	Sand
Ability level:	Intermediate to advanced
Best months:	Mar-Nov
Access:	Off the point
Hazards:	Crowds, pollution, more crowds and more pollution

Malibu has a place in surf history that no other break can rival. It not only spawned the modern surf lifestyle, it also gave its name to a piece of equipment that changed surfing forever. The scene that grew up around this California point break in the '50s contributed to the creation of 'youth culture'. After the austerity of the '40s, hanging out at the beach, surfing, playing music and having fun were suddenly things that could, and should, occupy huge amounts of time. Work was no longer the be all and end all. As the epicentre of a new movement, the reeling point at Malibu was not just a wave perfectly suited to the new style of surfing. What was it that made Malibu so special? "Simple," says Tom Morey. "It's the best and easiest wave to surf in the continental US during the summer. Period." It was also a cultural hang-out

and social 'drop-in drop-out' centre with characters like Tubesteak, Mickey Dora, Mickey Munoz, Kemp Aaberg, Dewey Webber and Mike Doyle leading the way. One of those attracted to the Malibu scene was a girl called Kathy Kohner. The tales she told her father of the exploits of the Malibu crew became the basis for the 1959 movie *Gidget*, and suddenly the surfing lifestyle was on cinema screens from Kansas to New York, fuelling the first boom of the modern surf era.

But Malibu isn't all about nostalgia. This right-hand point is still one of the best quality spots in the country with cutting-edge surfing taking place there every time it breaks – from new skool aerialists to progressive longboarders. "It's summertime's Rincon, " explains *Surfline*'s Marcus Sanders. "A perfectly shaped sand-bottomed wave, offshore in the afternoon seabreezes, open to most south swells, it allows you to pull out your full repertoire of turns."

This long wall is split into three sections. First Point is the furthest inside and smallest of the three. When it comes to quality its machine-like, long, curling lines make it hard to beat, despite the cluttered, heaving mass of longboards jostling to hook into just one of these gems. "First point is by far the longest ride of the three," says Gary Stellern, former President of the Malibu Surfing Association. "It is arguably the best right point wave in California and maybe in the United States. Even on a 4-ft wave, with the tide etcetera all synchronized, you can get a ride of 100 yards or more. Then, when the swell increases to overhead, it is sometimes possible to ride to the pier, which is well over 200 yards away from the main take-off spot. And all this without it closing out in front of you. This very long, beautifully shaped right is what makes Malibu such a special location." Next up is Second Point – a shorter, faster wave that is

Malibu Board

9'8" Robert August Wingnut Noserider

Shaper: Mark Martinson

9'8" x 23½" x 3⅛"

Design concepts from the classic nose riding models of the '60s blended with current design make this ideal for Malibu!

Modern tail-rocker and a custom single fin, allow it to rip in any conditions.

2+1 fin set up.

ⓘ Boards by **Surftech**
www.surftech.com info@surftech.com

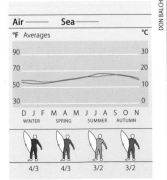

DON BALCH

Above: Autumn Malibu on a south swell produces clean lines and a busy line-up.
Opposite page: Five on the nose at First Point.

more susceptible to conditions such as tide and swell direction. As such it is a lot less crowded but on some classic days it can run through and connect with First Point allowing for an awesome, mind-melting ride. Third Point, the furthest outside, is a fast, walling performance wave, home to a pack of wave-hungry wolves with a survival of the fittest culture that would make Darwin proud.

Peppered through the line-ups at Malibu is every kind of waverider imaginable, from hardcore shortboard rippers, surfskis and learners to some of the best longboarders on the planet. Don't underestimate the balding, overweight octogenarian who's paddling into the wave with priority just up from you. Chances are he'll be up hanging ten before you've even popped to your feet. Malibu is still home to some of the greatest names of the early surf era.

Pollution at Malibu can still be a problem – run-off from the lagoon after rains can cause bacterial levels to soar – but, on a clean swell, with classic lines wrapping along the point, there are always scores of surfers willing to paddle out in the pre-dawn darkness just on the chance of snagging a ride before the crowds descend. "I started surfing Malibu regularly in 1961," says Gary Stellern. "It was crowded even then. This was prior to computers and their two-edged-sword surf forecasts. Now, due to the computer, the larger Malibu south swells are often accurately predicted a week or more in advance. With such notice there will often be up to 100 surfers of all abilities crowded into First Point, pushing, shoving and yelling, trying to ride one glorious Malibu wave. Factor in the beginners on rental boards that have no idea of what they are doing, riders on tandem boards, shortboards and regular longboards, it is often a dangerous zoo at Malibu's Surfrider Beach. However, one ride – 100-200 yards long, and with extreme luck, solo – and the hassles are worth it."

Locals and legends

An A-Z of surfing's pioneers: Matt Kivlin, Tubesteak, Mickey Dora, Mickey Munoz, Lance Carson, Kemp Aaberg, Dewey Webber, Mike Doyle. Today Anthony Petruso, Pascal Stansfield, Kassia Meador, CJ Nelson, Josh Farberow and Cole Robins are regulars.

Nearby breaks West around the headland is the long stretch of **Zuma Beach** – just watch out for the serious shore dump here. Heading east from Malibu along Highway 1 you run into a series of right-hand points including **Topanga** and **Sunset Boulevard** whose lines, although fine, are less perfectly formed than those of the nearby prom queen. From here on in Santa Monica Bay descends into a series of beachies punctuated by jetties, piers and breakwaters.

Surfers' tales
California screamin' Bruce Savage

Take Tinkerbell for example, over the years, with all the magic dust stored in that burlap bag of hers, making some classic droppings. Remember Miki Dora, Johnny Fain, Lance Carson, Noodle, Jack Lameroux, Red Gaines, Mickey Munoz, Tom Powell, Don Wilson, even the Sip 'n' Surf in the Canyon. Many wonderful capers took place at the Cottage Bar. Like Lee Marvin and Keenin Wynn roaring in on their Harleys and Indians. Capers such as slamming shut and locking the massive Malibu Pier oaken doors, stranding hundreds of sightseers on 4 July 1954. So many wonderful things happened which may, or may not be, duplicated. My favorite is Memorial Day 1960.

Dudley Jacobs was always smiling; maybe that's how he received the moniker, Happy. Yeah, Hap Jacobs! Hap watched from the porch of his surfboard shop, located halfway up Valley Drive in Hermosa Beach. Dave Puissinger's 1928 open-sided milk wagon sat in Hap's parking lot overlooking the railroad tracks. Surf-mobiles filled with surfers arrived early for the journey north to Malibu Beach, 35 miles up the PCH. A nighthawk arrived on the wing, talons clutching a helpless morsel, and settled amid the swirling fog. Its fledglings squealing their hunger, awaiting breakfast. Surfers alighted from their vehicles. It was no surprise to see Chubby Mitchell, 'Baby' Alan Gomes, Buddy Boy Kaohi, Dewey Webber, Kimo Hollinger, Duke Brown, Ricky Hatch, Peff Eick and all the usuals. Beach beauties Sparkle Eyes, Monkee, Melinda Lust and Skeeter Deeter hung the last shreds of crêpe paper from the roof's interior, inflated the colorful balloons and attached the red, white and blue tassels to the inner roof. They were set to go. Puissinger revved the engine. She sounded good. Puissinger pictured himself as a member of the Third Reich. The others returned to the procession vehicles, gave Hap Jacobs the 'V' sign, and off they went to Malibu. It was 0800, Memorial Day, 1960…

The 1928 milk wagon, with over inflated 18-inch tires on wood-spoked rims, chugged and belched its way up the coast. The seven-car entourage following passed Standard Oil pier at El Segundo, over Ballona Creek, along Speedway by the Saucy Dog, the biker's meeting place. The scene was unbelievable. In the Saucy Dog's parking lot, surrounded by a dozen Harleys, a biker swirling and popping a 12-ft bullwhip stood over a terrified looking, leather-clad broad with bleached blond hair. "Let's get out of here," said a nervous Puissenger, and off they went. After a while they

headed up the PCH, past Topanga Point, The Raft, the Zoo, The Reel Inn, and the Topanga Ranch Motel and Market – next stop the Malibu Pier.

All the while during the 35-mile early morning ride, Chubby Mitchell kept the vodka flowing like there was no tomorrow. They passed the Drift Inn and Foster Freeze, The Malibu Outrigger Club, The Cottage, and the old Rendezvous Restaurant. Chubby Mitchell stood, proposing a toast with the passengers, the real Tubesteak, Buddy Boy, The Manong, Mike Zuetell and the four ladies: Sparkle Eyes, Monkee, Melinda Lust and Skeeter Deeter.

Kemp Aaberg prepared himself for what seemed to be a 'gravy day', thinking about how lucky he was to be here at the pier and not Zuma Beach. His tower on the bluff overlooked the cove, behind him the PCH. A hundred yards south towards the pier, and across the highway in Malibu Inn's parking lot, sat six Highway Patrol squad cars, the drivers on another break. Dave Puissinger – Herr Puissinger as he wanted to be called – was a young, five-ten, slicked down, combed over brow, Adolph Hitler lookalike. He sat straight as a board behind the oversize steering wheel. He wore a Gestapo jacket borrowed from Jack Haley. Almost at journey's end, he sped past the pier, threw a huey at Serra Retreat Road, pulling up to the number one parking place directly beneath Kemp Aaberg's tower. Puissinger extended the choke to get a full mixture of air and gasoline, revved the engine, quickly turned the ignition on and off, causing a massive explosion, 'KAABALOOM', shattering Aaberg's nerves, causing its passengers to double over in hysterics.

It didn't take long for all the beach to gather up on the highway. Singing, dancing, shouting – it was now a fiesta. Kemp Aaberg, visibly shaken from the milk wagon's gnarly arrival, looked down at El Manong, Tubesteak, Chubby, Buddy Boy, and the four ladies, laughing and giggling, barely able to stand. Skeeter Deeter yelled, "Buckle your seatbelts, it's a bumpy road ahead." That was all Kemp could take. He grabbed the emergency phone and called Sheriff's headquarters, "Lifeguard needs assistance, tower sixteen," hung the phone and waited.

More revellers found their way to the milk truck but it was impossible to get in – vodka flowed, jitters were eased, and it was only 1000. Chubby Mitchell, engulfed by all the commotion, seized the moment, leaped from the milk truck – clad in black Frisco jeans, white Penny's T-shirt, purple velvet slaps – sprinted to the median in the middle of PCH, faced Ventura, unzipped his laundry, laying a wicked BA directly in front of northbound traffic but mainly in clear view of a CHP cop, his black and white responding to Aaberg's 'lifeguard needs help' call. The beach bums see the cop, yell at Chubby to get back to the milk wagon. Because of the holiday traffic, the officer had to go to the cut out at Serra Retreat Road in order to U-turn. By the time he made the turn, Chubby returned to the milk wagon, took off all his clothes and made a beeline for the ocean, Kemp Aaberg wisely requesting, "officer and lifeguard needs assistance". Chubby Mitchell floated 50 yards offshore, when the police arrived. Aaberg refused to leave his tower, but he stood on the deck, bull-horn in hand, shouting instructions to Chubby, "Will the swimmer please return to shore immediately", said Aaberg. All the bums, CHP, Malibu Sheriffs, stood on the bluff, adjacent to the 'Pit' now laughing at the scenario. Chubby, his tanned head, curly black hair, stark naked, floating like a like a seal, refused to come ashore. Aaberg repeated his command. Still no response. Now everyone on the bluff, from police to tourists, could no longer refrain from laughing, it was just too funny.

Herr Puissinger's milk wagon was in an awful condition, caused by all the merry-makers partying like there's no tomorrow. Buddy Boy was out like a light on the milk wagon's floor, sloshing around the swill of vomit and spilled alcohol. Skeeter Deeter lay on the curb, she too incapacitated by vodka. The real Tubesteak, Sparkle Eyes and Monkee seemed to sense the outcome of the fiasco, and adjourned to the safety of The Malibu Sports Club at the entrance to the Malibu Pier, their window booth affording them full view of all celebrations. Patrolman Hal Dairywimple responded "Code Three" to the 'lifeguard needs assistance' call and parked adjacent to the milk wagon abandoned except for Buddy Boy wallowing unconscious in the swill. Officer Dairywimple acknowledged Aaberg, proceeded to the officers involved in the Mitchell matter. Out of sight two beach rats, Denny and Harold Fred, emerged from the shadows, crawled to the manhole cover set between Aaberg's Tower and the Coast Highway. They cracked the cover enough to insert a devise made from a book of matches and a lighted cigarette. Malibu in those days had no useful sewer system. The manhole in which they placed the timing device was filled with trapped volatile gas fumes. Suddenly, a huge bang, shaking the earth, sending the

125 lb manhole cover 100 ft into the murky sky. This was too much for Guard Aaberg. He leaped from his tower, ran to the officers standing on the bluff yelling "Get me outta here, I can't take any more."

Even the patrons in the Malibu Sports Club were terrified; it was the worse noise they'd ever heard. Tubesteak peered out the window towards the guard tower. Traffic was at a standstill. Spectators were circling around the fallen manhole cover which landed and bounced haphazardly in the middle of PCH. Amid all the confusion, Duke Brown, Kimo Hollinger and Mike Searcy scampered down PCH to their cars, parked at the Malibu Inn. Searcy opened the trunk pulling two cans of Bardhal from it, keeping one for himself, and one for Duke Brown. They started the motor, opened the cans pouring the contents into the carburettor. Bardahal is an engine cleaner causing all carbon to burn out of the engine creating a massive smokescreen, shutting down the highway.

Aaberg's tower was a disaster – explosions, smoke, fumes, police running around trying to maintain law and order. Kemp leaned against the base of his tower, looked to the heavens saying, "Lord, give me Puddingstone Dam, just get me out of here!" Amidst all the confusion, Herr Puissinger loaded all the available passengers into his milk wagon, burst through the wall of smoke heading home to safety in Manhattan Beach.

Lower Trestles

◈ **Location:** Lower Trestles, Orange County, California	
● **Break type:** A-frame peak	
● **Conditions:** All swells	
● **Size:** 2-8 ft	
◐ **Length:** 100 m	
◉ **Tide:** Mid	
◎ **Swell direction:** Southerly, southwesterly	
◉ **Wind:** Easterly	
● **Bottom:** Sand and rock	
◉ **Ability level:** All levels	
● **Best months:** Summer	
◎ **Access:** Famous walk in via tracks and rail lines	
◉ **Hazards:** Crowds, Amtrak	

From the start of the Malibu era, Trestles proved an irresistible draw. A series of classic surf spots nestled in pristine parkland sitting in the heart of Orange County. No boardwalks, no beachfront cafés or summer hordes. A chance to lose the crowds and chaos of the urban breaks and score some perfect waves with a few friends. There were the tempting walls of Upper Trestles, the peeling lefts at Cottons and the A-frame peaks of 'Lowers'. The only drawbacks were the 20-minute walk down to the beach via a sketchy section of railway line (hence the name Trestles) and the fact that the waves were incarcerated behind the barbed wire of Camp Pendleton, protected by testosterone-fuelled US marines. What better temptation to the original

waveriding counter-culturalists? "Trestles was the forbidden fruit," explains *Surfer Magazine* founder John Severson. "My defining moment there was making a bottom turn and facing a glassy green wall that just waited… for me. I remember wishing there was another surfer out to share the moment." As the surfers became more determined to access the waves at Upper and Lower Trestles, so the soldiers became more determined to prevent them. Tales of marine ambushes or packs forced to paddle north to the safety of the San Clemente State Park have become the stuff of legend.

But it wasn't just the challenge of accessing the hallowed waves of Trestles that drew surfers from across the county. Conditions combine to produce world-class walls that can make even the most mediocre surfer feel like they should be packing in their nine-to-five and heading out onto the qualifying tour. The long, tapering walls of Lower Trestles are a surfer's dream. In perfect conditions, when a clean south or southwesterly swell comes rolling out of the southern hemisphere, the corduroy lines feather into an A-frame peak, pouring out lefts and rights along the sandbank formed by the outflow of the San Mateo Creek. The lefts tend to be faster, hollower and more critical allowing for explosive manoeuvres but with shorter rides. The rights tend to be longer walls allowing multiple off-the-lip hits and cutbacks. Surfers have to make tactical decisions about whether the lefts or the rights will allow for maximum points in any given heat. As the only US mainland stop on the world tour, Trestles is among the top dozen elite spots in the world.

The days of lurking marines and chases down the beach may have ended in 1973 with the establishment of the state park but access to the beach is still less than straightforward. There is no beach parking and pilgrims still have to negotiate a series of trails and a short, well-timed dash along the railway lines. But if you thought that the crowds here at Trestles would be any lighter due to the lack of direct access, you'd be wrong. Sitting in the line-up and looking around at the jostling pack, it's interesting to note that among the hundred wave-hungry boardriders there is a whole spectrum of surfers represented. WCT stars past and present, local heroes, groms, old school longboarders and intermediates on funboards all trying to snag the next set wave. "There is still a whole mix of chaos and mayhem

JACK ENGLISH/SURF IMAGES

Left: Trestles offers such excellent performance waves that it has become a regular contest venue.
Opposite page: San Clemente super grom Kalohe Andino grabs some air time.

out there," says former world number two and local surfer Shane Beschen. "You got guys going left and right, the pack chasing every wave. But then it's hard to resist." As the jewel in Orange County's crown, 'Lowers' will always be a draw. "Trestles was the first famous wave I surfed," says ex world champ CJ Hobgood. "I remember thinking 'I'm surfing Trestles and I can't wait to tell my friends.'"

Despite massive protests, permission was granted in 2006 to build a controversial toll road through San Onofre State Beach Park. What impact this will have on the future of the surrounding environment as well as the water quality and sediment flow at Trestles remains to be seen.

Locals and legends

John Severson, Mike Doyle, Joyce Hoffman, Shane Beschen, Dino Andino, Mike Parsons, Taylor Knox, Rob Machado, Chris Ward, Gavin Beschen, Matt Archbold, Christian Fletcher, Greg and Rusty Long, Nate Yeomans.

Nearby breaks About 300 m to the north, **'Uppers'** is a good alternative to **'Lowers'** when the crowds are too insane. There is a much better chance of snagging set waves here and the quality is still excellent. **Cottons** is a few hundred metres north of 'Uppers' and a good option in bigger swells when there are excellent lefts and shorter, less punchy rights, and no crowds. The break sits in front of the so-called 'Western White House', where, during the Nixon era, surfers also had to dodge the eager guards. **Church** is not considered part of the Trestles breaks. In a good swell, it can produce long, right point-style waves with juicy days on offer in the winter. It can suffer from pollution from the San Onofre Creek run-off.

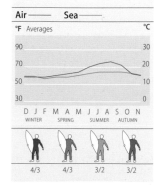

Trestles Board

5'10" Patterson Pat O'Connell Model

Shaper: Timmy Patterson

5'10" x 18" x 2¼"

Designed by Timmy Patterson and Pat O'Connell, geared for the high-performance surfer.

Single to double concave, extra rocker, super fast down the line, yet turns tight in the pocket.

Perfect for fast, bowly Lowers.

ⓘ Boards by Surftech
www.surftech.com info@surftech.com

Air ——	Sea ——		
°F	Averages		°C
90			30
70			20
50			10
30			0

D J F	M A M	J J A	S O N
WINTER	SPRING	SUMMER	AUTUMN
4/3	4/3	3/2	3/2

Blacks

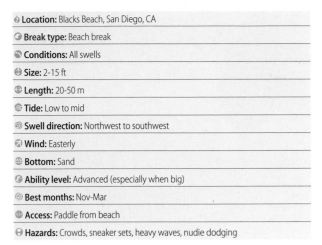

- **Location:** Blacks Beach, San Diego, CA
- **Break type:** Beach break
- **Conditions:** All swells
- **Size:** 2-15 ft
- **Length:** 20-50 m
- **Tide:** Low to mid
- **Swell direction:** Northwest to southwest
- **Wind:** Easterly
- **Bottom:** Sand
- **Ability level:** Advanced (especially when big)
- **Best months:** Nov-Mar
- **Access:** Paddle from beach
- **Hazards:** Crowds, sneaker sets, heavy waves, nudie dodging

Blacks Board
6'3" Rusty Pro-ject
Shaper: Rusty Preisendorfer

6'3" x 18¾ x 2³/₁₆"

Moderate rocker, triple concave, with a slight release vee through the tail.

Shines brightest in waist-to-overhead waves.

Designed and tested by Rusty teamriders in the wedging peaks at Blacks

Futures FEA fins.

ⓘ Boards by **Surftech**
www.surftech.com info@surftech.com

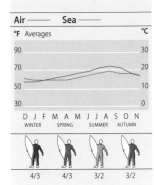

Air ——— Sea ———	
°F Averages	°C

```
90                          30
70                          20
50                          10
30                          0
   D J F  M A M  J J A  S O N
   WINTER  SPRING  SUMMER  AUTUMN
```

| 4/3 | 4/3 | 3/2 | 3/2 |

San Diego is just about as far south as you can go on the US west coast. Blessed with a warm, Mediterranean climate, the beaches are popular with tourists in the summer and surfers year round. Here, the water rarely gets below the mid-50s and the coastline turns it on in both the summer's southwest and the winter's northwest swells. It's also the last stop before Mexico and the fabled waves of Baja. The Windansea and La Jolla areas have a strong surfing tradition, producing a raft of surfing's stalwarts – among them Mike Diffenderfer, Waimea pioneer Pat Curren and the original Pipemaster Butch Van Artsdalen – who were drawn to the North Shore of Hawaii in those pioneering days of the 1950s and early '60s. More intriguingly, it is also home to the Scripps Institution of Oceanography. Despite the fact that the unique waves found between La Jolla and Blacks Beach are pretty complex creatures, they are probably the most understood and studied in the whole USA.

Blacks consists of two distinct breaks: North Peak and South Peak. Offshore sits an area of ocean bed that helps give the waves their distinctive characteristics and trademark unpredictability. The northern head of the Scripps Submarine Canyon, a large undersea valley gouged out by an ancient river, is not just an oceanographer's delight, it also focuses swell energy straight into the beach. The waves refract and peak, bent by the complex canyon bathymetry, as the

energy and swell lines converge. It is for this reason that the surf at Blacks can be pumping when just up the coast it is half the size. One resulting quirk is the infamous 'outside sets' phenomena, when surfers caught daydreaming on a clean 4-ft day can suddenly find themselves scratching to get over a series of reprimanding eight footers swinging in to wake up the line-up.

Those who have sampled the world's best beach breaks rank Blacks up there alongside the legendary sandbanks of Hossegor and Puerto Escondido for sheer power and class. These thundering waves can be found at the base of a stretch of crumbling cliff, just to the north of La Jolla. The precipitous view from the glider port can give a slightly misleading image of the surf breaking 300 ft below. That is until the tiny paddling dots help bring the whole scene into focus and the true scale of the 'small' lines appear as the grinding 6-ft barrels that they

JACK ENGLISH/SURF IMAGES

Right: Local surfer Jonathon Dupont.
Opposite page: The after work crew make the most of an evening glass-off.

really are. This is not the kind of place where you want to misjudge the size of the surf. Both the walk to the break and the sheer power of the surf can be punishing, especially if you chose a 5'10" wafer when a 6'9" mini-gun is the order of the day.

The surf can be fun here with innocuous, walling chest-high set complete with nice little hollow sections but once it hits head high things can get serious. This is no place for beginners. Cavernous barrels reel consistently with board-breaking ferocity. Those caught inside describe going through a washing machine cycle to rival anywhere. The North Peak throws up long, hollow lefts and shorter, faster rights and South Peak is an A-frame. Both peaks have a committed, loyal and hardcore crew who are on it from the first rays of sunlight through to the last glow of sunset. Although the long walk down the cliffs to the break hampers those in need of a quick lunchtime dip, the crowds are still heavy – in both senses. They have grown up in a competitive line-up close to an urban centre of 1.2 mn people that also boasts four universities. At a heavy break, where drop-ins can be costly on body, mind and board, respect is a prerequisite.

Blacks is not a glamorous wave. It does not feature in high profile videos or have a celebrity clientele and if it does find its way into a magazine, it's usually an obscure clifftop shot. It takes near military-level discipline to get comfortable out in the line-up here. But Blacks is no mere 'grunt'. This is a tough, sergeant-major of a wave, going about its business with as little fuss as possible. Make a mistake and it will beat you senseless but work hard and you might just earn your stripes.

Locals and legends
Brad Gerlach, Rob Machado, Joel Tudor, Skip Frye, Rusty Preisendorfer, Randy Lind, Peter King, Chris O'Rourke, Mike Hynson.

Nearby breaks To the south, **Scripps Pier**, overlooked by the Scripps Institute of Oceanography, is a popular beach break whose banks – either side of the pier – can be epic in a decent swell. Continuing further down the coast you hit the **La Jolla Reefs** including the fickle and sheltered **La Jolla Cove** – a left that needs a big winter swell to be running before it even thinks about working (just watch out for the caves) – and **Windansea**, a low to mid tide peak with a long and proud surf heritage that breaks over rock and sand. Heading north of Blacks, the big swathe of **Torrey Pines State Beach** offers plenty of opportunity to sample some beach break action.

DON BALCH

It is often said that Britain and the USA are two countries separated by a common language. For the USA and Canada, the geographical and cultural mileage may be less great, but a short trip across the water from the Seattle skyscrapers to the beaches of Vancouver Island can still be a whole world away.

Even from this distance, high up in the tree, his profile was unmistakeable. Head held high and proud, he surveyed his surroundings with the knowledge that this was his domain. The surface of the clear, green water lost its dappled matt appearance, indicating that the rain had eased from a heavy downpour to light drizzle. I had long since turned my back on the approaching sets, having paddled far enough out to just sit in the line-up and watch – the land. This is not normal practice for me. This is not normal practice for any surfer. But then this didn't feel like an ordinary surf experience. The bald eagle eased into the sky from his perch on the skeletal cedar tree and lazily circled over the dark, sandy bay before banking and gliding towards the small offshore island. The sun had broken through over the snow-capped mountains of the interior, causing a rainbow to display its palette across the lush green of the ancient rainforest. This was a ridiculously beautiful sight. I looked around the line-up at the other surfers bobbing in the clean, 4-ft swell. They too were completely clad from head to toe in neoprene. In the chill of the water, chatter was obsolete – we were all anonymous. This only seemed to add to the scale of the situation and the insignificance of our band of small, black dots floating in this huge, green ocean.

Vancouver Island is dominated by the intense green temperate rainforest. Lichens cling to tree trunks and mosses hang like fringes from every branch. It is the land where secret spots are reached by driving huge 4WDs down maze-like logging roads that terminate suddenly in disorientating clearings. Here the promise of the ocean echoes in surround-sound but gives no clue as to the direction in which the hidden gem may be found. From here it's on foot but there are no well-trodden trails to follow. There is a perpetually damp feel about the land, fuelled by the seemingly endless rain that pours from the grey skies. I thought I knew about rain, coming from Britain – I was wrong. In most countries rain is a barrier but here, clad in jackets designed for the summit of some Himalayan peak and trusty rubber gumboots, it is something that the locals seem to have grown impervious to. Surprisingly, after a week, the downpour had become just another fact of life on the island. Rain is one of the few predictable things here.

Sitting off the western coast of Canada, you'd probably assume that Vancouver Island is home to some decent waves. After all, it is open to the huge swell window and immense fetch of the Pacific Ocean. But the waves that break here year round are surprisingly good, if a bit on the cold side (winter temperatures can dip as low as 43°F). Surfacing from a duck-dive you realize you are immersed in 'ocean lite'; high on rainwater, low on salt. The clear green waters have a ghostly, Nor-Cal

feel to them. It has that chilly, sharky edge, though the locals will reassure you that – surprisingly – this is not Great White country. If you thought that encounters with bears were pretty common, you'd be right. Every surfer I met had a handful of bear stories. Then there are the cougars, the killer whales, the wolves…

There is also a large and diverse surfing community on the island that has been around a lot longer than you would expect. Wayne Vliet can cast his mind back 40 years to a time when life on Vancouver Island revolved around logging and fishing. Wayne and a couple of friends, having successfully built skimboards out of plywood, decided surfing was the next challenge. How hard could it be? "We put our brains together, decided we were going to make ourselves surfboards and we went down to the lumberyard. In the plywood section there were all these instructions about how to make a kayak, how to build a sailboat and how to build a surfboard paddleboard. So, with the help of my friend's Dad, we built ourselves a couple of heavy, hollow paddleboards. We took them out at Jordan River and then we found out there was maybe half a dozen other surfers out there that had real surfboards. That was 1965." From that moment on, the life of Vancouver Island's small, dedicated band of surfing brothers echoed the trends and styles set in motion thousands of miles away by the likes of George Greenough, Bob McTavish, Mark Richards and Simon Anderson. "Almost immediately the shortboard revolution was on," says Wayne. "It started in the late sixties, so we only surfed these new longboards a couple of years before we were chopping our boards down to keep current – and that's how I got into shaping."

Today, Tofino has become the island's surf capital and a perfect microcosm of the modern surfing world. There is a boom in women's surfing, retro has been and gone, surf schools are still packing them in and the explosion in coastal property prices is hitting locals hard. It is a place where two worlds collide but both manage to flourish. On one side of the street *Surf Sister's* large, bright surf boutique, complete with coffee shop and all-female team of surf instructors, has played an important role in the huge women's surf scene on the island. On the opposite side of the road sits *Long Beach Surf Shop*. The owner Ralph stands in front of a vintage pinball machine, and behind a beard to rival ZZ-Top. The boards on sale are as diverse as the collection of old skateboards on the wall. Gerry Lopez repro single fin pintails sit alongside modern funboards and thrusters. And what of the future? Local surfers Sepp and Raph Bruhwiler have scored sponsorship deals, been profiled in *Surfer Magazine*, are towing in at outside reefs and exploring the northern section of the island where road access is impossible. It's a truly hardcore surf experience where there is no margin for error. "We've found some amazing spots," says Sepp. "But there is so much potential up there – it's mind blowing." He's not wrong.

Opposite page: Wayne Vliet. [RICHIE HOPSON]

Surfers' tales
Crossing the water

Central America and the Caribbean

Pat Drummy, East Cape,
San José del Cabo, Mexico.

DAVID PU'U

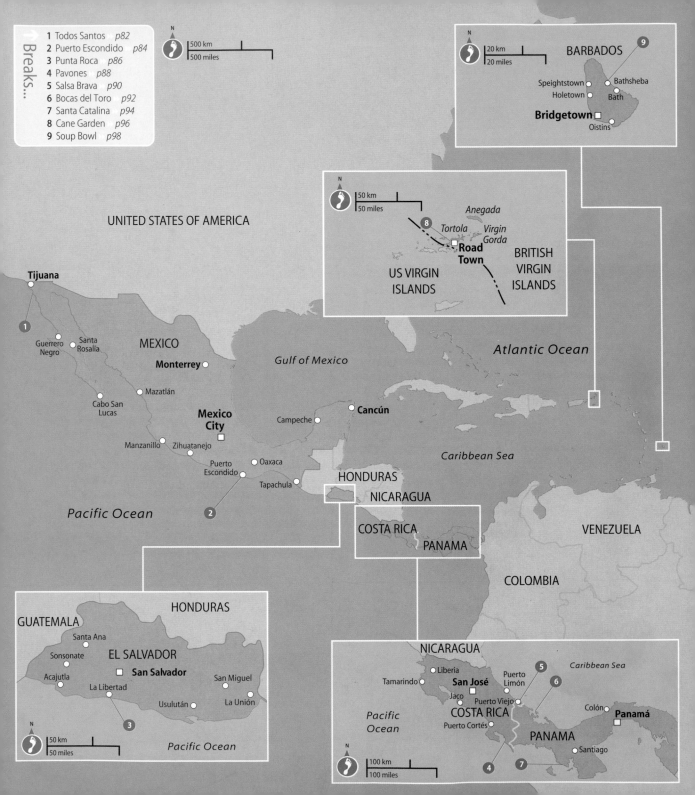

N
500 km
500 miles

N
20 km
20 miles

BARBADOS

Speightstown   Bathsheba
Holetown   Bath

Bridgetown

Oistins

N
50 km
50 miles

Anegada

Tortola   Virgin
Gorda

**Road
Town**

US VIRGIN
ISLANDS

BRITISH
VIRGIN
ISLANDS

UNITED STATES OF AMERICA

Atlantic Ocean

Tijuana

Guerrero   Santa
Negro   Rosalía

MEXICO

Monterrey

Gulf of Mexico

Cabo San
Lucas

Mazatlán

**Mexico
City**

Cancún

Campeche

Manzanillo   Zihuatanejo

Caribbean Sea

Puerto   Oaxaca
Escondido

Pacific Ocean

HONDURAS

Tapachula

NICARAGUA

COSTA RICA

PANAMA

VENEZUELA

COLOMBIA

GUATEMALA

HONDURAS

EL SALVADOR

Santa Ana

Sonsonate

Acajutla   **San Salvador**

La Libertad

San Miguel

Usulután   La Unión

NICARAGUA

Caribbean Sea

Liberia

Tamarindo   **San José**   Puerto
Limón

Jaco   Puerto Viejo

Pacific
Ocean

COSTA RICA

PANAMA

Colón   **Panamá**

Puerto Cortés

Santiago

N
50 km
50 miles

Pacific Ocean

N
100 km
100 miles

The boats slipped ashore under the cover of darkness. It wasn't the first time that they had carried out this kind of strategic operation and it wouldn't be the last. Central America was important to the regime back home – they had big plans and this area was key. No rival superpower was going to get their hands it. They were a superior force with superior weaponry. Gunpowder and ruthlessness allowed them to take what they came for. Here, in the 16th century, the Spanish, French and English fleets squabbled over the isthmus that forms a land bridge between the continents of North and South America. They saw only a place to plunder for gold and any other commodity they could pack into their ships. Waiting around the islands of the Caribbean, buccaneers and pirates, many sponsored by rival European states, were waiting to plunder the very cargoes that had been plundered from the native Indians in the first place. The crazy days of the Reagan administration, with the Sandinistas, contras, revolutions, counter-revolutions, plots and secret bases, were still a long way off and regime change was a concept that hadn't been thought of yet. It was still just good old-fashioned robbery.

The region of Central America and the Caribbean is a cauldron – a ring of volcanoes flanks the azure depths of the Caribbean Sea, some lie dormant biding their time, some are temperamental, prone to blow at a moment's notice. They seem to sum up the turbulent history of this region. However, this is an area with a rich social tapestry and one of the most exciting coastlines on the planet. In a turbulent world, surfers are the last travellers to desert a region and the first to return. Danger is all relative and if the pay-off is big enough, risks will be taken. During the political instabilities of the seventies and eighties, the CIA weren't the only crazy guys creeping around in the outback. Trucks piled high with boards were inching down tracks to discover new breaks, to clear spots for tents and hammocks, to find a place away from the rat race. Centuries ago they would probably have dodged the buccaneers and pirates to check out a promising point break on some remote Caribbean outpost. Today, with newfound political stability, surfers are at the vanguard of tourism – pushing boundaries out into the remotest regions and swarming over the safest. Surfing's frontline troops have lifted the curtain and suddenly the rest of the world wants to follow. But hasn't that always been the way?

Surfing Central America and the Caribbean

BEN SELWAY

Central America wasn't 'discovered' by the European sailors who braved the Atlantic Ocean crossings in the 16th century. Their voyages of discovery stumbled across a region that had already been home to some of the most advanced civilizations on the planet. The Maya built huge pyramids and sophisticated societies between AD 250 and 900. They had mastered mathematics and astrology and their influence spread across many countries, including Guatemala and Honduras, before mysteriously dying out. With the establishment of transatlantic routes to the so-called New World, the Caribbean Islands became vital trading posts; important ports on the trade routes between South America, North America, Africa and Europe. The incredible feat of linking the Pacific with the Caribbean through the 77-km-long Panama Canal, which opened in 1914, ensured that the region would always maintain its pivotal role in world trade.

Pros & cons

Central America

✅ Pros

Varied and undulating coastline.

Consistent swell catcher.

Good transport infrastructure.

Outside Costa Rica the cost of living is very low.

Warm weather and water year round.

Awesome point breaks.

Huge unexplored potential.

Culturally rich.

❌ Cons

Pockets of crime and banditos.

Busy around most well-known surf breaks.

Roads can be impassable in wet season.

Basic health care outside Costa Rica.

Malaria and dengue fever present in certain areas.

Pros & cons

Caribbean

✅ Pros

Good tourist infrastructure.

Warm waters and great climate.

Home to some world-class breaks.

Beautiful, volcanic landscapes.

❌ Cons

Flights and accommodation can be expensive.

Onshore trade winds at many breaks.

Many spots are inconsistent.

Limited number of breaks.

Main breaks get crowded.

Opposite page: El Salvador still offers a chance to lose the crowds, as Cornwall's Dan Joel demonstrates.

California's growth in surf numbers during the 1950s and '60s saw surfers pushing out and exploring new pastures. Baja was a natural extension of this territory and as they drove south, their adventures and misadventures became the stuff of legend and inspired more to follow. The first trips onto the mainland were spearheaded by a hardcore bunch of guys who found deserted beaches, excellent fishing and bandit country. Costa Rica meanwhile became a natural bridgehead for surfing as it spread through this central zone. In a region renowned for instability, Costa Rica was seen as a fairly safe introduction and offered a glimpse at the true potential of the classic, warm waves on offer along these coastlines. The Pacific breaks of Pavones and Tamarindo, and the Caribbean spots like Puerto Viejo were soon seeing a steady stream of surfers heading their way. During the eighties this flow intensified and, while Indo was the Aussie explorer's dream, Central America offered amazing adventures on the USA's doorstep.

The old image of Central America as a region rife with political instability, revolutions, military corruption and summary executions is gradually being replaced by a new one: lush countryside, comparatively uncrowded surf breaks and outstanding potential in a much more stable and secure environment. Costa Rica is currently experiencing a massive growth in surf tourism. Antonio Pilurzu, president of Costa Rica's Federation of Surf has stated that the 222,659 surfers who visited Costa Rica in 2004 was more than double that of 2001, and he predicts that

that number will double again over the next three years. Those who visited in 2004 generated US$273.3 million for the country. That's big bucks in anybody's language, and though Costa Rica's neighbours can only look on enviously for now, they may soon get their share. With a big increase in coverage in surf magazines around the globe, it seems only a matter of time before the boom spreads throughout the region. As the January 2005 edition of *Surfing Magazine* said, "Word is out that Costa Rica's less fortunate neighbours have everything to offer – world-class surf, empty line-ups, tropical paradise – and nothing to lose." The number of surf camps in Nicaragua, El Salvador and Panama are increasing every year, and many locals see this as a great way to help rebuild economies blighted by outside interference, successive corrupt and incompetent governments, and natural disasters. Unlike certain other destinations, this is a region that positively welcomes surf travellers and the money they bring. With the publicity generated by the visit of the Indies Trader and the new generation of local talent, it seems there has never been a better time to strike out into the tropical reaches of Central America.

Position

Central America runs like an umbilical cord between North and South America. At the top end, San Diego melts into Baja – a finger of land pointing south from the Californian border – while the bulk of Mexico is anchored to the good old-fashioned values of Arizona, New Mexico and

ALEX LAUREL

Texas. To the west is the vast Pacific Ocean and to the east, the Gulf of Mexico fringes the southern US states of Louisiana and Mississippi before squeezing through the gap between Florida and Cuba to meet the Atlantic Ocean. To the south, the Gulf of Mexico becomes the Caribbean Sea, lapping the shores of Belize, Honduras, Nicaragua, Costa Rica and Panama before docking onto Colombia and South America. Off Central America's east coast lies a string of thousands of islands, keys and reefs running from Mexico's Yucatán Peninsula to the Orinoco Delta in Venezuela. Cuba, the largest of the islands, is at the north of the chain and Trinidad and Tobago, just 11 km off the northeast coast of Venezuela, is at the southern end. These islands mark the limits of the Caribbean Sea with the Atlantic Ocean to the east.

Culture

The Central American mainland was home to an extensive and advanced Maya culture throughout the first millennium. Their pyramids and large urban settlements were already in terminal decline by the time the Spanish arrived in 1519. The Conquistadors claimed the region and, apart from a British presence in Belize and part of Honduras, this isthmus became a huge colony ruled from Madrid. The Spanish also laid claim to the whole of the Caribbean, but their settlements were mainly restricted to the larger islands. Other European powers such as Britain, France, Holland and Denmark established colonies of their own throughout the Caribbean region and the area was soon rife with bickering and squabbling. By the 18th century buccaneers were harassing French and Spanish shipping with the blessing, and backing, of the British, and many Caribbean ports were getting rich off the back of the marauding pirates.

Mainland Central America became an independent state in 1823 and formed a federal republic along the lines of the USA. This short-lived nation included the states of Guatemala, El Salvador, Honduras, Nicaragua and Costa Rica. Today, Central America and the Caribbean is a healthy tapestry of independent states, with a degree

of political stability even in the some of the traditionally volatile hotspots. Tourism is an important economic factor in opening up countries such as Haiti, El Salvador and Cuba and helping to stabilize a region with a very short fuse. Don't forget that this is where El Salvador and Honduras went to war over the outcome of a World Cup qualifying soccer match.

Climates and seasons

While northern Mexico and the majority of Baja are in the northern hemisphere's dry sub-tropical region, the rest of Central America and the Caribbean lie firmly within the tropics (though there are huge variations in temperature according to altitude). The cold Californian current travelling south through the Pacific to the tip of Baja lowers the water and air temperature and also serves to lower the rainfall of the region. North of the Tropic of Cancer the average annual rainfall is only around 250 mm, increasing as you travel further south. For Oaxaca, Mexico, the majority of the rainfall occurs June to October. September, with an average rainfall of around 350 mm, is the wettest month while the rest of the year is relatively dry. The year-round average is 28°C with temperatures rising by around a degree to coincide with the rainy season.

The mountain chain that runs down the spine of Central America acts as the boundary line between the two coastlines. The rainy season runs roughly from May to October and the dry season from November to April. However, with the persistent northeasterly to easterly trade winds carrying moisture off the sea, the Caribbean coast endures a longer, more intense wet season (sometimes double the rainfall of the Pacific coast). June to November is the hurricane season for this part of the world. In El Salvador, temperatures hover around 26°C throughout the year with around 8 mm of rain in January and 300 mm in July. Nicaragua's east coast is one of the wettest zones in the region with around 2500-3750 mm of rain per annum. West coast temperatures remain around 26°C throughout, rising to an average of 28°C from March to May. June to October are the wettest months on this

ALEX LAUREL

Above: Having a *Captain Zero* moment.
Right: Kevin Johnson, Pacific Coast, Panama.

coastline with approximately 20 wet days a month. January sees just 5 mm of rain. Northeasterly trade winds blow offshore for the majority of the year while in winter the Papagayo winds kick in over the lakes. High pressure systems move in from North America while areas of low pressure form over the Pacific. As air pressure regulates, it is funnelled through the break in the mountain chain backing the lakes, which causes the wind to intensify, often to gale force strength. The wind pushes out over the Gulf of Papagayo on the Pacific coast, causing a drop in sea surface temperatures at this time. Costa Rica and Pacific coast Panama have similar climates. They are somewhat cloudier than the rest of Central America and temperatures remain around 27°C from December to July, dropping to around 26°C from August to November. Rainfall can be intense but comes in short bursts averaging 25 mm in January and 180 mm in July. The Caribbean coasts enjoy similar temperatures but with increased rainfall.

The Caribbean islands are in the path of the consistent easterly trade winds that blow year round, tempering the humidity levels and temperatures to around 25°C in January and 27°C in July. In terms of rainfall, Barbados receives around 66 mm in January and 147 mm in July. This also marks the beginning of the hurricane season for the region, which runs through to around November. Most hurricanes pass Barbados by but it doesn't manage to escape the accompanying heavy rainfall. The higher positioned British Virgin Islands do lie within the hurricane track, with August to October being the peak risk period. Rainfall is, however, lower here with around 69 mm in January and 81 mm in July.

Wavewatch report by Vic DeJesus
Central America This tropical area receives swell from a variety of sources. Large south to southwesterly groundswells of anywhere from 4 ft to 20 ft, generated by intense winter storms in the southern hemisphere, slam into this area consistently from May

◢☁ W A V E W A T C H	Dec-Feb Winter	Mar-May Spring	Jun-Aug Summer	Sep-Nov Autumn
CENTRAL AMERICA				
Wave size/direction	NW/S 2-4'	SSW 3-5'	SSW 4-6'	SW 3-5'
Wind force/direction	ENE F4	ESE F3	SE F4	ESE F3
Surfable days	10-15	20-25	20-25	15-20
Water/air temp	27/27°C	28/27°C	28/27°C	27/27°C
CARIBBEAN				
Wave size/direction	NW 4-6'	NW/ENE 2-4'	ENE 1-3'	NW/ENE 3-5'
Wind force/direction	E F4	E F4	E F4	SE F3
Surfable days	15-20	10-15	5-10	10-15
Water/air temp	26/25°C	27/28°C	28/28°C	27/27°C

Despite the rain, conditions stay generally clean. Passing tropical waves and cyclones cause poor conditions periodically. During the winter and spring months, powerful North Pacific storms send in large northwesterly swells into select open areas. The Caribbean coast is often neglected, but can see large tropical cyclone surf in the summer along with occasionally powerful trade swells in the winter and spring months.

Caribbean Many islands of the Caribbean are to the east coast of the US what Hawaii is to its west coast. Winter months from November through to March prove to be the most consistent months of surf with large northwesterly to northeasterly groundswells impacting exposed locations. During the summer and early fall, tropical cyclones provide quality, punchy groundswells, although timing is essential. The Caribbean lies in the tropical latitudes so consistent trade swell also occurs year round for windward coastlines.

Geography and breaks
The geology of Central America and the Caribbean is predominantly volcanic in nature. The Caribbean basin is a volcanic cauldron with a ring of volcanoes running down the Central American isthmus joining North and South America, as well as a series of islands running back up the eastern fringe of the sea where upwellings of lava have risen above sea level. Many of these volcanoes are still active, though some have long since lost their fiery temper. The predominant breaks in this region are therefore a mix of lava-based coral reefs, black boulder points, black sand and white sand beaches.

In Central America, spots like Pavones in Costa Rica and La Libertad in El Salvador offer the trademark black boulders (see below) and many of the beach breaks in Costa Rica, Panama and Guatemala have that ashen black sand that gives the water a dark, bottomless, eerie feeling. The same is seen on the Caribbean islands with a mix of boulder points, coral reefs and sandy beaches. Spots like Soupbowl in Barbados offer a sandy beach leading into a quality right-hand coral reef whereas Cane Garden is a boulder and reef point. Some spots are images of paradise where blue water breaks on golden sand under a swaying palm.

Health and safety
With a spine of volcanoes running the length of Central America and through the Caribbean islands, this region really is a cauldron of fire and as such is at risk from natural disasters including earthquakes and eruptions. Due to their location, the countries are also affected by the hurricane season which, as well as high speed destructive winds, brings rain and the threat of flooding and landslides.

Despite the fact that Central America is more politically stable, it still has crime hotspots in some parts of Mexico, Guatamala and El Salvador where carjacking and kidnapping do occur. Other problems include the threat from robbery and pick-pocketing with the more serious crimes occurring in and around cities and major towns. As with many developing countries, roads bring their own particular set of problems and driving at night is not recommended.

Health care standards are varied and prevention is better than cure. Check yourself for ticks and avoid being bitten by mosquitoes which, depending on season, time of day and destination, could be administering dengue fever or malaria. Cover up, use a decent repellent that includes DEET and talk to your doctor before your trip about which course of anti-malarial prophylactics to take.

The water throughout the region is not safe to drink, so get a good supply of bottled water (check the seal), avoid ice in your drinks and peel fruit and veg before you eat it. If you do succumb to traveller's tummy, remember it's better out than in, stay out of the sun and keep fluid levels up to avoid dehydration. If you have diarrhoea for more than three days, pass blood or are in any doubt, seek immediate medical attention.

There are numerous sharks in the region on all coastlines but the actual number of shark attacks is extremely low. There are urchins to watch out for but a less obvious foot-related hazard is the black boulders, which line many points. In the midday sun these can heat up to foot-scorching, skin blistering temperatures.

Surfing and the environment

Central America as a whole faces a number of major environmental issues. Deforestation for firewood, for agricultural land or for development has seen the area of rainforest across the isthmus decimated. In Guatemala huge swathes of land have been peeled back so that little woodland remains, especially in coastal regions. In El Salvador, a country once completely shrouded in dense jungle, only 6% of the land remains forested, mainly due to the high population density. Panama has set aside large areas as national parks but protecting the greenery from illegal logging and enforcing park boundaries is a huge problem.

Deforestation not only robs the countryside of its natural vegetation, but has other far-reaching effects. Many forest species now top the endangered list across the continent as their habitat disappears, from insects and butterflies through to larger mammals such as jaguars. Trees and plants also absorb rainwater and their extensive root

WILLY URIBE

systems hold the soil together. Without this natural cover, flooding and landslides become much more common as the soil is literally washed off the hillsides. Flash floods and landslides have become an increasing problem across the region. This was demonstrated by the massive loss of life in landslides and flooding associated with Hurricane Mitch in 1998. At least 1000 people died in a single mudslide at the Casita volcano in Nicaragua. In addition to this, silts and soils washed into the rivers flow into sea and choke marine environments. Reefs are buried under sediments and the cloudy waters decrease the amount of light, killing off the corals.

Many rivers and lakes across the region have become polluted with garbage, sewage and chemicals as they are regularly used as dumping grounds. The area around Panama City is a prime example as sewage is dumped straight into coastal waters and rivers and streams have become garbage dumps. The sheer smell from the seafront here, where vultures pick through the debris, can be bad enough but the risk of infection is considerable.

In the chase for tourist dollars industrial expansion can be rampant and prime environmental locations lost to development and construction of new hotel complexes. The loss of land and resultant pollution are all too easily brushed under the carpet as developers try to present this as a small scale issue that will bring benefits to the whole community, but development is taking place across the whole of the Central American region to the point where many coastal habitats are now threatened. On the flip side, recognizing the importance of the link between green issues and tourism, Costa Rica established the Blue Banner Beaches system in 1996. This rewards the most ecologically sound beaches and since its inception, the number of awards presented have risen from 10 to over 50 in 2005.

Above: A spot of surfing, a spot of fishing and a bit of exploration.
Opposite page: Iconic View – Witches Rock, Costa Rica.

❝ ❞

Word is out that Costa Rica's less fortunate neighbours have everything to offer – world-class surf, empty line-ups, tropical paradise – and nothing to lose.

Surfer Magazine, January 2005

In the Caribbean the tourist boom has brought many development issues: the wave at Cane Garden was recently threatened by a marina development, larger hotel complexes are always on the horizon and discharge from the increasing numbers of cruise liners is an issue that environmental groups have been campaigning on in recent years. To find out more about the environment, check out organizations such as **Friends of the Earth**, www.foe.org, **Greenpeace**, www.greenpeace.org, or **Rainforest Action Network**, www.ran.org.

Surfing resources

Central America has a maturing surf scene with several countries setting up ISA affiliated associations including Costa Rica, Panama and El Salvador. *Planeta Surf La Revista*, www.planetasurflarevista.com, is the Spanish language surf publication for Baja and Mexico. The quarterly magazine is available across Mexico and some parts of the USA, featuring trips, news and interviews. As well as the global surf resources, *Wavewatch* and *Surfline*, good local resources include www.crsurf.com for English language surf reports, and www.purosurf.com for news and information on surfing in Costa Rica, www.purosurf.com is a great resource for Panama while www.barbadossurfcams.com has useful info on the Barbados surf scene plus forecasting and webcams for the area.

Todos Santos

◈ **Location:**	Todos Santos, Islas Todos Santos, Baja, Mexico
◔ **Break type:**	Right-hand reef break
◑ **Conditions:**	Medium to big swells
◔ **Size:**	8-30 ft +
◔ **Length:**	50-100 m
◔ **Tide:**	Mid to high tides
◉ **Swell direction:**	West to northwest
◔ **Wind:**	Light east to southeasterly
◔ **Bottom:**	Rock and boulder reef
◔ **Ability level:**	Expert
◈ **Best months:**	Oct-Mar
◔ **Access:**	Boat only
◔ **Hazards:**	Big waves, heavy hold downs

It was a sea change. A moment where people stood and stared. Tow-in surfing had blown minds at Pe'ahi and now here was Taylor Knox dropping down the vertical glassy blue face of a 52-ft wave under his own steam. It became *the* image of the new era of big wave surfing and highlighted a shift in just who these men where out there scaling these previously undefined peaks. Taylor Knox, Mike Parsons, Brad Gerlach, Flea – weren't these guys contest and small wave chargers? As the focus had shifted from the old Hawaiian stalwarts like Waimea, so a fresh crew of summiteers had emerged to take them on, and by 1998 the K2 Challenge showed just what was going on in the world of paddle-in big wave surfing.

Below: Greg Long – through the boils and bumps of a Todos bottom turn.
Opposite page: Scott Chandler – towing-in at Killers.

During the '80s feeding frenzy of Thatcherism and Reaganomics, money talked and it was a growth market – by '84 the world tour had swelled to include in excess of 20 internationally rated events and '88 saw Tom Carroll become the first surfer to sign a million dollar contract. Everything was to excess – except the size of the waves people were riding. Rhino chasers became the preserve of the old guard whose brand of surfing no longer lit up the pages of the surf magazines. During the '90s, as challenging peaks beyond the bounds of the North Shore began to impact on the surfing consciousness, momentum was building once again behind the 'men who ride mountains', heralding the start of big waves for big money contests. Taylor Knox's wave at Todos Santos took the K2 title, US$50,000, and signalled a new movement that would practice their art on fresh canvases around the globe.

Islas de Todos Santos are actually two islands, the flat Norte and its hillier sister Sur. Watched over by an imposing red and white lighthouse, the northwest point of Norte is home to 'Killers', a right-hand reef whose name should not be taken with a pinch of salt (but with a serious dose of mescal). Picking up almost double the swell that reaches mainland Mexico, this grunting wave can be ridden from anywhere between 8 ft and 50 ft and is a challenge at whatever size it breaks. During the northern hemisphere's winter months, waves steam in out of deep water and are best with a northwesterly or westerly swell direction and light offshore winds, as these allow longer waves to form. When the Tanner Bank buoy is showing 18-20 ft and 20 seconds, the committed crews will have hit the road south to be in

TOM COZAD

Todos Santos Board

9'6" Brewer Doerner Gun

Shaper: Dick Brewer

9'6" x 20½" x 3⅛"

Go big! Dick Brewer designed this board with Darrick Doerner.

Plenty of flotation to get in early and just enough rocker to keep the nose above the surface and as steep and deep as you dare go!

Futures fins.

ⓘ Boards by Surftech
www.surftech.com info@surftech.com

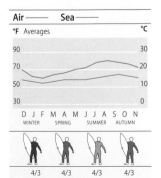

Air ——— Sea———

°F Averages °C

	90		30
	70		20
	50		10
	30		0

D J F M A M J J A S O N
WINTER SPRING SUMMER AUTUMN

4/3 4/3 4/3 4/3

TOM COZAD

the line-up for dawn. This crystal-blue, cool water creature now jacks up into one of the tallest waves on the planet offering elevator hell drops into the pit. From here on, the face can have many moods and it requires every ounce of focus and power to make it safely into the channel. As Todos veteran Brad Gerlach said of his Billabong XXL winning wave of 2006: "I didn't even know how big the wave was because you can't look behind you. You've got bumps and boils to concentrate on and the last thing you want is to catch a rail out there." Take a tumble in the impact zone and, as any Todos veteran will explain, you are in for one of the heaviest beatings of your life.

Lying in the Pacific about 12 miles offshore from Baja, in the migratory path of the grey whale, the only way to access the islands is by boat or jet ski, usually from Ensenada Harbour. Although there are a number of breaks here, most people only make the journey for the main draw card. "It's (about) the whole experience," explains *Planeta Surf La Revista* editor Mario Dillanes Valverde. "You have to go to the island in a boat, then when you get there you'll find a perfectly shaped wave. The bigger it is, the better the shape, even up to 20 ft!" Despite access issues, increasing numbers are heading for Todos Santos meaning that the line-up can become very crowded, especially on those medium sized days. Whereas at many big wave spots there is a compromise between the tow-in crew and the paddle surfers, here at Killers there have been serious

confrontations on days that fall between 'too big to paddle' and 'too small to tow-in'. As the number of people drawn to big wave surfing increases every year, it seems that the less legally restrictive Mexican waters are where these issues are being brought to a head, meaning a new and dangerous element is being added to an already life-threatening line-up.

Despite the media attention that Mavericks and Pe'ahi attracts, Todos Santos is also right there at the cutting edge. With K2 challenge wins, Billabong XXL awards and those heroic performances that don't seem to make the headlines, this continues to be the benchmark for big wave riding – a place where even the mightiest challengers sometimes just stand and stare. "Todos is just for those surfers with a real heart for adventure," explains Mario. "And with no fear of dying."

Locals and legends
Mike Parsons, Brad Gerlach, Taylor Knox, Ken 'Skindog' Collins, Ross Clarke-Jones, Peter Mel, Greg and Rusty Long plus all the central figures of the big wave scene have put their time in here.

Nearby breaks Despite the fact the spot is often referred to simply as Todos Santos, the main attraction is actually called Killers. The Islas de Todos Santos are home to a number of breaks including the North Island south coast right **Chickens** and south island spot **Thor's Hammer**.

Puerto Escondido

- **Location:** Puerto Escondido, Oaxaca, Mexico
- **Break type:** Beach break
- **Conditions:** All swells
- **Size:** 2-10 ft +
- **Length:** up to 50 m
- **Tide:** All tides
- **Swell direction:** Southwesterly to westerly
- **Wind:** East to northeasterly
- **Bottom:** Sand
- **Ability level:** Intermediate to advanced
- **Best months:** Apr-Oct
- **Access:** Paddle out from beach, difficult in bigger swells
- **Hazards:** Big, powerful waves, many close-out

Puerto Escondido Board

7'5" Brewer Sunset

Shaper: Dick Brewer

7'5" x 18¼" x 2⁵/₁₆"

Designed with North Shore charger, Myles Padaca.

It has the paddle power to get you over the ledge early with the drive to pull into and escape from the deep barrels of the Mexican Pipeline.

Futures fins.

Boards by **Surftech**
www.surftech.com   info@surftech.com

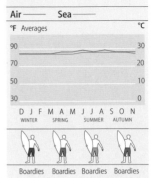

Air ——— Sea ———

°F Averages												°C
90												30
70												20
50												10
30												0

D J F M A M J J A S O N
WINTER SPRING SUMMER AUTUMN

Boardies Boardies Boardies Boardies

If surfing was an organic entity, it would be one of the most pernicious and invasive forces in nature. It has spread to virtually every corner of the globe, actively seeking out fresh territory. Just how many Pacific reef passes, Norwegian boulder points and Uruguayan beaches have been touched by this unstoppable movement is impossible to tell, but one thing is for certain – of all the stretches of sand around the globe that have been surfed over the decades, Puerto Escondido is consistently quoted as the most powerful beach break in the world. But Puerto Escondido isn't a wave, it is a small Mexican town that overlooks a number of beaches and bays. One of these is Playa Zicatela, whose trademark huge, heavy green barrels draw the brave and the crazed from a rainbow of nations. On a big swell, the sand-bottomed waves can rival any at Backdoor, but just paddling out could turn into the biggest car crash moment of your life. "Our Mexican Pipeline is the test for any surfer," explains Mario Dillanes Valverde, editor of *Planeta Surf Revista*. "Compared to other waves in Mexico it is monstrous. Once you have surfed in Playa Zicatela, you will know that you have gained another level – most guys don't even try".

When the first surfers ventured south from the familiar points of Baja onto mainland Mexico in the late 1950s and early '60s, they were searching for something on which to glide their heavy longboards. The thumping close-outs of Puerto Escondido were not part of the plan. It wasn't until the shortboard era and the boom in travellers of the 1970s that word of this hollow beach began filtering through the surfing grapevine and soon photos and articles, such as Tim Bernardy's 'Mexico Memoirs', brought surfers and backpackers to a town rapidly expanding on the back of tourism. Playa Zicatela lost its trademark zicatela plants to a wave of development expanding along the beachfront during the last few decades of the 20th century, and the beach beyond Far Bar is now free from the banditos that used to add an extra jalapeno-spiced edge to those early years.

Zicatela starts to work in small swells when peaks appear along the huge length of sand, offering up walling lefts and rights with a propensity to throw into powerful speeding barrels. Visit during the prime summer months and any Puerto Escondido veteran will give you the same advice when asked: bring your favourite semi-gun and then add an identical replacement to your quiver for when you snap

WILLY URIBE

Right: Size isn't everything – sometimes just surviving is enough.
Opposite page: Local Oscar Moncada at Playa Zicatela.

it. When a big southern hemisphere groundswell or westerly hurricane swell comes grinding out of the offshore ocean trench the place is transformed into a gladiatorial pit where the sympathetic 'Ooohs!' from the watching tourists on the beach outnumber the cries of jubilation at a well-timed barrel exit. Some punters don't even make it into the line-up as a thumping set can shatter even the best duck dived board on a badly timed paddle-out. This is one of the reasons why the board repair here is some of the most efficient and speedy in the world. In these bigger swells, The Right, a shifty right-hand sandbank, can throw up some epic waves, but it can just as easily transform into a screaming close-out. The appropriately named Far Bar sits along the beach and is an equally fickle left-hander that likes a south swell and a light offshore. It is not unusual for these banks to throw up waves at double to triple overhead. But what makes this place so special? "The fact that for sure you will get the barrel of your life, but you also could die," explains a matter of fact Mario Dillanes Valverde. "In order to surf Playa Zicatela, you have to have a lot of 'huevos' just to paddle into the wave. This is the most heavy and dangerous wave in all of Mexico, and maybe in the world. The water is full of sharks, but there are hundreds of barrels waiting for you, if you have the guts to get into it."

Puerto Escondido is a town where there is some serious partying to be had. The bars rock and during a flat spell the night-time activity can reach legendary levels. But to score it epic means hitting the line-up at first light. The winds will be favourable and the waves less crowded. Sitting out back in a macking swell and you'll soon see why this place inspires such a reputation. "When we paddled out it was a decent size but this swell just kicked in," says Al, a travelling surfer staying in Puerto Escondido. "Suddenly it was massive and breaking straight onto the beach. I have never been so happy to set foot on dry land as I was when we finally managed to snag a smaller one into the beach." This is definitely a destination for those who like it extra hot and extra spicy.

Locals and legends

Listing the 'heavy' locals in the Playa Zicatela area, Mario Dillanes Valverde cites Carlos 'Coco' Nogales, Roger Ramirez, David Rutherford, Oscar Moncada, Sergio Ramirez, Celestino Diaz, Jorge Valle, Roberto Salinas, Cristian Corzo, Angelo Lozano.

Nearby breaks Carrizalilla is a small bay just to the west of Zicatela and is a sheltered spot popular with beginners and tourists. To the east of Zicatela is **The Point**, a quality left that is the place to head when big swells hit the main beach. It also handles the afternoon winds better as they blow side-shore here. Hop in a taxi as the walk is longer, and hotter, than you think.

Punta Roca

◈ **Location:** Punta Roca, La Libertad, El Salvador

◔ **Break type:** Right-hand point break

◉ **Conditions:** All swells

◈ **Size:** 2-12 ft +

◉ **Length:** Up to 200 m +

◉ **Tide:** All tides

◈ **Swell direction:** Southwesterly to southerly

◉ **Wind:** Northwesterly to northeasterly

◉ **Bottom:** Cobblestone

◉ **Ability level:** Intermediate to advanced

◉ **Best months:** Feb-Nov

◉ **Access:** Well timed paddle off the point

◉ **Hazards:** Polluted water, some localism, robbery

BEN SELWAY

Many people consider Punta Roca to be one of the world's most hardcore surf spots – and that's before you even get in the water. If you follow the valuble advice offered by veteran gringo travellers who've braved this world-class right-hand point, you might just make it into the line-up unscathed. To start with, you'll leave any valuables you have safely locked away in your hotel, which will probably be out of town. No watches, money, even sandals. Hiking up the point you'll probably have hooked up with a few other surfers to get that 'safety in numbers' feeling and the early start will have reduced the chances of running into any crack-crazed robbers. This won't bother you too much as you've had an early night (it's too dangerous to wander the streets after dark). Obviously you won't be carrying your favourite board in

case its shiny new whiteness disappears off into the bushes under the arm of a local psycho bandit. By sticking close to the shore you'll avoid the rabid dogs that lurk around the tempting grassy areas near the point. You'll have had all your jabs but the water quality may still make you think twice about actually launching off the boulders (what's that chemical smell?). In the line-up you'll try to speak a bit of Spanish with the locals but the earplugs you are wearing to ward off infections make it difficult to hear what people are saying in response. You'll try not to swallow any water when you take a beating after being dropped in on. Yes, there's nothing like a trip to tropical paradise to help you relax and forget about the stresses of home.

But is this really what Punta Roca is like, and if so, why do so many surfers still head there? Firstly, the wave at La Libertad is certainly a world-class point break offering up some of the best waves in the whole of Central America. Swells come out of the South Pacific and reel along this cobblestone point for over 200 m in the right conditions. The take-off is fast and hollow and can barrel before wrapping around and onto the point where the wave walls up and starts to speed along towards the town. There are a couple of possible cover-ups and on a low tide the rocks can be close to the surface. During the peak season, between April and May, swells can reach over 12 ft, but the average range is between 4 ft and 6 ft. The next section (which can sometimes link up with first) starts in front of the cemetery and peels down the inside of the point towards the restaurant where the third section of the wave, La Paz, produces mellow waves suited

Punta Roca Board

6'1" Byrne HP
Shaper: Phil Byrne
6'1" x 18⅜" x 2⁵⁄₁₆"
High-performance shortboard ideally suited for the long hollow lined up point waves at Punta Roca.
Single to double concave.
FCS fins.

ⓘ Boards by Surftech
www.surftech.com info@surftech.com

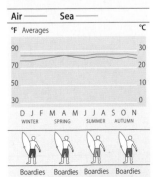

Air ————	Sea	
°F	Averages	°C
90		30
70		20
50		10
30		0

D	J	F	M	A	M	J	J	A	S	O	N
WINTER			SPRING			SUMMER			AUTUMN		

Boardies   Boardies   Boardies   Boardies

Above: The long walls of the cobble stone point help put the hazzards and hassles into perspective.
Opposite page: Dan Joel rocking la Punta.

to longboarders and beginners. There are, and always have been, issues with the quality of the water around La Libertad. Surfers returning in the seventies had tales of illness and putrid waters, and the sea can still be less than inviting today.

When it comes to issues outside the water, none, some or all of the scenarios above can apply depending on how lucky (or unlucky) you are or how much Central America experience you've clocked up. Even experienced travellers can find La Libertad an intimidating and uncomfortable place. "My favourite place in Central America is Panama," says Javier Amezaga, editor of Spanish surf magazine *Tres60*. "I have seen better surf spots in El Salvador, in La Libertad area, El Zunzal or El Zonte, a lot of very good spots in a short distance, but the place is especially dangerous and you feel you are risking your life all the time." La Libertad is not an affluent town and does have its share of issues. Many travellers advise visiting with reputable surf tours or staying at surf camps nearby.

"Punta Roca is an amazing wave," says Damian Tate. "It has a barrelling take-off and a racetrack that's great for down the line speed followed by hacking cutbacks. The town itself is a real experience. Not all surf trips are a tropical paradise and lush green forests. There are camps in the area and a first-time visitor might benefit from staying with one of those." There is talk of the point being redeveloped with new high-rise blocks being built as well as a marina and breakwater. Some claim that this will threaten the wave ("The only reason to visit the town," says one surfer), and others claim that the wave will be preserved. It is worth remembering that this is a spot sitting in the heart of a developing country, and for all its drawbacks and bad points, this certainly is a wave with personality – which face it shows you can be part of the adventure.

Locals and legends

Jimmy Rotherham is one of Central America's hottest young talents. His father Roberto Rotherham first arrived at the point in the seventies and owns the local Punta Roca Hotel and Restaurant.

Nearby breaks **Rio Grande** is a nearby rivermouth break found to the west of La Libertad and is worth checking if Punta Roca is too big for your tastes. **Zunzal** is a little further west and is a right-hand point break that is the most popular wave in the region. It offers pretty easy walls that can hold a decent size without getting too critical. For this reason it is also very busy. Try to catch it early.

BEN SELWAY

Pavones

◈ **Location:** Pavones, Pacific coast, Costa Rica

◔ **Break type:** Left point break

◔ **Conditions:** Big swells

◔ **Size:** 3-8 ft +

◔ **Length:** Up to 200 m +

◔ **Tide:** All tides

◔ **Swell direction:** Southerly

◔ **Wind:** Easterly to northeasterly

◔ **Bottom:** Cobblestone

◔ **Ability level:** Intermediate

◔ **Best months:** Apr-Nov

◔ **Access:** Easy paddle-out

◔ **Hazards:** Crowds

Hot and sweat-soaked, sitting at the side of the road, waiting for the next bus on the Pan American Highway. A heavy single-fin propped against a tree. Dense rainforest encroaching on either side as a lorry roars by, belching smoke. The sounds of the tropics are deafening, as birds and insects compete to be heard over the battering rain accompanied by the occasional rumble of thunder. Chasing down leads, hitching and hiking down claustrophobic trails, paddling across rivers and hacking through the undergrowth to reveal wide volcanic beaches or peeling rivermouths: a flashback to the pioneering days of the early seventies or a modern traveller pushing the exploration boundaries minus the ubiquitous 4WD. Central America is a pretty wild place. A place where you feel you could easily disappear and no one would notice. Even in the

seventies, Costa Rica was different from the rest of the continent; ripe for exploration, but politically stable. It wasn't that it was safe, but it was safe enough. There were still snakes, sharks, spiders, malaria and dengue fever, but there was less chance of encountering banditos and even less chance of corrupt army officers demanding bribes (Costa Rica doesn't even have an army).

When Christopher Columbus first set foot in Costa Rica he was so impressed by the friendly locals and the wealth of the land that he christened the place 'Rich Coast'. Abundant in natural beauty, its mind-bending waveriding potential has been attracting gringos since the late sixties. Pavones has always been a major draw, and despite the fact that it is inaccessible and inconsistent, surfers seem to appear from nowhere every time it breaks. The waves of this region are home to an expat community that seems to survive in a fragile state of peaceful coexistence. There are land issues at some of the breaks and squabbles in and out of the line-up, but this is still a compelling location that continues to attract more surfers every year. They all came here to enjoy a tropical paradise away from the crowds, but the crowds have now followed them to their quiet corner of the globe.

The Golfo Dulce is a large inlet on the southwestern Pacific coast of the country. The bay faces southwest and a number of breaks can be found around its mouth, but nestled in the more sheltered inner recesses of the inlet is Pavones. Big southerly swells wrap around Punta Banco, reeling along the southern fringe of the bay. The long, cobblestone-lined section at Pavones is perfectly angled and the

Below: Steven Chew, Pavones.
Opposite page: You don't need to read between the lines to understand this.

Pavones Board

5'8" Surftech Soul Fish
Shaper: Randy French
5'8" x 20¾" x 2½"
Blends the curves and outlines of yesteryear with bottom contours of today.
Drivey off the front foot, nice and wide for increased paddling power, twin keel fins for added drive and stability.
Custom twin keels fins.

ⓘ Boards by **Surftech**
www.surftech.com info@surftech.com

Air ——— Sea ———

°F Averages °C

90	30
70	20
50	10
30	0

D J F M A M J J A S O N
WINTER SPRING SUMMER AUTUMN

| Boardies | Boardies | Boardies | Boardies |

GEOFF RAGATZ

GEOFF RAGATZ

walling lefts peak and peel for what can be over 600 m, spinning down the lush, forest-lined point. Many consider this to be one of the longest lefts in the world, and seeing it in all its glory you would be hard-pressed to disagree.

"If you catch a good set, you start well up on the point and can make it past three 100-yard sections at each end of the rivermouth and past the Esquina del Mar cabinas," explains Greg Gordon from *CRSurf*. "Keeping up your speed and being able to smack the lip will keep you in the pocket and you can ride for another 200 yards to where the fishing boats are kept. That's over a quarter-mile ride, and when you're done your legs ache. Forget about paddling back against the strong current, most just follow a beachside path back to the rivermouth and then paddle across it to make it back to the peak." If the swell arrives during the night, sun up will see many waiting to paddle out. The wind sweeping down off the hills in the early morning means this is often the best time to catch these endless walls as they are groomed into glassy, ruler-topped lines. "When the sun warms up the land, the wind switches onshore and the heat rises to create rainstorms that hit or miss for the rest of the day and into the evening," says Greg. "The accompanying lighting and wind can make it sketchy staying out in the line-up."

Driving into the area, blanketed with dense, verdant forest, still gives you a sense of getting away from it all. You and the rest of the crew that is! "On larger days there may be 80 people out," says Greg "but the swift current quickly separates the crowd and the best surfers know exactly when to paddle for the horizon to catch the waves that line up the best. More than just great surfing, however, Pavones is the full sensual experience. It serves up a feast of sights, sounds and feelings. Greg explains, "Out in the line-up you get an amazing view of the Osa Peninsula, jungle-clad mountains, and if you're lucky the unique calls of the scarlet macaws and howler monkeys." It's moments like this that demonstrate why this is truly Central America's 'Rich Coast'.

Locals and legends
America's Ted Marzas, Marshall McCarthy, and Gonzo writer Allan Weisbecker, author of *In Search of Captain Zero*. Local Circuito Nacional competitors Durby Castillo and Laura Pecoraro are lighting up the ranks.

Nearby breaks Further inside the inlet is the beach break at **Playa Zancudo**, which picks up less swell but is pretty uncrowded. **Punta Banco** to the south of Pavones is more exposed and usually has waves. Around this point there are plenty of beaches and reefs to explore when Pavones is flat.

Salsa Brava

◎ **Location:**	Salsa Brava, Puerto Viejo, Caribbean Coast, Costa Rica
◐ **Break type:**	Right-hand reef
◒ **Conditions:**	Medium to big swells
◍ **Size:**	4-8 ft +
◑ **Length:**	up to 100 m
◓ **Tide:**	All tides
◉ **Swell direction:**	Easterly
◎ **Wind:**	Westerly
◒ **Bottom:**	Coral reef
◐ **Ability level:**	Intermediate to advanced
◉ **Best months:**	Dec-Feb
◎ **Access:**	Via small, rippy channel
◒ **Hazards:**	Heavy barrel, shallow reef

Salsa Brava is a truly hot and spicy wave that lives up to its name. It's either a sauce that's only for the brave, or you need 'brave sauce' pulsing through your veins before you take on this Caribbean beast. Who would have thought that the most powerful and deadly wave in Costa Rica would sit on the eastern coastline facing out into the relatively small Caribbean Sea, famed for its idyllic still waters. When Salsa Brava is firing, it's a spectacle to behold, whether you are sitting on the grassy bank ocean-side, or have front-row seats staring into the grinding barrel from the line-up. For many people in Puerto Viejo, life revolves around this wave. Some left behind money, mortgages and marriages to set up camp here. Salsa Brava can be a dream, but she can also be a cruel mistress. There can be long flat spells, huge macking swells, broken boards and close-outs that mean a trip across the grating reef. But still the faithful stay because the rewards are some of the most perfect barrels in Central America.

"Salsa Brava is a world-class reef break because it can hold giant surf and throw barrels that last over 100 yards," says Greg Gordon of *CRSurf*. "The powerful wave breaks across an L-shaped reef rock, with a challenging paddle out beginning in a 3-ft-wide channel. The local surfers know exactly where to sit, while the novice can be confounded by the two shifting peaks and deceptive currents. It's known for its rights, but also has a speedy left with a steep drop. The biggest I've surfed it was double overhead, but stories have been shared of 20-ft-plus faces, with not a trace of wind and only a handful of people out. On a medium-sized swell it can get crowded with a large local contingent that one should respect if they plan on getting any waves."

"I was travelling through Central America and stopped off at Salsa Brava with a friend," says British surfer Anthonia Atha. "It's a super heavy wave and before long we'd snapped a board. But the waves were so good we stayed in the line-up and shared the one board, taking it in turn catching barrels and treading water. A few weeks later I was in Panama and I heard this guy going on about these girls charging Salsa Brava sharing one board and I wanted to lean over and go 'That was us'." This is a wave that most people liken to the North Shore of Oahu for sheer grunt and power. There are two peaks at Salsa. First Peak has a tight take-off with steep drops onto the ledgy reef producing fast and hollow rights. First peak can also have the occasional short left and is dominated by locals and expats. Just to the north is the Second Peak, a more shifty take-off zone that helps to spread the crowds around a bit. "I guess the locals thought we were a bit crazy, these girls taking it in turn to swim around the line-up while the other caught waves," says Anthonia. "Looking back, maybe it was a bit."

The prime season to catch the Caribbean coastline is December to February, but it can extend into April when easterly swells can still fire in off the warm sea. Although pictures of Salsa Brava first started to filter out of Central America in the seventies, there has been a boom in visitors to Puerto Viejo over the past ten years. This seemed to intensify after the wave was featured in *The Search for Captain Zero*, a book about a surfer's journey through Central America and his time

JS CALLAHAN/TROPICALPIX

Left: Salsa sign.
Opposite page: Paul Reineke tucking into some salsa.

spent in this Caribbean town. It's not just the settlement that's changing either. Through natural disaster and the consequences of human actions, the reef has changed too. "Salsa Brava has been altered by an earthquake that took place in 1992," explains Greg Gordon. "That made the reef even shallower in some spots. It helped in some ways but supposedly made the ride shorter. The earthquake, along with the pesticides for the banana crops and human development along the coast, has killed the reef that creates the wave. At low tide, the stream that leads out to the beach sometimes is polluted from septic tank run-off. And without the strong opposition by the locals, Salsa Brava might have had oil drilling platforms far enough offshore to be out of sight, but not out of range of potential toxification of the line-up." The surfers and fishermen of Puerto Viejo are trying to protect their beach and their reef – trying to ensure that the brave will continue to be able to take on the 'Caribbean Pipeline'.

Locals and legends

Gilbert Brown won the CNS tour in 2001 and has competed on the WQS. Germain 'Niño' Medrano was the 2004 Costa Rican champion. Other standouts include Gabriel Araya ('Topo'), known for his fluid style, Andy Hilton and expat Tequila who has the place wired.

Salsa Brava Board

6'6" Channel Islands K-Model

Shaper: Al Merrick

6'6" x 18¾" x 2⅜"

A high-performance board for thick, powerful waves.

Single to double concave for down the line speed with extra nose rocker for steep take-offs and under the lip snaps!

FCS K 2.1 fins.

ⓘ Boards by **Surftech**
www.surftech.com info@surftech.com

Air ——	Sea ——	
°F Averages		°C
90		30
70		20
50		10
30		0

D J F	M A M	J J A	S O N
WINTER	SPRING	SUMMER	AUTUMN

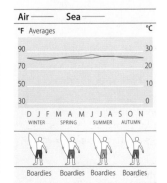

Boardies	Boardies	Boardies	Boardies

Nearby breaks Limón is the port town where the road takes a south turn for Puerto Viejo. There are breaks around here such as **Isla Uvita**, a left that breaks along the side of the offshore island and is only accessed by boat. To the south of Limón, **Westfalia** is a very German sounding stretch of beach that has miles of peaks to explore – closes out in bigger swells though. Just south of Puerto Viejo lies **Playa Cocles**, an okay beach break that's worth checking low to mid tide.

Bocas del Toro

Location:	Bocas del Toro, Caribbean Coast, Panama
Break type:	Reefs breaks
Conditions:	All swells
Size:	3-6 ft +
Length:	Up to 50 m +
Tide:	All tides
Swell direction:	Northeasterly to easterly
Wind:	Southwesterly
Bottom:	Coral and rock reef
Ability level:	Intermediate to advanced
Best months:	Jan-May, Jul and Aug
Access:	Boat
Hazards:	Go explore

Below: Gary Savadra – matadorian magic at Bocas del Toro.
Opposite page: Shane Dorian enjoying a bit of Caribbean island life.

The long, thin skiff cuts through the glassy sheen, water lazily lolls around the bottom of the boat, mottled with the rainbow colours of spilled gasoline. The air is a mixture of salty spray and two-stroke exhaust. When the sun breaks through the patchy cloud cover, its intensity makes the hairs on the back of your arm stand up. The boat approaches the headland from the west but already the spinning right-hander is visible, grinding down the reef; the translucent blue green waters transformed into a huge open barrel with a steep wall, wrapping along the submerged rock and coral. The headland clothed in tropical rainforest is a scene so familiar to the surfing psyche, be it from the Indian Ocean or the Pacific. But here in the Caribbean it feels strange to be waxing up a 7-ft pintail with the hard tropical wax that you

bought back home when preparing for the trip. The essence of coconut released by the fresh top coat brings a familiar reassurance as you prepare to paddle into the line-up at Silverbacks, a wave that surely boasts one of the best names anywhere in the surfing world. Like the silverback gorilla, this is a wave that doesn't tolerate fools lightly, and has the power to dismiss pretenders with a mere backswipe that can send you spinning into the channel, later retrieving the pieces of your favourite stick.

Some breaks are deemed great despite their locations, diamonds lying in the rough. Others are made, purely by their surroundings. Here in the Bocas Del Toro island chain, off the northeast coast of Panama, there are some classic waves in a lush and tropical setting. Some have no real business hiding away in this quiet corner of the Caribbean, amongst the post-colonial architecture and the golden sand beaches. The provincial capital, Bocas del Toro, was a turn-of-the-century boomtown boasting a population of 25,000, feverishly employed in the day-to-day running of the United Fruit Company. By the 1920s the banana industry had withered due to a plague of blight and the town was left as yet another isolated outpost, testament to both the expansiveness and the ruthlessness of multi-national corporate enterprise. Today the grand wooden buildings have been transformed into restaurants, cafés, bars and hotels to accommodate the many travellers, divers and eco-tourists drawn to this pristine environment. Meanwhile, the virgin forest and the white sand of the Bastimentos Island National Marine Reserve provides safe nesting for three species of sea turtles.

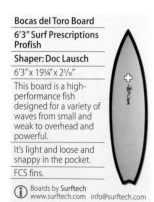

Bocas del Toro Board

6'3" Surf Prescriptions Profish

Shaper: Doc Lausch

6'3" x 19¼" x 2⁵/₁₆"

This board is a high-performance fish designed for a variety of waves from small and weak to overhead and powerful.

It's light and loose and snappy in the pocket.

FCS fins.

Boards by Surftech
www.surftech.com info@surftech.com

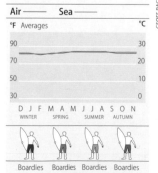

Air —— Sea ——

°F Averages °C

90 — 30
70 — 20
50 — 10
30 — 0

D J F M A M J J A S O N
WINTER SPRING SUMMER AUTUMN

Boardies Boardies Boardies Boardies

GEOFF RAGATZ

Surfers have been drawn here since the seventies, but it is still fairly off the beaten track. The surf seasons are brief and the science behind swell generation remains something of a mystery. Waves can appear overnight lighting up the breaks for no apparent reason, and on days when ideal weather scenarios arise the water can sleep like the dead. However, between the end of December and the beginning of April, the winter season brings with it the probability that something will stir during a visit, as does the June to August window. When a swell does kick in it can turn on an amazing array of surfing possibilities dotted through the chain. On the main island of Colón, the main spot, known romantically as Dumps, is a shallow, fast-breaking left reef that bowls along a rock and coral ledge. In a big swell it is transformed into a hollow racetrack boasting stand-up barrels for the brave. It has a less critical inside section known, surprisingly, as Inside Dumps. (The nearby beaches tend to be predominantly close-outs). Across the channel, a short boat ride will bring you to a left point that peels along the northern edge of Isla Carenero. This popular spot is home to long walling waves that break from 4 ft to 8 ft. Across the channel to the east, on the tip of Isla Bastimentos, Silverbacks rests out on the point,

and beyond it are miles of open coastline waiting to be explored. It's just a case of hiring the right boat, slapping on the sunscreen and waxing up your best board. Motoring off to the southwest, you never know what you might find out there in this lost archipelago.

Locals and legends
Mostly visiting surfers. As yet no surf shops or facilities.

Nearby breaks On Colón, **Bluff Beach** is a 5-km long beach which is fickle and tends to close out. **La Curva** is a short and fast A-frame that can have some fast, barrelling waves over a shallow reef. To the southeast, **Outside** and **Inside Dumps** offer lefts that range from the shallow fast tubes to longer walling rides. **Isla Carenero** has a long, left reef point that needs a bigger swell to filter through. Just a short boat trip from Bocas town **Silverbacks** has been compared to Pipe. You may get lucky.

Santa Catalina

⚐ **Location:** La Punta, Santa Catalina, Southwest Panama	
◗ **Break type:** Right-hand point break with short left	
◔ **Conditions:** All swells	
⊖ **Size:** 3-8 ft +	
◉ **Length:** up to 200 m	
◓ **Tide:** Mid to high	
◈ **Swell direction:** Southwesterly to southerly	
◑ **Wind:** Northerly to northeasterly	
☺ **Bottom:** Lava reef	
◉ **Ability level:** Intermediate to advanced	
✿ **Best months:** Apr-Aug	
✇ **Access:** Straightforward paddle wide of peak	
⊖ **Hazards:** Shallow at low tide	

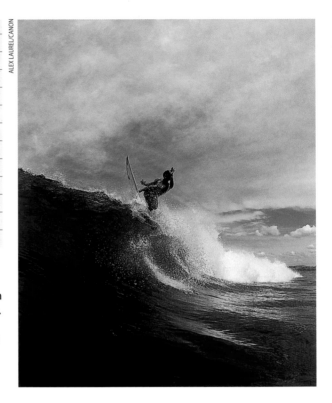

ALEX LAUREL/CANON

It's cold. Not just chilly but cold. You pull the hood up on the sweatshirt you thought you'd never need, even though you'd been warned you would. The guy sitting next to you is wearing a beanie. The coach has stopped to deposit another passenger on the edge of the Pan American Highway, but looking through the window all you can see in the consuming blackness, that devours everything up to the very edge of the dense rainforest, are fireflies dancing in the trees. The claustrophobic heat of late-night Panama City is of stark contrast to the turbo-charged air conditioning blasting through the comfortable, but almost empty coach. Not long now until the turn-off and the road south, where you'll be released from this frosty confinement and set free onto the bus for Santa Catalina and the warm, welcoming waters of the Pacific.

Back in 1970 the journey was not quite so simple. A group of surfers from Panama City pushed out to the southwest searching for virgin waves along the pristine Pacific coastline. Ricardo Icaza, Freddy Dietz, Max Castrellon and Ricki Fabreca were following the rumour trail which, like the rainforest track, was vague at best. By pure chance they stumbled out of the bush at a spot near the tiny fishing village of Santa Catalina. "That was the start," says Ricardo. "We came down here as much as possible over the next few years and managed to keep it secret for quite a while." Here was a world-class wave being shared between a few friends who learnt the moods and nuances associated with shifting tides and swell directions. The guys had struck gold, and in order to fully enjoy their discovery, they invested in plots of land in the village. After years of empty perfection, Ricardo opened the first

Santa Catalina surf camp in the mid-eighties. Reputation brought the first visitors and soon magazine features revealed the true quality of this classic, hollow right-hander to the world. Suddenly Santa Catalina was one of Central America's biggest surfing attractions.

The wave is a classic point that spins along a shallow reef producing reeling barrelling rights that can run for over 100 m. There is also the option of the shorter left, which produces some fast walls. At the southern edge of Panama's Pacific coastline, this region is one of the most consistent in the country. The long, flat lava reef tapers out into the vast blue, perfectly angled for the predominantly southerly and southwesterly swells which roll through the peak season. It has taken a while for the crowds to catch on, but today there can be over 40 surfers paddling around the peak. In a good swell, the waves come thick and fast and the stream of surfers are soon spread along

Above: Caribbean surfer Jason Apparicio.
Opposite page: Iker Fuentes being a Panamaniac at Santa Catalina.

the point. Mid to high tides provide the best, and safest, times for the jagged basalt bottom. Low tide is really the domain of the Hellmen as water is drawn off the reef and the inside bowl section can often suck dry.

When it comes to seasons, there are a number of options. May to October is the wet season. Southwesterly swells are pretty consistent at this time of year and can peak in the 8 ft plus region. Winds switch onshore around lunchtime but the daily rains can help soften their impact on the waves. November to January is the dry season but it can also be a barren time for decent groundswells as only the biggest northwesterly swells reach this region and the southwesterly

groundswells dry up. However, the new surfing season kicks in during the February to April window when daylong offshores can coincide with good weather and fine waves.

There is a growing number of local surfers who charge here, inspired by regular visitors like Tom Curren. Since the fall of General Noriega, Panama has become a relatively safe country to visit. Aside from the threat of petty crime in large urban areas, the country offers a much more laid-back surf experience than in the seventies and eighties. Recently a large corporation earmarked Santa Catalina for development, buying up huge swathes of land to create a major tourist destination. The village has reached a crossroads. What this means for the locals and the wave at Santa Catalina is uncertain. Hopefully progress will not bring an end to this perfect point and the wave will be preserved for future generations of surfers.

Locals and legends
Some of the names associated with the wave include the likes of Ricardo Icaza, Freddy Dietz, Max Castrellon, Ricki Fabreca, Alejandro 'Cholito' Alfonso and Peter Novey while visiting pros like Tom Curren have helped to raise the profile of the wave.

Nearby breaks Punta Brava is located just to the southeast and is a beach with a low tide left reef. Good up to head high and a place to check when Santa Catalina is too shallow to surf. The outer islands of **Cebaco** and former penal colony **Coiba** have a number of quality reefs that are only accessible by boat. There are charter companies in Santa Catalina offering trips to these consistent and less crowded breaks.

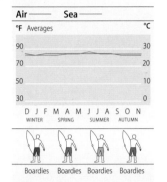

Santa Catalina Board		
6'2" Rawson Hyper Skate		
Shaper: Pat Rawson		
6'2" x 18¼" x 2¼"		
Designed for all around surf in the 2' to 8' + range.		
Fast and drivey through turns and cutbacks with enough stability to hold in the steep hollow sections.		
Futures FTP1 fins.		

ⓘ Boards by **Surftech**
www.surftech.com info@surftech.com

Air ——— Sea ———

°F	Averages	°C
90		30
70		20
50		10
30		0

D J F M A M J J A S O N
WINTER SPRING SUMMER AUTUMN

Boardies Boardies Boardies Boardies

WILLY URIBE

Cane Garden

◊ Location: Cane Garden, Tortola, British Virgin Islands

◗ Break type: Right-hand point break

◐ Conditions: Medium to big swells

◑ Size: 4-8 ft +

◒ Length: 75-200 m

◓ Tide: Mid tide

◔ Swell direction: Northeasterly to northwesterly

◕ Wind: Southeasterly to southwesterly

◖ Bottom: Coral and rock reef

◗ Ability level: Advanced

◐ Best months: Sep-Mar

◑ Access: Paddle off the point

◒ Hazards: Heavy, shallow inside, fickle

Cane Garden Board
5'11" Stretch Fletcher 4
Shaper: Stretch
5'11" x 18.75" x 2.375"
Designed with world-class aerialist, Nathan Fletcher. Full nose and tail which straightens out mid-section inducing speed.
Four fin makes it ride like a tri-fin with more drive and acceleration.
Ultra responsive and fast!
FCS GX/M5 fins.

ⓘ Boards by **Surftech**
www.surftech.com   info@surftech.com

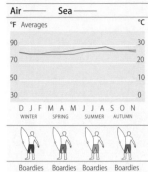

Air ——— Sea ———

°F Averages   °C

| D | J | F | M | A | M | J | J | A | S | O | N |
| WINTER | | | SPRING | | | SUMMER | | | AUTUMN | | |

Boardies   Boardies   Boardies   Boardies

A long, winding point wave wraps around the lush green northern edge of a sheltered bay. In the protected cove, a pristine white yacht rests at anchor, the sun reflecting off it like a diamond in the blue. The houses that cling to the hillside and the crystalline oceanic hues immediately identify this piece of paradise as lying firmly within the bounds of the Caribbean. Cane Garden is a dream wave in a dream location. This safe haven could well have been a favourite anchorage for the fabled local outlaw Black Beard and his pirate fleet, or a place where Sir Francis Drake stopped off to resupply his ships. Today it draws a different kind of mariner cruising the rich islands, and a new breed of buccaneer in search of waves to plunder.

The Leeward and Windward islands form a huge arc delineating the boundary between the Caribbean and the North Atlantic. The British Virgin Islands sit at the northern apex of this curve, heading up the Lesser Antilles and putting themselves in an excellent position to pick up swells coming out of northern waters. This independent island state is volcanic in origin, as are the majority of Caribbean territories. Occasionally one of these sleeping giants awakens and, on small landmasses such as these, the results can be devastating. Neighbouring Montserrat lost her capital, harbour and airport in 1995, when a huge eruption forced over two thirds of the population to flee the now grey, ash-smothered landscape.

Sitting at one of the beachfront bars in Cane Garden Bay, however, this is the furthest thing from your mind. The subtropical climate ranges from sunny and warm in the summer to sunny and warm in the winter. The white sand beach is the perfect place to kick back and wait for one of those hurricane swells to hit. "What makes this wave so special is its beautiful setting," says Andy Morrell, local surfer and owner of the HIHO brand. "It's the best break on our island and the fact that it's also a world-class spot makes it kind of cool for us Tortola surfers." The long, azure walls wrap around the point at Cane Garden creating a number of sections that, on the right day, can produce rides of up to 200 m. "I remember once surfing until dark and as the sun set over St Thomas the moon rose over the hill behind us," says Andy. "There was a moment when both the sun was up and the moon was visible. These are some of the memories that make this place so special."

Below: Total connection Tortola perfection.
Opposite page: Lines of sell bend around the headland and into the bay to produce long, reeling crystaline righthanders.

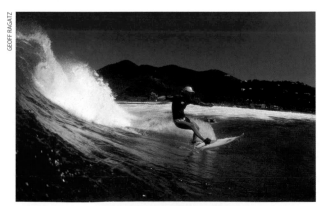

GEOFF RAGATZ

GEOFF RAGATZ

Cane Garden Point sits at the northern fringe of a westerly facing bay on the island of Tortola, the largest of the British Virgin Islands. During the peak surf months of October through to April low pressure systems roll off the American mainland and onto an easterly trajectory over the Atlantic towards Europe. These spinning storms push groundswell down from the northern Atlantic waters until they eventually hit the shores of these lush islands as clean, combed corduroy. There can also be some magical days during the hurricane season, when frenetic storms heading through the Gulf and off into the Sargasso Sea can be the bearers of epic conditions. Lines bend around the headland and into the bay, and at over 6 ft begin filtering along the point producing long, reeling right-handers. These waves barrel and wall down the shallow rocks and coral, offering up some challenging rides. Cane Garden may only break between ten and 15 times a year, but it can work for days at a time with the right conditions, and the increase in hurricanes occurring year on year means this wave may be one of the unwitting beneficiaries of global climate change. The point really starts working when the swell hits head high, the geography of the spot allowing it to hold its own when even the biggest storm swells kick in. Its westerly facing aspect means that the trade winds coming from the east are funnelled into feathering offshore breezes, but this is a flexible wave that will even work during light onshores.

Although the wave has only come into the public domain since the 1990s, the growth in general tourism has had some impact. "There is minimal environmental awareness here and throughout the Caribbean," says Andy Morrell. "Unchecked development is harming the marine environment." This became evident in April 2006 when the break at this laid-back idyll was threatened by a potential new breakwater development. Shock waves went around the local surf community and word spread across the Internet. Luckily the scheme seems to be on hold, but in a world where big money talks, developments can appear out of the woodwork with little or no warning. In a region where offshore often refers to financial matters, it's up to the surfers to keep an eye on the practices of the modern-day privateers.

Locals and legends

"The best local surfer to ride Cane is JC Pierce," says Andy. "But in a good swell 20-30 surfers might be on the water at once."

Nearby breaks Tortola has many wonderful, pristine bays but most of them are sheltered and more suited to sunbathing than surfing. **Josiah's Bay** is considered the most consistent break as it faces north and picks up any swell going. The banks don't really handle swell of any size though. **Capoons Bay**, south of Cane Garden Bay, is home to a nice A-frame reef. It tends to cope well with bigger swells and its orientation makes it offshore in the trade winds.

Central America & the Caribbean Cane Garden

Soup Bowl

Location:	Soup Bowl, Bathsheba, east coast, Barbados
Break type:	Right-hand reef break
Conditions:	Small to medium swells
Size:	3-8 ft
Length:	50 m +
Tide:	All tides
Swell direction:	Northeasterly to southeasterly
Wind:	Westerly
Bottom:	Coral topped limestone reef
Ability level:	Intermediate
Best months:	Oct-Mar
Access:	Paddle out in channel
Hazards:	Heavy take-off, shallow inside section

ALEX LAUREL

"I had a day when it was about 15-ft-plus faces and a huge set came through," says Zed Layson, thinking back to his most perfect moment at his home break. "Only about six of us were taking off and I was a bit too deep. I yelled for it, I was about 6 ft behind the peak, others guy who wanted it were looking at me and pulling back, I barely made the drop and decided to pull into the massive barrel, which was safer. I got the longest and biggest barrel of my life. The entire beach was screaming." Soup Bowl has a reputation that has quickly developed from a windy winter warmer to a world-class performer as the increasing number of surfers leaving Barbados singing its praises has continued to rise year after year. And when the likes of Kelly Slater say they've had one of the best surfs of their lives there, you know that people are going to sit up and take notice.

The Isla Los Barbados, or Island of the Bearded Ones, was inhabited by the descendents of migratory tribes of South American Indians when it was stumbled upon by Portuguese explorer Pedro Campos in 1536. He named the islands after the fig trees whose aerial roots he likened to huge beards. Life on this outpost, however, was never easy and by the time the British arrived in 1620 the place was deserted. This island nation is set apart from its neighbours both geographically – sitting east of the main chain of Caribbean Islands – and geologically – Barbados is not volcanic in origin. The limestone and coral landmass sits out in the Atlantic Ocean, open to swell from the persistent easterly trade winds and passing North Atlantic low pressures and hurricanes. The exposed eastern coastline is home to a number of surf breaks, with Soup Bowl being the headline act. This open beach near Bathsheba is home to some quality waves, a left that works in smaller swells and an excellent and consistent right-hander that can be a fun, whackable wall or a grinding barrel. "Soup Bowl is one of the most unique waves to surf for a number of reasons," says Zed. "It is very consistent given that it faces the Atlantic Ocean and receives swell from all directions, it is very powerful on a north swell. Soup Bowl is a tight and powerful barrel, vertical lips and aerial sections with nice round-house sections, all packed into one wave. When it's big it can make your heart jump in your throat."

The real beauty of Soup Bowl is that there is nearly always a rideable wave here. "Soup Bowl has the unique set up," says Zed "and it always has waves, probably 355 days a year." Even though the easterly winds can be a near-constant companion, the set-up here means that quality waves can still break in the light onshores. It can even offer up barrel sections when the light trades are blowing. The bowling peak throws out on take-off meaning a steep, ledgy drop in shallow water. The right-hander then reels away into another wedgy section that offers some nice lips to hit. The inside is a tuberider's dream and the heavy barrels break powerfully over the reef here. This is a wave that likes a swell with some north in it. When small, there is a left that springs up while on a big swell the whole place gets a lot more serious and a lot meaner. There can be heavy rips and the reef has a liberal covering of spiny urchins – a massive contrast to the relaxed, chilled scene that awaits once you reach the safety of the beach.

Above: Local Mark Holder getting his fill at Soup Bowl.
Opposite page: Caribbean dreams are made of this.

Barbados has a long history of beach culture and waveriding. In 1966, the year the island gained its independence from Britain, the Barbados Surfing Association was established. The year-round excellent climate combined with the fact that Soup Bowl is the most consistent break in the Caribbean chain, has seen the break become the region's most famous spot. For Zed, the highs of being a Bajan surfer outweigh the lows. "We have great waves in warm conditions all year, it is sunny and we are a friendly nation. The lows are, as a competitor, it is difficult to get noticed and very expensive to travel to events, and sponsors are not available because our industry is small and still growing."

Barbados is still increasing in popularity as more and more surfers trade destinations like Hawaii, with its hardcore waves and hardcore line-ups, for the consistency and enjoyment to be found on this idyllic island. And when the big groundswells kick in, there are waves here to challenge any location on the planet. As pro surfer Sam Lamiroy says, "I've had some of the most perfect barrels ever in Barbados. It's one of my favourite spots on the planet."

Locals and legends
Mark Holder, Anderson 'Hoggie' Mayers, Alan Burke, Peter Hill, Zed Layson, Stewart Stoute, Jake Corbin, Stefan Corbin.

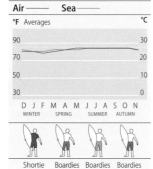

Soup Bowl Board

6'1" Channel Islands K-Model

Shaper: Al Merrick

6'1" x 18¼" x 2¼"

Single to slight double concave for lots of drive and lift with extra nose rocker for steep take-offs and under the lip snaps!

FCS K2.1 fins.

(i) Boards by **Surftech**
www.surftech.com info@surftech.com

Air ——— Sea ———
°F Averages   °C
90   30
70   20
50   10
30   0
D J F M A M J J A S O N
WINTER SPRING SUMMER AUTUMN

Shortie   Boardies   Boardies   Boardies

Nearby breaks High Rock is to the south of Soup Bowl and is named after the rock jutting out to sea. It produces both rights and lefts in smaller swells. **Parlours/Parlors** is a peak that picks up more swell than Soup Bowl, but is a less critical wave. The crowd factor is much lower, but the paddle out in bigger swells needs to be well timed due to the lack of a channel.

Central America & the Caribbean Soup Bowl

ALEX LAUREL

Surfers' tales

Caribbean dream Sam Lamiroy

I'm biased, take note. When it comes to describing Barbados and the waves to which it plays host, my rose tinted glasses are firmly in place. On my visits to the island I have had waves and experiences that will stay with me until eternity ends! I feel it would be somewhat amiss to simply describe the best wave on the island, as in Soupbowls, (allegedly, though there are still some secrets!) without touching on the whole Bajan experience. Barbados seems to have a magic mix of distant exoticism and a homely, somewhat British, European feel to it. In fact this trait seems to be quite prevalent through out most of the Caribbean region.

You just have to love the instant, emotive impact that these islands evoke. Be it Barbados, Martinique, Trinidad, Tobago, Dominica or any of those islands on the outer and thus more swell catching edges of the Caribbean basin. Wherever you decide to go, the chances are that if you have figured out the right time for the optimum swell/trade wind combination and done a little home work about the particular island

you're visiting, you will be blessed with warm water, clean, fun waves, usually in the 2-6 ft range and predominantly friendly locals – just be sure to be courteous and respectful. The other great thing about all these islands is the fact that they can cope with most swell and wind directions. If one side of the island is blown out, simply jump in the car, nip around to the other side and score some clean surf. Easy!

It sounds like a cliché to talk about palm trees, turquoise waters, white sandy beaches, and perfect waves, but the simple fact of the matter is this, clichés have to start somewhere. The genesis of the proverbial 'tropical paradise' definitely seems to stem from around these here shores. Allow me to illustrate with a brief recollection of some of my own personal highlights here…

It all started a little while ago, when my oldest sister fell in love with, married and had kids with a well-known local Bajan Surfer. Obviously it was our collective familial duty to visit them on a regular basis –

ALEX LAUREL

ALEX LAUREL

what a drag! So for the past few years not only my family, but also my girlfriend's family (most of whom surf) have made many visits to this Fair Isle. Wives, kids, aunties, uncles, grannies, all have had a great time here and all for different reasons. This is what makes surfing here such a joy. Obviously for me it is always work, but more about that later. In all my years of travelling I have never been to a place that can make so many people happy on so many different levels. The quality of the waves are good enough to keep even the most hard core of surfers content, while there is enough cosmopolitan entertainment to keep the 'land lubbers' and sun worshipers satisfied as well.

As far as my 'work' is concerned, one particular trip does seem to stand out. We were doing a photo trip to one of the islands 'near' Barbados, getting really fun overhead waves, just having an absolute blinding time, when word got to us that there was a contest on in Barbados that weekend. A couple of flights later and there we were – solid 6ft barrels, just perfect Soupbowls caverns, surfing heats with

only 3 other guys out. It felt most peculiar to be getting barrelled for points instead of the usual contest grovel surfing.

Now remember that Kelly Slater had a session here recently when it was a little bigger, and called it 'possibly the best day of surfing in my life'. To put that into perspective, the place has potential! As far as surfing trips go you could do a lot worse than spending some quality time around these parts, after all this time I should know, and you can bet I'll be back. See you there!!

Sam Lamiroy is one of Europe's top professional surfers as well as a globe trotting surf explorer. In 2004 he won the Barbados Independence Pro Surfing Classic in front of 5,000 fans at Soupbowls in pumping 6 to 8ft barrels.

Above: Sam Lamiroy burries the rail at Soupbowls.
Opposite page: Sam Caribbean dreamin' on a winter's day.

Local Javier Romero,
El Colegio, Chile.

ALFREDO ESCOBAR

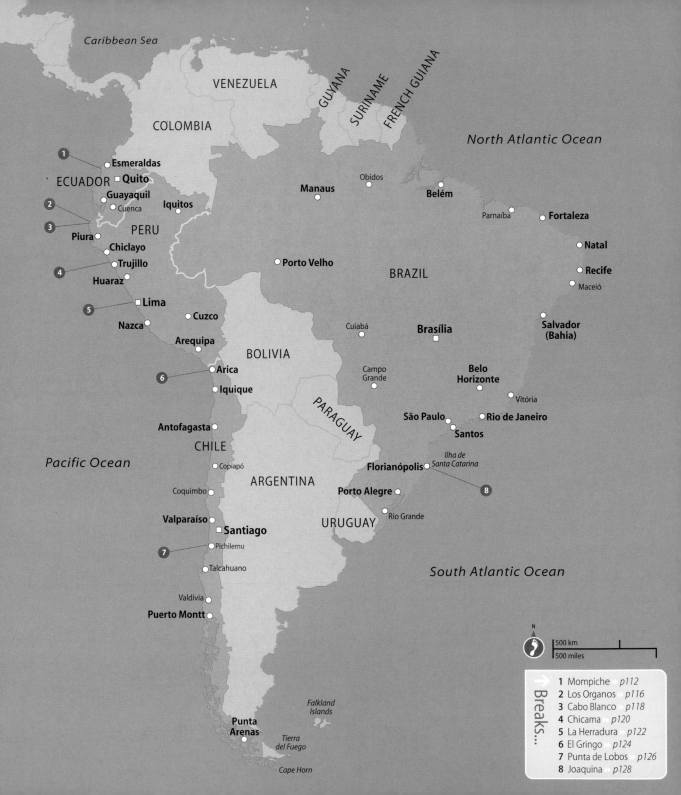

Caribbean Sea

VENEZUELA

GUYANA

SURINAME

FRENCH GUIANA

COLOMBIA

North Atlantic Ocean

Obidos

Manaus

Belém

1 Esmeraldas

Quito

ECUADOR

Guayaquil

Cuenca

Iquitos

2

3

Piura

PERU

Chiclayo

Trujillo

4

Huaraz

5

Lima

Cuzco

Nazca

Arequipa

6

Arica

Iquique

BOLIVIA

Parnaíba

Fortaleza

Natal

Recife

Maceió

Porto Velho

BRAZIL

Cuiabá

Brasília

Salvador
(Bahia)

Campo
Grande

Belo
Horizonte

Vitória

PARAGUAY

São Paulo

Rio de Janeiro

Santos

Antofagasta

CHILE

Pacific Ocean

Copiapó

Coquimbo

ARGENTINA

Valparaíso

Santiago

7

Pichilemu

Talcahuano

Valdivia

Puerto Montt

Ilha de
Santa Catarina

Florianópolis

8

Porto Alegre

Rio Grande

URUGUAY

South Atlantic Ocean

N

500 km

500 miles

Punta
Arenas

Falkland
Islands

Tierra
del Fuego

Cape Horn

Breaks...

1 Mompiche *p112*
2 Los Organos *p116*
3 Cabo Blanco *p118*
4 Chicama *p120*
5 La Herradura *p122*
6 El Gringo *p124*
7 Punta de Lobos *p126*
8 Joaquina *p128*

It's 1965 and a youthful Nat Young is walking down to the ocean at Miraflores. An assistant is trying to carry his Mal but Nat is resisting. At the Waikiki Club surfers don't have to carry their own boards. Their beachfront retreat is resplendent with showers, a bar, a restaurant, masseuses, locker rooms and a pool where gorgeous girls sun themselves. After surfing, the locals retire to the balcony to enjoy a cool beverage and watch over the ocean. They own state-of-the-art cars that they race in the streets, scaring the long-haired beauty queen in the passenger seat into squeals of fear and delight. It is the World Surfing Championships and Peru is proving to be a generous host. However, for the visiting Australian and American surfers, used to bumming around the North Shore or scraping a living together near the California points, this is a strange world. What may have seemed so decadent back in the sixties might sound very familiar if you look at professional surfing today. Seems like the Peruvians were just ahead of the game, by about three decades or so. But then they did have a head start, by a few millennia. Over three thousand years ago the 'caballitos de totora' rode the Peruvian waves standing on reed 'wave skis' (think Laird on his stand-up paddle board) as they returned with the day's catch. Some historians believe it was here, in South America, that surfing was originally born.

This continent offers the surfer an amazing array of experiences. The beaches of Brazil are a frenetic blend of sun, sand, salsa and surf. There is enough energy in a bustling line-up here to power a whole city. Brazilians attack everything with the same degree of passion, expression and showmanship so it has been no surprise to see that they have risen quickly to become a true surfing superpower. Across the Andes, the cold of the Humboldt Current cools the waters of violent reefs and powerful pointbreaks spread over the 6435 km of the Chilean coastline. Here the surf can go from fun, head-high peelers to XXL overnight. It has bred a nation of fearless big wave chargers who can adapt to whatever the mighty South Pacific throws at them. To the north of Peru and into Ecuador, the warming Equatorial Current bathes the northerly facing breaks that promise summer days in boardies, sunscreen and leg-meltingly long rides. Yes, if you had to pick just one continent to surf for the rest of your life, it would be hard to look beyond the shores of South America.

Surfing South America

South America Surfing

South America is a continent dominated by its incredible natural environment and peppered with political uncertainty. Since independence from their erstwhile colonial masters, the majority of countries here have flip-flopped between military juntas and corrupt governments back to military juntas. When it comes to politics, the leaders of South America have steadfastly sailed a course towards troubled waters and then dropped anchor – through the bottom of the boat. Today things have stabilized somewhat, but the chat show-hosting, America-baiting President Hugo Chavez of Venezuela proves that this region still has its mavericks.

Pros & cons
West coast South America

✅ Pros

Best left points on the planet.

Consistent swell catcher – 180° swell window.

Many unexplored areas.

Relatively inexpensive, although Chile is now less so.

Something for everyone – from big wave spots to mellow beginner walls.

Stunning landscape.

Rich culture and environment.

Few sharks.

❌ Cons

Certain regions unsafe.

Crime.

Pockets of malaria and dengue fever.

Dangerous roads – infrastructure poor and bus crashes common in some regions.

Be aware of drug trafficking.

Pros & cons
East coast South America

✅ Pros

Beach lifestyle rules!

Birthplace of Carnival and the G-string.

Pumping nightlife around the cities.

Consistent beachies.

Mostly warm water.

❌ Cons

Extreme poverty in certain areas.

Relatively small surf.

Trade winds can blow onshore messing up afternoon sessions.

Main breaks get extremely crowded.

Super, super competitive line-ups.

Crime – especially in urban areas.

Sharks, no-surf zones.

South America Surfing

Opposite page: Cristián Merello, Lebu, southern Chile.

This huge continent has 13 countries from the equatorial north to the frigid southern tip, 11 of which boast a surfable coastline. Although the Pacific fringe begins with Columbia, in reality the western coast's most northerly accessible spot is Mompiche, close to the port of Esmeraldas. Although the landscape is lush and green, the town is a place where you get an adrenalin rush just walking into a bar. "Hazards in Esmeraldas include being mugged, stared to death, or scared to death by rats the size of farm livestock," says Alan Murphy, Footprint South American writer. But the wave at Mompiche can make the rigours of getting there worthwhile. "This wave is as close to a machine as I have ever surfed," claims top longboarder Chris Griffiths. On the tip of the continent, some 6000 km south, the Patagonian coastline hides untapped potential. It is a land of cold waters with southern ocean swells bombarding a system of inlets and bays that hide an endless array of possibilities. To the east, in Brazil, a country of staggering social differences, the beaches and the line-ups are places where the richest playboys and the poorest kids from the favelas can all compete for the same waves, in that typically frenetic Brazilian style.

But modern surfing isn't new to these shores. Peru hosted the 1965 World Championships, an event won by local legend Felipe Pomar. "Peru was also the first country to create the first International Surfing Federation – ISF (created on 13 February 1965, before the ASP)," says ex-Peruvian Champion Roberto Meza. "The first president of this institution was Eduardo Arena Costa, and the first rules to regulate tournaments were designed by Peruvian big wave surfer Guillermo 'Pancho' Wiese, and are practically the same rules that ASP use nowadays." Today 2004 world champion Sofía Mulanovich is a national hero in Peru where she ranks as highly as any of the nation's sports stars. But the country that has risen to the status of surfing superpower is Brazil. They host an annual leg of the prestigious WCT, and while away from home, the elite Brazilian surfers who account for around one fifth of the top 44, are a tight knit, supportive unit. Perhaps their togetherness has contributed to the fact that Victor Ribas, Paulo Maura and Peterson Rosa are among some of the world's most successful surfers.

Position

The equatorial line slices through the northern tip of Ecuador, the southern quarter of Columbia and the top fringes of Brazil, to leave Venezuela, Guyana, Suriname and French Guiana stranded in the northern hemisphere while the lion's share of the continent rests in the southern hemisphere. Columbia is the border nation to Panama and Central America. Continuing eastward, South America is washed by the Caribbean to the north while the eastern coastline, dominated by vast Brazil to the north and Argentina in the south, is open to the Atlantic. Rounding the southern cone and the notorious Cape Horn, the tail ends of Argentina and Chile are separated from the frozen Antarctic by Drake Passage. Bordered by the vast Pacific, the sliver that is Chile runs up the west coast, before meeting Peru, which borders Ecuador. The Galápagos Islands rest on the equator 1050 km off the west coast of Ecuador and comes under its jurisdiction.

Culture

The waves of immigration over the past 500 years have left a huge impression on everything from the language to the music and dance, and the food. The native Amerindian population of what is now Ecuador, Peru and northern Chile, had, by the middle of the 15th century, been subsumed into the great Inca empire. The arrival of the Spanish conquistadors resulted in an almost complete destruction of the technically sophisticated Incas. Their temples were destroyed, their cities built over, their agricultural systems were disrupted and many were taken into slavery to work in mines. As if that weren't enough, the European invaders also brought with them diseases such as measles, smallpox and flu which killed off those who didn't die in the gold and silver mines. The ruins of Machu Picchu in Peru remain as a stunning reminder to a lost civilization.

The arrival of the Spanish, Portuguese and French also meant an influx of slave labour from Africa, used as replacement workers for the native Indians whose numbers were decreasing rapidly. There are over 60 million people of African descent. In the state of Santa Catarina, the Bavarian architecture of some of the towns gives a clue to the origins of the wave of immigrants that settled in this corner of Brazil. Today Brazil has a population of over 188 million people with major urban centres such as São Paulo and Rio de Janeiro sitting on the surf-rich southeastern coastline.

Climates and seasons

With the equator cutting through the top of South America, the majority of the continent rests within the southern hemisphere with seasons running opposite to her neighbour the USA roughly as:

ALFREDO ESCOBAR

spring – September to November; summer – December to February; autumn – March to May; winter – June to August. Straddling the equator between 1° north and 5° south, Ecuador's coastline has high temperatures and humidity levels year round. Rainfall varies widely between the north – up to around 2000 mm per year – and the south, which can have as little as 200 mm. Esmeraldas, also known as the Green Province, is a lush, wet area with high rainfall year round, showing a marked increase from December to April. January temperatures average 26°C with 240 mm rain, July sees temparatures drop slightly to around 24°C and around 20 mm rain. Peru's coastal desert climate is created by the effects of the Humboldt or Peruvian Current. This cold, low salinity, nutrient-rich current starts at around 44-45° south and flows northward past Chile and Peru before veering west around Piura in northern Peru and merging with the warm south-flowing currents to become part of the west-flowing south equatorial current. The Humboldt is one of the major upwelling systems in the world, creating a rich marine eco-system and also ensuring the waters of Peru are colder than their tropical position suggests. Another characteristic generated by the current is the propensity of low cloud and damp coastal fog. December to April sees the warmest weather with the greatest sunshine periods and barely a wet day. January averages 24°C and around 3 mm of rain, dropping to around 17°C in July with around 8 mm of rain on the coast. Inland, temperatures begin to drop as the Andean mountains rise up. The periodic and cyclical El Niño sees a dramatic change in weather patterns and in ocean-atmosphere interaction. The easterly winds weaken and warm east-flowing water from the equator dominates and displaces the Humboldt Current, causing a rise in sea water temperatures (up to 2-3°C), a rise in sea water levels, an increase in rainfall and flooding, and a drop in the nutrients in the surface water.

Chile is also affected by the Humboldt Current and the mountainous spine of the Andes. With a vast coastline, covering around 40° in longitude, climate varies widely, seeing a north to south temperature decrease and rainfall increase. Northern Chile and the Atacama Desert is one of the driest regions in the world although temperatures are cooler than the latitude indicates. For Arica, January temperatures average 23°C and 16°C in July with no rain. As with Peru, however, the coastline endures low cloud and damp fog as well as low sun hours. Around Santiago, the climate is more Mediterranean with warm, dry summers and mild, wet winters. Temperatures average 21°C in January with around 3 mm of rain and a cool 9°C in July with around 76 mm of rain.

Brazil faces out into the Atlantic. The tropical coastline is warm and humid with a tempering sea breeze. Near the mouth of the Amazon, there is rainfall year round, more so from December to May. Fortaleza

Left: Punta de Lobos – the jump off point...
Opposite page: Sunset at Panic Point.

to Bahia is mainly dry, with the wet season falling May to August. Around São Paulo however there is some rainfall year round with the wet season falling November to April. Outside of the tropics, around Porto Alegre the coast is warm and temperate with rain year round. January sees temperatures of around 25°C and around 89 mm rain, while in the cooler months – April to September – it is slightly wetter. July averages 17°C with 115 mm rain.

Wavewatch report by Vic DeJesus

South America West coast The west coast of South America consists primarily of the Chilean and Peruvian coastlines and is one of the most consistent year-round surf destinations. Large low-pressure systems travelling eastward in the mid latitudes of the South Pacific send westerly to southwesterly swell year round, although largest in the southern hemisphere winter months from May to September. During other months of the year these swells continue, but are much smaller. Also, during the northern hemisphere winter from November through March, large northwesterly swells travel thousands of miles impacting this area with small to moderate size on average. Planning a trip to this area merely depends on one's taste in surf. Flat days become less common the further south one travels along the coastline, but then again conditions also become less favourable, especially in the wintertime. With the Humboldt Current flowing northward the water also becomes colder, staying generally cool for the whole coast throughout the year.

South America east coast The east coast of South America gets a variety of swell. The largest and best quality swell usually originates from intense Antarctic lows passing eastward in the mid latitudes. South facing breaks often see the largest swells from May through August. Further north, many of the south swells bypass the area, but high-pressure windswells from the east to northeast are common with small to moderate size. Like many east facing coastlines, this area

PAUL KENNEDY

receives its fair share of storm surf followed by offshore winds as fronts pass with maximum intensity during late autumn through the winter months. Most agree that overall size and shape are best in the southern hemisphere autumn months from April through May.

Geography and breaks

The landscape of South America is dominated by the towering Andes, the longest mountain range on earth, which runs like a spine down the western side of the continent and is home to many active volcanoes as well as seismic activity. It has a huge effect on everything from climate patterns to the very nature of the environments that develop here. To the west of the mountains, the narrow coastal plain is dry and barren, with the Atacama Desert claiming the record of the driest place on earth. To the east of the mountains, snow and rainfall is channelled down into the immense Amazon Basin, feeding the biggest expanse of tropical rainforest on the planet and providing the water for the largest river, the Amazon. Continuing eastward, the land then rises again, this time forming a high plateau, before a narrow coastline meets the Atlantic.

For Ecuador, the north and south reaches of the coast are a series of cliff-backed bays and capes forming rock and sand point breaks while the estuarine Gulf of Guayaquil is fringed by mangroves and mudflats. Peru's 2400-km coastline is a series of points interspersed by bays and often backed by cliffs. The arid environment created by the Humboldt Current means that the points are mainly rocky points groomed with a layer of sand, leading into sandy bays. The coastline of Chile is over 4200 km long. Pounded year round by swell, the deep ocean trench lying offshore sinks to more than 8000 m in depth, ensuring they hit with both power and speed. It is a patchwork of points and reefs – areas such as Arica and Iquique in the north have a series of high quality reef set-ups, as does the majority of the central coastline. For Brazil, the southeast coastline faces into the brunt of the south Atlantic swells. This is where most of the surfing takes place, with the hotspots of Florianoplois, São Paolo and Rio soaking up vast quantities of highly

◎ WAVEWATCH	Dec-Feb Summer	Mar-May Autumn	Jun-Aug Winter	Sep-Nov Spring
WEST COAST SOUTH AMERICA				
Wave size/direction	SW/SW 3-5'	SW 4-6'	WSW 8-10'	SW 4-6'
Wind force/direction	S F2	S F2	S F3	S F3
Surfable days	10-15	15-20	25+	25+
Water/air temp	20/30°C	28/22°C	17/18°C	19/22°C
EAST COAST SOUTH AMERICA				
Wave size/direction	SSE 2-3'	S 3-5'	SE 4-6'	SSE 3-4'
Wind force/direction	S F3	S F3	N F2	S F3
Surfable days	5-10	10-15	15-20	10-15
Water/air temp	23/31°C	20/27°C	18/25°C	21/29°C

South America Surfing

PAUL KENNEDY

Left: Some historians claim that waveriding actually originated with the 'caballitos de tortora' in Peru some 3000 years ago.
Opposite page: There's something left around every headland in Peru.

charged surfers. Brazilians are known for the beach break prowess, so it's little surprise that the coastline is littered with quality beachies, interspersed with points. The region of Recife, on the most easterly tip of the country, has a large section of coastline where surfing is banned. This followed a prolonged series attacks by large tiger sharks, drawn to the region as marine development altered currents. The islands of Fernando de Noronha, lie 200 miles off the eastern tip of Brazil and are often referred to as Brazil's Hawaii due to their volcanic nature and fact that their exposure leaves them open to any large swells prowling the Atlantic.

Health and safety
With the Nazca tectonic plate abutting the Pacific coastline of South America, the Andean Mountain is highly charged with active volcanoes and the region is at risk from earthquakes. The coastland of Ecuador suffers occasional flooding, which can also be a hazard for the rest of the west coast, specifically during El Niño years. Large parts of South America remain as unstable politically and economically as they are geologically. The perennial problems of poverty and the cocaine trade mean that crime is prevalent, particularly in and around cities and towns, ranging in scale from pick-pocketing to less frequent but far more serious carjacking and kidnapping. Bus 'hold ups' can occur in Peru and Brazil (specifically around Rio, Recife and Salvador), and even traditionally safe Ecuador has its own dangers, especially around the northern border with Columbia. As with many developing regions, roads bring their own unique blend of issues and driving or indeed travelling at night is not recommended.

Avoid being bitten by mosquitoes as there have been dengue fever outbreaks in the Pacific lowlands of Ecuador, the north coast of Peru and some areas of Brazil. Malaria is fairly high risk in the Esmeraldas region of Ecuador with some risk in Piura region of Peru. Cover up, use a decent repellent that includes DEET and talk to your doctor before your trip about which course of prophylactics to take to protect against malaria.

Water quality varies throughout the region, so best to drink bottled water, avoid ice in your drinks and peel fruit and veg before you eat it.

If you do succumb, remember it's better out than in, stay out of the sun and keep fluid levels up to avoid dehydration. Generally speaking, if you have diarrhoea for more than three days, pass blood or are in any doubt, seek immediate medical attention.

There are sharks on the west coast of South America, although so far these hunters have remained well fed by the fish swimming in these rich, chilly waters. The main shark risk occurs on the east coast, where tiger sharks and bull sharks are not uncommon. The main problem area around Recife had a well-publicized spate of attacks that saw surfing banned in the area. The regional government is now implementing a netting programme similar to the one employed in Durban, which will see surfing back on the menu, instead of the surfers.

Surfing and the environment
South America has the greatest levels of urbanization in its coastal regions and, due in part to unregulated development, these urban areas continue to expand. Poor infrastructure and economic limitations have resulted in huge amounts of untreated sewage and industrial waste being pumped directly into the sea or into the vast waterways that feed the oceans. Surfers across the continent are rallying to raise awareness of these issues and lobbying hard to protect the fragile environment. Below, Chile's Proplaya and Surfrider Foundation Brazil give an overview of the issues facing their coastlines. Inland, the Amazon Basin is home to the world's largest rainforest – often described as the lungs of the world. This huge area of vegetation helps regulate the amount of carbon dioxide (an important greenhouse gas) in the atmosphere through absorption. Unfortunately this valuable resource is being felled and burnt down at an alarming rate. For more information check out www.amazonwatch.org.

Proplaya by co-founder Joshua Berry

Coastal environmental problems threaten Chile's international image as a clean, coldwater surf destination of snowy mountains, green rivers, dense forests and remote reefs and point breaks. A breakneck pace of large-scale natural resource extraction (tree pulp, fish farming, drift netting, industrial agriculture and precious metals mining) and a booming coastal population are conspiring to forever change thousands of miles of coastline. In southern and central Chile numerous pulp mills dump their chlorine-treated waste and heavy metals by-products directly into the Pacific Ocean and nearby rivers. In the logging town of Constitución in the VII Region, several point breaks have been unridden for over 10 years after numerous local and travelling surfers experienced nausea, vomiting, shortness of breath and other physical ailments from surfing the town's polluted waters, caused by the operation of a beachfront pulp mill. In the VIII Region a battle is underway between surfer-environmentalists and the tree pulp industry, which is constructing a huge pulp-producing facility on the banks of the Itata River. Much of northern and central Chile's coastline is now falling prey to unregulated urban development, a complete lack of town planning and summertime crowds. Due to these imminent threats, surfers in Chile are now organizing through Proplaya and smaller local environmental groups to conserve Chile's wild heritage of ocean, mountains and forest. Proplaya now works with local and international groups in government lobby, public policy, community activism and environmental education. Contact: www.proplaya.cl.

Surfrider Foundation Brazil by Giselle Firme

Established in 1996, the Surfrider Foundation Brazil is based in Rio de Janeiro. In contrast to many countries, Brazil does not have a problem with beach access, since all beaches are public, according to a national law. Most issues surfers face, however, are pollution-related. Beach littering is a common problem throughout the Brazilian coast, mainly owing to a lack of public awareness as the government does provide trash cans. Surfrider Foundation promotes Beach Cleaning Days to educate the population about the harm such beach littering causes and to bring awareness of the importance of taking care of the coastal environment. Outfalls are another problem for Brazilian surfers as most have no form of treatment and raw sewage pours into the sea. The authorities claim that as long as the outfall pipe is far enough from the beach, this does not cause problems for the population, but many surfers have been infected with hepatitis or suffer some form of skin rash after surfing at polluted beaches. Currently the Rio de Janeiro government is pushing the opening of an ocean outfall at Barra da Tijuca, one of Rio's best surfing beaches. The Surfrider Foundation is opposing this plan by raising public awareness, publishing scientific papers, and working with local politicians to force the Rio government to finish the primary treatment plant first devised for the project but later ditched. At a recent Jack Johnson concert, the Surfrider Foundation was able to gather over 2000 signatures for a petition requesting the Rio governor to finish the treatment plant before the outfall starts working.

Peru was also the first country to create the first International Surfing Federation... the first rules to regulate tournaments were designed by Peruvian big wave surfer Guillermo 'Pancho' Wiese, and are practically the same rules that ASP use nowadays

ex-Peruvian Champion Roberto Meza

The best success story to date of the Surfrider Foundation Brazil was a protest against the development of the Grumari beach in 2000. It has since become an area protected by environmental law for the enjoyment of surfers and beach enthusiasts alike. For more information and to find out what you can do to help, check out www.surfrider.org.br.

Surfing resources

South America has a maturing surf scene. In Peru there is *Tablista* surf magazine while www.peruazul.com.pe has surf news and info plus webcams and forecasting resources. *Olas Peru Surf Travel*, www.olasperusurftravel.com, run by former champion Roberto Meza, offer trips to Peru's premier breaks. The site also has a useful rundown (with images and video) of the spots. Chile is home to *Marejada*, www.marejada.cl, the surf magazine for the country as well as *Surfeando*, www.surfeando.cl, a crossover boardsports magazine. Other good resources include www.surfchile.cl and www.chilesurf.cl with every forecasting tool you need from tides to swell to wind as well as local surf news and info. Go to www.proplaya.cl to find out what you can do to help protect the beaches, points and reefs of Chile. Brazil has the excellent and long running *Fluir* magazine. For forecasting and news check out http://waves.terra.com.br.

ALFREDO ESCOBAR

Mompiche

- ⬧ **Location:** Mompiche, Ecuador
- ◗ **Break type:** Left-hand point
- ☁ **Conditions:** Medium to big swells
- ⬡ **Size:** 4-8 ft +
- ⬤ **Length:** up to 400 m
- 🌊 **Tide:** All tides
- ⟫ **Swell direction:** Northwesterly to westerly
- ⬑ **Wind:** Southeasterly
- ☺ **Bottom:** Rocky ledge to sand
- ◉ **Ability level:** Intermediate to advanced
- ❀ **Best months:** Dec-Mar
- ⬳ **Access:** Paddle from jump-off point
- ⊖ **Hazards:** Hollow on take off close to a cluster of rocks

Mompiche Board

6'3" Channel Islands Flyer II

Shaper: Al Merrick

6'3" x 18¾" x 2⅜"

One of the most versatile shortboards on earth, made for long lined up point waves.

Works best in waves from knee high to a few feet overhead.

Single to double concave.

FCS fins.

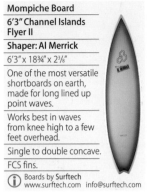

ⓘ Boards by Surftech
www.surftech.com   info@surftech.com

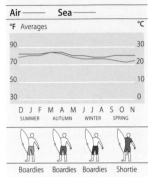

Air ——— Sea ———

°F	Averages		°C
90			30
70			20
50			10
30			0

D J F M A M J J A S O N
SUMMER   AUTUMN   WINTER   SPRING

Boardies   Boardies   Boardies   Shortie

Welcome to the world of the goofy-foot and left-hand point break perfection. South America's huge Pacific profile boasts a 180° swell window as well as an accommodating coastline that provides a diverse and undulating geography with just enough points and headlands to catch swell year round. While the most northerly state, Columbia, undoubtedly has some quality waves, its reputation as a place to avoid dictates that they aren't exactly top of every surfer's wish list. Mention speeding lines there and you might find yourself bundled into a dark, smoke-filled room with some guys in trademark shades and moustaches who want to talk about distribution. Ecuador, on the other hand, is limping out of the shackles of instability and turmoil and stumbling into position as one of the region's burgeoning surfing destinations.

2004 saw surfers from across the globe gathered here for the World Surfing Games – a success, despite the Ecuadorian army's presence as contest compound security, and the fact that the Mexican team, hijacked by gunmen, had their quivers liberated on the way. But the warm sea, great waves and abundance of swell has led to more people wanting to give the country a try.

Then there's Mompiche… nestled inside a tropical bay, this is a left-hand point that just keeps on running, long after others would have given up. Any other wave would be happy to offer an initial burst, a bit of high-quality action before easing into a slack shoulder and the relief of the channel. But not here. This baby refuses to back down. Northern hemisphere winter lows push down through the Pacific, lighting up the Hawaiian Islands on the way. Sitting way out back on a clean 6-ft swell the green, clear lines that break on the very outside of the point are always tempting you to go deeper as you stare into the hollow barrels that reel towards your take-off spot in front of the rocks. But the drop-in here is a hollow, sucking affair and not one you'd like to blow. Make it down the face and pull in, charge through the spinning tubes with a race for the daylight and out onto the shoulder. Time to catch your breath because it's only just getting going. It's at this point that the wave pivots and bends to hug the contours of the point with a steep pocket and big open walls that wind through for another 200 m. Just when you think that it has nothing more to give, you reach the inside section where, on a big day, the wave straightens out and carries on walling for a further 400 lip-bashing metres. By the end your legs have been liquidized and your brain fried.

Left: Sitting on the equatorial line, this spot gives a sense of balance and equilibrium.
Opposite page: Mompiche – long and lush.

The point at Mompiche lies on the northern coastline of Ecuador in a region known as Esmeraldas. Falling in the shadow of the equator, the lush green landscape is the result of the tropical weather patterns that roll through here, the abundant plant-life, fed by an annual rainfall of over 2500 mm. While the natural environment of this region may have conspired to produce a wave of mind-bending perfection, Ecuador remains the archetypal banana republic and not quite the tropical idyll it may appear. The history of government here is consistent in nothing but its inconsistency. Ecuadorian politics has seen a rolling wave of coups, juntas, reforming Presidents arrested for corruption followed by reforming Presidents forced from power by scandal. Here the phrase 'four more years!' doesn't usually refer to campaigning for another term in office, it's more likely a term of exile. A week is a long time in politics but in Ecuador it's a career. Then there's the long-running dispute with neighbouring Peru over land boundaries. All this in a country that has benefited from deposits of oil.

Unless you're planning on running for office, the main concern travelling into this region is disease. Malaria is a problem and food hygiene and water quality are both poor. Top pro longboarder Chris 'Guts' Griffiths scored classic Mompiche for a week but their trip was not without its little hitches. "One of our guides came down with cerebral malaria while we were there and nearly died," explains Chris. "I caught amoebic dysentery and thought I was turning inside out for about 10 days… There are downsides to finding the perfect wave." However, with a bit of luck, and a bit of traveller's sense, you too could score some of the longest, most seriously mind-bending waves anywhere on the planet. As Chris says "This really is a set-up where just one wave will give you everything you could ever want from a surfing destination." Just stay out of the politics.

Locals and legends
Eddie 'Nato' Salazar Jepsen, Daniel 'El Flaco' Velasco, Rene 'La Rana' Burgos.

Nearby breaks Heading south there are a couple of other point breaks including **Suspiro** – another quality sand-covered rock-reef left. If sandbars are more what you're looking for, continue south into the Manabí region and head for Canoa and the 10-km stretch of consistent beachies.

Surfers' tales
The green, green points of Ecuador Chris 'Guts' Griffiths

TOM KOERBER/SEALENS

In 2000, I was fortunate enough to be invited on a surf exploration trip with my good friends Beau Young and Sam Bleakly. The destination was to be the South American country of Ecuador. At the time I knew nothing about the place, other than it was sandwiched in between Peru and Columbia and that it was one of the most unstable countries in the world, having suffered the upheaval of over 10 military coups in just over a 12-month period prior to our trip. Oh well, it's a good job surfers are hardy travellers and not easily swayed when they have the scent of the pristine waves in their nostrils.

For the month we were there we explored the coast in 4WD trucks and surfed everything from an abundance of average beach breaks to a couple of semi classic reefs. However the highlight of the trip was one of the longest, most rippable points in the world, an absolute classic set-up called Mompiche.

Mompiche is situated in the Esmeraldas, Ecuador's northern province, and is only accessible by enduring an hour-long boat ride down the coast from the nearest fishing town. It lies in a secluded bay surrounded by miles of dense jungle and the set-up is absolutely classic. The take-off spot is out at the end of a rocky point that sticks out about half a mile out into the sea on the left hand side of the bay. The drop-in can be as difficult as you want to make it, as you can push yourself deeper and deeper on the point so you are eventually taking off right in front of the rocks. This is the hollowest section and barrels off for about 60 yards before starting to pinch shut. At this point the wave slows a touch and bends around the point and starts to hug the rocks down the inside. This section covers about 300 yards and has a steep concentrated pocket where you can do hack after hack until your legs go to jelly. If you are sill riding and have any energy left then you will be looking at the third phase of your amazing 1-mile ride, which is where the wave stops hugging the rocks and starts to straighten out along the crescent bay. It's at this point that you see the wall start to extend for another 500-600 yards in front of you.

Although the tube riding time at Mompiche is short, it can be intense and the price for hesitation can be high, however, what it lacks in hollowness it more than makes up for in length and shape. If you can't perfect your manoeuvres here then there is no hope for you because this wave is as close to a machine as I have ever surfed! Couple this with an empty line-up and stunning backdrop of Ecuadorian rainforest and it doesn't get much better! We got to surf Mompiche for five days straight with waves ranging from 3 to 6 ft. The locals told me they had surfed it at twice the size we had it. The mind boggles. Can you imagine a solid 10-ft wave that peels for almost a mile?

There are downsides to finding the perfect wave mind you. This area of Ecuador has a massive problem with malaria, the cerebral type too. One of our guides came down with this strain while we were there and nearly died. I caught amoebic dysentery and thought I was turning inside out for about 10 days. Then one of the camera guys with us managed to split his face open while filming in the water and was doing a pretty good impression of one of the baddies from Blade 2 (bottom lip split open down the middle to his adam's apple, skin flapping in the breeze) for a day or so until we could find a surgeon to fix him up. Also it might pay to keep an eye on where you eat. I don't remember seeing too many cattle in Ecuador but when I ordered beef steak in mushroom sauce I didn't expect to find out it had never said moo or eaten grass in its life. Judging by the small patch of grey fur I found hiding under the sauce it's more likely it had barked and licked its nether regions. Even with dog dinners, the mosquitoes and the dysentery to contend with, this is a spot that makes it all worthwhile. I don't think I have smiled so much in a week of surfing as I did at this wave.

Chris 'Guts' Griffiths is a professional longboarder from Wales. He finished fifth in the World Longboard Championships and runs Guts Surfboards. www.gutsurfboards.com.

Below: Mompiche wasn't the whole point of the trip.
Opposite page: Guts chowing down on a slice of Mompiche.

TOM KOERBER/SEALENS

Los Organos

Location:	Piura, Northern Peru
Break type:	Rock reef
Conditions:	All swells
Size:	3-8 ft
Length:	up to 50 m
Tide:	Mid
Swell direction:	North to northwesterly
Wind:	Southerly
Bottom:	Rock and sand
Ability level:	Intermediate to advanced
Best months:	Dec-Apr
Access:	Easy paddle from side of break
Hazards:	Crowds and reef

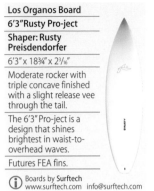

Los Organos Board
6'3" Rusty Pro-ject
Shaper: Rusty Preisdendorfer
6'3" x 18¾" x 2³⁄₁₆"

Moderate rocker with triple concave finished with a slight release vee through the tail.

The 6'3" Pro-ject is a design that shines brightest in waist-to-overhead waves.

Futures FEA fins.

ⓘ Boards by Surftech
www.surftech.com info@surftech.com

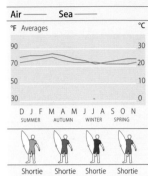

"Peru is known as the place where humans first started to surf, at least 3000 years ago – way before Hawaiian and Polynesian people started to practise the art of riding waves," says Roberto Meza who runs Olas Peru Surf Travel and is a former national champion. **"There are archaeological pieces of ceramic and paintings that demonstrate this theory, and all of them are thousands of years old, belonging to the Caral, Viru, Mochica and Chimu cultures."** Ancient fishermen, the 'caballitos de totora', spent years learning the moods and behaviour of their local waves. Getting in and out of the huge rollers on their reed craft was a daily routine, and at the end of each day they would ride the long point break waves back to the safety of their village with their catch. It is still possible to see this ancient craft in certain areas around the coastline to this day. Perhaps this link with the ocean and the past helps to explain how amazingly popular surfing is in this South American country. It is also one of the few countries (USA, Australia and South Africa aside) that can boast both male and female world champions.

"Peru is a special surf destination because the immense variety of beaches and all kinds of waves, the good weather, the excellent food and the fact that our country has waves all year long," says Roberto. "Peru is characterized by its long left-handers, thanks to its geographical location in the middle of South America in the heart of

the South Pacific." However, Los Organos sits in the upper region of this amazing coastline, away from the winter southwesterly swells that bombard the majority of Peru. One of the advantages of surfing 'round the corner' is that, while most of the country is washed by the cold Humboldt Current, this northern section of the Peruvian coastline is distinctly warmer, the Humboldt having taken on a westerly diversion just to the south of nearby Cabo Blanco. The waters here benefit from the warming effect of the Equatorial Current, meaning boardies and rashies, while just a few miles to the south it's more wetsuit temperatures.

Los Organos is one of Peru's most famous spots. Unlike many of its cousins, this is not a long, winding point but a short powerful reef. This left-hander only works in the northerly swells that strike the coastline between the middle of November and the end of March. These long

PAUL KENNEDY

Right: Classic low tide Los Organos.
Opposite page: National surfing champion and Organos local Titi de Col.

PAUL KENNEDY

travelled waves come all the way from the Alaskan waters via the warmth of Hawaii. By the time they arrive at Los Organos, the trade winds are blowing offshore from a southwesterly or southerly direction helping to groom the hollow lefts that barrel across a reef ledge. The wave here can produce a couple of excellent tube sections with mid tide seeing the best waves feeling their way along the contours of this epic spot. Although swells are generated thousands of miles away, when they peak at the end of the reef, they produce powerful, chunky lips that will pitch at 6 to 8 ft, offering late drops and the chance to tuck in before busting out the fins and lining up again. The ride finishes in the sand-bottomed channel where an easy paddle takes you back to the peak.

Peru is nothing if not flexible. Should the northerly swells not arrive, and the reefs and points of this coastline remain sleeping, then it's only a short trip south back around the corner. This will bring you into the familiar southwesterly facing points, waiting to hoover up that roving Southern Ocean corduroy. Oh, and if you're heading south, don't forget to pack your neoprene.

Locals and legends
Magoo de la Rosa, Marco Antonio Ravizza, Titi de Col, Germán Aguirre, Cesar Aspíllaga, Coco Landeo, Bruno Mesinas, David Fioriani, Coqui Carbajal.

Nearby breaks Just to the north **Organitos** and **Casablanca** offer up beginner sessions and cruisey walls. Continuing up the Pan American Highway, **Máncora** is home to a mellow left-hand point which works in a northerly through to a southerly swell (making it pretty consistent) and is best at mid to high tides. A kilometre north, **Punta Ballenas**, is yes, you've guessed it, a left point. It delivers a shorter but more power ride than Máncora, with some hollow sections. Works best at higher tides (to avoid the rocks) and in decent southerly swells. The road south leads on to the challenging **Cabo Blanco**.

Cabo Blanco

Location: Piura, northern Peru	
Break type: Left point	
Conditions: Medium to big swells	
Size: 3-10 ft	
Length: Up to 75 m	
Tide: Mid to low	
Swell direction: Northwesterly to northerly	
Wind: Southerly	
Bottom: Sand and rock	
Ability level: Advanced	
Best months: Nov-Feb	
Access: Jump-off point	
Hazards: Crowds, heavy fast barrels	

PAUL KENNEDY

The black and white picture still hangs on the wall. A little faded after five decades, but the details are clear. Ernest Hemingway is being served a drink in the Cabo Blanco Fishing Club. This exclusive establishment was owned by oil tycoons whose companies came here with the black gold rush. Membership was vetted – with the right connections and US$10,000, you were in. And when Texas oilman Alfred C Glassell landed a world-record marlin (the first of more than 1000 lbs), the likes of Howard Hughes soon began dropping in for a spot of deep-sea fishing. In 1956 Hemingway came to Cabo Blanco with Warner Bros: his goal to catch a huge black marlin. The footage was to be used in the upcoming film adaptation of his novella *The Old Man and the Sea*. During his weeks in northern Peru he spent his days on the ocean and his evenings in the club. One legend suggested he was inspired to write the piece here, but it was actually based on a Cuban fisherman. What isn't in doubt, however, is the quality of the underwater geography. The waves of Cabo Blanco certainly match the quality of the fishing to be had in these waters.

Cabo Blanco sits in an amazing arena. It is framed to the south by dark cliffs and to the north by the angle of the fishing pier, the numerous bobbing boats and the Meccano-like oil platform provide a busy backdrop. However, once you see a set roll through and start to pour onto the reef to your left, your attention is fixed on one place alone. This dark, sand-covered reef produces a super-fast and super-hollow left-hand cavern that drains away, just offshore, sucking hard into a barrel that winds along the shoreline right in front of the waiting rocks. The hungry pack has to paddle south against the rip to stay on the peak, making this line-up a real survival of the fittest endurance test. The drop is a heart-in-mouth moment as the bottom disappears from your world. Blow the take-off and you'll be pounded through to the inside. Make it, and it's time to pull in and race the speeding curtain. It's not uncommon to see surfers here pumping for extra speed while in the barrel. With a bit of luck and a bit of skill you may find yourself exploding out onto the safety of the shoulder. On a good swell here it's all about the tubes. Hey, that's why they call it Peruvian Pipeline.

Above: Cabo Blanco – Piura perfection.
Opposite page: Peruvian surfing champion Magoo de la Rosa demonstrating some of the skills he passed on to former world champ, Sofía Mulanovich.

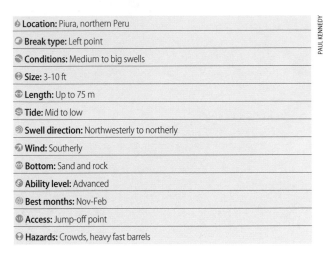

Cabo Blanco Board

6'3" JC SD-3

Shaper: John Carper

6'3" x 18.15" x 2.2"

John Carper designed with Shane Dorian for steep hollow waves.

Round pintail, single to double concave, finely tuned rails.

Fits deep tubes, flies down the line and turns tight in the pocket.

Futures JC1 fins.

ⓘ Boards by Surftech
www.surftech.com info@surftech.com

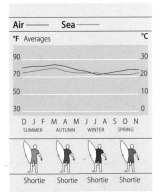

Air ——— Sea ———

°F	Averages	°C
90		30
70		20
50		10
30		0

D J F M A M J J A S O N
SUMMER | AUTUMN | WINTER | SPRING

| Shortie | Shortie | Shortie | Shortie |

But if it wasn't for the action of a group of campaigning surfers, this line-up could look very different today. In fact, you'd be able to walk right out through it. In 1992 local fishermen planned to build a pier that would have pushed through the very heart of the wave. ACOPLO is a Peruvian surfers' environmental group that successfully campaigned to save a number of waves along the coastline. They sat down and talked to the fishermen who agreed to move the pier to the north of the break. Having a wave like Cabo Blanco breaking under your pier would probably not be the best idea when it comes to the safety of the structure. See this baby breaking big and you'll know why. Not that the locals mind when it's thumping. They like it big, and one thing they have mastered is how to barrel ride.

The Peruvian Pipeline wasn't discovered until 1979 when Peruvian surfer Sergio 'Gordo' Barreda came to check out the potential of the area. Since that day, the steady trickle of Cabo addicts has turned into a constant stream. Surfers just scan the Internet forecast and hit the road by the car-load, many from as far south as Lima. The take-off spot here is small and the competition fierce. With a pack of 30 in the water, the line-up is saturated and drop-ins are commonplace. This can make for some painful watching as it's commonplace to see a

surfer make a hell drop and tuck into a great tube, only to have the curtain brought down by a guy dropping from the shoulder.

Cabo Blanco is still more famous around the globe as a fishing village than as a surf destination. Check the place out on the internet and you'll get more advice on hooking a big sailfish than hooking into a big barrel. These guys are still out there, roaming the coastline, studying charts and checking the weather with religious zeal. Charts, searching for secret spots, checking the forecasts? Sounds familiar. Now where's my copy of Hemingway's lost masterpiece *The Old Man and the Mal*.

Locals and legends
'Magoo' de la Rosa, Titi de Col, Germán Aguirre, Cesar Aspíllaga, Coco Landeo, Bruno Mesinas, David Fioriani, Coqui Carbajal.

Nearby breaks Just south round the headland is **Punta Panico** or Panic Point to the gringos. This powerful left works best on a southerly or southwesterly swell and delivers long rides with tubing sections.It can get crowded. Continuing south, **Lobitos** is yet another hollow left that breaks over a sand and rock bottom and is best in swells from the southern quadrant. Wind here can be strong and picks up in the afternoon.

South America Cabo Blanco

ALFREDO ESCOBAR

Chicama

🜂 **Location:**	Chicama, northern Peru
🜨 **Break type:**	Left point break
🜁 **Conditions:**	Medium to big swells
🜔 **Size:**	3-6 ft
🜏 **Length:**	up to 2 miles!
🜍 **Tide:**	Low to mid
🜊 **Swell direction:**	South to southwesterly
🜎 **Wind:**	Southeasterly
🜐 **Bottom:**	Sand
🜖 **Ability level:**	All levels
🜑 **Best months:**	Mar-Sep
🜒 **Access:**	Easy paddle-out from end of point
🜓 **Hazards:**	Stamina and lack of it!

Many of the world's premier waves know how to work it. Seasoned pros, they can turn it on for the camera, offer themselves up for that cover shot, framed in a single snap of the shutter. Photographers clamber up to higher ground, sacrificing a bluebird session with a clean, lined swell for that perfect overview. These flawless images – liquid glass, geometric walls, telescopic barrels fringed with icy fresh white water, set against an azure sky with only the occasional cloud discerning air from liquid – stir the imagination of surfers across the globe like few other photographs. All the better if it can be captured with just a few surfers out, maybe early morning or during a contest. But Chicama is a reluctant A-lister, a gangly beauty that doesn't quite fit the scene. This is a wave that is just too long for one mere 35 mm transparency. She is often too hazy or overcast, which doesn't exactly enhance the cool brown water. One of the most famous waves in the world is still a relative unknown. The result is that the line-up here is probably the least busy of any world-class wave. And what a line-up it is.

"I really think Chicama is the 'Disneyland of Surfing'," says Peruvian legend, Roberto Meza. "Surfers, longboarders, kneeboarders, bodyboarders kitesurfers and even bodysurfers can enjoy this incredible gift." Since this wave was discovered back in 1967, it has become the name synonymous with the quest for the world's longest wave. Ask any surfer and they will tell you, Chicama is the longest left on the planet. Ask if they've been there, chances are they haven't. But why? Do we need glossy line-ups and crisp, fresh surf porn to tempt us into making the trip to check it out? What if the images don't do the wave justice? "Visually, Chicama is a masterpiece, the perfection of the waves are really amazing, they are hollow, fast, tubular and very, very long," says Roberto. "Located 600 km north from Lima, Chicama is a beautiful fishing town. Chicama, also known as Puerto Malabrigo, is not only the longest wave in the whole world, but on a good day you can surf a wave that runs for more than two miles, connecting the five different sections that become only one. The name of these five sections, in order, are: La Isla, El Cape, El Point, El Hombre and El Pueblo. When the waves become bigger, Chicama offers more sections. Actually, from the town, you can see more than 50 lines of waves coming to the shore, I really think that's overwhelming because all the waves break perfectly. And last but not least, Chicama is so big, that you can have more than 100 people in the water and you won't feel it's crowded."

Not that you will often find 100 people in the line-up here. You are more likely to see just a handful scattered down the line, with a couple making the long walk back up the point. Ah, maybe that's the drawback, the walk back. After a four-minute ride – or eight 30-second waves – the last thing you want to do is to hike 20 minutes back up the point. "That's why, along the pier near the town, you can find the friendly local taxi cabs (they're motorcycles with a cabin installed over), that charge you only one sol (30 cents) to take you back to the place where the wave begins in about five minutes." As Roberto points out, they seem to have ironed out that little problem. It's like a surfing equivalent of a ski lift.

PAUL KENNEDY

Right: Classic walls demanding classic lines.
Opposite page: Two miles, five sections and one long ride.

PAUL KENNEDY

Chicama Board

6'2" Webber Squash

Shaper: Greg Webber

6'2" x 18½" x 2¼"

High-performance shortboard designed for advanced surfers.

Single to double concave for down the line speed, yet turns tight in the pocket.

FCS fins.

(i) Boards by **Surftech**
www.surftech.com info@surftech.com

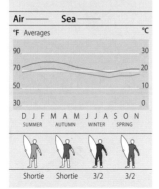

Air ——	Sea ——	
°F Averages		°C
90		30
70		20
50		10
30		0
D J F	M A M	J J A	S O N
SUMMER	AUTUMN	WINTER	SPRING

Shortie	Shortie	3/2	3/2

For Peruvians it is a matter of national pride that this natural phenomenon lies within the boundaries of their homeland. "When someone asks me why do I feel proud to be Peruvian, I always think about Chicama," says Roberto. "Of course, all Peruvians feel proud about Chicama, and there's practically not a single Peruvian surfer who is not counting the days to come back. Once I surfed a magical wave from the beginning to the end. As I was passing the different sections (always in the same wave), I had the feeling that I was surfing different beaches at the same time, and that was because all sections cherish you with different characteristics." Leg burn aside, this sand-bottomed beauty is probably one of the easiest world-class waves to ride considering its size, shape and the fact that it is, in essence, a huge long angled beach.

"It's a classical feeling to watch those perfect waves breaking along the bay," says Roberto, "you hear the shouts of the surfers inside the barrels and you know that the next wave will be yours. If God is a surfer, I'm sure he created Chicama for his own personal delight. You have to visit Chicama, my friend, the experience is worth it and you will always have the unforgettable pleasure to know that you have ridden the longest wave on Earth." .

Locals and legends

Sofía Mulanovich, Analí Gómez, Gabriel Villarán, Gabriel Aramburú, Salvador Voysest, Sebastián Alarcón, Matías Mulanovich, José 'Jarita' Gómez, Gonzalo 'Chendo' Velasco, Edson Padilla, Cristóbal de Col, Carlos Mario Zapata, Jesús 'El Zorro' Florián (Chicama's local legend), Titi de Col, César Aspíllaga, Roberto Meza, 'Magoo' de la Rosa, Jonathan Gubbins, Javier Swayne, Gustavo Swayne, César Siles, Claudio Balducci, Herbert Mulanovich, Sebastián 'Toto' de Romaña.

Nearby breaks Chicama is just one long, long left in a series of long left-hand point breaks – to the south there are the fun walls of **Punta Huanchaco**, just above the city of Trujillo. Heading north, **Poemape**, susceptible to the southerly winds, and **Pacasmayo** – both of which are good swell catchers.

La Herradura

Location:	Chorrillos, Lima, Peru
Break type:	Left point
Conditions:	Big swells
Size:	4-10 ft +
Length:	100-400 m
Tide:	All tides
Swell direction:	Northwesterly to southwesterly
Wind:	Southeasterly
Bottom:	Boulder and rock
Ability level:	Advanced
Best months:	Apr-Sep
Access:	Well timed paddle from jump-off point
Hazards:	Heavy waves, boulders on exit

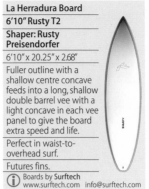

La Herradura Board
6'10" Rusty T2
Shaper: Rusty Preisendorfer
6'10" x 20.25" x 2.68"
Fuller outline with a shallow centre concave feeds into a long, shallow double barrel vee with a light concave in each vee panel to give the board extra speed and life.

Perfect in waist-to-overhead surf.

Futures fins.

Boards by Surftech
www.surftech.com   info@surftech.com

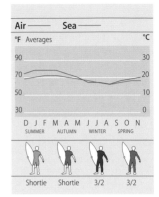

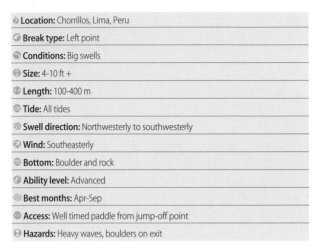

The beaches of Miraflores are a mix of boulder and dark, sandy breaks, nestled between breakwaters and laid-out beneath a fringe of ashen brown and ochre cliffs. The poetic nomenclature of this stretch of coastline brings to mind the very roots and soul of modern day surfing. The breaks of Waikiki, Makaha, Ala Moana and Laniakea offer clues to a link between Peru and Hawaii that goes back generations. When Carlos Dogny returned from Hawaii in 1942 to found the elite Waikiki Beach Club here on the beaches of Lima, he found a location that offered the essence of the surfing experience that first attracted him to waveriding. While the less than lush Costa Verde may lack the fine sand, palm trees and crystal blue waters of Oahu, it did offer the promise of regular breaking waves, consistent rollers, the feeling of sun on face and water on skin, before retiring to the club to discuss the day's exploits over martinis.

Today, the city of Lima has spread to the very edge of the cliffs that overlook the beaches and surfing has also expanded to become the nation's second sport behind football. While the breaks of Miraflores may offer some occasionally good sessions, it is the point break that nestles under the rusting peak at the south of the bay that is the star attraction. La Herradura is a dramatic wave in a dramatic frame. When a big swell lumbers out of the chill, green Pacific, thick, chunky walls grind along the point under the towering rocky faces.

"La Herradura is an incredible surfing spot because the quality of its waves and amazing location is beautiful and overwhelming at the same time," says former national surf champion Roberto Meza. "You can feel God's mighty creation when the waves make the rocks tremble, creating a frightening sound. Surrounded by dolphins and sea lions, and many seabirds, all Peruvian surfers are waiting for the big swells to ride these waves."

With a northwesterly aspect, this emerald pinwheel needs a well-travelled groundswell of a decent size before it peaks out on the end of a headland and reels into this quiet bay. "It has three very defined sections," points out Roberto. "The wave breaks along a huge mountain and runs for over 400 m. The First Section has a difficult drop and a very long wall of water. The Second Section is where the wave becomes slower but the wall is long enough to allow a number of manoeuvres before the Third Section, a hollow tubular section, fast and wild, yet perfect." This constantly changing wavescape allows the

Right: Peru's Germán Aguirre.
Opposite page: The horse shoe showing how lucky it is.

PAUL KEENEDY

surfer to sample the sheer power of the hollow sections with their challenging barrels, as well as the big open faces, perfect for power gouges and big slashes. It is no wonder that the line-up attracts the top surfers from the Lima district and has been the training ground for many of the country's top surfers past and present.

The sheltered nature of the headland and its proximity to the capital has made this a site that developers have looked on with envious eyes. A concerted effort was made to push through a proposal for a marina that would have decimated the wave. As Roberto explains, it took an almighty effort by the whole surfing community to fight off this plan. "The wave was threatened by marina development, with La Herradura facing extinction. Just because some politicians were trying to build a marina for yachts – but Peru is not such a wealthy country and there are not many people who own yachts, as opposed to 80,000 Peruvian surfers. To protect La Herradura, the most prominent Peruvian surfers, including 2004 ASP World Champion Sofía Mulanovich, organized an annual event called the Quiksilver Pro La Herradura Invitational. The best 100 Peruvian surfers wait for the biggest swells of the year to compete at La Herradura in all its splendour and power. In Peru, surfing is the second most practiced sport after soccer, and it's incredible to see what we're capable to do together when it comes to protecting La Herradura, as a sanctuary of Peruvian surfing. With coverage from TV, newspapers, magazines, radio and different websites, Peruvian surfers have stopped an insane

and illogical construction to defend the waves of La Herradura, proposing other places where the marina can be built."

Unlike the nearby beach breaks, La Herradura lacks a Hawaiian moniker so has had to create its own reputation, identity and fortune. It was the profile of the bay, funnelling swell in so expertly, that influenced the given name. But it must be more than by happy coincidence that La Herradura, 'the horseshoe', forged from an alchemy of rock and fire, is a lucky talisman. That this wave has faced extinction on more than one occasion, and is still here, is a testament to good fortune. But it is the fact that the local surf community exhibits the fire and strength to withstand the onslaught of developers and prevail that is the real stroke of luck.

Locals and legends
1965 World Champion Felipe Pomar, Joaquín Miro Quesada, Guillermo 'Pancho' Wiese, Eduardo Arena Costa, Salvador 'Tato' Gubbins, Milton Whilar, 7-time Peruvian Champion Luis Miguel 'Magoo' de la Rosa, Roberto Meza, César 'Mr Tubo' Aspíllaga, Titi de Col, Sebastián 'Toto' de Romaña, Sebastián Alarcón, up and coming Cristóbal de Col.

Nearby breaks Head north along the coastal highway for a Hawaiian tour through Lima's beach breaks, separated by jetties and piers including **Ala Moana**, a decent left that works well in big winter swells, and **Laniakea**, a good right. Further north there is also **Makaha** whose beginner rollers don't quite live up to its namesake.

GEOFF RAGATZ

El Gringo

◈ **Location:** El Gringo, Arica, Chile	
◔ **Break type:** A-frame reef	
☁ **Conditions:** Big swells	
◉ **Size:** 3 to 10 ft +	
◑ **Length:** up to 50 m	
◒ **Tide:** Low	
◎ **Swell direction:** Southwesterly	
◉ **Wind:** Northeasterly	
◔ **Bottom:** Rocky reef	
◉ **Ability level:** Advanced	
◈ **Best months:** Apr-Sep	
◉ **Access:** Paddle wide of break from rocks	
◉ **Hazards:** Shallow, heavy, rocks	

El Gringo is a violent, unpredictable character. Think Lee van Cleef in a Sergio Leone western. Don't look him in the eye too long or you may lose your nerve. He's best tackled early in the still of the bright morning light. The crystal-clear water of the line-up shows just how little ocean separates the partially submerged board you are sitting on from the waiting rocks below. In the approaching set this is a spot where you can see the good, the bad and the ugly all roll through, one wave after the other.

Below: Brad Gerlach towing in at the powerful A-frame reef.
Opposite page: Chile's Ramón Navarro, El Gringo.

Obviously there's only one suitable place for such an adversary to rest – a border town. Arica sits on the very northern edge of the Chilean coastline, only a few miles from Peru. In fact, the town that has grown on the banks of the Rio Lluta was actually seized from the Peruvians in the War of the Pacific, which ended in 1883. It is also the gateway to the Atacama Desert – reputed to be the driest place on earth. If you want to avoid rainfall on your holiday, this is the place to come. It can go years without a single drop. Its position makes it a popular tourist destination, but from a surfers point of view, the nature of the breaks here mean it's a place where it pays to pack a gun. And a back up.

Ex-Isla Alacran. It used to be Isla Alacran, or Scorpion Island, but the man-made peninsula that now tethers the island has led to a down-grading of this former free-floating soul. Although the boulder peninsula has helped to create a safe harbour for small boats, it has also allowed access to the many breaks of Scorpion Island. When swells come out of the north they will wrap along the northern side of the island to create a quality left point wave known as La Isla. When it's on, waves bend and pinwheel, throwing up fast walls and barrel sections that reel over the waiting rocks. Further outside and just to the south breaks El Toro Viejo, 'The Old Bull'. This beast doesn't raise its head very often but when it does, powerful walls gouge the headland in front of the watching lighthouse. A low tide and a big southerly swell are both needed to raise the Bull from its torpor, and when that happens only the region's hell-men will paddle out to take on the beast.

The most famous wave on Ex-Isla Alacran is the one that crowns the headland – El Gringo, also known as Chilean Pipeline. This is a wave that certainly lives up to its name. It is a hard, fast and shallow

GEOFF RAGATZ

El Gringo Board
6'6" Channel Islands K-Model
Shaper: Al Merrick
6'6" x 18¾" x 2⅜"
A high-performance board for thick, powerful waves.
Single to double concave for down the line speed with extra nose rocker for steep take-offs and under the lip snaps.
FCS K2.1 fins.
ⓘ Boards by Surftech www.surftech.com info@surftech.com

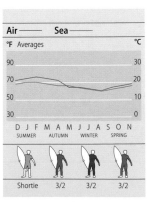

Air ———	Sea ———
°F Averages	°C

D J F M A M J J A S O N
SUMMER AUTUMN WINTER SPRING

| Shortie | 3/2 | 3/2 | 3/2 |

A-frame that breaks incredibly close to the rocks and is safe only on a low tide. Well, safe is a relative concept here. Rides are a do-or-die mix of super-fast tubes and pounding close-outs. In the early morning, before the wind kicks in, El Gringo can be the purveyor of clean, 4-ft glassy barrels or 10-ft death pits. For the watching crowd, the brave few really do put on a show. Chilean Pipeline produces a classic right and left set-up as the triangular rocky reef points straight into the jaws of roving southwesterly swells. These can hit 10-15 ft and the huge fetch of the southern reaches of the Pacific helps to lengthen the period and clean up the lines.

After years of being charged by a dedicated crew of locals, travelling surfers have arrived in this northern town to take on El Gringo. In huge swells, there have even been tow-sessions spearheaded by some top riders from the US. The boundaries of El Gringo are still being pushed

by guys with that steely look and custom-made guns that they hope will help them take down this cold, chilling adversary. One thing is for sure, on the dry, dusty, rock-strewn Scorpion Island there rests an opponent with a sting in the tail. Handle with care.

Locals and legends
Diego Medina, Ramón Navarro, Reinaldo Ibarra, Sebastian Noguiera, Christian Aguirre, Giovanni Visconti, Makiol Pacheco, Raul Cubillos, Hugo 'Tatu' Henríquez, Jorge Moscoso, Edward Potrocarrero.

Nearby breaks The ex-island is home to several excellent breaks. Running north to south **El Brazo** (the arm) is a hollow A-frame, sand covered rock reef that delivers the goods (big and punchy) in a big swell accompanied by southwesterly winds. The left-hand reef **La Isla** works well on a mid-low tide with southeasterlies serving up long walls and barrel sections. Next up **El Toro Viejo**, producing rare but seriously powerful lefts, is best left to experienced surfers only. Resting off shore from Playa El Laucho, **El Buey**, the area's big wave spot, comes to life in big swells. It does offer up a right but is better known for it's hollow powerful left. It is best surfed in the morning or with light south easterlies. If grinding reefs aren't your thing then head off the island and drive northwards to the beachies at Playa Chinchorro.

ALFREDO ESCOBAR

Punta de Lobos

- ⬥ **Location:** Punta de Lobos, Pichilemu, Chile
- ◗ **Break type:** Left-hand point
- ◔ **Conditions:** All swells
- ◉ **Size:** 3-20 ft +
- ◔ **Length:** Up to 400 m
- ◔ **Tide:** Low to mid
- ◔ **Swell direction:** Southwesterly
- ◔ **Wind:** Southeasterly
- ◔ **Bottom:** Rock and sand
- ◔ **Ability level:** Intermediate to advanced
- ◔ **Best months:** Mar-May
- ◔ **Access:** Jump-off point on rocks
- ◔ **Hazards:** Breaks in front of rocks

WILL HENRY

The 20-ft swell has travelled from the far reaches of the freezing southern ocean, where the circumpolar current drives the water ever eastward and spinning storms lash vessels that hunt these volatile waters for their rich harvest. Twin peaks of rock crown the headland, pinnacles of sandstone that watch over the take-off point that has moved outside the bay, closer to the ledge on which they are planted. A huge crest rears up, throwing out a lip that drives into the calm of the impact zone, transforming the green glass into a fizzing mass of white water. Local surfer Ramón Navarro is already bottom turning and carving out onto the open face, driving down the line. As the wall runs close to the headland it throws into a gaping barrel which Ramón unflinchingly backdoors. The crowd on the headland holds its breath. The wave exhales with a huge plume of spray, spitting the Chilean surfer out onto the safety of the shoulder. The last wave of the annual Ceremonial Punta de Lobos sees Ramón claim another epic win. The point has put on yet another epic display.

Punta de Lobos is Chile's iconic spot, its incredible waves made instantly recognizable by its distinctive headland. Like the church overlooking Mundaka, or the lighthouse at Todos Santos, it is a unique feature that identifies this break like a surfing fingerprint. This has always been seen as one of the continent's classic set-ups but its reputation has only grown in stature with the sheer size and calibre of waves that South America's top surfers have been charging here. The waves on offer just seem to keep building with the swell size, from 3-ft fun peelers through to the realm of the XXL winner's circle. Lobos seems to sum up the Chilean surfing experience. It's a raw, open spot that can handle anything that Mother Nature throws at it. Whereas many spots max-out, Lobos just shifts around a bit, moves the line-up down the point and starts again. On 25-ft days the rocks are a looming threat in front of the brave, as the region's top chargers paddle into these big, walling monsters. However, on small days this is a break that can be transformed into a long walling point with little barrelly sections thrown in for fun. Once it gets into the overhead range the wave hots up and sections start to connect, through the magic of kinetics. Suddenly laid out before you is the full length of the point,

Punta de Lobos Board
6'1" Surf Prescriptions F-85

Shaper: Doc Lausch

6'1" x 18¼" x 2⅜"

A full body shortboard with lots of drive.

Single to double concave for rail to rail turns and down the line speed.

FCS fins.

ⓘ Boards by **Surftech**
www.surftech.com info@surftech.com

Air ——— Sea ———			
°F Averages			°C
90			30
70			20
50			10
30			0

D J F	M A M	J J A S	O N
SUMMER	AUTUMN	WINTER	SPRING
3/2	3/2	4/3	4/3

Above: Twin peaks define the Lobos line-up.
Opposite page: Locked in at the point.

offering a variety of steep, speeding walls and juicy tube rides. The sheltering nature of the cliff-lined headland allows for clean, glassy conditions when other spots are blown out by the cutting southwesterlies that can blow in during afternoon sessions. March to May is probably the best time to take on the point. Not that the rest of the year is lacking surf; it's just that the autumn season offers the best combination of weather, wind, sea temperatures and means that the sand will have been combed along the inside section, ironing out any rocky anomalies that may pop up on smaller days.

During the peak seasons and at weekends, surfers from Santiago will head for nearby Punta de Lobos but crowds are generally not large and usually pretty chilled, like the water. "I don't know if this is a spot for all surfers because it's big, cold and far from anywhere but it's still a really nice and mystical place for surf," says Alfredo Escobar of *Marejada* surf magazine in Chile. "My advice would be don't think these waves are empty because we have a lot of surfers around. It is a really calm place with a lot of waves and it is super consistent. If you come to Chile you'll need to pack a 3/4 wetsuit and booties." One problem for the locals heading out to the point must be which board

to pack. There are not many waves that can match the amazing transforming act that Punta de Lobos goes through on a day-to-day basis. Imagine if Mavs changed into a super-long, high quality point in medium swells, and a fun place to rip in small swells. This is a spot for all sessions and requires a quiver to match, from a full on rhino chaser through to a wafer-thin aerial chip. For local chargers like Ramón though, they like it plenty when those huge days light up the point, and the crowds are reduced to watching from the gallery.

Locals and legends
Ramón Navarro, Cristián Merello, Tristán Aicardi, Fernando Zegers, Diego Medina.

Nearby breaks Punta de Lobos lies to the south of **Pichilemu**, home to one of the country's better-known breaks. To the north of the village lies the long, reeling left point and although it doesn't pick up as much swell as Lobos, in the right conditions it's a longer wave and less life threatening as it breaks over sand and there aren't the rock jump-offs to deal with.

Joaquina

◈ **Location:**	Joaquina, Florianópolis, Ilha de Santa Catarina, Brazil
◔ **Break type:**	Beach break
◍ **Conditions:**	Small to medium swells
◉ **Size:**	3-8 ft
◎ **Length:**	Up to 100 m
◔ **Tide:**	All tides
◍ **Swell direction:**	Southerly to east-northeasterly
◔ **Wind:**	Westerly to northwesterly
◍ **Bottom:**	Sand
◉ **Ability level:**	All
◍ **Best months:**	Apr-Oct
◎ **Access:**	Paddle from beach
◔ **Hazards:**	Crowds

Brazil. Just the word conjures up images of beautiful women, golden sandy beaches, surf, sunny days and hot nights. Obviously nowhere could actually live up to a reputation like that. Or could it? Welcome to Ilha de Santa Catarina, home to the city of Florianópolis and over 40 beaches. During the summer it is a tourist honeypot for the beautiful people of Brazil, Argentina and Uruguay – a place to play on the beach and party the night away. During the rest of the year it is still the home of the beautiful people who like to surf all day and party all night. Ah, Brazil.

Santa Catarina was first settled by the Portuguese, who made the tortuous journey from the Azores around the mid-1700s. There then followed a second wave of immigration from Germany 100 years later,

meaning that the region has a real European feel. The legacy includes the Bavarian-style architecture of a number of towns and the traditional beer drinking of the Oktoberfest found in Blumenau each autumn. From a surfer's point of view, Ilha de Santa Catarina is a paradise found. Apart from the consistent surf and great climate, the whole of the western coastline of this island is peppered with an endless series of sandy bays, including the huge expanse of Praia do Moçambique and the classic Praia Mole. "It's a place with good waves specially during the autumn and winter," says Luciano Ferrero of Brazilian surf magazine *FLUIR*. "There are beautiful and remote beaches, great hospitality and very beautiful girls."

The most famous break on the island is Joaquina, a classic stretch of sand that offers everything from quality speeding tubes through to mellow, playful walls. As a WCT venue, the beach has become one of Brazil's best-known surfing locations, but it deserves its reputation for quality. In a clean swell, peaks spring up all along the bay, from the busy northerly stretch through to the quieter south. One of the most popular spots is a left that breaks out behind and outcrop of smoothed off, rounded boulders and reels through to the safety of the inside. "Of the 10 km of beach, the most famous wave breaks behind a rock named Pedra do Careca," says Luciano. "It's a high quality left-hander that's very long." With a wave like this on offer, you can bet the locals are on it. In Brazil, the level of competition in the water is amazing. It's not so much localism as a wave-feeding

Below: With a 10-km stretch of beach, there are enough sandbars to accommodate everyone – just about....
Opposite page: Fabricio Machado making himself at home in one of Jaoquina's beachfront shacks.

Joaquina Board

6'2" Byrne Six Channel

Shaper: Phil Byrne

6'2" x 18⅜" x 2⅜"

State of the art performance board. Slight concave into six channels through the tail.

Works great in hollow, powerful beach breaks and designed for waves from 2ft to 8ft.

FCS fins.

ⓘ Boards by **Surftech**
www.surftech.com info@surftech.com

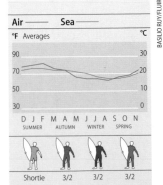

Air ———	Sea ———
°F Averages	°C

D J F M A M J J A S O N
SUMMER AUTUMN WINTER SPRING

Shortie   3/2   3/2   3/2

BASILIO RUY/FLUIR

frenzy. You think you're being vibed out and paddled round, but then out of the water the locals are chilled and friendly. It's just the competitive nature of surfing here. And this is a region that breeds top competitive surfers. Guys like Flavio and Neco Padaratz, Fabio Gouveia and Paulo Moura have all made the top echelons of surfing with a competitive drive honed in these waves.

Santa Catarina sits on the Atlantic coast to the south of São Paulo. It is exposed to swells from the east but really comes alive in swells from the south or southwesterly direction. Storms generated by deep depressions tracking past Cape Horn and into the southern reaches of the South Atlantic push lined-up groundswell towards the east coast of the island. In a northeasterly wind the beaches will go off with powerful barrels and thumping tubes. Despite summer air temperatures that can sometimes hover near 40°C, the winter water can still have a chilly enough edge to require a good 3/2 steamer. Although night-time temperatures can occasionally drop into single figures, the heat given off by the collective partying on the island must be a major contributor to global warming.

Brazil may have cornered the beach lifestyle market, created the ubiquitous dental floss bikini (women only please). They may have invented carnival and now be one of the three surfing superpowers, but one thing they have yet to master is football. So next time you're chilling on the beach at Joaquina after a classic surf session, a good idea would be to break out the football, do a few keepy-ups and lay down a challenge to the locals. Show them how the *jogo bonito* is really played…

Locals and legends
Former WCT surfers Flavio Padaratz, Neco Padaratz and Fabio Gouveia, WCT charger Paulo Moura who has lived here since 2002, plus Guga Arruda, Fernando Moura, Rafael Becker.

Nearby breaks Praia do Moçambique is a huge stretch of sand where, with a bit of hiking, you may find a few quiet peaks. It works through the tides with the northern end picking up the most swell. **Praia Mole** offers a bit of shelter when the wind picks up. To the south of Joaquina is **Campeche**, a long beach with easy access.

THIAGO MACHADO

AL MACKINNON

Europe

Dawn at Thurso East, Scotland

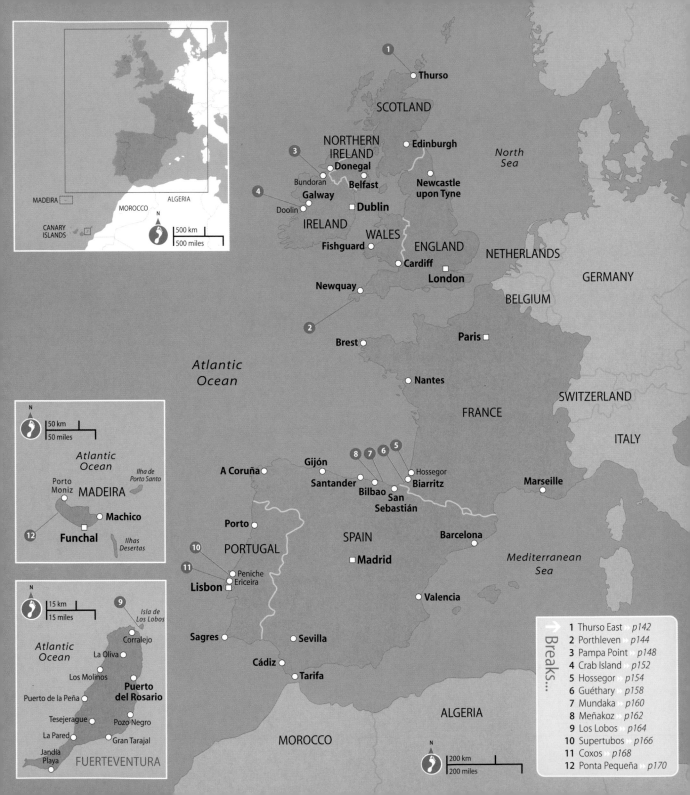

MADEIRA
ALGERIA
MOROCCO
CANARY ISLANDS

500 km
500 miles

N

1 • Thurso

SCOTLAND

NORTHERN IRELAND

• Edinburgh

North Sea

3 • Donegal
Bundoran
• Belfast

Newcastle upon Tyne

4 • Galway
Doolin
■ **Dublin**

IRELAND

WALES

ENGLAND

NETHERLANDS

GERMANY

• Fishguard

• Cardiff

■ **London**

BELGIUM

Newquay

2

Atlantic Ocean

• Brest

■ **Paris**

FRANCE

SWITZERLAND

• Nantes

ITALY

N

50 km
50 miles

Atlantic Ocean

Ilha de Porto Santo

Porto Moniz

MADEIRA

• **Machico**

12 **Funchal** ■

Ilhas Desertas

• A Coruña

• Gijón

8 7 6 5

• Hossegor

• Santander

• Biarritz

• Bilbao

• Marseille

• San Sebastián

• Porto

SPAIN

• Barcelona

PORTUGAL

■ **Madrid**

Mediterranean Sea

10

11 Peniche
Ericeira

Lisbon ■

• Valencia

N

15 km
15 miles

9 Isla de Los Lobos

Atlantic Ocean

Corralejo

La Oliva

Los Molinos

Puerto del Rosario

Puerto de la Peña

Tesejerague

Pozo Negro

La Pared

Gran Tarajal

Jandía Playa

FUERTEVENTURA

• Sagres

• **Sevilla**

• **Cádiz**

• **Tarifa**

ALGERIA

MOROCCO

N

200 km
200 miles

→ Breaks...

1 Thurso East » p142
2 Porthleven » p144
3 Pampa Point » p148
4 Crab Island » p152
5 Hossegor » p154
6 Guéthary » p158
7 Mundaka » p160
8 Meñakoz » p162
9 Los Lobos » p164
10 Supertubos » p166
11 Coxos » p168
12 Ponta Pequeña » p170

When surfing arrived on European shores, it was hardly a 'storming of the beaches' style invasion. It kind of got off the bus with its huge board under its arm, put its feet up and chatted with the ladies in its quaint foreign accent. Today surfing is whizzing round every corner of this continent on a scooter at high speed, without a helmet or a care in the world, in nothing but a pair of boardies. Over the past couple of decades it has become a frenetic and exciting lifestyle with a true European twist to it. There are local operations as well as multi-national brands – a thriving European surf industry with expanding teams of locally sponsored global riders, each with their own identities and characteristics moulded by the distinctive environment in which European surfers have developed.

Northern Europe offers those ice cream-headache duck dives, cool, clear waters, long, winding reefs and punchy beach breaks. There are mornings when the sand underfoot is still crunchy and frosty in the shadow of the cliffs, long before the sun has worked its warming magic. Summers on the French beaches can seem a long way off with their sunny afternoons of surfing in boardshorts, eating baguettes and cheese, with the distraction of reeling barrels and topless sunbathing. The surf communities of Spain and Portugal are filled with the same passion and enthusiasm that keeps fiestas rolling long into the night on the streets of San Sebastián and Lisbon. Europe even has her own 'islands', complete with monstrous waves and lava reefs. Waves steeped in stories of life and death, of being trapped out in the line-up at dusk with the swell rising and no way in through the rocks.

The world tour loves its European leg. A chance to charge in Hossegor and to power down the line in Mundaka, to sample the fine food and enjoy the culture on offer. This is what tempts many Aussies into a van that's seen better days – that classic Euro road trip from the beaches of Cornwall south towards Africa and the adventure that waits on the far side of the Mediterranean Sea.

European surfing may be a late developer but it is making up for it with a growth spurt that can make your head spin. While each country has its own character, culture, language and heroes, Europe is a continent united by its differences. So whether you're surfing the vagues, olas, ondas or waves of Europe – vive la difference!

Surfing Europe

Europe likes projects and, when Europe decides to get into something, it really gives its all. Like wars for example. They start local, but pretty soon Europe will get everyone involved. Empires as well. From the Romans to the British, no one did it better than the Europeans. But those things are old hat now. The youth of Europe has always been at the cutting edge when it comes to trends. From the Mods and Rockers of the sixties through to Punks and New Wave, they like to have their fingers on the pulse. The surf booms of the sixties and seventies kind of passed Europe by. The beach lifestyle and watersports traditions stopped after the 'conquering new kingdoms' phase. But the advent of new wetsuit technology in the eighties and nineties allowed Europeans a chance to sample what Americans and Australians had been hooked on for decades. And they liked it. A lot. European surf culture was suddenly bursting out of its bridgeheads in Cornwall and southwest France and it had a lot of lost time to make up for.

Pros & cons
UK and Ireland

Pros

Warm summers with cool water.

Regions have distinct geographical and surf characteristics.

Still potential to explore quieter regions.

Extensive surfing infrastructure.

Excellent standard of living – ok food but good nightlife.

No sharks!

Cons

Cold winters and year round wetsuits.

Inconsistent summer swells.

Busy around most well known surf breaks.

Expensive, especially fuel and accommodation.

Pros & cons
Mainland Europe

Pros

Great culture and scenery.

Geographically diverse with an endless assortment of points, sandy beaches, classic rivermouths and hollow reefs.

Lots of potential to explore.

Excellent standard of living and good food.

No sharks!

Cons

Inconsistent summer swells.

Main breaks are crowded.

Expensive food and accommodation.

Cold winters.

Opposite page: Four-time world champion Lisa Andersen hitting the spot somewhere along the 225-km stretch of beach which runs between Pointe de Grave and Anglet in southwest France.

Southwest France – Biarritz and Hossegor – is the European base camp for some of the world's surf giants – Rip Curl, Billabong and Quiksilver. Today, the European surf marketplace rivals that of the US and Australia as one of the biggest on the planet. It has taken surfing to its heart to such an extent that there are now 2½ million surfers across the continent. To surf in Europe is a truly unique experience. It is not just the quality of the waves, which can be exceptional, or the range of breaks on offer, which can seem endless, but the whole experience of travelling on a continent so rich in culture and tradition. From the soft, purple moorland of the northern reaches of Scotland through to the fractured volcanic landscape of the sun-scoured Canary Islands, this continent is as varied as the people who call it their home. "You can travel for days in Australia and never even leave the state," says top European surfer Sam Lamiroy. "Whereas in Europe, after two days on the road, you can have gone from France, to Spain and on to Portugal. Each has its own unique language and culture. That's what makes Europe to special."

European surfers are big travellers both within the confines of the continent and across the rest of the world's coastlines. Some have good reason. Those from countries that are somewhat lacking in the wave department – such as Switzerland and Holland – are some of the keenest globetrotters. Germany has even produced successful professional surfers like Marlon Lipke, currently enjoying success on the WQS. When it comes to the world of contest surfing, the top Euros have been stacking their boards in the competitor's tent for decades. Guys like Nigel Veitch, Nigel Semmens and Carwyn Williams enjoyed some success but today the likes of Russell Winter, Eric Rebière, Marie Pierre Abgrall and Micky Picon have been ranked in the elite top 44, while Tiago Pires, Eneko Acero and Patrick Bevan are knocking on the door of the World Championship Tour circuit.

Position

While Europe is the second smallest continent, it is probably one of the most diverse. Its reach stretches from the Russian Federation in the east to Portugal in the west, the balmy islands of Greece in the south through to Iceland in the north. Studying a world map it is easy to see that, while the southern most reaches are fringed almost exclusively by water (including the Caspian, Black, Aegean, Adriatic and Mediterranean Seas), it is the western coastline, facing out into the Atlantic, that is the business end of the continent for the surf community.

Culture

While Europe offers amazing surf potential, one of the beautiful things about this continent is that it is steeped in tradition and culture. And you don't have to venture far to immerse yourself. The nightlife of Paris and London offers an endless variety of options for the party goer, but the raging fiestas and festivals in Spain and Portugal can run

THIERRY ORGANOFF

WILLY URIBE

for days and even the coming of the morning sun cannot dampen the fervour. This is a continent where soccer is king and where good wine and food are celebrated. In Spain and Portugal in particular lunch is not just about nourishment – it is an event which sees business suspended and everything else put on hold. The borders may have largely gone since the advent of the EU, but local identities are celebrated with an undiminished passion. Although English is widely understood, even a bad attempt at the local language can win you many friends. A little bit of groundwork here can pay big dividends.

Climates and seasons

Located in the northern hemisphere, the seasons in Europe are the opposite of Australia and South Africa and run roughly as follows: spring – March to May; summer – June to August; autumn – September to November; winter – December to February.

The continent of Europe covers a range of climactic zones from the frigid Arctic north through to the warm Mediterranean climes of the Italy and Spain. When it comes to weather the British are obsessed with it. And for good reason – as an island state they have a lot of it. Northern Scotland is home to some excellent surf, but sees winter temperatures regularly dip below freezing and daylight can be as short as five hours. In Cornwall the average summer temperatures can climb to a balmy 20°C after a winter low of around 6°C. The Irish coastline enjoys the effects of the North Atlantic drift which keeps the winter temperatures around the 5°C mark but also means that there is an annual rainfall level of around 1000 mm in western coast areas. Why else is Ireland so green? During the summer, temperatures rise to 15°C with water temperatures to match.

The west coast of Mainland Europe is usually a cool and wet place to be during the winter months with predominantly southwesterly through northwesterly winds blowing in off the Atlantic. Temperatures in southwest France average 7°C with around 90 mm of rain in January while Lisbon in Portugal can remain relatively mild at around 11°C with around 110 mm of rain. In the summer months, the Atlantic helps to keep temperatures at a comfortable 20°C in France and 23°C in Portugal with relatively few rainy days.

Madeira and the Canary Islands enjoy warmer weather than the rest of Europe, more on a par with neighbouring Africa. Summer sees highs averaging 23°C with negligible rainfall while winter experiences lows of around 17°C. But while the Canaries sees an average of 36 mm rain in January the Garden Island of Madeira has around 89 mm.

Wavewatch report by Vic DeJesus

Low-pressure systems travelling through the North Atlantic serve as the primary swell source for Europe. Maximum intensity at the lowest latitudes occurs during the winter months. Europe will see its largest, most consistent surf during this season, although conditions can often be poor – and it's cold. The probability of large surf with the best and warmest conditions occurs from September through early November. The summer months often see smaller swells, but are notorious for long flat spells.

Geography and breaks

The 21,000 km of shoreline that surrounds Britain and Ireland is as diverse as the landscapes around it. Britain was joined to mainland Europe until the end of the last ice age when the melting of the ice sheets caused sea levels to rise, flooding the channel region and cutting off southern England from northern France. But though part of the European Union, the political distance remains a bit greater than the 35 km of the English Channel. The UK and Ireland have an incredible collection of coastal environments. The flat rock beds of Caithness, Yorkshire and Sligo offer some of the best reefs and

---

Above left: Tom Carroll powering down the face in Isla Canarias.
Above right: Gorka Yarritu celebrating the return of the world's best left.
Opposite page: Rusty Long sampling some of the simple pleasures Ireland has to offer.

MICKEY SMITH

points in Europe interspersed with some excellent beaches. The sedimentary rock laid down over the millennia forms a perfect foil for the swells that arrive at regular intervals through the peak surf seasons. The complex geology and geography of regions such as Sutherland, Devon and Cornwall, with their undulating coastline and rocky points, forms a number of excellent beach breaks but are somewhat lacking in reefs.

Mainland Europe allows surfers to sample a complex coastline within a relatively small area. Europe's 9260 km of shoreline includes the rugged coastline of Brittany, so reminiscent of Cornwall, and runs south through the endless sandy beaches of Gironde and Les Landes, with their backdrop of sand dunes and pine forests. The Basque region runs into Northern Spain with its 5000 km of undulating coastline. "You can always find a place to surf," say Spanish pro Dani Garcia. "In any swell, from one to 20 ft, in any wind direction and at any tide." Spain is all about flexibility. Top local rider Michel Velasco agrees. "You have a real variety of waves for all the surfing levels. You can surf all year due to the swells consistency and you can always escape the crowds."

Heading into Portugal you are faced with some of the best beaches and reefs on the continent, spread along just 830 km of coast. João da Câmara Valente, editor of *Surf Portugal* loves Portugal's ever-changing countryside. "The uniqueness of surfing in Portugal is directly related to its geography. Although it is a somewhat small coast, it displays an enormous variety of breaks within very short areas. Point breaks, reef breaks, beach breaks, rivermouths, whatever – Portugal has it all. Sometimes I think to myself how lucky we are that the whole Portuguese coast is not made of just an enormous beach break monotony."

WAVEWATCH	Dec-Feb Winter	Mar-May Spring	Jun-Aug Summer	Sep-Nov Autumn
EUROPE				
Wave size/direction	W 6-8'	NW 5-7'	NW 3-4'	NW 5-7'
Wind force/direction	SW/NW F5	NW F4	NE F2	NW F3
Surfable days	20+	20+	5-10	10-15
Water/air temp	10/7°C	14/12°C	16/18°C	15/13°C

Health and safety
No specific immunizations are needed for the European counties covered in this guide and for minor problems, chemists are an excellent first port of call. Across Europe, opportunist thieves have become wise to the fact that surfers often stash keys on their vehicles so break-ins have seen an increase.

There are sharks in the waters around Europe but so far, except in the Mediterranean, they have not been an issue for surfers or other water users. The only other sea creatures to look out for are those that cause (usually) minor aggravations. Weaver fish are small fish that lurk in the shallows just beneath the sand on sunny, low tide days. If you do tread on one, you'll know about it and although pretty painful, their sting is not usually fatal. (Certain people may experience allergic reactions to the venom.) Immerse injured body part into water as hot as can be tolerated, to break down the protein-based poison and stop the pain. Leave to soak for 10-15 minutes. Urchins are found on rocky reefs and are most prevalent in warmer climes such as Portugal, Canaries and Madeira. If you are unfortunate enough to stand on an urchin, the spines – which are as brittle as pencil lead – usually break off and lodge in your foot. Better

out than in, spines can be carefully picked out with a sterile needle but prevention is better than cure so wear boots if you are in any doubt.

Surfing and the environment
The European coastline is a collection of very diverse environments. Across the continent surfers have often been at the forefront of campaigning to clean up polluted waters, to restore damaged ecosystems and to prevent environmentally damaging developments from taking place. In many countries raw sewage was routinely dumped into the sea, even at bathing beaches, until the EU Bathing Water Initiative introduced Europe-wide standards in bathing waters. There are still places where this practice still takes place and, as we all know, surfing isn't limited to bathing beaches. There is also the thorny issue of discharges from chemical plants, industrial complexes, nuclear power stations and oil refineries.

Campaign groups like **Surfers Against Sewage** have became a model of how a group of concerned individuals can come together to form a successful pressure group to pursue environmental causes at the highest level. Formed in the Cornish village of St Agnes, SAS has grown into one of the UK's most respected environmental organizations.

Live. Surf. Travel.

An indispensable guide to Britain which every surfer should own
Wavelength Magazine

Price £14.99   ISBN 1 904777 40 6

An invaluable resource – a one-stop guide to surfing across the continent
Surfer Magazine

Price £24.99   ISBN 1 904777 07 4

DOCUMENTING THE BEST OF
BRITISH SURFING

wavelength

SUBSCRIBE BY LOGGING ON TO
WWW.WAVELENGTHMAG.CO.UK

"In 1990, surfers were getting sick of the state of the sea and sick *because* of the state of the sea," says Andy Cummins of SAS. "At the time the general attitude towards sewage was pump it out to sea and dump it there untreated. Surfers and other water users were bearing the brunt of this outrageous dumping practice as raw sewage floated back to shore with the winds, waves and tide. The general public however remained unaware of the risk and the extent of the problem. SAS took on huge industries and governments in order to get the changes everybody deserved. To do this successfully, SAS has always strived to present a solution-based argument of viable and sustainable alternatives. SAS highlights the flaws in current practices, attitudes, and legislation, challenging industry, legislators and politicians."

As well as organizing clean-ups, a key aspect of SAS is education and information, raising awareness from classroom level all the way up to the corridors of the European Parliament. To find out more about SAS, check out www.sas.org.uk.

Surfrider Foundation Europe was formed in 1990 by Tom Curren and today has 15 chapters all dedicated to a single purpose – acting now to protect Europe's oceans and coastlines. They combine educational initiatives with direct action such as beach clean-ups. They run the annual Initiatives Océanes each spring where over 5000 people are involved in a co-ordinated clean up of around 150 locations. The also publish an annual Black Pennants report highlighting the most polluted beaches on the French coastline. Find out more about SFE on www.surfrider-europe.org.

Surfing resources

Europe has the largest and most diverse surf media in the world. The UK has a strong and ever-expanding surf media. Established in 1981, *Wavelength* (www.wavelengthmag.co.uk) is the UK's longest running surf magazine. *Carve* (www.carvemag.com) came into the picture in 1992. The environmentally minded magazine *The Surfer's Path* (www.surferspath.com) has now expanded into the US. In 2004 core magazine *Pitpilot* (www.pitpilotmag.co.uk) burst onto the scene to establish itself firmly at the heart of the British surf scene. New on the scene is *Slide* magazine (www.slidemag.com).

On the continent, France is home to the ever-stoked *Trip Surf* (www.trip-surf.com) and *Surf Session* (www.surfsession.com). Spain has a strong surf media including *3Sesenta* (www.3sesenta.com) and *Surfer Rule*. Portugal is home to *Surf Portugal*, one of the most established surf magazines in Europe. Ireland now has *Fins* (www.finsmag.com) – a watersports magazine that covers surfing. Elsewhere in Europe, where there are surfers, there are magazines – Germany has the excellent *Surfers* Magazine (www.surfersmag.de),

> **6699**
>
> In Europe, after two days on the road, you can have gone from France, to Spain and on to Portugal. Each has its own unique language and culture. That's what makes Europe so special.
>
> Sam Lamiroy, top European surfer

Italy is home to several magazines including *Revolt* (www.revolt.it), the Netherlands have *Reload* (www.reload.nl) and *6 Surf*, even the Swiss, with absolutely no coastline, have *Seventh Sky*. *Surf Europe* (www.surfeuropemag.com) is a pan-European magazine published in several languages across the continent. There are plenty of good surf resources for each individual country but a good starting point and comprehensive swell predictions site is *Magic Seaweed* (www.magicseaweed.com). For news from across the planet head to French-based *Surfers Village* (www.surfersvillage.com). For the best guide to surfing in Europe check out *Surfing Europe*, the fully comprehensive surf travel guide (www.footprintbooks.com).

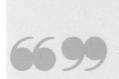

Thurso East

◈ **Location:** Thurso rivermouth, Thurso, Caithness, Scotland

◓ **Break type:** Right-hand reef

◓ **Conditions:** Medium to big swells

◒ **Size:** 3-12 ft

◔ **Length:** 50-100 m

◑ **Tide:** All tides, best quarter to three quarter tide on the push

◈ **Swell direction:** Huge westerly, big northwesterly or any northerly swell

◈ **Wind:** Southeasterly

☺ **Bottom:** Slate reef

◐ **Ability level:** Intermediate to advanced

◈ **Best months:** Sep-Dec, Apr-Jun

◈ **Access:** Off the rocks, or via the river in big swells

◈ **Hazards:** Cold, rock bottom, heavy when over head-high

Over the centuries the county of Caithness has survived attacks from marauding Vikings, economic hardship and the relentless battering of the violent storms that roll out of the Arctic. The area made its living from herring fishing and from the huge deposit of flat slabstone, a sedimentary rock much sought after for paving stones and house building. Slate from Caithness was exported around the world during the 19th century. This same flat slate also makes the region one of the most amazing surfing playgrounds in the world. Many bays host flat rock beds that slant into the sea and have been groomed by the ocean over the centuries to produce high quality points and reefs. One such reef sits at the mouth of Thurso River.

Below: Local charger Chris Noble hooks into another cold water classic.
Opposite page: Dawn at Nias by any other name.

Thurso East is one of those waves that is instantly recognizable from a photograph. The trademark brown, peaty water and the distant white lighthouse, a stark contrast to the otherwise green backdrop, are just some of the clues that give it away. The other is the hollow, reeling right-hander looking more 'North Shore' than 'Norse Shore'. Many monikers have been attached to this break, but the one that is most commonly used is 'cold water Nias'. Thurso East offers serious tube time, without the threat of razor sharp coral lurking just below the surface. "You've gotta put Thurso in any top ten, it's up there with any wave in the world," sums up top longboarder and former world number five, Chris Griffiths. "The amazing thing is it would have more people surfing it if it was hidden on some tiny island in the middle of the Mentawis."

Thurso is Britain's most northerly mainland town, an 18-hour drive from the traditional surfing heartland of Cornwall. The famous reef is overlooked by a 17th-century castle ruin while the farm to the north provides the perfect vantage point to witness the beauty of a 10-ft swell unleashing Indonesian-style rights at the mouth of 'Thor's River' – the raw power of an Arctic storm condensed into a huge, perfect barrel. The topography of the set-up couldn't be better if it was computer generated. The smooth, kelp-covered reef waits for big swells to roll out of the North Atlantic and into the northerly facing bay. The angle of the approach is critical. A big swell out of the west bends into the bay, producing fast, hollow barrels whereas a swell from the north angles down the reef to produce long, steep, critical walls. As a wave

DEMI TAYLOR

Thurso East Board

6'6" Channel Islands K-Model

Shaper: Al Merrick

6'6" x 18¾" x 2⅜"

A board to harness the energy of this powerful break.

Kelly Slater rides this board when it's not quite big enough for a gun.

Added nose and tail rocker for steep take-offs and snaps!

FCS K 2.1 fins

ⓘ Boards by **Surftech**
www.surftech.com info@surftech.com

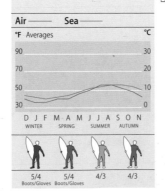

Air ———	Sea ———	
°F Averages		°C
90		30
70		20
50		10
30		0

D J F M A M J J A S O N
WINTER SPRING SUMMER AUTUMN

5/4	5/4	4/3	4/3
Boots/Gloves	Boots/Gloves		

approaches the reef, it starts to rear up into a peak. The wave bowls slightly and the brown, peat-stained lip throws over. It is then a race to the finish with the barrel spiralling along the rock-bed, always threatening to nip shut. Pick the right one and with the right line it will be a perfect tube ride, though the freezing water will test even the hardiest surfer. "I remember being in Thurso for the European Championships," says top French surfer Didier Piter. "The waves were excellent, but the water was so cold! We were not prepared and brought only our 3/2 summer suits. It is truly a hardcore surf spot". Even the 24 hours of daylight in summer does little to warm the waters ready for the September sessions.

Thurso was first ridden by a visiting English surfer, Paul Gill, back in 1975. Pat Kieran came north of the border to work at the nearby Dounreay nuclear power plant, drawn to the town by photos of the nearby waves. He moved into a cottage overlooking the reef and helped bump-start the local surf community. "It was a brilliant spot," says Pat. "I was a single bloke surfing and shaping boards in the barn and the bedroom next door. Surfers from all over the country used to drop in and stay, even when I wasn't home. I never locked my door. When I moved out a few years later, I picked up the key to hand it back to the landlord and it left a key-shaped hole in the dust."

Thurso still has a relatively small but amazingly hardcore surfing community, but as with everywhere, numbers in the line-up are increasing. "There has been heightened media attention over the last couple of years," says local charger Chris Noble. "The recent contests have brought the best surfers in the UK to Thurso and the wave has featured in a couple of DVDs. People only used to have photos to go by and this never really showed the wave's full potential." In the peak autumn season the wave can now become quite crowded. Even a bleak afternoon in December can see up to a dozen surfers in the line-up, but if visitors are calm and respectful they will find a warm, friendly line-up. If not, the welcome will be as frosty as the water.

Locals and legends
Paul Gill, Pat Kieran, Neil Harris, Chris Noble, Andy Bain.

Nearby breaks Across the rivermouth is **Shit Pipe**, a high quality right reef usually smaller than its more famous neighbour. Further west, **Brims Ness** (Norse for surf point) is an exposed point that hoovers up any swell around. It is home to **The Bowl**, (1/4 to 3/4 tide fast, shallow, barrelling right reef), **The Cove** (same characteristics as The Bowl but a bit less extreme) and **The Point** (longer left, watch out for rips). Travelling east, **Dunnet Bay** is an ideal beach break for beginners while **Gills Bay** is an experts-only left point that can hold waves of over 10 ft.

AL MACKINNON

Europe Thurso East

Porthleven

🜂 **Location:**	Porthleven village, south coast of Cornwall
◐ **Break type:**	Reef break
◓ **Conditions:**	All swells
◑ **Size:**	3-10 ft
◈ **Length:**	50-75 m
🌊 **Tide:**	Just off low to three quarters
🜁 **Swell direction:**	Southwesterly
◔ **Wind:**	Northeasterly
🜨 **Bottom:**	Rock reef
◉ **Ability level:**	Intermediate to advanced
🜚 **Best months:**	Sep-Dec
◍ **Access:**	Off the rocks
⊖ **Hazards:**	Shallow near low, crowds and more crowds

Cornwall isn't famous for its reef breaks. It has a plethora of beaches scattered between the many rocky headlands but the lack of reefs and points is something that niggles in the background, like an itch that can't be scratched. The complex, fractured, granite and sandstone geography just doesn't allow for quality reef formation. However, there is one ray of light. Nestled away on the south Cornish coast sits the small community of Porthleven. Once a thriving fishing village, it is now a popular holiday spot and an unlikely surfing Mecca, for at the western entrance to 'Leven' harbour sits a bona fide quality reef break.

The rocks above the western side of the harbour give a wide reaching view over the reef and beyond. The expanse of the Lizard peninsula stretches south, terminating at Britain's most southerly point, while, to the west, the coast curves around Mount's Bay, past Penzance, and swings round the corner to Lands End. It's a beautiful setting for a special wave. Porthleven is probably the most famous reef break in the south of England. It faces southwest and is somewhat sheltered from the dominant northwesterly swells that hit the north coastline of Cornwall. Although 'Leven breaks year round, it really comes to life in a clean southwesterly swell out of the mid Atlantic or Bay of Biscay. It can also fire during a big winter westerly or wrapping northwesterly swell. As Cornwall boasts one of the largest and most dedicated surfing communities in Europe, this means one thing. Porthleven is something of a crowd magnet.

Heaven can wait, but 'Leven can't. When the swell's up, you've got to be on it. News spreads by mobile and email. Cars descend on the village but the locals are already in. "Due to the shape of the reef, Porthleven forms one of the heaviest waves in the UK," say local surfer Will Boex. "Unfortunately it's no longer the all local line-up from yesteryear but when 'Leven is on, it's certainly a privilege to surf." Will and brothers Jake and Sam, as well as Robyn Davies and Dan Joel will probably be first in the line-up, along with the north coast crew headed by Robin Kent, Minzie and James Hendy. The good days will see the UK's top surfers duelling it out for the hell drops, pulling in and getting kegged. "The thing about Leven is that when it's good it's so competitive there's only a handful of guys actually getting waves," says James Hendy. "Some people just paddle out to say they were in."

Below: Cranking at 6ft – the dots on the left give the wave some perspective.
Opposite page: Cornwall's Robin Kent leading the charge at 'Leven.

CHRIS GRIFFITHS

Porthleven Board

6'3" JC SD-3

Shaper: John Carper

6'3" x 18.15" x 2.2"

Designed for down the line speed, late drops and tight turns, with finely tuned rails to fit you deep in the barrel.

Offers plenty of paddling to battle the winter crowds.

Futures JC1 fins.

ⓘ Boards by Surftech
www.surftech.com info@surftech.com

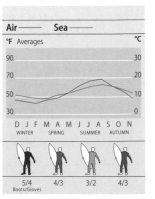

Air ——	Sea ——	
°F Averages		°C
90		30
70		20
50		10
30		0
D J F M A M J J A S O N		
WINTER	SPRING SUMMER	AUTUMN

| 5/4 Boots/Gloves | 4/3 | 3/2 | 4/3 |

MICKEY SMITH

The wave itself sits to the west of the harbour channel and ledges up onto the reef, throwing out right-hand barrels with the occasional left squeaking through. On classic days the line-up will look like a perfect A-frame, the rights feathering off towards the channel with the bowling wall racing ahead. The wave works best from just off low through to just off high. The rocks are jagged and unforgiving. The take-off is steep and there is a keen crew of body boarders who like to charge the big days with a hardcore crew of stand-up surfers. Get it right and there can be classic open barrels, get it wrong and you can be picking bits of your favourite stick out of the rocks. "Leven can be a real board eater," says Minzie. "I recall one session where I'd just snapped my board and I was scooting in on what was left of it and I saw Chops (Lascelles) paddling out. He saw me and started laughing.

Luckily I had a spare board with me so I grabbed it, put my leash on and jumped back off the rocks. I'm paddling out and guess who I meet coming in on the remains of his board?"

Locals and legends

Sam Boex, Jake Boex, Will Boex, Robyn Davies, Dan Joel, Robin Kent, James Hendy, Minzie.

Nearby breaks Praa Sands is a stretch of beach that sits to the northwest of Porthleven. It is a popular choice with local surfers when the big winter swells hit and the winds are coming from a north or northeasterly direction. It breaks all through the tides but better at low to mid. If winds are easterly, **Sennen Cove** is an exposed stretch of beach break found on the toe of Cornwall that picks up any swell from the North Atlantic.

Pampa Point

- **Location:** Southwest edge of Bundoran, County Donegal, Ireland
- **Break type:** Left reef break
- **Conditions:** Medium to big swells
- **Size:** 4-12 ft
- **Length:** 25-75 m
- **Tide:** Mid to high
- **Swell direction:** Northwesterly
- **Wind:** Southerly
- **Bottom:** Ledge reef
- **Ability level:** Advanced
- **Best months:** Sep-Dec
- **Access:** Well timed paddle off the rocks
- **Hazards:** Heavy wave, rips

MICKEY SMITH

Ireland is a land of rolling hills, a place where the autumn sun illuminates a vibrant spectrum of colours, from purple heathers to the pink fuchsias that form huge blooming hedgerows, all set against a background of every shade of green known to nature. Country roads duck into tiny villages where terraces of brightly painted cottages line the narrow main street, and new-build bungalows punctuate the landscape, giving just a hint of the recent economic boom that has taken place here. Eire lies off the west coast of Britain and, with nothing standing in its way, bears the full brunt of passing Atlantic lows. Its coastline is blessed with pristine beaches and some awesome flat reefs, where the cool crystal-blue waters conspire to utilize those pressure systems and produce some of the world's most epic waves. Ever since the first

waves were ridden in Irish waters by Kevin Cavey back in 1960, surfing and Ireland have been destined to have a special relationship. "I love the whole Irish surfing experience," says journeyman surfer Dan Malloy. "The surfing is amazing but it's like a bonus on top of everything. It's a whole different thing to surfing in Hawaii or California. It's freezing and that's one of the things I like about it."

Bundoran is Ireland's unofficial surf city. It is home to one of the best known waves in the country, The Peak, a wave threatened by a proposed marina development until local surfers stepped in and rallied support to save it. The Peak now sits in one of only two surfing reserves in the world. To the southwest of the town lies another famous reef break, PMPA, or Pampa Point, which was brought to the attention of the surfing world in the movie *Litmus*. When Aussie pro Joel Fitzgerald charged huge, gaping lefts here in the 1990s, it really opened people's eyes to the potential that lies around the Irish coastline. Pampa was named after a PMPA Insurance sign that stood near the break – and good insurance is probably a wise thing to have at this ledgy point break that offers some fast, challenging and hollow lefts. As the size increases, so does the danger level of the wave. It can be transformed into a frighteningly fast, gaping race for survival. "Pampa is one of my favourite waves in the world," say Irish hell-man John McCarthy. "The reef is so shallow but somehow there have been very few accidents out there. As the wave gets to 8 ft it moves onto the outer ledge. When you look at the 10-footers Joel Fitzgerald surfed

Pampa Point Board

6'7" Wayne Lynch Free Flight

Shaper: Wayne Lynch

6'7" x 18¾" x 2⅜"

Solid semi-gun perfect for the ledgy hollow tubes of Pampa Point.

Single to double concave with extra nose and tail rocker to handle the elevator drops when it gets big.

FCS G7 fins.

ⓘ Boards by **Surftech**
www.surftech.com info@surftech.com

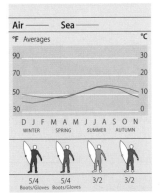

Air ——	Sea ——	
°F Averages		°C
90		30
70		20
50		10
30		0

D J F M A M J J A S O N
WINTER SPRING SUMMER AUTUMN

5/4 | 5/4 | 3/2 | 3/2
Boots/Gloves | Boots/Gloves | |

Above: The innermost limits of pure Pampa.
Opposite page: The wave jacks up onto a shallow ledge opening up into a wicked, barrelling left but watch out for the rips pushing eastward.

in *Litmus* – that's the second ledge. When it gets to that size it takes on a whole different and much more serious persona."

The take-off at Pampa is steep and the wall bowls round and soon the lip is racing away. The aim is keep as much speed as possible going into the tube. "It's just so challenging riding backside," says John. "I'm having a good session out there if I make 20% of my waves. But whether you make the wave or not you're going to clock up four or five seconds of tube time on each wave." Pampa is a serious wave for serious surfers, not the kind of spot to paddle out at if you haven't

racked up some serious time at some serious reefs. After all, at a surf spot named after an insurance company, the only thing you want to claim is the barrel you just pulled out of.

Locals and legends
Kevin Tobin, Joel Fitzgerald, Richie Fitzgerald, John McCarthy, Cain Kilcullen, Mike Morgan, Fergal Smith from County Mayo, David Blount.

Nearby breaks To the east, **The Peak** at Bundoran is a flat reef that offers hollow lefts and rights. Works best at low tide in swells from 3 up to 8 ft. "We've been trying to save The Peak by demonstrating that surfing brings a lot into this town," say Richie Fitzgerald, local surfer and shop owner. So far the surfers have run a successful campaign and development plans have been put on hold. To the west is the right-hand boulder point **Tullaghan** – best in medium to large swells.

THE GILL

Surfers' tales
Come on, Aileen John McCarthy

Since the explosion of big wave surfing outside Hawaii, new spots have been challenged around the globe from the skulking beasts at Mavericks to the great white hunting ground of Dungeons. Europeans have been riding bigger and better waves on an almost yearly basis, from Belharra in France to Punta Galea in Spain. The latest recruit to this elite band can be found off Ireland's west coast. For a small continent, it's certainly discovering its big wave riding feet.

Lahinch was once just famous for its exclusive 18 -hole links course. Today it has become a surf town, the epicentre of Irish surfing on the west coast. There's a long tradition of waveriding in the town, there's been a club here since the early seventies and the European Championships rocked up here, in 1976 I think, but it was flat for two weeks so the event was called-off. But this rich tradition and the hard charging role models in the line-up has started to push through the best junior surfers in Ireland, guys like Damien Conway who is the Irish U16 and U14 champion. The Lahinch area is blessed with a variety of points and reefs, some fickle and some less so and in the Liscannor Bay area there are over 20 breaks that work on different swell, tide and wind conditions.

I started surfing 20 years ago in Tramore, Co.Waterford in Southwest Ireland, where there was a really good club set up run by Hugh O'Brien Moran, which really helped bring through the kids. My most amazing trip was with my partner in crime David Blount, leaving Hawaii we drove from California through Central America to get to Panama and onto Columbia and Brazil. That was six years ago and we've been basing our searches for waves in Ireland since then. Aileen was waiting nearby. Waiting 'til we were ready.

The Cliffs of Moher are the regions biggest tourist draw and a spectacular natural phenomenon. The tallest cliffs in Ireland fall in a head-spinning sheer plunge into the sea just to the north of Lahinch. Breaking far below is a huge thundering wave. Photographer Mickey Smith saw the wave in Oct 2004 and told me about it. I watched in awe for almost a year with my friend David Blount trying to figure out how big it was. On a couple of huge days it looked kind of Jaws size so we didn't know if we were interested, but luckily it seems not to be as big as it looks from the cliffs. The wave is like your dream head high perfect right hand barreling peak, but in a form five times bigger and about 10 times thicker. It's got so much power and grunt. What makes it more amazing is the location. The Cliffs are completely vertical so if you get washed in, it is pretty ugly. It's a truly amazing place. We named the wave 'Aileens' which is from the Irish name of the headland Aill na Searacht. We finally got the cash together to get the ski in August of 2005.

It was first surfed the day we all went out there in mid October 05 with Rusty Long, Robin Kent, Mickey Smith, Dave Blount and myself. The swell was really huge, maybe five or six times overhead at Crab Island and really gusty and cloudy. We were all hummin and hawwin about whether to try it or not but I think Rusty made the call to get out there. We paddled in that day, as the wave was more standing up than just bowling over. Lining up under the cliffs for the first time was difficult, as we didn't really know what we were doing. It took about 30 minutes before we got any waves. We were all just so stoked with the whole thing, none of us could believe what was happening. Rusty was obviously totally in the comfort zone and was leading the way just picking off the right ones without messing up once.

Yep, people are just blown away by what's been seen so far, the photos kind of say "Come on over to Ireland and surf a freezing cold'n fickle Nuclear rated slab underneath the largest vertical cliffs in the country but remember – fall off your surfboard and there's a good chance your fucked onto slabs the size of tennis courts!" I don't know if that many people will take up the offer. The potential in Ireland is obvious but when the waves are big in the winter, Ireland is bloody, freezing cold so you have to be kinda crazy or very keen to be going out on a jet ski or boat. It's hardcore shit doing this with a 6/5/4 suit, hood and gloves. It's just the same ol' thing in Ireland, where you have to hang around for a couple of months to get a few good days, but that's what keeps it what it is.

John McCarthy lives in Lahinch, County Clare, Ireland. He started and runs Lahinch Surf School which is "hands down Ireland's best surf school". At other times you may find him in the line-up at Sunset, charging a huge point in Madeira or tucking into a barrel at some hidden Indo reef. Check out more about Aileens at www.lahinchsurfschool.com/cliffs.

Opposite page: John McCarthy limbering up on a 'smaller' day but he's ready for Moher. [AL MACKINNON]

Crab Island

◈ **Location:**	Doolin, County Clare, Ireland
◔ **Break type:**	Right-hand reef
◍ **Conditions:**	All swells
◉ **Size:**	3-12 ft plus
◑ **Length:**	50-75 m
◔ **Tide:**	Low to mid
◈ **Swell direction:**	Northwesterly to southwesterly
◍ **Wind:**	Light easterly to southeasterly
◔ **Bottom:**	Jagged reef
◉ **Ability level:**	Advanced
◍ **Best months:**	Sep-Nov
◔ **Access:**	Paddle from the harbour
◈ **Hazards:**	Reef, rips, long paddle

The lush, green, countryside of Western Ireland gives way to the bleak limestone pavement of The Burren as if some ancient giant had peeled away the carpet of grass to reveal the flat, grey rock beneath. This is an ecological landscape found in few places around Europe, and nowhere can rival the sheer scale of The Burren. The huge slabs of rock are separated by cracks that hide unique plants, crouched in the shade and sheltered from the howling wind that scours the open countryside above. This topography gives a massive clue as to why the nearby coastline is such draw to European surfers. The flat limestone that gives this land its distinctive make-up also shapes the reefs and points, providing wonderful hollow playgrounds for the adventurous, but also jagged punishment for the careless.

The road into Doolin runs downhill for a couple of miles before it hits the bridge. On the right-hand side of the road sit a couple of pubs that are world-renowned for their cold Guinness, warm fires and excellent live music. They attract visitors from all parts of the village and all corners of the globe. But carry on another half mile to where the road terminates and you'll be met by a low harbour wall, with breathtaking views of the towering cliffs to the south. Out in front of the harbour lies a small, unassuming, low-lying island, home to one of the least famous world-class waves in Europe. "When you come over the hill from Lahinch, you can see how the wave is breaking from way above," says local charger John McCarthy. "It's an amazing sight as you pass by the old castle in the foreground. The most awesome thing about surfing Crab Island is the view when you're out there in the line-up.

Just a mile to the south are the 700-ft Cliffs of Moher, which are one of the most scenic areas of Ireland." These cliffs are so sheer they would test anyone's head for heights. It's as if a large chunk of western Ireland's coastline had been sliced off by a giant cheesewire. "Out in the other direction are the Aran Islands. There's no housing estates or shops and the water is perfectly clear. It's just an amazing place."

The bay at Doolin boasts a couple of excellent waves, but the real gem hides on the far side of Crab Island. The carboniferous limestone of the local geology lends itself to the production of wonderful flat, though somewhat jagged, beds for the consistent Atlantic swells to break on. Walking down to the water's edge at low tide will give you an idea of what lies in wait if you blow the jacking take-off. The uneven erosion of the bedrock has left sharp fingers and ankle-deep fissures. The reef at Crab has left more than the odd lasting impression on unwary visitors and this gives a clue as to why helmets are not a rare sight in the line-up.

From the harbourside the island looks tantalizingly close. "To get to the wave at Crab you have to cross a 200-m channel and then paddle around the back of the island," says John. "Fortunately there's no such thing as a shark attack in Ireland as it's the kind of paddle I wouldn't consider in Australia or South Africa." Paddling around the corner gives a sudden, awesome view of the pitching, glassy, barrelling right as it lunges out of the deep, cold, blue water and onto the shallow shelf, the inside a boiling contrast of white turbulence. It is a vertical

Below: The 8-ft Crab detonates in the evening sun.
Opposite page: Local charger John McCarthy tucks into a bit of fresh crab.

drop and then a race-track that bowls around towards the channel. Make the drop, bottom turn and then pull in, taking aim for the daylight. "The wave can be a really nice barrel, from 2 ft to 8 ft," says John. "Crab is quite short but has a lot of intensity. At full low tide it's only a couple of feet deep so the take-off can be very challenging, but you can get some perfect tubes. If you get a big west or southwest swell with no wind, you can surf it at 12 ft and maybe bigger. There are always some random peaks that can catch you out, but if you get to know the wave you can avoid most of the swimming." Tom Buckley of the nearby Lahinch Surf Shop adds a sobering thought. "It is a serious wave that has broken many boards and leashes, dislocated a few shoulders and put out a few backs. If you lose your board the swim home can be very difficult due to the currents between the island and the mainland." But for John there are few waves to match the surfing paradise that sits on his own doorstep. "Sometimes when I surf it alone I'll think how much busier it would be if it was a regular spot where you could park right in front of the break. The paddle and the heaviness of the wave definitely keep the crowds down. It's pretty special."

Locals and legends

Andy Burke, Saul Harvey, Alvin McCullough, Bill Keane, Tom Doidge-Harrison, John McCarthy.

Nearby breaks To the south of Doolin lies the regional surf capital **Lahinch**. It is home to a consistent beach break with a number of good left-hand reefs to the south including **The Left**, **Cornish Left** and **Aussie Left**. Further south lies one of Ireland's most famous spots, **Spanish Point**, with its three waves. This was one of the first Irish waves to come to the attention of the outside world.

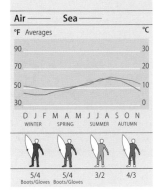

Crab Island Board		
6'1" Byrne Tom Carroll		
Shaper: Phil Byrne		
6'1" x 18⅜" x 2⅛"		
Designed with two-time world champion Tom Carroll, this highly responsive round pin works well in just about any surf from 2 ft- 6 ft.		
FCS fins.		

ⓘ Boards by Surftech
www.surftech.com   info@surftech.com

Air ——— Sea ———	
°F Averages	°C
90	30
70	20
50	10
30	0

D J F M A M J J A S O N
WINTER SPRING SUMMER AUTUMN

5/4
Boots/Gloves   5/4
Boots/Gloves   3/2   4/3

Europe Crab Island

AL MACKINNON

Hossegor

◈ **Location:**	Les Landes, southwest France
◐ **Break type:**	Beach break
◐ **Conditions:**	All swells
◉ **Size:**	2-15 ft
◉ **Length:**	10-150 m
◉ **Tide:**	All tides
◉ **Swell direction:**	Northwesterly to westerly
◉ **Wind:**	Easterly
◉ **Bottom:**	Sand
◉ **Ability level:**	Beginner to advanced
◉ **Best months:**	Sep-Nov
◉ **Access:**	Off the beach
◉ **Hazards:**	Crowds, heavy waves, rips

WILLY URIBE

Hossegor provides an almost perfect combination of everything a surf trip should contain. The sidewalk cafés are where the bold and the beautiful sip their café au lait in the warm glow of September. After sundown the open terraces of the restaurants offer classic French fare washed down with fine local wine and cognac from a neighbouring region. Then it's back to that nice little hotel you've discovered that's doing good off-season deals, or to the campsite that has become the exclusive domain of a United Nations of surfing nationalities. The climate is hot, but not stifling and life revolves around the beach. And why not? It is long, perfectly formed and, on a clear day, you can look to the north and to the south, past the heat haze rising from the sand, and it's impossible to see where this huge stretch of gold begins or ends. Then there's the surf.

Hossegor is not just a single break, or a small local beach. This region boasts endless golden sands sculpted into some of the planet's best banks. To put a figure on it, 225 km of west-facing, pure, unadulterated beach runs from Pointe de Grave in the north to Anglet in the south, broken only by the occasional rivermouth and the Bassin d'Arcachon. Unlike some spots around the globe, which can offer either thumping close-outs or frustrating mushburgers, Hossegor has a seemingly endless array of surf conditions on offer every time a new swell kicks in: from the sickest stand-up barrels to the most fun walls you can imagine,

lefts, rights, peaks and, as the tide changes, so do the banks. "Hossegor, France – super-punchy, wedging beach break that spits you out of tubes right at some of the craziest air sections you can find anywhere in the world", says Chris Cote, editor of *Transworld Surf*. It's like a big surfing wonderland. Put in the groundwork and you'll soon work out where the best spots are for each tide or size swell. Just strap your boards to the roof, hop in the car and drive north. "I love it here because I spend my days at the beach," says soul surfer Dan Malloy. "I pack a bag and an umbrella, food for the day, put on some sun block and just surf all day. Hike down the beach and look for sandbars. It's fun to check it out, be on it, eat lunch, then be on it again when the tide drops."

One of the most famous sandbanks in Hossegor is La Gravière. With an underwater trench to channel the energy, this super-fast, hollow wave can produce Pipeline-like conditions – in terms of both the pleasure and the pain – when big, clean swells hit. "It really is like Hawaii out

Above right: Patrick Bevan slashes up Hossegor.
Opposite page: Hossegor – La Gravière.

Hossegor Board
6'3" Rusty Pro-ject
Shaper: Rusty Preisendorfer
6'3" x 18¾" x 2³/₁₆"
Moderate rocker with triple concave finished with a slight release vee through the tail.
A design that shines brightest in waist-to-overhead waves.
Built for the perfect sand bars of Hossegor!
Futures FEA fins.
ⓘ Boards by Surftech www.surftech.com info@surftech.com

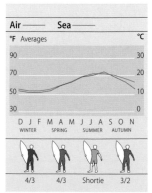

Air ——— Sea ———		
°F Averages		°C
90		30
70		20
50		10
30		0

D J F M A M J J A S O N
WINTER · SPRING · SUMMER · AUTUMN

4/3	4/3	Shortie	3/2

there," said North Shore local Kalani Robb speaking at the 2005 Quiksilver Pro France. "I almost drowned out there the other day and I just broke a board. It's pretty gnarly for sure. It was like 10 ft – that's big." One man who knows all about the best French beach break is *Trip Surf* editor Franck Lacaze. "La Gravière is my number one wave, because I've surfed there some of the most perfect waves of my life. Just intense and powerful barrels. Absolute beach break perfection." But it isn't just French patriotism speaking. Hossegor has universal appeal and has featured on countless top tens, from 'CT surfers such as Damien Hobgood through to ASL's Jimmy O'Keefe and Tahitian-based photographer Tim McKenna who sums this up as simply the 'best beach break'.

To the north of La Gravière are the breaks of Estagnots, Bourdaines and Le Penon. To the south are the breaks of Capbretton, La Piste and VVF. During the peak months of August and September the sea will be heaving with surfers from across the world as well as every name on the WQS and WCT. The car parks at the main breaks are a collage of campervans, their occupants cooking up breakfast on their stoves and donning wetsuits to catch the morning glass. Crowds are a real issue here but it's worth that short walk away from the main access points. It's still possible to score empty peaks with just a little effort.

One of the problems with Hossegor is its almost magnetic effect. It's easy to slip into the French way of life, the French way of doing things. Sometimes it can be hard to drag yourself away. "Oh, I love France, I love Hossegor and the French lifestyle," says Lars Jacobsen, editor of *Surfers*. "Baguettes, café au lait and beautiful girls. This together with those powerful beach breaks makes Hossegor and Les Landes one of my favourite places to be." Even for the hardened travelling pro, Hossegor is still a special place. "I just love surfing their beachies," says tour veteran Neridah Falconer "They're consistent and powerful. I love their long summer days as well. The only place I miss not travelling each year not being on tour. A very special place in my heart!"

Locals and legends
Micky Picon, Fred Robin, Eric Rebière, Robbie Page, Jean-Lou Poupinel, Sébastien St Jean, Vincent Verdier, Maurice Cole, Gérard Dabaddie.

Nearby breaks To the north of Hossegor the huge stretch of sand continues through Les Landes and a seemingly endless series of small coastal towns and villages, including **Messanges**, **Moliets**, **St Girons** and **Biscarrosse**. Each offers some great and relatively uncrowded beach break surf.

WILLY URIBE

Guéthary

◈ **Location:**	Parlementia, Guéthary, south of Biarritz, France
◔ **Break type:**	Reef break
◔ **Conditions:**	Medium to big swells
◔ **Size:**	4-15 ft +
◔ **Length:**	50-200 m
◔ **Tide:**	Low to mid tide
◔ **Swell direction:**	Northwest to westerly
◔ **Wind:**	Easterly
◔ **Bottom:**	Rock reef
◔ **Ability level:**	Intermediate to advanced
◔ **Best months:**	Sep-Dec
◔ **Access:**	Huge channel to left of peak
◔ **Hazards:**	Sneaker sets, heavy waves, crowds

Guéthary is a *pression* outside the Bar Basque on a sunny autumn afternoon. Guéthary is the rapid fire of pelota in the local sports hall. Guéthary is the whitewashed walls of the grand old Basque houses, offset by the burgundy of the shuttered windows. Guéthary is the old guys lugging their big single fins down the hill to surf the huge peaks at Parlementia. This is a traditional Basque village, home to a tight-knit community of ex-pats alongside some of France's original surfers, many of whom shun the packed beaches to the north but will break out that magic board for those magic Guéthary sessions. This is a wave of tradition.

The bench here – the one that the whole community turned out to dedicate to its most famous (and infamous) resident, Mickey Dora –

provides both a monument to Guéthary's core values as well as panoramic views across the bay. To the south of the harbour reels the heavy, barrelling left-hander of Les Alcyons, a world-class wave that throws down the gauntlet to the region's strongest chargers with every big, clean swell. This is a death-or-glory, hell drop kind of a wave where mistakes can be punished with a brutal trip over the inside reef. Further out beyond Les Alcyons lies the region known as Avalanches, a big wave spot that is patrolled by only a very few of France's most proficient big wave chargers. A long paddle across the channel to the north lies Parlementia, dominating the view from the benches and drawing the eye of onlookers. The wave sits at the head of the household and the tip of a huge reef that stretches out to sea for half a mile. At this distance the waves look small and fun, like gentle, slow motion rollers devoid of sound, but do not be fooled. Any paddling dots in the line-up will soon add the necessary scale.

When big, clean swells come rolling out of the Atlantic, this reef is one of the first pieces of the local coastline that they encounter. Tucked away in the southwest corner of France, this is a wave that is often likened to Sunset Beach on the North Shore in Hawaii, as it is unpredictable and offers that same heart-in-the-mouth drop. Huge walls rear up and bear down on the line-up, shifting from north to south in a game of cat and mouse with the paddling surfers. A big board is needed here to get into the wave as it rises inexorably into a huge peak before avalanching down the face, chasing the dropping surfer and daring a bottom turn before the trough is reached. It is a test of nerve to hold for the right moment before easing onto the toes

Below: Breaking out the big boards as Guéthary begins to warm up.
Opposite page: Feathering peaks – the view from Dora's bench.

Guéthary Board
7'5" Brewer Sunset
Shaper: Dick Brewer
7'5" x 18¼ x 2⁵/₁₆"
Designed with Hawaiian veteran, Myles Padaca, the 7'5" Sunset is the perfect board to handle the elevator drops and big walls of Guéthary.
Single to double concave.
Futures fins.

ⓘ Boards by **Surftech**
www.surftech.com info@surftech.com

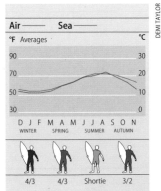

Air —— Sea ——

°F Averages °C

| D | J | F | M | A | M | J | J | A | S | O | N |
| WINTER | | | SPRING | | | SUMMER | | | AUTUMN | | |

4/3   4/3   Shortie   3/2

DEMI TAYLOR

and allowing the fins and rail to bite into the huge expanse of the face. Parlementia is a wave that is famous for the exhilarating right, but can also offer a long walling left. The risk is that the wave behind may be bigger and may have broken further out. The right offers the security of the deep, wide channel, always waiting to offer sanctuary. It often fizzles out into a big, gentle shoulder, but with the right momentum and some patience it can reform onto the inside reef to offer a bit of heart-stopping speed.

There are many breaks in places like California and Hawaii that ooze tradition and history. Although the wave at Guéthary is often very crowded, and attracts many surfers with no idea of its tradition of waveriding and waveriders, it is still one of the few places in Europe that can boast some true surfing soul. This is not a flashy wave for flashy manoeuvres; here size and style are everything. This is a classic big wave, which requires a class act.

Locals and legends

Christophe Reinhardt, Marc Bérard, Bernard Marcel, Cyril Robert, Mickey Dora, Jeff Hakman, Gibus de Soultrait.

Nearby breaks To the north is the fickle beach break of **Bidart** which is more sheltered from the swell but can close-out easily. Further north sits the grand old resort town of **Biarritz** and the start of a massive run of beach breaks. **Plage de Côte des Basques** is a popular longboarding spot that works from low to mid tide. From **VVF** north are the **Anglet** beaches, a quality stretch of sand that culminates in **Les Cavaliers**, a world-class peak.

Mundaka

- ⬧ **Location:** Ria Mudaka, Euskadi
- ◔ **Break type:** Rivermouth sandbank
- ◑ **Conditions:** Medium to big swells
- ◉ **Size:** 3-10 ft +
- ◉ **Length:** 50-200 m +
- ◔ **Tide:** Low to mid
- ◉ **Swell direction:** Northerly to northwesterly
- ◑ **Wind:** Southerly
- ◉ **Bottom:** Sand
- ◉ **Ability level:** Intermediate to advanced
- ◉ **Best months:** Sep-Apr
- ◉ **Access:** In the river flow
- ⬧ **Hazards:** Rips, crowds, heavy waves, shallow sandbank

Mundaka Board

6'6" Wayne Lynch Round Pin

Shaper: Wayne Lynch

6'6" x 19½" x 2⁹∕₁₆"

A little extra overall volume and softer plan shape curves, creates great paddling qualities plus the ability to maintain speed and make every section of the long sandbar lefts at Mundaka.

FCS fins.

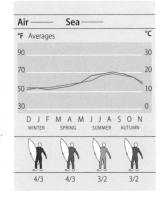

ⓘ Boards by **Surftech**
www.surftech.com info@surftech.com

Air ——— Sea ———

°F Averages   °C

90		30
70		20
50		10
30		0

D J F M A M J J A S O N
WINTER SPRING SUMMER AUTUMN

4/3   4/3   3/2   3/2

Rivermouth sandbanks are one of nature's true architectural masterpieces. Particles picked up high in the mountains are carried for hundreds of miles through a meandering and turbulent course until the river finally flows into the ocean. The loss of kinetic energy causes the suspended particles to be dumped at the rivermouth. Once deposited, this sand and sediment is shaped and sculpted by tide and swell to produce sandbanks. In some estuaries these are in a perpetual state of change, but in others they remain a constant. The tiny Basque village of Mundaka looks out over the tidal estuary at the mouth of the Urdaibai Biosphere Reserve, blessed with a long sweeping sandbar of near-mathematical precision. When a big northwesterly swell comes out of the Bay of Biscay, this curved bank of sand produces a wave that mirrors the contours of the sea bed lying a few feet below, one continuous sweeping barrel that can roll without sectioning for up to 300 m. This is why it is one of the most perfect waves in the world.

A jump off the rocks or a gentle paddle from the harbour and soon a surfer is mere flotsam in the river's current, carried north towards the pack of black neoprene-clad locals jostling on the peak. Many wear helmets, a clue that this is no ordinary sandbank. Best to paddle past the peak and inside to the second take-off spot to get the lie of the land. There have always been crowd issues at Mundaka, even in the age before computers and the Internet. "Even in the early '80s it wasn't uncommon to get over a 100 guys out on a weekend," says Nick Lavery, who grew up here. Mundaka breaks well from 3 ft up to 10 ft plus, and the nature of the sandbank allows the wave to break, even in massive swells, when other spots might simply close out. It can provide anything from leg-crampingly long walls through to unending barrels that thunder along the super-shallow sandbank. On the paddle back to the peak it's possible to see the most incredible tuberiders threading their way towards the inside. "The quality of this wave is well known, maybe the best in all of Spain," says Spanish pro Michel Velasco.

Just because the wave breaks on sand, doesn't mean it isn't punishing. "It can be a bit nerve-wracking with the crowds," says Nick. "Often guys will drop in on you when you are deep in the barrel. It was about 6 ft and I was in the barrel and I saw this guy frantically paddling up the wave, and kicking with his feet – a no-no as it brings the curtain down. I thought he might be caught in the lip as the curtain closed down. I punched through it and put my hands up in case he landed on me. The lip landed on my arms pushing them behind my head, the force dislocating both my shoulders."

Northern Spain and Mundaka have become a lesson in how delicate the ecological balance can be. In 2002, the *Prestige* oil tanker sank off the coast of Galicia, causing one of Europe's worst environmental disasters. Then, in 2005, dredging of the Mundaka rivermouth caused extensive damage to the sandbank and the wave disappeared. Local surfers lost a

WILLY URIBE

Above: Alfonso Fernández.
Opposite page: Master architecture of the Ría de Mundaka.

Europe Mundaka

whole season and the local economy suffered due to the cancellation of the 2005 Billabong Mundaka Pro and the resultant loss of revenue. Mundaka has gradually recovered but the incident sent shockwaves around the globe.

Many people drop in to Mundaka on a mad mission to grab some waves and then blow out of town, hair still wet, eyebrows encrusted with salt – just another particle in the wind. But sometimes it pays to slow down a little and absorb some of the atmosphere of your surroundings. Like the course of the Ría de Mundaka, the Basque region has had a meandering and turbulent history, one that has helped shape the lives of present-day *Euskerra*. Take a little time to sit outside the Hotel El Puerto, to sample some local *pintxos* and hear tales of Mundaka past and present, perhaps an anecdote relating the horrors of the 1936 Civil War, or some other fragment of the rich mosaic that is the history of this region. Sometimes it pays to take more away from a surf spot than just a few waves.

Locals and legends

"At Mundaka some of the best surfers (in my opinion) are: Alfonso Fernández, Ibon Amatriain, Nacho Fernández, Iker Acero, Kepa Acero, Iker Fuentes, Craig Sage, Gorka Yarritu, Henry Hunte, Guillermo Lekunberri... and more. Legends? There are no real legends at Mundaka, I think... but I'll give you a list of some of the best world surfers we've ever seen at Mundaka... and we know that all of them were stoked. Mark Paarman, Maurice Cole, Tom Curren, Wayne Lynch (one of the few surf photos on my office wall shows Wayne in one of the best waves I've ever seen there) and Kelly Slater. I made the list in collaboration with Alfonso Fernández and Craig Sage." Willy Uribe.

Nearby breaks **Playa de Bakio** sits to the west and is a good quality beach break in small to medium swells. Half and hour west sits the regional surf centre of **Sopelana**, with a number of good beaches. To the east is **Playa de Laga**, a beautiful beach with good banks nestling under spectacular cliffs.

Meñakoz

Location:	North of Sopelana, Euskadi
Break type:	Reef break
Conditions:	Medium to big swells
Size:	6-18 ft
Length:	up to 200 m
Tide:	Mid to high
Swell direction:	Northerly to northwesterly
Wind:	Southeasterly
Bottom:	Rock
Ability level:	Advanced
Best months:	Sep-Apr
Access:	From the bay
Hazards:	Heavy wave, dangerous rocks

Meñakoz Board

6'8" JC Peter Mel Machine

Shaper: John Carper

6'8" x 19½" x 2⅝"

Designed with big wave charger Peter Mel.

Blends medium rocker and single to double concave to give lots of paddling power to get in early and plenty of speed off the bottom and through tight turns.

FCS G5 fins.

ⓘ Boards by Surftech
www.surftech.com info@surftech.com

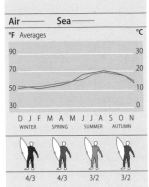

Air ——— Sea ———

°F	Averages			°C
90				30
70				20
50				10
30				0

D J F M A M J J A S O N
WINTER SPRING SUMMER AUTUMN

4/3   4/3   3/2   3/2

While Mundaka is the picturesque face of Euskadi (El País Vasco), Sopelana, to the west, is a bustling, workaday town and surfing heartland of the Basque country. Although part of the Bilbao commuter belt, the surf shops that line the main coast road give clues to the waiting waves that lay tantalizingly close to this busy trunk road. Take a right turn down one of the roads signposted *hondartza* and you'll discover that poker-faced Sopelana has a few aces up its sleeve. It is home to a wonderful stretch of northwesterly facing beaches, which produce consistent and quality surf and are the breeding grounds for some of the best surfers in Europe. Sitting on the clifftop at La Salvaje and watching the A-frames of La Triangular, it's easy to see why this area is such a hotbed of surfing. The long finger of reef points straight out into the Bay of Biscay, beckoning to all available swell and shaping it into long peeling lefts and rights. In a big swell the lines will stack to the horizon and, looking to the east and west, the huge open vista of the coastline seems to offer so many surfing possibilities. From this vantage point, however, your attention will be drawn to one particular feathering peak, way off to the right, which stands out from the rest.

This can't be the road, it just can't be. Obviously there's no sign. If there ever was one it would have been removed years ago, broken up, burnt and the ashes buried. The rough track stops abruptly at the clifftop and suddenly this *is* the place. It's the perfect location for this rampaging bull of a wave. One of the first European big wave spots to come to the attention of the outside world, this is a kind of brooding beast that roams through an equally intimidating setting. The cliffs tower over the break and the shore is littered with huge rocks. Ask anyone about Meñakoz and they will tell you it is a place where you have to put your time in, learn the ropes. "Meñakoz is an extreme example of 'You just can't paddle out there first time and have it wired,'" says oceanographer Tony Butt, a Brit who has spent many years learning the nuances and moods of this place. This big, powerful right-hander is definitely an experts-only proposition. "Meñakoz is a huge beast of a wave which heaves out of deep water and breaks into the huge cliffs," says pro surfer Gabe Davies. "It's an intimidating place."

WILLY URIBE

Right: Jaime Fernández drops in on wintertime Meñakoz.
Opposite page: Asier Ibañez takes on the beast.

Simply accessing the wave is not for the faint-hearted and the line-up is very focussed and local-dominated. It is definitely the domain of the paddle surfer and those classic 'gunnie' shaped boards are king. Meñakoz offers immense drops and huge, fast walls with gaping barrels opening up for the wave-wise. But watch out for the inside section. "Beside the huge cliff there, another danger is the rock that sticks out of the water the size of half a bus," explains Gabe. "Also a current runs out through the seemingly calm bay, it takes you sideways faster than a bottle of tequila." There's rips, rocks, outside sets and massive hold downs. "With Meñakoz, you will pay your dues, it's just a matter of time."

"I have always associated Meñakoz with being a man!" says Nick Lavery. "Although not the most perfect wave, it never closes out, so it really is up to you how big you ride it. When I was eight years old I remember going with my Dad when he surfed it and before I was officially a surfer, in the middle of the winter, with steam rising off the water, and massive offshore winter swells rolling in from the North Atlantic. It's a classic place."

Locals and legends
Tony Butt, Pepetoni, Peio Etxeberria, David 'Zumo' Bustamante, Guillermito Gananderian, Jaime Fernández, Nacho Fernández, Txema Fernández, Aritxa Saratxaga, Iñigo Careaga 'El Pajaro', Xavi, Axier, Jaime 'el Pequeño', José Olaso, Aitor 'Tuto' Larradogoitia, Jon 'El Loco', Adam Tye, Jesus Suarez.

Nearby breaks   To the west Sopelana offers a number of excellent beach breaks. **Playa Atxibiribil** and **Playa de Arrietara** work in small to medium swells and need winds from the southeast. The next bay is **La Salvaje**, home to the excellent A-frame reef break, **La Triangular**. This is a very popular spot with long walls and barrel sections on both the right and left. **Playa de Aizkorri** offers the best chance of some less crowded waves and even has some good left point waves to the south.

WILLY URIBE

Europe Meñakoz

Los Lobos

Location:	Western coast, Isla de Los Lobos, Canary Islands
Break type:	Right-hand point break
Conditions:	All swells
Size:	3-8 ft
Length:	up to 300 m
Tide:	All tides
Swell direction:	North to northwesterly
Wind:	Southeasterly
Bottom:	Lava reef
Ability level:	Intermediate to advanced
Best months:	Nov-Feb
Access:	Via ferry to island
Hazards:	Sharp reef

THE GILL

Above: Taking the high line at Lobos.
Opposite page: Laval Los Lobos.

In the still, morning air it's a relief to be on the water, making the short crossing from Corralejo to the small peak that lies straight ahead, sticking out of the blue Atlantic like an orange shark fin. Isla de Los Lobos, 2 km to the northeast of Fuerteventura, is the tip of an undersea volcano and was named after the *lobos marinos* (sea wolves), or monk seals, that used to inhabit its coastline. The seals are no longer around but any regret may be outweighed by the knowledge that you're not floating around amongst lots of little shark snacks.

The Canary Islands is a volcanic archipelago that lies off the western coast of North Africa. To European tourists they mean winter sun, cheap holidays and cold beer. To European surfers they mean winter sun, cold beers, Atlantic swells, warm waters and clear seas. The north coast of Fuerteventura is a dusty, inhospitable stretch of lava reefs reached by a gnarled old track that has been the graveyard to many a board-stacked hire car. On a clear, windless day the clean swell lights up a string of reefs and points with speeding walls and rolling barrels. But when a big swell hits, the whitewater on Los Lobos is telling you that the point is reeling – taunting you from afar.

Lobos is a dreamy point wave that ticks all the boxes. It can produce those classic, ruler-topped walls that seem to race forever, never sectioning and always giving more. It can offer the fast, speeding days and opportunities for special, clear water cover-ups with those 'Greenough-like' down-the-line images from within the barrel. Just getting there requires a little more effort and makes this wave feel a bit more special. The geography of this break is also special. "If you walk to the top of the volcano and look down onto the wave, through the light blue, almost Caribbean blue, you can see how perfectly the wave peels," says Nick Lavery. As the swell angles down the side of the island it reels off these endless right-handers. "After the take-off barrel section, you can get some nice re-entries off the lip, quite challenging on your back-hand," he continues. As the swell builds, so the waves become more powerful, hollow and challenging. "The wave barrels on take-off like J-Bay," says English surf photographer Paul Gill. "Once you're off and riding it can be a 300 m ride – unless you fall off!" At 8 ft it goes all the way through – all day. On smaller swells you can get it offering a couple of more distinct sections. But the reef here is a sharp lava bed strewn with

Los Lobos Board

6'1" Byrne HP

Shaper: Phil Byrne

6'1" x 18⅜" x 2⁵/₁₆"

High-performance shortboard ideally suited for the long lined up point waves at Los Lobos.

Single to double concave.

FCS fins.

ⓘ Boards by Surftech
www.surftech.com info@surftech.com

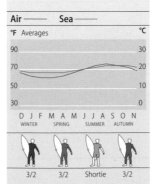

Air ——	Sea ——	
°F	Averages	°C
90		30
70		20
50		10
30		0

D J F M A M J J A S O N
WINTER SPRING SUMMER AUTUMN

| 3/2 | 3/2 | Shortie | 3/2 |

urchins where mistakes can and will be punished. As the tide pushes onto the reef the wave bowls along the lava heads. Entry and exit become a matter of critical timing.

"Lobos is one of those set-ups like Coxos, Jeffreys Bay or Boilers where the entry and the exit are pretty tricky. You're going in over lava reef," explains Paul Gill. "I was there years ago, before it got busy. There are a couple of jump-off rocks and this Aussie guy was running down to the water's edge in front of me, but I'd been watching and the sets were big and surging up the rocks. I started to follow but I saw this big set out the back so I backtracked about 50 ft to safer ground. The Aussie in front turned and I said 'I think I'll wait 'til after this set.' He just scoffed at me and turned round just in time to get hit by the first wave. It knocked him off the rock and the set washed him right down the point. I saw him later that evening and he looked like Edward Scissorhands had applied suntan cream over the whole of his legs."

Today, many local surfers will make the crossing to the island in their own small boats, so that they can be on it at just the right tide, leaving the traditional ferry crossing to the visitors. However, with the correct permit, it is possible to camp on the island, sleeping out in the stark lunar landscape under the chill of the huge, bright night sky. Then, in the first light of dawn, it's possible to beat the crowds to those precious, machine-like rights that taunted you through the darkness of the night.

Locals and legends

Welsh surfer Roger Cooper and Keith Beddoes made the ferry crossing from Morocco to the Canaries in the mid-seventies and pioneered many spots including Lobos. The Canaries now have surfers making a big impression on the international stage including Jonathan González and Adelina Taylor. Other top riders from the Fuerteventura include José Casillas, David Hernández and Sonnia.

Nearby breaks The north shore of Fuerteventura is home to some well-known waves. **Hierro Right** or **The Bubble** is an A-frame reef with fast hollow rights and slightly less intense lefts. It has a small take-off zone which doesn't help with the crowds. Moving east there are a series of lava reefs including **Majanicho**, **El Mejillón**, **El Generoso**, **Shooting Gallery** and **Harbour Wall**. Expect crowds.

THE GILL

Supertubos

◈ **Location:** Southern outskirts of Peniche, Portugal	
◷ **Break type:** Sandbar with lefts and rights	
◉ **Conditions:** Small to medium swells	
◉ **Size:** 2-10 ft	
◷ **Length:** Up to 50 m	
◉ **Tide:** All tides, better around mid	
◈ **Swell direction:** Southwesterly to northwesterly	
◷ **Wind:** Easterly	
◉ **Bottom:** Shallow sandbar	
◉ **Ability level:** Intermediate to advanced	
◉ **Best months:** Sep-Nov	
◉ **Access:** Off the beach in the channel	
◉ **Hazards:** Pitching take-off, powerful, shallow compacted sandbar, very crowded	

Peniche is a traditional, hard-working fishing town and doesn't make any apologies for the fact that it is a little rough around the edges. Beautiful wooden trawlers are still hand-crafted in the shadow of the formidable, grey walls that fringe the old town. Formerly an impregnable island fortress, Peniche now stands on a rocky peninsula, joined to the mainland by the massive, umbilical sandbar that carries the main arterial road. Within its walls an imposing fortress casts a watchful eye over the harbour as the busy fishing fleet scampers in and out of the Atlantic fishing grounds. From the south-facing windows, there is a clear, unimpeded view of a huge crescent-shaped sandy bay. This 16th-century stronghold is also a former political prison – the legacy of an era when the Portuguese Military junta ruled the country with an iron fist. Those days came to an end in April 1974 when the town of Peniche rose up and stormed the prison. It was a people's revolution that spread across the whole country. Following those heady days of freedom, a young Aussie surfer was camped up on that crescent beach, enjoying the unique waves that break here. "I remember going to Peniche in the seventies and surfing Supertubos before it was even called Supertubos," says Phil Jarratt. "We camped near Mohlo Leste (a short walk to the north of the break) and just surfed these epic waves all summer. It's one of my favourite places."

There is an old cliché about Supertubos – that you can always tell when it's offshore by the smell of putrid fish that wafts over the break. That's one of the endearing qualities that makes this such a great place, albeit a bit smelly. Peniche hasn't been polished and sanitized by a tourist authority. This town is alive and kicking. As is the line-up at Supertubos, on any given swell. The small car park will quickly fill with an assortment of vehicles, from locals' cars to campervans driven by virtually every surfing nationality on the globe. For this is a wave that lives up to its impressive moniker. Looking down the beach, about 200 m to the south, the currents have conspired to endow this long, curving bay with a concentrated tract of shallow sandbanks that produce a shifting, but constantly world-class wave.

The wave here is a fluid phenomenon. Depending on the tide, currents and swell direction, Supertubos can be a left, a right, a peak or a peak with another right sitting just across the channel. Whatever the state of the sandbank, the waves have one thing in common – they are shallow, fast and hollow. "This beach break is like a mini-Pipeline, without the dangerous reef," says Nick Lavery. "It also looks like Puerto Escondido when it breaks. Lefts and right walls, just pull into the barrel really close to the beach." Javier Amezaga, Editor of *3Sesenta* surf magazine agrees, "Supertubes is the best because it offers the best quality tubes, and breaks just in front of the beach."

The banks here work in any swell, from 2 ft up to 10 ft plus, and when it's clean and offshore, the hollow waves rear up and pitch onto the shallow sandbars, offering excellent ringside views. The peak can be crowded with local bodyboarders and surfers as well as a good

Below: Surf photographer prepares for some water time in Portuguese Pipeline.
Opposite page: A Brazilian samples a supertube.

DEMI TAYLOR

THIERRY ORGANOFF

Supertubos Board
6'10" Minami M-1

Shaper: Glen Minami

6'10" x 18⅜" x 2⅜"

For the steep drops and deep barrels of Supertubos, you'll need the 6'10" Minami M-1.

Built with extra rocker to to handle those late take-offs and a tight round pintail to fit you deep in the barrel.

FCS fins.

ⓘ Boards by **Surftech**
www.surftech.com info@surftech.com

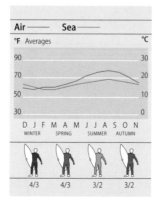

Air ——	Sea ——	
°F Averages		°C
90		30
70		20
50		10
30		0
D J F	M A M	J J A	S O N
WINTER	SPRING	SUMMER	AUTUMN

| 4/3 | 4/3 | 3/2 | 3/2 |

Michel Velasco. "It's my place in Portugal." However, it can also be punishing. As the swell picks up, the wave can become a board breaker and a heartbreaker. Don't be fooled by the fact that this 'Pipe'-like wave breaks on a sand bottom. The sandbank is shallow and surprisingly hard. But as the people of Peniche proved over three decades ago, obstacles are there to be overcome.

Locals and legends
Nuno Silva, Pedro Morgado, To Gama, João Antunes, Pedro Silva, Diogo Gonçalves.

sprinkling of travelling Aussies, French, Brits and Americans, all competing for these world-class barrels. It is brutally competitive with the locals usually snagging the lion's share of the set waves. But a good session here will remain a lifelong memory and patience is definitely rewarded. If you make the steep drop, set the rail and hang on, you'll soon be locked into a completely round, dredging barrel. "I like this beach break because you can get really good barrels," says

Nearby breaks As a peninsula, Peniche is one of the most flexible surf locations in the country with breaks facing in virtually every direction. Northeast of Peniche (and east of Baleal) is the popular but urchin-infested left-hand reef **Lagide**. It likes small to medium swells and southeasterly winds. It also has a tiny take-off point and, situated just in front of a car park, can get very busy. West of Baleal, on the other side of the car park, is the long sweeping bay **Praia do Baleal**, home to some good beach break waves. Between the sections of beach here, which face north, and Supertubos, which faces west, there is usually somewhere offshore to surf.

Coxos

Location: Ericeira, Portugal	
Break type: Reef point break	
Conditions: Medium to big swells	
Size: 3-12 ft	
Length: 50-100 m +	
Tide: Low to mid tide	
Swell direction: Northwesterly to southwesterly	
Wind: Easterly to southeasterly	
Bottom: Sharp, rock reef	
Ability level: Advanced	
Best months: Sep-Dec	
Access: Well timed paddle off the point	
Hazards: Badly timed paddle off the point, rocks, rips, crowds	

DEMI TAYLOR

The sign pointing down to the turn-off at Coxos is more than just a quaint, tiled directional marker. It's a sign of the times. Even after surfing really caught on in Portugal, this remained a secret spot. And even when word got out, it was still a spot that you had to search out – a case of trial and error down dirt tracks that led off the coastal road. Granted, the fact that the guys at Semente surfboards had chosen to locate nearby was a big clue. Today, local councils are not slow to point out their newly realized assets – 'Surfing this way'. In Portugal the main breaks are marked out in brown and orange with their own little surfer icon. The sign for Coxos, however, is of a more thoughtful design – one that speaks of traditions, craft and respect and befitting what is one of the best right-hand point breaks in Europe.

Coxos Board

6'6" Bushman Pancho Model

Shaper: Jeff Bushman

6'6" x 19³/₈ x 2½

Jeff Bushman designed with Pancho Sullivan for hollow, powerful waves on and beyond the North Shore; perfect for Coxos.

Single to double concave for down the line speed and power gouges in the pocket.

FCS fins.

ⓘ Boards by **Surftech**
www.surftech.com info@surftech.com

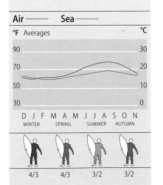

In an area of quite amazing surf potential, Coxos is certainly the ace in the hole. Just an hour's drive north of the sprawling capital Lisbon, Ericeira is at the centre of the Portuguese coastline. While this traditional whitewashed fishing village, with cobbled streets and working harbour, reflects the industrious heart of Portugal, its fine reefs define Portugal's surfing soul. "The uniqueness of surfing in Portugal is directly related to its geography," explains *Surf Portugal* editor João da Câmara Valente. "Although it is a somewhat small coast, it displays an enormous variety of breaks within very short areas. Point breaks, reef breaks, beach breaks, rivermouths, whatever – Portugal has it all. Sometimes I think to myself how lucky we are that the whole of the Portuguese coast is not made of just an enormous beach break monotony".

A drive down the dusty dirt track leads to a small, somewhat plain bay. Along the northern edge is a point composed of a long, flat bed of rock that has an almost Martian appearance. The rock is jagged and flecked with reds, orange and yellows. It slants away into the sea for the length of the point, providing the occasional ledge on which to sit and admire the clear, azure blue of the Atlantic. As with many of surfing's greats, on a calm day it is difficult to see what all the fuss is about but when a solid groundswell stacks the horizon with corduroy lines, the spot is transformed. From deep water swell approaches the end of the point with linear precision. But the lines quickly meet the ledge waiting innocuously a few feet below the surface, causing the energy to

Above: The writing's on the wall.
Opposite page: After a session at Coxos there's nothing like kicking back, taking it in.

compress into a square and critical take-off section. The local crew scramble into position as one makes the vertical drop and immediately nips into the barrel. From here on the wave offers so many variations, depending on the swell, from multiple barrel sections through to fast, open walls, for laying down serious, buried-rail bottom turns followed by huge, carving off-the-tops. Once you are out onto the face the world is your oyster. Just don't blow the take-off on the first wave of a set or you'll be left bobbing like a cork in front of the unforgiving rocks with a whole freight train of waves bearing down on you.

This region is the epicentre of surfing in Portugal and has produced a number of excellent surfers including runner up at the 2000 Sunset Pro, Tiago Pires: "My favourite break in Europe has to be Coxos," says the local WQS surfer. "Coxos every time; 8-10 ft on a southwest swell – perfect!" This wave is a 'shoe-in' on virtually any European top ten. "Coxos is one of the best point breaks in the whole of Portugal," enthuses Spanish pro surfer, Michel Velasco. "It is a really good right-hander where, depending on the swell conditions, you can have good barrels and crazy turns." And when the Atlantic turns it on, the reefs around Ericeira can fire for weeks. "The winter of 2001/2 was the best winter I've ever experienced in my life," says Tiago. "There was three months of offshore and the waves didn't drop the below the 4 ft range! I had some days where I would surf perfect 6-8 ft Coxos in the

morning low tide, surf White Rock in the midday high tide and then have another perfect, low tide evening surf at Coxos, that would make me touch heaven at night. I couldn't stop laughing!"

Due to its proximity to Lisbon, this is a popular area for both local and visiting surfers. Ericeira has become a compulsory stop on the European road trip for good reason – the amazing cluster of excellent reefs and points, consistent swell and good climate. "Coxos is probably one of the best point-break waves in Europe," says *Trip Surf* editor Franck Lacaze. "I've had some challenging surfs at Coxos and the biggest barrel I've ever surfed in Europe. The Portuguese lifestyle is really cool, the people are cruisey and mellow, there's great food and wine, and it's cheap too. All in all, it makes Coxos one of my favourites."

Locals and legends
Nick Uricchio, Miguel Katzenatein, Miguel Fortes, João Pedro, José Gregorio, Tiago Pires.

Nearby breaks Just to the north of Ericeira lies the excellent, walling, right-hand point of **Ribeira d'Ilhas**. Very popular, especially with longboarders, it breaks between 2 ft and 10 ft. Within the boundaries of the town are a series of excellent spots such as the super shallow **Reef**, the left barrelling **Pedra Branca** and the less crowded **Praia do Norte**.

DEMI TAYLOR

Ponta Pequeña

⬙ **Location:**	Southwest coast, Madeira
◐ **Break type:**	Right-hand point break
☁ **Conditions:**	Medium to big swells
◉ **Size:**	6-12 ft +
⬡ **Length:**	100-200 m
🌊 **Tide:**	Mid tide
📶 **Swell direction:**	Northwesterly
💨 **Wind:**	Northeasterly
▦ **Bottom:**	Rocks and boulder
◔ **Ability level:**	Advanced
◷ **Best months:**	Oct-Mar
⊕ **Access:**	Tricky access from the rocks
⊖ **Hazards:**	Rocks, heavy waves

Madeira is an extreme land, created by extremes of nature – huge geological pressures forcing an upwelling of molten rock. The island, the largest in a group of three, sits proudly in the middle of the Atlantic Ocean, the summit of a huge mountain, over 6000 m high. Described as a 'floating garden', Madeira's precipitous landscape has been cultivated into lush green terraces that thrive in the high rainfall and rich volcanic soil while vines, bananas and dense forest cling to the steep slopes that drop away into the ocean.

Sitting off the coast of Africa between the Azores to the north and the Canary Islands to the south, Madeira stands directly in the line of fire for all those North Atlantic swells that come rolling towards Morocco. It looks ideally placed as a surfing destination, but a cursory glance at the geography would persuade many otherwise: a complete lack of beaches, big bouldery points and sheer cliffs. No, thanks – back on the plane. But then, some people like a challenge. "The first surfer in Madeira was in 1974," explains local charger Orlando Pereira, "according to my father and the people from Jardim, (they) say that it was a French surfer – Gibus de Soultrait, editor of *Surf Session*."

The change in surfing styles and the type of big waves being ridden over the last couple of decades caused some surfers to look again at Madeira. When swells reached the 6-ft-plus region, the waves cleared the rocky inside and acted like perfect points, but on a massive scale. Big walls reeled for hundreds of metres and monstrous barrels opened up. But it wasn't until two decades later, in 1994, when the *Surfer Magazine* crew charged the island, that Madeira caught the attention of the surfing world. The article blew the lid and suddenly Europe's top big-wave chargers where on the case. Jardim do Mar became the European big wave challenge of choice with huge, dangerous sessions splashed around the globe. (The wave also became the focus of a concentrated global campaign by surfers to prevent a sea wall being built there, see page 13.)

However, there are other classic waves scattered around this jagged coastline. Near to Jardim sits the somewhat modestly named Ponta Pequeña, or 'little point'. This is also a walling right-hand point break but it starts to work on smaller swells and can offer waves that fall into the more manageable category of size. Surfable even when small, the wave bowls round the point and rolls for a couple of hundred metres, but also offers big open walls in bigger swells. "Ponta Pequeña is what most people would want in a surf spot," says Will Henry from the Save the Waves Coalition. "Imagine Rincon but with warmer (and cleaner) water. An easy take-off leads to a 100-m-long screaming wall of turquoise pleasure. It can handle any swell direction, and is surfable from 2 ft to 25 ft."

"Ponta Pequeña is a mix of Jardim do Mar and Paul do Mar," says Orlando Pereira. "Jardim is a massive wave where you don't make many barrels. It is a big wall and heavy to surf, and Paul do Mar is very hollow wave and shallow, but is a great wave where you can get the

WILL HENRY

Right: Looking down over Ponta Pequeña.
Opposite page: Robin Kent – glass house on the floating garden.

longest barrels in your life. Ponta Pequena, however, is the longest wave in Madeira – that makes all the difference. It's very easy to get out and in, you have the channel and when you are outside you can get a wave with 4-m faces or more. The wave starts very easily but when you arrive inside the wave can get double the size and barrel."

"I had one of my most memorable sessions ever at Ponta Pequeña," says Irish big wave charger John McCarthy. "Greg and Rusty Long and Dave Blount surfed it one morning at about 10 ft, we went for lunch and just watched from Cecilia's, it kept getting bigger. After lunch we jumped back in and had it to ourselves at five or six times overhead and rolling for 200 m. The wave can rumble you pretty bad but it's such a down-the-line, sweeping cutbacks rush. Immediately after lunch we all got the biggest wave of the day on the head. It was like Pequeña telling us, 'I'm not so pequeña'."

Locals and legends
Legend has it first surfed by Gibus de Soultrait. As well as Orlando Pereira, other local chargers include Belmiro Mendes, Manuel Mendes and Adriano Longuiera.

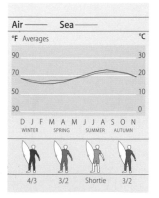

Ponta Pequeña Board

6'0" Stretch Ratboy

Shaper: Stretch

6'0" x 18⅝" x 2¼"

Surfing Magazine's 2005 Shaper of the Year, William 'Stretch' Reidell designed this 6'0" round pin with Jason 'Ratboy' Collins.

From steep drops, fast walls, wobbly sections and open face bliss.

Futures F4 fins.

ⓘ Boards by **Surftech**
www.surftech.com info@surftech.com

Air —— Sea ——

°F Averages °C

	D	J	F	M	A	M	J	J	A	S	O	N	
		WINTER			SPRING			SUMMER			AUTUMN		

4/3	3/2	Shortie	3/2

Nearby breaks   Jardim do Mar, once a grunting, right-hand, classic Atlantic big wave spot, has been altered following the construction of the controversial sea wall and coast road and locals say it is not the wave it was. It only breaks properly in really big swells and only on the lowest part of the tide.

PAUL KENNEDY

The Dunes, Cape Town.

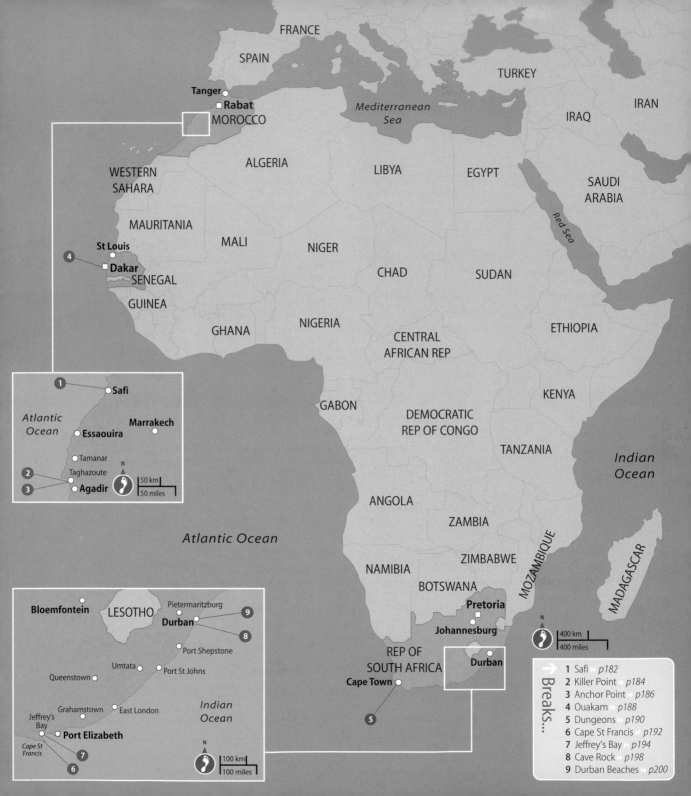

FRANCE

SPAIN

MOROCCO

Tanger
□ **Rabat**

Mediterranean Sea

TURKEY

IRAQ

IRAN

ALGERIA

LIBYA

EGYPT

SAUDI ARABIA

WESTERN SAHARA

MAURITANIA

MALI

NIGER

CHAD

SUDAN

Red Sea

St Louis
□ **Dakar**
4
SENEGAL

GUINEA

GHANA

NIGERIA

CENTRAL AFRICAN REP

ETHIOPIA

KENYA

GABON

DEMOCRATIC REP OF CONGO

TANZANIA

Indian Ocean

ANGOLA

ZAMBIA

ZIMBABWE

NAMIBIA

BOTSWANA

MOZAMBIQUE

MADAGASCAR

Pretoria
□
Johannesburg

REP OF SOUTH AFRICA

Durban

Cape Town
5

N
400 km
400 miles

1
Safi

Atlantic Ocean

Marrakech

○ **Essaouira**

Tamanar
2
Taghazoute
3
Agadir

N
50 km
50 miles

Atlantic Ocean

Bloemfontein

LESOTHO

Pietermaritzburg
9
Durban
8

Port Shepstone

Umtata
Port St Johns

Queenstown

Grahamstown   East London

Jeffrey's Bay

Port Elizabeth

Cape St Francis

7

6

Indian Ocean

N
100 km
100 miles

The sun is rising at the point just north of Taghazoute. It is so close to the big name breaks of Anchor Point and Boilers that the waves here have remained largely overlooked, even though they offer long, reeling rights on a par with anything at its more famous neighbours. The point is fringed by a small cliff of crumbling sedimentary rock stained orange and yellow. The twisted, gnarled trunks of the Argan trees are topped by a thorny, brush-like canopy that keeps a herd of goats busy grazing, somewhat surreally, in the treetops. The whitewater pushes over a ribbed reef running the length of the headland, resembling the backbone of a Jurassic skeleton. Launching off the jagged platform the emerald water has a chill that doesn't chime with the rising warmth that comes from the sun. Two duck-dives and it's a straight paddle-out, up the headland towards the glassy line-up.

Five thousand miles to the south, across burning desert, arid savannah lands and intense green jungle, a figure is huddled checking the surf, hands nursing a cup of fresh coffee. Stretched out ahead, the first light of dawn presents a scene of smooth oceanic brush strokes feathering in the light offshores. J-Bay is alive with a fresh swell born in the cold southern oceans. At the surfer's feet lies a damp wetsuit, there to take the edge off the chill green sea, even though the skies promise to be clear and the sun bright. Despite the distance, at this moment the two surfers are sharing an essentially African surf experience, part of the same vast landmass and separated by a mere two hours' time difference.

Africa has had a bi-polar waveriding evolution. Surfing arrived in Morocco via a winding coastal route. Like a vine spreading along the edge of a forest, staying close to the light to maintain its sustenance, so the hippy trail wound its way south from Europe along the green fringes of the Atlantic, until it came to rest in the shadow of Cap Rhir. Here the climate, lifestyle and surf combined to provide a habitat that still draws greater numbers year by year. In South Africa the colonial beach culture meant a more traditional evolution through the surf lifesavers' progression onto the smooth-planing of the balsa board. Two pockets of surfing, established in two paradoxical regions, implanted by separate means, but evolving towards the same goal. In between lies a vast area of titanic potential, though even in warm African waters there are still plenty of 'icebergs' to watch out for. The discoveries in Mozambique, Angola, Namibia and Mauritania demonstrate that as political stability spreads, surfing is quick to follow. For a continent that was once said to have a 'Heart of Darkness', it is proving to be clothed in sparkling light.

Surfing Africa

WILLY URIBE

They're like non-identical twins separated at birth; they share the same DNA but their appearance and their personalities are completely different. The flowing right-hand points of Taghazoute, Morocco, and the reeling right-hand points of St Francis Bay, South Africa, may be from the same stock, but they are poles apart. Morocco is very much an African country and an Arabic state, her undulating coastline blessed with some of the most incredible point breaks on the planet. The northerly coastline fringes the Mediterranean while the west sits exposed to the long-distance swells of the North Atlantic. Five thousand miles away, South Africa lies in the opposite hemisphere washed by the South Atlantic to the west and the Indian Ocean to the east. Its countryside is a picture-perfect representation of all we expect from an African landscape. The wandering wildebeest and ever-watchful lions may be confined to the sprawling game reserves but the burnt red sunsets and arid savannah are the essence of this huge continent. The colonial history and regional wealth of South Africa means it has no peers when it comes to surfing on the African continent.

Pros & cons
Northwest Africa

Pros

Warm winters with cool water.

Wealth of culture.

World-class right points abound.

Easily accessible from Europe.

Cheap.

Great food and friendly people.

No sharks!

Cons

Dangerous roads.

Inconsistent healthcare.

Petty crime and car break-ins.

Busy around well-known surf breaks.

Little nightlife and limited access to alcohol.

Little surf infrastructure, even in major surf areas.

Pros & cons
South Africa

Pros

Great culture, scenery and wildlife.

Geographically diverse coastline.

Lots of potential to explore.

Excellent standard of living and good food.

Consistent.

Cheap.

Cons

Main breaks are crowded.

Country breaks can be isolated.

Relatively cold water.

Crime.

Sharks.

Opposite page: Abdel El Harim – Morocco's rising star, with his eyes set firmly on the top.

Morocco is an emerging nation struggling to its feet, both economically and in surfing terms. Waveriding crossed the Mediterranean with the hippy trail in the sixties, its destination Taghazoute, where it found the perfect winter getaway from the cold of Europe. It became a Baja for the Old World's 20th-century explorers. The promise of warm surf close by with a rich culture and a spirit of adventure flavoured with a hint of danger. By the nineties a boom in Moroccan travel saw surf camps spring up all along the coast, mostly owned by Europeans. The line-ups have filled, but while Morocco is blessed with awesome resources, translating that into a surf industry has been a struggle. Today, Taghazoute is a melting pot of Arab culture and Euro-surf influence. However rich the village is in culture and however warm the welcome, what little equipment there is in Morocco remains extremely expensive for the locals. It used to be forbidden for foreigners to leave boards behind, even broken ones. They were literally counted into the country and counted out again. This seems to have changed and programmes have been set up in France to encourage the donation of boards to Moroccan surf clubs. Young surfers also have a successful role model in Abdel El Harim, a WQS competitor who raises the profile of Moroccan surfers every time he competes and in every interview he gives in international surf magazines.

At the southern end of the continent surfing has spread from the urban heartlands and is now pushing out into neighbouring countries like Mozambique. "The guys who pioneered the Durban waves were guys like Max Wetteland, Harry Bold, the late Baron Stander, Frenchy Fredericks, Ant van den Heuvel and John Whitmore," says one of South Africa's brightest stars, Jordy Smith. "They basically all started riding crocka skis which were made of a wooden frame and shellacked canvas. Harry Bold then returned from California with the first foam board which became a revolution in South Africa around 1956 and this is when the surfing industry in South Africa started." South Africa has been a surfing superpower since the 1970s when young Shaun Tomson changed tube-riding forever, dominated on the North Shore of Oahu and became only the second official surfing world champion, in 1977. Wendy Botha became the first South African women's world champ in 1987 and today surfers from the rainbow nation are regulars on the WCT and WQS.

Durban is still the continent's 'Surf City'. It boasts a bustling, modern waveriding scene and The Gunston 500, held there annually, is the second oldest surf event on the competitive calendar. When it comes to surf travel, however, the country doesn't attract the numbers that fellow wave-rich superpower Australia seems to. "I think South Africa is often overlooked as a surf trip destination because of the threat of sharks (which, unfortunately, is sometimes very real and other times imagined), lots of cold water and its longstanding reputation as quite a volatile place," says Will Bendix editor of *Zigzag Magazine*. "Fortunately, the latter

JS CALLAHAN/TROPICALPIX

rainforests where traditional tribal culture and language has mixed with colonial and Christian influences to create a number of independent states with many common links, but also with enough differences and divisions that conflict – often brutal – is never too far away. Post-colonial southern Africa has, for decades, been dominated by white South Africa, the fragile political balance determined by the politics of Pretoria. The post-apartheid era has seen a degree of stability in most of the region, with Zimbabwe being a notable exception.

Climates and seasons

Northern hemisphere seasons in Morocco and Senegal run the opposite of Australia and New Zealand as follows: spring – March to May; summer – June to August; autumn – September to November; winter – December to February. In southern hemisphere South Africa they run: spring – September to November; summer – December to February; autumn – March to May; winter – June to August.

The Moroccan coast enjoys a Mediterranean climate with hot summers and warm winters, although the Atlantic coastline is somewhat cooled by the Canaries current and evenings can be surprisingly chilly. Travelling further south towards the western Sahara, the coastal climate becomes drier and hotter. January in Agadir hovers around 18℃ with around 42 mm of rain and in July hovers around 25℃ with no rain.

Senegal has a tropical climate with a single short rainy season from June to September (peaking August to September), accompanied by warm, humid west/southwesterly winds. The average July temperature for Dakar is 28℃ with around 89 mm of rain. Dry season sees the climate cool slightly and wind switch round to offshore for Ouakam. The harmattan winds blow from the northeast bringing in the hot, very dry, dusty air from the Sahara. Temperatures average 22℃ in January with no rain.

has changed to a degree. Of course there's reason to be wary, but if you're half street-smart and are dialed into what's happening on the ground, it's no gnarlier than travelling around a place like mainland Mexico. I also think people aren't always aware of the great potential that some of our coastline offers."

However, as Will explains, this is a country where you can experience all aspects of the waveriding experience. "You can surf world-class beachbreaks in the city with world-class surfers (and intense crowds), and then drive 45 minutes along the coast and surf a sketchy but cooking semi-rural point, alone, with cows grazing down to the beach... even though you're only five minutes away from a major highway. It's crazy!"

Position

Africa is the second largest continent, straddling the equator with its huge landmass lying between 35° north and 35° south. It is bounded on all sides by water – Atlantic Ocean, Indian Ocean, Red Sea, Mediterranean Sea – apart from a tiny land bridge across to the Middle East at the head of the Red Sea (where the Suez Canal cuts through to the Mediterranean). The 14-km-wide Straights of Gibraltar once joined the continents of Africa and Europe before they were breached by the Atlantic, creating the biggest waterfall in the Earth's history and flooding the area that is now the Mediterranean.

Culture

The continent of Africa is a spectrum of nationalities, religions, cultures and environments. The arid north is predominantly Muslim with a history of religious tolerance. In many major cities in Morocco it is not uncommon to find synagogues and mosques standing virtually side-by-side. As a moderate Islamic state, alcohol does not flow freely but is often available from supermarkets and urban tourist bars. Lone women travellers can quickly attract (often unwanted) attention so dress moderately and be prepared to be firm but fair. The huge swathe of the Sahara leads into the lush, tropical central African equatorial

WAVEWATCH	Dec-Feb Winter	Mar-May Spring	Jun-Aug Summer	Sep-Nov Autumn
NORTHWEST AFRICA				
Wave size/direction	NW 5-7'	NW 3-5'	N 2-3'	NW 4-6'
Wind force/direction	S F2	W F3	NE F3	N F3
Surfable days	15-20	10-15	5-10	10-15
Water/air temp	17/21℃	19/24℃	23/27℃	20/27℃
SOUTH AFRICA	(Summer)	(Autumn)	(Winter)	(Spring)
Wave size/direction	S 3-4'	S-W 4-6'	S-W 6-8'	SW 4-6'
Wind force/direction	SW F5	W F4	W F4	W F4
Surfable days	5-10	15-20	15-20	10-15
Water/air temp	21/27℃	17/23℃	18/17℃	20/23℃

South Africa lies between the Atlantic and Indian oceans so climate varies. The eastern coastline is warmed by south-flowing tropical currents, the west is affected by colder currents flowing northwards and the south can be influenced by the weather patterns of the Southern Ocean. The Durban climate is tempered by sea breezes, enduring wetter summers and enjoying warmer winters, ranging from an average 24°C with around 110 mm of rain in January to around 17°C and 28 mm of rain in July. The Eastern Cape has relatively little rainfall year round and a slightly cooler climate averaging 21°C with 31 mm rainfall in January to 13°C in July with around 48 mm of rain. Cape Town sees occasional summer rainstorms with around 15 mm falling in January and temperatures averaging a respectable 21°C. Winters are changeable and wet yet mild, with the main precipitation from May to August. July sees peak rainfall – around 90 mm – and temperatures averaging 13°C.

Wavewatch report by Vic DeJesus
Northwest Africa This desert climate receives its biggest and best surf during the winter months. From November through to April powerful North Atlantic storms push in large northwesterly swells in the 6 to 10-ft range, often larger. During this time conditions are usually most favourable with clean mornings and light to moderate northeasterly winds in the afternoons with occasional southerly winds associated with passing fronts mainly in the winter months. Late spring through to summer is typically smaller with very few days exceeding 3-4 ft. Conditions are also much hotter and winds are stronger.

South Africa South Africa is a southern hemisphere standout location for consistent and large swells during the winter months from May through September. During this time intense low-pressure systems travelling eastward in the Roaring Forties send in large south to southwesterly swells usually lasting from two to four days each with periodic strong offshore winds for many areas as fronts pass. Summer months are typically smaller and flatter with periods of large swell from tropical cyclones in the southwest Indian Ocean during the southern hemisphere warm season from October through to March.

Geography and breaks
Africa is a big place. As the second largest continent it has a coastline that stretches for over 25,000 km, however, the gentle arcs and curves mean that it is relatively modest compared to its landmass. It lacks the undulations and inlets of Europe or the island archipelagos of Oceania. Vast sections of this coastline remain virtually unexplored by waveriders and are off the surfing map. The reasons for this are varied. Access is difficult in many regions, and political instability and conflict contribute to the lack of knowledge for specific countries.

Along the north, the Mediterranean coast looks like it should be a wave-free zone. However, there are regions of Libya and Egypt that offer surprisingly good surf in specific conditions. Just ask Italian surfers about the potential of this small body of water. During the northern hemisphere autumn to spring season, numerous low pressure systems track through the North Atlantic and push swell towards the coastlines of Morocco, Western Sahara, Senegal and the Cape Verde Islands. The rocky sandstone headlands of Morocco offer a perfect foil and many are home to excellent, mostly right-hand point breaks. Between points, sand is corralled into miles of beaches, many of which may be cliff-lined as you move into the south of the country. Here, rivermouths or reef outcrops can provide some classic set-ups. Senegal offers up a combination of big sandy beaches as well as quality reef breaks.

Namibia picks up swells from the southern Atlantic Ocean with waves regularly battering what is known as the Skeleton Coast. This region is barren, sandy and vast and areas are fairly inaccessible. The water is

JS CALLAHAN/TROPICALPIX

Right: Locals out to watch the African sunset.
Opposite page: Victor Ribas slotting into Durban's North Beach.

cold and great white sharks feed on huge colonies of seals, which line some of the reeling point breaks. Neighbouring Angola has suffered years of instability and armed conflict. There have, however, been a number of surf expeditions to check out the fabled left points that reel along the coast and rumours persist that the potential here is pretty good. South Africa has a seemingly endless array of points, beaches and reefs. The country is bounded by two oceans, with the western coastline fringed by the South Atlantic and bathed by the cold of the Benguela Current. This moves frigid waters from the Southern Ocean in a northerly direction, keeping temperatures cool and making the sea around Cape Town a rich environment for sea life. Western Cape is geographically diverse, packing sandstone mountain ranges and fertile valleys into the region, with headlands punctuated by sandy bays and steep cliff edges plunging into the ocean. Eastern Cape is a mix of rocky points interspersed with beaches. The eastern coastline faces into the Indian Ocean and the beaches of Durban and KwaZulu-Natal are warmed by the Agulhas Current, which brings warm water down from the equatorial region.

Health and safety
Africa is a wild place. From the insects and animals you may run into on land to the huge, skulking sharks that ply the depths to the equally hazardous roads, this is a place where you need your wits about you and a good deal of luck on your side.

In Morocco and Senegal untreated tap water is not safe to drink so make sure you have a good supply of bottled water to keep you well hydrated. Avoid ice in your drinks and peel fruit and veg before you eat it. Also be aware of sewage contaminated water, common around urban breaks. If you do succumb to traveller's tummy, remember it's better out than in, stay out of the sun and keep fluid levels up to avoid dehydration. If you have diarrhoea for more than three days, pass blood or are in any doubt, seek immediate medical attention. Both Senegal and certain areas of South Africa, including northern KwaZulu-Natal, are at risk from malaria. There have also been outbreaks of yellow fever in Senegal. Check with your doctor on the best course of action for the area you are travelling to.

2003 saw Casablanca in Morocco targeted by suicide bombers. However, in today's political climate, the threat from terrorism is ever present everywhere around the world. Certain urban areas of South Africa, such as Cape Town and Johannesburg, have serious problems with violent crime. Other more common issues across Africa include pick-pocketing and van break-ins. Seasoned travellers recommend against driving after dark.

There are snakes, scorpions, spiders, ticks and so on but the main wildlife issues here are aquatic, namely sharks. They cruise the line-ups of Senegal but have so far posed little threat. South Africa, with its hungry

GARTH ROBINSON

Below: Sharks like Africa. Just don't think about it.
Opposite page: Samuel Mabetshe, J-Bay local.

GARTH ROBINSON

> 66 99
> You can surf world-class beachbreaks in the city with world-class surfers (and intense crowds), and then drive 45 minutes along the coast and surf a sketchy but cooking semi-rural point, alone, with cows grazing down to the beach...
>
> Will Bendix, editor of *Zigzag Magazine*

great whites, tiger and Zambezi (bull) sharks, has a bad reputation, not all of it deserved. Counteracting this, shark nets have been strung along sections of the KwaZulu-Natal beaches. They are not a barrier but act to reduce the chances of people and sharks coming into contact. According to the Natal Sharks Board there were no fatal shark attacks on netted beaches between 1990 and 2004. On the un-netted Eastern and Western Cape, the same figures show there have been 74 attacks and nine fatalities in the same period (which averages out to less than one fatality a year). For more info check out: www.shark.co.za. To minimize risks, let logic dictate: don't pee in your wetsuit; don't surf with a bleeding wound; don't surf at dusk and dawn, or during heavy rains; and don't surf at flooded rivermouths or when the sardine run is on.

Surfing and the environment

As with most regions of the world, in Africa the ocean environment is viewed in many ways – a precious commodity, a tourist attraction, a food source and a dumping ground. Which of these takes priority has to do with a number of factors – economics usually being the overriding force. Pollution of coastal waters with sewage takes place in pockets around many urban environments in developing countries where the local sewage infrastructure offers no form of treatment before discharge. This can be seen in heavily populated areas such as Casablanca and Rabat in Morocco, Lagos or Dar es Salaam and to a lesser extent around many towns and villages. This can lead to water-borne diseases entering the ocean as well as adversely affecting delicate ecosystems such as coral reefs. There are also pollution issues arising from untreated waste being discharged into rivers or straight into the sea from the outfalls of chemical plants and industrial factories. In developing countries safeguards tend to be minimal or not enforced at all. In Nigeria there are regular leaks from oil pipelines, which contaminate vast areas of land, groundwater and coastline, while Angola suffers chemical and mineral contamination from mining operations.

In most parts of developing Africa the 'beneficial' effects of building developments on the local economy override the effects on the local environment. Breakwaters or marinas can affect the flow of currents or destroy surf breaks but these considerations are generally of secondary importance. Areas where the marine environment takes precedent tend to be those where it is seen as a resource and as a tourist attraction. Resorts in countries such as Tanzania, Madagascar and Kenya have sprung up to target western holidaymakers. This change in how the ocean is viewed may hopefully become more widespread.

Surfing resources

The major surf title on the continent is South Africa's long-running and excellent *Zigzag Magazine*, www.zigzag.co.za. Another good resource is the website www.wavescape.co.za which is a good source for surf reports, news and information. www.satides.co.za has detailed tidal information for South Africa and Namibia. **Fédération Royale Marocaine de Surf et Bodyboard**, www.fedesurfmaroc.com has news and event information for the country (it's in French but hit the translate button on your search engine). It also has tide info for Casablanca as well as forecast models for the coastline.

Safi

Location:	North of Safi, Morocco
Break type:	Right-hand point break
Conditions:	Big to huge swells
Size:	4-12 ft
Length:	200-400 m
Tide:	Low to mid
Swell direction:	Northwesterly
Wind:	Northeasterly to easterly
Bottom:	Sand and rock point
Ability level:	Intermediate to advanced
Best months:	Nov-Mar
Access:	Off the rocks
Hazards:	Heavy, dangerous when big

Morocco is the land of the right-hand point break. They seem to be everywhere, almost as common as beach breaks in southwest France. Perhaps common is not the right word. Maybe abundant is better. Common can mean something ordinary, everyday, and the right-hand points of Morocco are far from ordinary. The country nestles on the northwestern tip of Africa, perfectly angled to catch those North Atlantic low pressure generated swells; the geography of the coastal landscape conspires to produce a long series of headlands, capes and bays, each with the potential to gather the shifting sands blown in from the Sahara. Particles captured and laid down as seamless sandbars. No, common would not be the word. They are more like a natural phenomenon.

Below: Safi, so good.
Opposite page: Abdel El Harim enjoying some home comforts at Safi.

Positioned halfway between Agadir and Casablanca, the town of Safi lies in the lee of one such cape. Just north of the town is one of the world's most enigmatic, yet terrifyingly perfect, point breaks. Ride a screaming, hollow reef and it might be like Pipeline, a powerful beach break, and it might be like Puerto Escondido, but ride a 600-m-long, 10-ft reeling point offering endless barrel sections and where do you find a comparable wave? "It's like a mix between Kirra and J-Bay," says top French surf Didier Piter. "Like a reverse Mundaka", says British pro Gabe Davies. "Like Burleigh only longer and more hollow," says Tom Carroll. One man who knows the wave better than anyone is Laurent Miramont. "Even compared to Mundaka, the speed is higher. The base of the wave is so perfect and impressive, but you also have the sand filling the holes, which can only add some degrees to the perfection of the wave." According to Laurent, the bathymetry of the offshore region adds to the velocity and power of the waves here. "There's a booster process with the 30-km Cape of Bedouza and the proximity of deep water. The swell, if it has the potential, size and power to pass the cape, is much faster than all the coast of Morocco. You have to be lucky though, because it doesn't happen as much as we used to get. Low pressure systems seem to pass higher than before on the Atlantic and we get less and less!"

The wave at Safi is a fast, walling and barrelling machine that seems to never end. It starts its magic at 4 ft and can break up to 12 ft plus. The middle to end sections have been ridden since the mid 1980s with a tube-riding, lip-bashing ferocity, but the first section is a challenge for even the world's best. The take-off leads into a racing, hollow sprint in

Safi Board	
6'7" Wayne Lynch	
Free Flight	
Shaper: Wayne Lynch	
6'7" x 18¾" x 2⅜"	
Solid semi-gun perfect for the thick barrels at Safi.	
Single to double concave with extra nose and tail rocker to handle the elevator drops when it gets big.	
FCS G7 fins.	
Boards by Surftech www.surftech.com info@surftech.com	

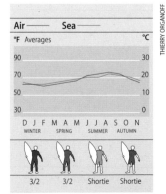

Air — Sea —
°F Averages °C

D J F M A M J J A S O N
WINTER SPRING SUMMER AUTUMN

3/2 | 3/2 | Shortie | Shortie

THIERRY ORGANOFF

front of unforgiving rocks. As Laurent says, it's not for the faint-hearted. "That's a dangerous place, specially from the top. There's a 200-m section, which is at a very close angle with the cliff, and the scheme of rocks is very bad. Until now, no one has been caught in this area, but just a few surfers engage from this peak. The very first one to take-off there was Ross Clarke-Jones. He opened the door! We had to wait for such an experienced surfer. I do worry about someone getting caught in this area though."

While the waves of Taghazoute have been ridden since the late sixties, Safi eluded the media spotlight until the 1990s. The wave has had a somewhat controversial history with a reputation for localism that is now luckily diminishing. "I remember in April 1986 on the way back to my home in Oualidia, after a super surf trip to 6- to 10-ft Anchor Point. I heard from a famous surfer-writer from *Surfer Mag* that the best potential seemed to be between Oualidia and Safi. So I checked on the way back; it was a huge swell, and on my first stop on the cliff it was so insane that I will never forget that day. I jumped in the water, it was 10-12 ft, and I was shocked... my concept of surfing completely changed that day." And the best session of all? "I can't talk of one session, but periods, when the swell pumps for three, six, ten days.

And can you imagine 30 days of swell with waves not less than 6 ft, peaking at double that size? Insane, square, blue, green – with 12- to 20-seconds barrels!" How do you put that into words, and is there a spot that you can compare such waves to?

Locals and legends

Some of the first surfers include Gérard Dabaddie and Luc Soutiff. Laurent Miramont, Karim Laaleg, Karim 'Ghier' Chiabat, Ross Clarke-Jones, Tom Carroll.

Nearby breaks To the south sits the town of **Essaouira**, with a beach popular with windsurfers. Just south is **Cap Sim**, an excellent right point that is difficult to find, and **Sidi Kaouki**, a wide beach which picks up heaps of swell. Further to the south lies **Immessouane**, an often overlooked world-class right that reels for hundreds of metres.

Killer Point

Location:	Killer Point, Taghazoute, Morocco
Break type:	Right-hand point break
Conditions:	All swells
Size:	2-10 ft +
Length:	50-200 m +
Tide:	Low to three quarter
Swell direction:	Northwesterly to westerly
Wind:	Northeasterly to easterly
Bottom:	Sand covered reef
Ability level:	Intermediate to advanced
Best months:	Sep-Mar
Access:	Paddle from beach at The Source
Hazards:	Gets crowded, rips, breaks in front of cliffs

PAUL GILL

It's funny that we tend to think of killer whales as the cute creatures that perform at Sea World – intelligent and gentle giants that watch us with that knowing look in their eyes, like an oversized, friendly dolphin. What we don't tend to think of is the huge, black-and-white death-bringer that rips huge seals to shreds as they loll around in the shallows looking remarkably like surfers. That is until they pop up next to us in the line-up. "I looked across and the fin was easily a metre high," says Mike McNeill of his first visit to Morocco back in 1976. "My next conscious thought was 'I'm on the rocks and I'm still paddling.'" This place isn't called Killer Point because of the good waves – it's to do with the big guys who sometimes pop up to cruise the line-up.

Just to the north of Anchor Point, the road loops, climbs up a cliff and around the headland giving a view over the point at Killers. From the vantage of this elevated position the coastline to the south is lost in a sunny, dusty haze before it reaches the city of Agadir. Below, the animated, jostling pack are scattered over a huge area about 300 m out from the base of the cliff. While Anchor Point may be the best-known wave in the area, many will contend that Killers is actually superior in terms of quality. It is more exposed, so picks up more swell, and when it's on it has a tendency to produce steeper, more hollow waves than its nearby brother. However, as with the whole Moroccan experience, whether you are rewarded on your journey depends on pure luck. You may have the perfect low, in the slot, pumping out a groomed 10-ft swell, but if the sand has not been distributed properly out on the point, this corduroy could be transformed into a cauldron of sections torn to pieces by a ruthless rip. If, on the other hand, the sandbanks are favourable, it will look like that perfect right point you used to draw on your school exercise book when you were a grommet. '*Inshallah*' – if God is willing.

If Killers is on, prepare to do a lot of paddling, as well as riding, the waves of your life. The main peak is about a 300-m paddle-out in a 6-ft swell, maybe more when bigger. The rip will spread out the pack, but the sets bear down on the line-up like a fleet of *Mack* trucks. The peak shifts around so it pays to sit wide and get your bearings before venturing deeper. The drop here is steep and fast and the wave bowls round into a speeding racetrack that just keeps reeling and reeling, occasionally slowing for a cutback, occasionally throwing into a barrel

---

Above: Paul Canning slashes off the top at Killers.
Opposite page: Cliff view over Killers' line-up.

Killer Point Board

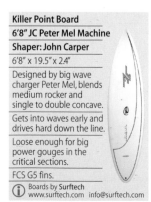

6'8" JC Peter Mel Machine

Shaper: John Carper

6'8" x 19.5" x 2.4"

Designed by big wave charger Peter Mel, blends medium rocker and single to double concave.

Gets into waves early and drives hard down the line.

Loose enough for big power gouges in the critical sections.

FCS G5 fins.

ⓘ Boards by Surftech
www.surftech.com info@surftech.com

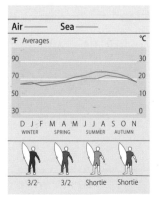

Air ——	Sea ——	
°F Averages		**°C**
90		30
70		20
50		10
30		0

D J F M A M J J A S O N
WINTER · SPRING · SUMMER · AUTUMN

3/2	3/2	Shortie	Shortie

section. When it's big you'll be using every inch of your semi-gun, as the pintail hangs in the vertical face. Try not to blow it near the take-off because, although it's a long way to the cliffs, fate nearly always dictates that the waves behind will be bigger, and the caves have claimed more than a few shiny new thrusters sacrificed by a less than trusty leash. "An 8-ft wave unloaded behind me and snapped my leash," says British charger James Hendy. "The next wave landed virtually on my head and opened up my wetsuit all down my back and filled it with water. I'm under water like balloon man. I came up and proceeded to get another four on my head. I was still 300 yards out, really cold and tired. I was more bothered about getting my board back than survival. Later that day a Kiwi guy unwedged my board from the back of a cave and handed it back to me."

You'd think the fact that Killers is a little bit further away from Taghazoute should mean the crowds are kept down, but the truth is that most swells are either destined to light up Anchors or Killers. Not both. One of the beauties of this point is that it can conjure up waves, even when small. Out around the headland, at the most exposed part of the point, a wave can break at low tide in really small swells offering long, fun walls that are all but hidden from view from the beach at The Source – the place to paddle out to the line-up. But when the serious swells roll in, this spot is transformed from something playful and friendly to something a whole lot bigger and more powerful – something that it doesn't pay to underestimate. Something that could be transformed into a killer.

Locals and legends
Top locals in the area include Samir Boukhiam and Ramzi Boukhiam, Lachen Idouch, Chakib Bouskou and former Moroccan women's champion Aurelie Magnen.

Nearby breaks **The Source** is a playful sand-covered reef that breaks out in front of the spring that gives the beach its name. It has a short left and right in small to medium swells at low to mid tide. **Mysteries** is a right-hander that breaks between Killers and Anchors and has a tiny take-off zone that is usually crowded. Can be excellent but depends on the sand.

PAUL GILL

Anchor Point

Location: Anchor Point, Taghazoute, Morocco	
Break type: Right-hand point break	
Conditions: Medium to big swells	
Size: 3-12 ft +	
Length: up to 200 m +	
Tide: Low to three quarter	
Swell direction: Northwesterly to westerly	
Wind: Northeasterly to easterly	
Bottom: Sand	
Ability level: Intermediate to advanced	
Best months: Sep-Mar	
Access: Jump off rock near end of point	
Hazards: Gets crowded, needs well-timed entry and exit	

DEMI TAYLOR

These trees grow in only one other place on earth, a small region thousands of miles away in Mexico. Around Taghazoute the twisted, gnarled Argan trees eke out a harsh existence in the barren, ochre-coloured soil. Goats climb high in the thorny branches to snack on the olive-like fruit that appears in the winter months. The Argan seeds are harvested from the goats' droppings and processed into a valuable oil that has become the latest must-have anti-ageing panacea for women across the western world. From the faeces left behind by a moth-eaten goat to the faces of a raft of rich Beverley Hills socialites – it's all about our take on what constitutes a valuable resource.

During the late sixties and early seventies the hippy trail meandered down to the west coast of Europe, across the straits of Gibralta and ended up at the village of Taghazoute. The combination of warm climate, welcoming locals and cheap living made it a haven for the children of the revolution. As surfing had taken on the rainbow colours of the 'Age of Aquarius', these were surfers along for the free ride. The pioneers scored classic, empty points and returned with tales of right-hand reelers that peeled forever under a warm African sky, a contrast to the rain and drizzle of a European winter. "In 1976 I went to Taghazoute with Chops Lascelles and we had six weeks when the surf never dropped below 8 ft," says Mike McNeill. Mike had just left the North Shore where he glassed Lightning Bolts. "There were six or eight of us surfing. It was one of the best experiences I'd ever had – and I'd just come from Hawaii."

Taghazoute is still a small village, nestled in the shade of a series of long, rocky headlands, the old anchor factory sitting at the apex of the closest and providing the early surfers with a ready name for their perfect point. It now rests abandoned, one of the most prime pieces of surfing real estate left on the planet. When a big swell rolls out of the north Atlantic, lines stack to the horizon and peak out past the end of the point. Emerald backlit walls can reel for over a minute, a picture-perfect train of top to bottom speed. Prime season at Anchors is the northern hemisphere winter months, when regular lows tracking through the north Atlantic will light up the breaks of the region. Between late December and early January the waves around Taghazoute will be jammed whenever they break – this is the Christmas vacation destination of choice for many a European or Aussie traveller. However, Anchors itself is a break that only improves with size and at 8-ft plus, the huge walls pack serious power and the line-up quickly empties. At 10-ft plus some of the longest walls you've ever seen will roll down the point like a steamroller. Being the most sheltered point around Taghazoute, it may go a whole season without breaking this ceiling, but if it does, then break out the pintail and head for the line-up. But make sure you time your jump-off well or you'll soon find yourself washed all the way back to the village to make the long walk up the road again.

Like many Moroccan points, Anchors is a rock-fringed but sand-bottomed break and so the quality of the wave varies greatly from year to year. Depending on how the sandbar is laid down and how the currents mould the banks, it may do a flawless impression of

Below: Basque charger Haritz Mendiluze getting into some Anchor Point power.
Opposite page: Chris Nelson, evening lines at the point.

Lennox one year, and be a mass of sections the next. When it's perfect, it can break all the way through to Hash Point, a wave that sits at the heart of the village and was named after the early stoners who couldn't make the walk out to the end of the point. This would be a wave of over two minutes in length. From here it's just a short paddle down to the take-off point at Panoramas, after which you'll need a taxi back to the end of the point! "I had one of the best waves of my life here," says Roxy rider Sarah Bentley. "It is so good at about 4-5 ft and seems to break at the perfect speed for a forehand wave and allows you to do some really sweet feeling turns."

Taghazoute is a wonderful blend of traditional Moroccan life, mixed with essence of surf culture and a liberal sprinkling of the old Europe from the many campervans that rock up for the winter full of French, German, Italian and Swedish pensioners. It's a real melting pot that the locals are stoked to play host to and they do so in the most welcoming way. This is the area's true natural resource. The old hippy trail of the seventies has become quickly established itself as an annual pilgrimage for the new millennium.

Locals and legends

Top locals in the area include Samir and Ramzi Boukhiam. According to coach Laurent Miramont, Ramzi is a future champion with "style, motivation and vibes". Other locals include Lachen Idouch, Chakib Bouskou and former Moroccan women's champion Aurelie Magnen.

Nearby breaks This region has an abundance of excellent set-ups. **Boilers** is a right point about 30 minutes' drive north that picks up more swell. On the southern side of Taghazoute sits **Panoramas**, a pinwheeling right point that is fast and hollow at low to mid tide. Ten minutes' drive south, **Devils Point** is another quality right in the village of Aourir.

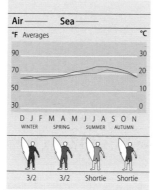

Anchor Point Board

6'3" M10 The Kid

Shaper: Geoff Rashe

6'3" x 18¾" x 2⅜"

Deep single to double concave with added tail rocker make this board super fast down the line yet it feels loose and accelerates through tight turns.

It'll bring out the kid in you.

Futures fins.

ⓘ Boards by **Surftech**
www.surftech.com info@surftech.com

Air			Sea	
°F	Averages			°C
90				30
70				20
50				10
30				0
	D J F	M A M	J J A S O N	
	WINTER	SPRING	SUMMER AUTUMN	
	3/2	3/2	Shortie	Shortie

Africa Anchor Point

WILLY URIBE

Ouakam

- **Location:** Almadies Peninsula, Dakar, Senegal
- **Break type:** A-frame reef
- **Conditions:** Big swells
- **Size:** 3-6 ft
- **Length:** Up to 100 m
- **Tide:** Not high
- **Swell direction:** Northerly to northesterly
- **Wind:** Northerly to northeasterly
- **Bottom:** Rock reef
- **Ability level:** Intermediate to advanced
- **Best months:** Nov-Mar
- **Access:** Easy paddle
- **Hazards:** Urchin-infested reef

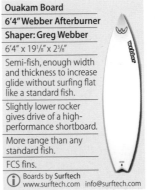

Ouakam Board

6'4" Webber Afterburner

Shaper: Greg Webber

6'4" x 19⅛" x 2⅜"

Semi-fish, enough width and thickness to increase glide without surfing flat like a standard fish.

Slightly lower rocker gives drive of a high-performance shortboard.

More range than any standard fish.

FCS fins.

ⓘ Boards by Surftech
www.surftech.com   info@surftech.com

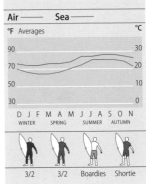

Sitting in the line-up the surrounding arena is a lesson in how to construct a complementary palette of colours. The sandstone cliffs are streaked with the sun-worn hues of yellows, oranges and browns. The cool, clear Atlantic has taken on a glassy, bottle-green tint as the hollow lefts and rights spin away from the tight take-off point. The sounds of the muezzin's call to prayer waft out over the ocean as returning fishermen skirt the reef heading for the beach. The twin towers of the commanding white mosque watch over the line-up while lines of bright rocks mark out a scrawl of symbols on the gently sloping hill that acts as a backdrop to the village. Even though this is one of the most westerly breaks on the African continent, it still rests within the bounds of the Arabic north. "Ouakam is placed in a Muslim cult

PHILIPPE CHEVODIAN

PHILIPPE CHEVODIAN

189

Left: The mosque watches over the break near Dakar.
Opposite page: Senegal's Didier Pitier getting pitted in Ouakam.

Africa Ouakam

place, which makes it a sanctuary for surfers," explains Didier Piter. "The break itself is also like a temple for Senegalese surfers. It is a pure pleasure wave in a perfect frame."

Ouakam village nestles on the western edge of the Almadies Peninsula, a finger of land that juts out into the Atlantic Ocean, pointing the way towards the distant shores of Barbados and the Windward Islands. The exposure of the peninsula means it picks up any swell coming out of the north. The Senegalese capital Dakar dominates the area and is home to an expanding surf community. Although Dakar is more famed as the destination for one of the most gruelling motor races on the planet than as a world-class waveriding destination, more and more surfers are drawn here every year by stories of the numerous breaks around this region. Along the northerly coastline and westerly fringe, this cape is blessed with beaches and reefs that offer up some classic, consistent surf. At Ouakam, a headland protects the bay from all but the biggest swells and ensures that the reef here is a gem that requires a specific set of conditions to come alive. And if it does, surfers from across the region will descend on the fabled line-up. When a serious Atlantic groundswell rolls out of the north, past the sharky break at Carp Bay, and bends round the bluff, the sleeping reef will be transformed into a perfect A-frame. The small take-off zone offers the instant reward of a 20-m barrel before running into a section with just enough time for two fluid moves over the urchin-covered rock reef. Backing off momentarily, the wave conserves its energy before accelerating into an inside barrel section that finally pours onto the beach.

The locals have the break wired, but for Didier this is a special place. "Ouakam is a really perfect wave but one that barely breaks, which means you never get enough of her," says the former European Champion. Didier has a special relationship with this wave, and this country. "It is my first surfing love and it is my birth country. Every time I go back I feel happy, relaxed and quiet, like a warrior back from a battle. I refuel a lot because the essence of surfing is always around." And the locals are always happy to see Didier return. Stories are traded, meals are shared and charts are fastidiously checked, waiting for the signs of swell to light up the region's jewel. For Didier each visit sees new faces in the line-up. "Surfing in Senegal has changed very much over the past 10 years. The problem before was there was no boards, no shops. Now there is everything and surfing can grow. Local Senegalese who are usually fishermen start to surf and they rip. There is now a Senegalese surfing association helping and developing surfing."

Sometimes the moods and colours of a location can create either a harsh, distracting discord or a bright, vibrant backdrop. In Senegal the ochre hues of Africa are washed by the iridescent Atlantic in a harmonious scene that merely enhances the whole experience of surfing the western fringe of this huge and diverse continent. In Ouakam the wave stands out as a bonus – and a very welcome bonus at that.

Locals and legends

"The surfing community around Dakar is like around 100 people," says Didier "plus all the former locals scattered around the globe who keep contact and keep the bounds. There is a true surf spirit there and unless you conduct yourself like an animal you will always receive a good welcome there and meet the locals. The best locals at Ouakam are Laurent Lardez, Oumar, Papé, Seb Barth..."

Nearby breaks   N'gor Right and **N'gor Left** are found on opposite sides of the island of N'gor on the northwestern edge of the peninsula. It was here that Hynson and August surfed in Endless Summer. They pick up lots of swell but are exposed to the wind and require a long paddle or boat ride to reach them. The southwesterly facing edge of the peninsula is home to a series of good reef offshores in northerlies, but need bigger swells. Check out **Secrets** and **Vivier**.

Dungeons

💧 **Location:**	Hout Bay, West Coast, Cape Peninsula, South Africa
◐ **Break type:**	Right-hand reef
🌀 **Conditions:**	Big to massive swells
🌊 **Size:**	10-25 ft +
🔁 **Length:**	100 m +
🌐 **Tide:**	All tides
📡 **Swell direction:**	Southwesterly
🌬 **Wind:**	Light north to northeasterly
⚓ **Bottom:**	Reef ledges
🎯 **Ability level:**	Advanced
🌼 **Best months:**	Apr-Sep
🚤 **Access:**	By boat from Hout Bay harbour
⚠ **Hazards:**	Super heavy hold-downs, currents, kelp, sharks, cold water

ALAN VAN GYSEN

The coastline of the Western Cape Peninsula is a fitting location for what must be one of the most hardcore waves to break anywhere on the planet. Offshore cloudbreaks overlooked by mountainous peaks, kelp-choked waters where seals play and lurking shadows stalk in silence waiting to strike. Huge, green, cold water peaks rear up from the deep and explode onto shallow ledges. It takes a special soul to paddle out here just knowing all the dangers to be faced before even considering the damage a mistimed take-off or a collapsing section could impose. The stretch of water between Cape Town and the Cape of Good Hope has been feared by sailors for centuries – and with good reason. Today it is a new frontier in big wave riding and home to a new breed of big wave surfers.

"The spectacle of the place is quite mind-blowing," says legendary South African big wave charger Ross Lindsay. "The waves break in the shadow of the Sentinel Mountain and for the morning sessions it is cold (both in the water and the air) and dark but when the sun breaks through the gap in the mountains, the whole place lights up from a gloomy and ominous big wave surf spot to a bright and awesome place. Throw in a seal colony right on the inside with its hundreds of seals flopping in and out of the surf from the island, and their predators, the great white sharks, and you have a hell of a mix of nature. Everyone is trying to survive – surfers included! Go figure the odds, and then you know why you are so drained after a session out there. Adrenalin pumps a-plenty no matter what is going on."

When a big swell comes out of the Roaring Forties, its open-ocean power undiluted by the restraint of a continental shelf as it impacts from deep water onto the flat reef, making sure you're in the right spot to take the elevator drops is crucial. "The waves start breaking from 10 ft upwards to 25-30 ft," says Ross. "The take-off zone is like a playing field of a couple of hundred square metres and you need to position yourself in the right place to get a great ride, or prepare to be pounded down towards the reef 2.5 m below in the powerful white water. The drops are critical; the rides (predominantly rights) are a few hundred metres long, with occasional gnarly tubes. The might of the Atlantic Ocean crashing into the majestic mountains on either side of Hout Bay makes this a big wave spot with a lot of drama and intrigue."

Just being in the water when these green, glassy peaks are throwing out huge, hollow wedges is a serious business – a life-threatening undertaking. It underlines the commitment these guys have to riding these waves. "My defining moment at Dungeons came when I was working on the K38 Water Safety team in one of the Red Bull Big Wave Africa events," says Ross, "and had to rescue Greg Bertish who was knocked unconscious by his board trying to paddle though a set wave of about 15 ft. We raced to his board and I pulled him up by the leash and dragged him onto our IRB to start CPR, as he had been down for about 45 seconds or so. He came round as I was getting ready to administer CPR as Pierre Du Plessis, my rescue partner at the time, raced us out of the impact zone and to the Medic boat. This incident brought home the fact that we are all vulnerable in the ocean, even

Above: It's behind you! From some Dungeons, there can be no escape.
Opposite page: The sun creeps over the Sentinel, casting a new perspective on the line-up.

ALLAN VAN GYSEN

amongst the best big wave surfers in the world, but with rescue techniques and vessels like the IRBs and PWCs we can keep each other safe and ready to surf again."

Imagine what it took to be the first guys to paddle out here? This outside bombora broke in clear visibility beneath the Sentinel Mountain, gazed on by surfers since the first days of surfing on this continent. It would require a massive paddle-out through the deep channels and kelp beds of a seal colony thick with white pointers. Then to take on these huge waves for the first time, in a shifting line-up with no clear exit point worked out? "It was watched way back in the '60s by the pioneer of South African surfing, John Whitmore, and his friends, but Pierre De Villiers and Peter Button were the first recorded surfers to ride at Dungeons in 1984," says Ross. "These guys are Dungeons legends for pioneering the spot alone with no back up for a couple of years – hardcore to say the least." With all the potential dangers posed by a break like this, it's hard to imagine a session here as a few friends out enjoying a few waves together. But in essence, that is still what a morning go-out at Dungeons is all about.

Locals and legends

Pierre De Villiers and Peter Button are legends who pioneered this spot. Others include Davey Stolk, Jonathon Paarmann, Justin Strong, Cass Collier and Ian Armstrong. Today's locals include Mickey Duffus, Chris Bertish, Sean Holmes, Dave Smith, Andrew Marr and Simon Lowe. Grant 'Twiggy' Baker, Jason Ribbink and John Whittle visit from Durban.

Nearby breaks This is a region where the swell is not the issue; finding the right exposure for the wind is more important. If the huge outside reefs aren't your cup of tea, the breaks at **Dunes** and **Long Beach** to the south or **Llandudno** to the north offer excellent alternatives.

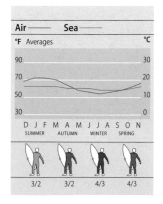

Dungeons Board

10' Clarke Gun

Shaper: Jeff Clarke

10' x 20" x 3½"

Jeff Clarke designed his 10' Gun specifically for big ledging mountains of water.

With plenty of thickness for great paddling to get you in early.

FCS GAM fins.

(i) Boards by **Surftech**
www.surftech.com info@surftech.com

Air —— Sea ——	
°F Averages	°C

D J F	M A M	J J A S	O N
SUMMER	AUTUMN	WINTER	SPRING
3/2	3/2	4/3	4/3

Cape St Francis

- **Location:** Cape St Francis, Eastern Cape, South Africa
- **Break type:** Right point break
- **Conditions:** Medium to big swells
- **Size:** 3-6 ft +
- **Length:** Up to 150 m +
- **Tide:** All tides
- **Swell direction:** Big southwesterly to easterly
- **Wind:** Southwesterly
- **Bottom:** Rock and sand
- **Ability level:** Intermediate to advanced
- **Best months:** Apr-Sep
- **Access:** Off the point
- **Hazards:** Sections can be heavy, others like Hullets good for less experienced

This is the wave that actually started the search. The 'Endless Summer' reached its solstice at Cape St Francis when Robert August and Mike Hynson walked out onto the point to be met by those reeling curls zippering down that rocky fringe. Bruce Brown's hyperbole reached epic proportions as his voice fought against the rising orchestral accompaniment. His mantra – suggesting that, day after day, perfect waves peel unridden along this point – struck a powerful chord with cinema audiences around the globe. The thought that they, too, could discover their very own Cape St Francis was like an electric shock to the collective consciousness. There really were perfect, machine-like waves out there just waiting for someone to board a plane and come and claim them. If Malibu was the wave that defined the end of the fifties era and the dawn of youth culture, Cape St Francis was the wave of the next generation. Suddenly the surfing world was a much bigger place.

Her reign, however, was a short one. Soon we were gleefully told of her flaws, that she was fickle and inconsistent. Like a starlet without her make-up, the myth couldn't live up to the reality; St Francis was not the picture of perfection promised on screen. Besides, a new queen had been crowned, and she just happened to live next door. J-Bay was to become the definition of a perfect point break. The irony is that had Hynson and August stumbled across perfect J-Bay instead of St Francis, they would probably have been unable to surf the spot to its true potential. As Shaun Tomson says, it wasn't until the end of the sixties that J-Bay was really ridden. "Back then [1968] we were, in fact, riding only the very tail-end of the ride. We would sit out in the line-up and watch these grinding tubes wind down for about a mile before they would get to us. We all called the spot south of us Indicators, and we all thought it was too fast and too dangerous to surf. It wasn't until later the next year, in 1969, that the real J-Bay was ridden and discovered, and eventually renamed Supertubes."

But the waves they found at Cape St Francis were perfectly suited to the equipment of the era. The longboards that Mike and Robert rode hooked into the curl and fired along the small, glassy tubes that wound down the sand-covered rocks in a virtually unbroken section; the wave that is to this day known as Bruce's Beauties (after the *Endless Summer* director Bruce Brown).

Below: The friendlier side of St Francis.
Opposite page: Bruce's isn't all perfect peelers and endless summers....

Cape St Francis Board
9'0" Robert August Wingnut II
Shaper: Dick Brewer
6'3" x 15½" x 1½"
Cape St Francis is a speed and trim oriented wave, exactly what Robert and Wingnut designed this for.
A narrow nose, flatter rocker and narrower tail fits up high in the pocket.
Make every ruler-edged section.
2+1 fins.
Boards by Surftech
www.surftech.com info@surftech.com

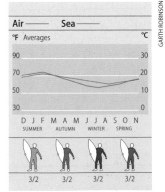

Air ——	Sea ——
°F Averages	°C

D J F M A M J J A S O N
SUMMER AUTUMN WINTER SPRING

3/2 3/2 3/2 3/2

GARTH ROBINSON

Today, the reputation of Bruce's may have changed, but so has the wave. Some blame the urbanization of the surrounding area for disrupting the sand flow. Although the wave isn't the most consistent along Africa's coastline, it isn't a sleeping beauty either. The cape bends to the east meaning only the bigger southwesterly swells light up the point, or the less common easterlies. The once barren headland is now sprouting a crop of houses and modern cottages. Garth Robinson explains "The point is now home to empty holiday homes for well-heeled English-speaking South Africans (Afrikaans-speaking ones prefer nearby Jeffrey's Bay). The white-walled houses make it look more like Greece than Africa, but given a decent easterly swell with a westerly wind the entire bay still lights up."

The variety of waves on offer on the cape means that there is something to suit all tastes. On occasions there are grinding, sucking barrels reeling just yards from the rocky fringe while just along the shore a more mellow wall will welcome the less reckless. "Choose from super-hollow lefts at Anne Avenue, the longboard perfection at Hullets and the legendary tubular rights of Bruce's Beauties," says Garth, "as well as a fair number of secret spots and you have a surfer's

dream destination. And that doesn't even take into account nearby Seal Point." Seal Point is the southerly section, crowned by the trademark lighthouse and serves up two more portions of the hallowed point. Bruce's still has its days when, sitting on the headland, watching a waist-high swell zip along the headland, you will see a longboarder crouched in the sweetspot, trimming in the curl, speeding so fast that for a moment you are transported back in time. Back to an era when the world was a very big place, and when every headland, on every map, offered the prospect of finding your very own Cape St Francis. She may no longer be the Queen, but she is definitely a very distinguished Queen Mother.

Locals and legends
Neville and Phillipa Hulet, Donald and Jonathon Paarman, Shorty Bronkhorst, Kenny Bygate, Anthony van den Heuvel, Max Wetteland, Bruce Gold, John Whitmore, Deon Du Toit, Eric Stedman, Jenny MacDonald, Edy Godfrey, Shavonne Hill, Helmie Tilder, Bob Pike.

Nearby breaks Cape St Francis is a number of breaks including **Bruce's Beauties** and **Seal Point**. Heading north into St Francis Bay there are plenty of other options including **Leftovers**, **Hullets** and a number of beach break spots before the coastline bends into the legendary pointbreak at **Jeffrey's Bay**.

Jeffrey's Bay

◐ **Location:** St Francis Bay, Eastern Cape, South Africa

◑ **Break type:** Right-hand point

◒ **Conditions:** All swells

◉ **Size:** 4-10 ft +

◔ **Length:** 100-600 m

◕ **Tide:** Low to three quarter

◗ **Swell direction:** Southwesterly to southeasterly

◖ **Wind:** Northwesterly to westerly

☺ **Bottom:** Rock and sand

◐ **Ability level:** Intermediate to advanced

◉ **Best months:** Apr-Oct

◍ **Access:** Tricky exit over sharp, mussel covered rocks

◉ **Hazards:** Look for the keyholes for entry, sharky, crowds

Ask a modern touring pro about Jeffrey's Bay and their description will probably be a short as their connection with the wave: "It's the best right point in the world"; "It's super fast"; or "Awesome". This is a generation that has only known the thruster and a new contest on a new continent every other week. Ask Shaun Tomson and you'll get a sense of a relationship that he invested time and energy into; a wave with which he has developed a special bond. "It is a purist's wave. Each turn, each manoeuvre must have meaning and significance. A surfer must write his own personal story on the face of the wave with style, rhythm and power. Unnecessary manoeuvres are wasted. Do only that which is essential to make the wave and feel the energy. It is the ultimate canvas for free expression."

JS CALLAHAN/TROPICALPIX

Right: Local Sean Holmes carving off a piece of J-Bay.
Opposite page: Lining up at J-Bay.

Jeffrey's Bay is a geological anomaly, a true freak of nature – yet one whose beauty casts a shadow over all other pretenders. In a community as diverse and disparate as the surfing family, it is one of the few areas of common ground. J-Bay *is* the best right-hand point break in the world. It offers challenging speeding walls, winding barrels, big gouging cutback sections and fragments where the curtain closes, but always offers the tantalizing promise that one day it may just grant that elusive connection to the next level. "Often called the fastest makeable wave on the planet, J-Bay allows one to fully express oneself on the ample and changing canvas," says Marcus Sanders. "Plenty of open face turns and barrels, it allows a surfer's style to shine through, as evidenced by Curren's first ride here in '92." For the slash and burn brigade, J-Bay forces a more cerebral style of surfing. On a set wave here you must think ahead, anticipate the waves changes and respond in kind. "This is the perfect wave for the natural footer," says top Spanish Pro Michel Velasco. "After the take off you have a long wall section that seems impossible to pass, but you start getting speed to do the best carves you can imagine. The different sections allow you to do really amazing turns with challenging barrels."

This wave has come a long way from its birth in a spiralling low pressure system in the Roaring Forties to the open ocean line rolling through the Southern Ocean to the feathering peak gaining height as the sea bed slows its northerly progress. A feathering offshore plume signals its lunge onto the end of the bay at Boneyards, the wave spinning right across the point towards the waiting pack at Supertubes. Here a speeding curtain of water begins zipping down the fringe of the point, before the lunge into Impossibles, the barrelling cavern that peels with the crispness of a scalpel through clean, white paper. Then from Tubes there is a tantalizing barrier before the final section, The Point. Each part of this amazing journey has been the scene of flowing, carving waveriding as an artistic form executed with the utmost skill; from dolphins gliding through the emerald face of Boneyards to Tom Curren carving huge arcs through Supers, to the board control of Shaun Tomson navigating an Impossibles' barrel to the final, leg-burning moments of Terry Fitzgerald's three-minute drive through the whole Jeffrey's line-up.

Imagining the empty line-ups of the late sixties and early seventies seems amazing now. Today the line-up has a heavy local presence and has a steady stream of visitors drawn to experience this surfing phenomenon at least once in their lives. J-Bay is also the site of an annual contest on the WCT. It's easy to see why this makes such an attractive tour venue, but at the same time it is on waves like this where the creative side of surfing is truly expressed. Waves from Tomson, Fitzgerald, Curren and Derek Hynd are seminal moments, and each generation is laying down their own. It is a place where equipment and style count for everything. "I was lucky enough to grow into a number of point breaks *before* I went to J-Bay" says Terry Fitzgerald. "Kirra, Burleigh, Bells, Winkipop and Sunset all contributed to setting me up with boards that rode high, a desire to ride lip lines and concaves... even back in the early seventies. So J-Bay was a walk-up start, a place where I could safely leave any of my boards and they would be in heaven."

Locals and legends

Max Wetteland, Tony van der Heuvel, Bruce Gold, Jonathan Paarmann, Shaun Tomson, Derek Hynd, Mickey Dora, Craig Els, Sean Holmes, Warren Deane.

Jeffrey's Bay Board

6'6" Lynch Round Pin

Shaper: Wayne Lynch

6'6" x 19½" x 2⁹/₁₆"

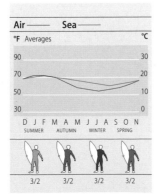

A little extra overall volume and softer plan shape curves, creates great paddling qualities plus the ability to run across flat sections and maintain speed.

Great for blazing speed runs at J-Bay!

FCS fins.

ⓘ Boards by **Surftech**
www.surftech.com info@surftech.com

Air ——	Sea ——	
°F Averages		°C
90		30
70		20
50		10
30		0

D J F M A M J J A S O N
SUMMER AUTUMN WINTER SPRING

| 3/2 | 3/2 | 3/2 | 3/2 |

Nearby breaks Albatross in the inside section of The Point works in big swells, and there are other breaks scattered nearby, but let's be honest, if you're not going to surf it, you should at least take time out to watch it.

Surfers' tales
Jeffrey's Bay, the ultimate speed line Shaun Tomson

JS CALLAHAN/TROPICALPIX

It starts with a gust of wind in the frigid Antarctic. The wind velocity increases as the barometric pressure drops. The wind howls across thousands of kilometres of open ocean, organizing chaotic chops into long bands of energy we call swells. These southerly ground swells march up the east coast of southern Africa and bend into a perfectly contoured point just south of Port Elizabeth, one of the country's most picturesque ports.

Jeffrey's Bay is the world's greatest right-hand point. No question. Nothing can compare. When a deep southerly swell meets up with a 20-knot southwest wind and a medium to low tide, the result is perfection. The wave itself is thick, fast and powerful. The sensation of speed is incredible. Each turn can be a 25-m arc. The only way to ride J-Bay is with power and rhythm. The wave is very easy to ride but extremely difficult to ride well. The wave is so perfect that it immediately shows up anything lacking in one's style or approach.

It is a purist's wave. Each turn, each manoeuvre must have meaning and significance. A surfer must write his own personal story on the face of the wave. Unnecessary manoeuvres are wasted. Do only that which is essential to make the wave and feel the energy. It is the ultimate canvas for free expression. When the offshores howl, a surfer can hang high on the face, holding an impossible trim while the wall feathers 50 m ahead of him. Hold the trim, hold it and then let go, flying faster than ever before, feeling every rail in your board's bottom curve, and feeling the fine, smooth texture of the wave's face through the soles of your feet.

Jeffrey's Bay has been ridden for around 40 years now. Two South African legends both claim to have discovered it in the mid-'60s. John Whitmore from Cape Town maintains he told Bruce Brown about the spot when he came to South Africa with Hynson and August to film the original *Endless Summer*. One of South Africa's all-time greats, Max Wetteland, claims he found it on the way to Cape Town.

I first surfed it in 1968. The shortboard revolution had shaken up the surfing world and my cousin Michael and I, escorted by my father Chony, were on our way to Cape Town to compete in the South African Surfing Championships. It was our first 'surfari' away from home and my father decided that we were to stop off for a week at Jeffrey's Bay en route to Cape Town. I remember arriving in the evening and checking into the town's only hotel, *The Beach*. We were 1000 km from home and my cousin and I could barely sleep thinking about the possibility of perfect surf.

The next morning we woke to a perfectly shaped 4 to 6-ft swell bending into the point – totally empty. We were the only surfers in the line-up and my enduring memory of Jeffrey's Bay is of the solitude and beauty associated with that first perfect day. That memory has remained close to my heart. I have surfed Jeffrey's Bay many times since that day in 1968 and many things have changed. Back then we were in fact riding only the very tail end of the ride. We would sit out in the line-up and watch these grinding tubes wind down for about a mile before they would get to us. We all called the spot south of us Indicators, and we all thought it was too fast and too dangerous to surf. It wasn't until later the next year in 1969 that the real J-Bay was ridden and discovered, and eventually renamed Supertubes.

J-Bay is actually five different waves that, on the right days, all mould together into the fastest, longest wave on the planet. Way out the back, at the top of the point, is Boneyards. At 8 ft, it's a heavy, ledging take-off made exceptionally difficult by being more exposed to the stiff offshore wind. Once you've made the take-off you can backdoor a long pitching tube, and if you're fast enough, you can race through to the main break of Supertubes. Supers is the heart and soul of the wave; an immense canvas of water perfectly suited to huge bottom turns and powerful, carving re-entries. It is here that you will travel faster than you have ever surfed before. Totally flat out, muscles straining – red-lining to the max!

Once you come burning through Supers, there is time for a quick cutback before setting up for Impossibles. Impossible is my favourite section, which for many years was considered 'impossible' to make. The section is square and dredges: not as hollow as Kirra or Backdoor, but perfectly suited to an attacking style of tube-riding. It is here, inside the long green barrels, that I developed techniques for turning and riding inside the tube, instead of trimming and running for cover.

After racing through the sections of Boneyards, Supers and Impossibles, muscle fatigue starts to set in. By now you may have had three deep tube rides and covered about 300 m in distance. The next section down the line is Tubes and it is very difficult to connect up unless the swell is perfect and you maintain a highline super-speed drive. I saw Terry Fitzgerald blaze through Tubes once, a ride of at least three minutes.

If all the conditions are perfect, your mind and body totally coordinated, you might just be able to make it through to The Point,

the place where we first experienced Jeffrey's. To do this is rare; extremely rare. I have done it once and have never seen it done again. I'm sure it's happened again. A young surfer connects with the perfect wave of the set and flies through section after section, surfing with style and power and rhythm. Some of the best things in life are almost unattainable. That thought of making it through again comes to me sometimes in the early morning, even thousands of kilometres away from its source. I can smell the powerful musky scent of Flymbos, a bush found only at J-Bay and nowhere else, like a distant skunk on the wind. And I can hear that Southwester' now; howling and growling, tugging at my thoughts with fierce gusts. I live far away now, and don't go back that often, but I feel like I've never left. That wave seems to stretch out infinitely before me, feathering forever, and I'm flying alone, flat out on the fastest wave on the planet, loving the feeling and living the memory over and over, for ever and ever.

Shaun Tomson redefined surfing with his barrel-riding and stylish attack in waves around the globe from Pipeline and Backdoor on the North Shore to his native waves of Durban and Jeffrey's Bay. He captured the 1977 World Title and inspired a generation with his surf style in the epoch-making movie Free Ride. *Today, based in California, Shaun is a respected figure in the surf industry and can be found in the barrel and carving up the faces of classic points, from J-Bay to Rincon.*

JS CALLAHAN/TROPICALPIX

Cave Rock

Location: The Bluff, Durban, KwaZulu-Natal, South Africa	
Break type: Reef break	
Conditions: All swells	
Size: 4-10 ft +	
Length: up to 50 m	
Tide: All tides, shallow on low	
Swell direction: Southeasterly to southerly	
Wind: Northwesterly	
Bottom: Rocky reef	
Ability level: Advanced	
Best months: Apr-Oct	
Access: Paddle from north side of pool	
Hazards: Shallow, heavy, hollow and powerful	

JS CALLAHAN/TROPICALPIX

It's all about getting in and getting out in one piece. Whereas J-Bay is about long, drawn-out turns, fades and lines, here at Cave Rock it's just about barrels. The bigger the swell, the bigger the barrels, and the lower the tide, the more critical they become. Cave Rock gets its name from the rock that sits in front of the break, giving the wave its distinctive setting, along with the concrete tidal pool that features in so many line-up shots. This is a short, intense, powerful right-hand barrel breaking over a shallow rock ledge. It is a wave that offers the brave a chance to grab the rail, make the vertical drop, backdoor the peak and tuck into a huge, round tube that would grace the North Shore. "Cave Rock is a great, hard fast wave," says Chris Leppan. "A very short ride but extremely hollow and powerful." It is little wonder that the wave has a solid following and when a swell kicks in, the line-up will fill with the best surfers from The Bluff and Durban.

Standing on Foreshore Drive looking out over Anstey's to Brighton Beach on a damp and windy easterly morning, you might wonder whether there was any decent surf on this section of The Bluff. "Upon first glance you would not think that this straight beach, with its scattered patches of reef can produce the goods," says Garth Robinson. "But given a combination of southerly swell and morning offshores it becomes the closest thing to Backdoor that South Africa has to offer. It's an elevator drop followed by a short wall and then tuck your gonads in and pull into a below-sea-level barrel section that can offer the deepest pits in the country." With a coastline as big as South Africa has to offer, all the points and all the beaches

that line it, and with all the swell it receives, this must be a pretty high calibre reef. "It has the flexibility to handle a light northeasterly, but it gets really crowded, snaps lots of boards and produces the longest and meanest hold-downs in the Durban area." This is no place for the inexperienced. The paddle-out alone can be a testing experience. Standing next to the tidal pool on a big day at low tide, with all the water moving around on the inside, the sets detonating on the reef and the odd rock popping its head above the white water, it's a matter of critical timing to make it out between the sets and avoid the ignominy of being washed back over the reef.

Rudy Palmboom Senior is probably *the* Cave Rock legend, having surfed there since the 1970s. "It's a challenging, dangerously good barrelling wave," explains Rudy. "The shallow, potholed, seaweed covered sandstone reef causes the wave to break almost below sea level on low tide. I have surfed many surf spots locally and on the North Shore [of Oahu] and I can honestly say it's an entirely different feeling when you paddle-out at the Rock. You almost have a sense of awe at the power of the place. You know instinctively that you have to respect this place, you will get the good with the bad – you will experience bad wipeouts (expect to get worked!) but the unforgettable barrels make it well worthwhile." When a 10 ft groundswell comes out of the southeast and hits the reef in the face of light offshore winds, this is truly a testing ground. Hardly surprising then that this is a wave that many of South Africa's top surfers have used as a stepping-stone to make the transition to the waves of the North Shore.

Above: Cave Rock.
Opposite page: South African ripper Frankie Oberholzer tucks into the Cave.

"I wasn't sure who the real pioneers were," says Rudy. "Spider Murphy says that he was a grom at the time and remembers that guys from the lifesaving club, like the late Wilbur Barrs, Darryl and Allan Ribbink and Raymond Brown, surfed the Rock in the early days. This was from 1960-65. George Thompson charged it from 65 onwards. I personally surfed The Rock with guys like Shaun Tomson, Mark Matthews, Paul Naude, Pierre Tostee, Greg Swart, Chris van Lennep from 1972 onwards." Despite its sheer quality and legendary status within South Africa, it's amazing that The Rock has managed to keep quite a low international profile. This is slowly changing and you can bet that Cave Rock is now as firm a fixture on any visiting surfers itinerary as J-Bay. Although it's one break where the wave itself is definitely more intimidating than the shark threat.

Locals and legends

Shaun Tomson, Rudy Palmboom Senior, Rudy Junior, Julian Wilson, Tristan Bransby, Ricky Basnett, Paul and Matt Daniel, and Grant 'Twiggy' Baker often strays to The Bluff for an epic surf session.

Cave Rock Board		
6'9" Byrne Tom Carroll		
Shaper: Phil Byrne		
6'9" x 18⅜" x 2¼"		

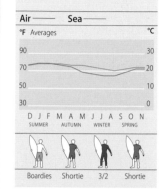

Ideally suited for the ledgy hollow waves at Cave Rock.

Design with 2-time world champion Tom Carroll, this highly responsive round pin works well in thick heavy barrels!

FCS fins.

ⓘ Boards by Surftech
www.surftech.com info@surftech.com

Air —— Sea ——

°F	Averages	°C
90		30
70		20
50		10
30		0

D J F M A M J J A S O N
SUMMER AUTUMN WINTER SPRING

| Boardies | Shortie | 3/2 | Shortie |

Nearby breaks Anstey's is a residential area of The Bluff, which offers a break with lefts and rights and picks up small swells, but works best in a medium-sized easterly swell. There is a right-hander that works in swells from a southerly direction and can handle some size. Further south **Brighton Beach** has some quality walling lefts and rights in clean swells. Both are good alternatives if The Rock is big and busy.

Durban Beaches

⬦ **Location:**	Durban, KwaZulu-Natal, South Africa
⬤ **Break type:**	Beach break lefts and rights with jetties
⬤ **Conditions:**	All swells
⬤ **Size:**	2-8 ft
⬤ **Length:**	up to 50 m
⬤ **Tide:**	Low to mid
⬤ **Swell direction:**	South to easterly
⬤ **Wind:**	Southwesterly to westerly
⬤ **Bottom:**	Sand
⬤ **Ability level:**	All
⬤ **Best months:**	Apr-Oct
⬤ **Access:**	From beach
⬤ **Hazards:**	Netted beaches, competitive line-ups

Durban Beaches Board
6'4" Patterson Pro 1G
Shaper: Timmy Patterson
6'4" x 18¾" x 2½"

It's your can't go wrong shortboard designed for punchy beach breaks.

Single to slight double concave to give you all the speed and drive you need to blow up the lip!

Futures fins.

ⓘ Boards by Surftech
www.surftech.com info@surftech.com

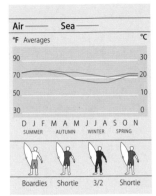

When it comes to the world's classic waves, there are not many beach breaks that are a shoo-in. Hossegor and Puerto Escondido aside, the line-up always seems to be dominated by points and reefs. Sandbanks are the equivalent of an unpredictable, slightly flaky partner on prom night. Never quite sure who's gonna turn up to the party: the perfect date of your life, the violent, screaming, adrenaline-charged seat-of-your-pants ride; or the whimpering, blubbering emotional wreck. Sometimes living with a stretch of sand can be a 'beach'… but in Durban, the odds have been redressed somewhat. A series of groynes and piers provide a degree of stability to the sand's usually shifty nature, and the Indian Ocean does the rest. Now where's that limo?

Aside from the waves, there are many things that make South Africa such a great surfing destination – the people, the countryside, the pure African experience. And Durban is the true surfing capital. It is home to the Gunston 500 – one of the world's longest running contests as well as a vibrant urban surf scene. Tight crews man each break along the wide curve of delineated and sectioned beach. From the north, Country Club, Battery Beach and Snake Park run through to the Bay of Plenty, North and Dairy beaches. The super-competitive New Pier, the Wedge and South Beach lead into the grommets' breeding ground of the south at Addington and the sleeping Vetchies Reef nestled in the lee of The Bluff. This concentrated stretch of east-facing coastline is home to some of the hottest surfing talent on the planet. "Durban has a wide variety and choice of beaches," says New Pier local and world-class junior, Jordy Smith. "This is because of its big bay that extends approximately 15 km from North Pier to Umhlanga Rocks. There are different breaks because of the location of piers that run off from the beach. This allows for numerous sandbanks to be formed causing both lefts and right-handers. Some can hold a big swell, which we have most of the year, as well as onshores and offshores, due to the protection from a headland called 'The Bluff'."

The geography and swells of Durban allow the classic grommet progression seen at spots like Steamer Lane in the US, where surfers advance from the smaller breaks, moving up the surfing ladder to the better spots and the tougher line-ups. It is a rites of passage followed by surfing legends such as Shaun Tomson and Martin Potter, as well as many of the current crop of top locals. "My dad, Graham surfed and

Left: Slipping through the green at New Pier.
Opposite page: Durban's pier pressure pays-off.

competed at these beaches before I was born and it was a natural thing to get me into the water as well," says Jordy. "He used to take me to Addington – which has a very small and flattish section with really small, surfable waves. I gradually progressed to my regular surfing spot, New Pier. I have competed in and won many an event here, the highlight being victory in the 2003 ISA World Junior Event in front of my home crowd."

In the winter, regular southerly and southeasterly swells roll out of the south Indian Ocean and are often accompanied by offshore southwesterly winds. The Bluff cuts out some of the southerly swell meaning that beachies such as Addington can be small when the northerly beaches are going off. However, during the November to April cyclone season, big, lined surf can hit this stretch, producing epic conditions for the whole of Durban. "After a cyclone, when a huge easterly swell rolls into the bay and the wind switches to a westerly offshore, you will find deep pits and long walls coming off the variety of piers," says Garth Robinson, "with New Pier and North Beach producing the best waves. Crowds are always thick and aggro attitudes can run high but the surfing is hot to trot. Sometimes the legendary Vetchies Pier (actually an underwater rockpile) will break

over a foot of water, reeling off fast, hollow rights." In good swells the banks will produce perfect tubes from 3 ft to 10 ft along the beach, the classic green water barrels spinning from out past the end of the piers. They can also throw up wackable lips just waiting for the latest new-skool manoeuvre. "The waves at New Pier can be really small," says Jordy, "but have quality and many little inside bowl sections, which run off the piers. It can also be huge and barrelling. But above all it's great fun!" What more could you want from a date?

Locals and Legends

Max Wetteland, Baron Stander, Graham Hynes, Ernie Tomson, Ant van den Heuvel, Shaun Tomson, Peter Daniels, Pierre Tostee, Martin Potter, Dan Redman, Travis Logie, Warwick (Wok) Wright, Ricky Basnett, Dave Weare. Also a good few juniors: Josh Redman, Brandon Jackson, Damien Farenfort, Chad du Toit, Rudy Palmboom, Jordy Smith.

Nearby breaks While the Bluff acts to cut out some of the swell from the Durban beaches, to the south there are more exposed spots such as **Anstey's** beach, an exposed left and right, and **Brighton Beach**, another popular spot that picks up heaps of swell. In between lies the legendary **Cave Rock**, a heavy, hollow break for experts only.

Surfers' tales
Mozambique: pitfalls and perfection Garth Robinson

GARTH ROBINSON

Since the civil war ended in 1992 surfers have been making exploratory forays into Mozambique in their quest for uncrowded waves. These journeys into the unknown are riddled with dangers making the stoke of discovering new spots all the more exciting and rewarding. After being warned by friends and family about all the various pitfalls I decided to go for it in 1994 and have since returned time and again to sample the country's exotic culture, friendly people and great, uncrowded waves. Some of those earlier warnings did indeed turn out to be true, but not to the extent that some old cynics had imagined. There are certain things about Mozambique that make journeys there somewhat dangerous. Here are some snippets from my misadventures, just to give you an idea of what a surf trip to this former Portuguese colony can entail.

Malaria
We hooked up with Mike after stumbling across the camp where he and his buddy were nestled in the lee of a great right point near Inhambane. Like us, they were travelling in an old beat-up VW Kombi. It was great to see other surfers after so many days of hard travelling; we shared our joints and tales of epic waves, and life was grand as we hung out and surfed the 4-ft rights rifling off the shelf and down an epic sandbar. After a week our time was just about up and we had to head back to South Africa. Mike needed a lift so he joined our crew in the back of the Kombi. On the way home we chanced upon a splitting right reef near a small fishing settlement and decided to camp out for a day to make the most of the dying swell. That night Mike started puking his lungs out and by morning he was as white as a sheet and running a high fever coupled with an extreme headache. What we did

not know was that, unlike ourselves, Mike had chosen not to take any malaria prophylactics. It was clear he had contracted the disease and needed to get to hospital or he was sure to die.

At this stage finding medical care locally was not an option and the nearest hospital was in Maputo, 500 km away. Anyone who has ever have seen the inside of a Mozambican hospital will tell you that the best option was for us to high-tail it back to South Africa. So began our nightmare journey to Empangeni Hospital, just over the Mozambican border. The Kombi's dual carburetors were being shaken off their mountings by the incredibly potholed roads. I had to stop every few hours just to keep the old girl running. Mike was part Native North American and was chanting between pukes into a bucket in the back. He looked terrible, pale with dark rings under his eyes, covered in sweat and shaking like a leaf and playing with a necklace made of bear claws. I truly thought he was going to die.

After two days of non-stop driving we finally made it to Empangeni. The Kombi was just about finished, as was the driver. The doctor told me if we had taken another day to get him to the hospital Mike would have been dead. We met up a few months later in Durban and although he was still rather pale and gaunt, he was on the mend. The *Surfers Journal* had run one of my photos from the trip showing Mike taking off on a perfect peak and he was stoked to see it, but the price he paid to find good waves almost cost him his life.

On later trips I have had to care for both close friends and total strangers who thought they would be fine not taking malaria prophylactics. To survive Mozambique you must cover up in the evenings, use insect repellent and take your anti-malarials so you can live to surf another day.

Sharks
In South Africa you often hear old fishermen say "Geez, Mozambique is so shark-infested, you won't catch me surfing out there!" I always thought they were full of bullshit until I started asking the locals about it. One old Bitonga guy told me how, as a teenager, he had been diving for crayfish off Tofo when his buddy got taken by a Zambezi shark right before his eyes. He never dived again. Another Portuguese lady told me a story of how she went flying over Inhambane with her pilot brother. As they passed over the entrance to the Barra estuary he pointed out the silhouettes of sharks in the current that flows out into the Indian Ocean.

She also remembered as a child before the civil war seeing helicopters taking shark attack victims from Xai-Xai to hospital in South Africa.

The clearest evidence of sharks I have ever encountered was while exploring what may be Mozambique's longest right point, Ponta Da Barra Falsa. We had surfed off the rock ledge that ran along the point, from where the small perfect rights ran onto a sandbar that extended over a kilometre down towards the mangrove estuary. This spot has a serious mysto sharky vibe about it and there is a deep channel you have to paddle over to reach the sandbar. The swell was waning so we decided to try down near the estuary. I was taking photos of a friend, Louis, who was unleashing his aerial attack on the tiny rights. A group of fishermen came along the beach with wooden planks on their heads, stacked high with what appeared to be meat from a large fish. As they neared us they gesticulated that we should not be surfing here. My grasp of the local dialect was pretty dodgy but then I noticed a large dorsal shark fin hanging over the one guy's head – the meat was actually from a large shark. They pointed down the beach to a series of poles that were placed at intervals all the way to the estuary mouth. We went for a closer look and realized the poles had massive Tiger shark jaws nailed to them to warn people not to swim here! Needless to say it was the end of our time surfing this particular point! Many surf spots in Mozambique are, in my mind, safe and relatively free of dangerous sharks. It is the breaks that are near rivermouths or estuaries that should be avoided. Never surf with cuts, don't piss in the water and try to sit with your feet up. Keep your eyes peeled and try to remember to try and keep your heart from thumping too loudly!

Landmines

One my first trip I stopped on the side of the EN1 national road for a call of nature. Without thinking I walked through some bush from where there was a great view of the Lebombo Mountains to the west. After the deed was done I suddenly realized I had broken a cardinal rule of travel in Mozambique: never wander from the road's edge. This country has one of the highest incidences of landmines in the world – especially alongside main roads and near bridges. I couldn't see my footsteps and gingerly treaded my way back to the car. If I hadn't already emptied my bowels I probably would have done through fear!

If you decide to visit this country you will notice how many locals have only got one leg. The prosthesis factories cannot keep up with the demand. Princess Diana even visited here to highlight the landmine problem. Nowadays most tourist areas have been cleared of mines, but due to the severe flooding mines may have shifted. Stay on the road or path, always ask the locals and keep an eye out for red flags indicating the presence of 'minas'.

And now for the good news...

After reading the above warnings about the dangers of surf travel in Mozambique you may decide this place is not for you. However, if you follow local advice and stick to a few general rules, this country is no different to any other third world surf destination. As the place recovers from its past and the infrastructure is rebuilt it will become a safer tourist destination. Fly-in options will limit the chances of accidents on the roads, anti-shark devices will make surfing, swimming and diving safer, and the ongoing landmine eradication programme will render the land safe again. The locals are friendly, the water warm and the tropical African culture and vibe is addictive. Once you visit Mozambique you will always return.

Garth Robinson is 38 years old, born and bred in Zululand, South Africa. He learnt to surf age 12 in Amanzimtoti, one of the world's shark attack capitals. Even seeing neighbour Breton Jones lose his leg in an attack hasn't kept him out of the water. He worked for Zigzag, *published his own mag* African Soul Surfer *and has contributed to* Tracks, Surf Europe, Surfer, Surf, Surfers Journal *and* Surfers Path. *He is presently an Art Director for Billabong in South Africa, and busy building a house at The Point in J-Bay with wife Yvonne and drinking way too much filter coffee.*

GARTH ROBINSON

Indian Ocean

Indo? Indon't? Indoes!

CORY SCOTT

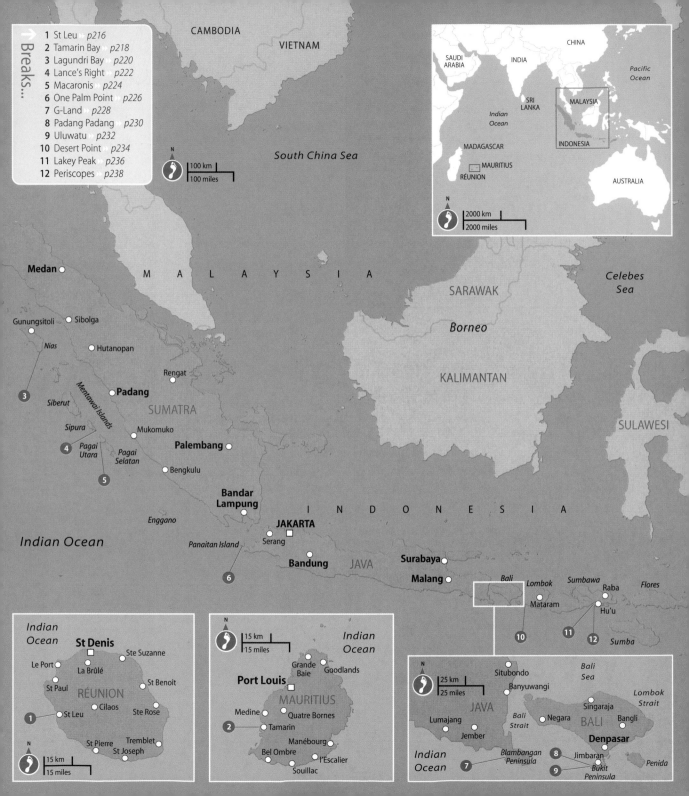

VIETNAM

100 km
100 miles

CHINA

SAUDI
ARABIA   INDIA

Pacific
Ocean

SRI
LANKA   MALAYSIA

Indian
Ocean   INDONESIA

MADAGASCAR

MAURITIUS

RÉUNION

AUSTRALIA

2000 km
2000 miles

Medan

MALAYSIA

SARAWAK

Celebes
Sea

Gunungsitoli   Sibolga

Nias   Hutanopan

Borneo

Rengat

3

Mentawai Islands

Padang

SUMATRA

KALIMANTAN

Siberut

SULAWESI

Sipura

Mukomuko

4   Pagai
    Utara   Palembang

Pagai
Selatan

5   Bengkulu

Bandar
Lampung

INDONESIA

Enggano

JAKARTA

Indian Ocean

Panaitan Island   Serang

Bandung   JAVA   Surabaya

6   Malang   Bali   Lombok   Sumbawa   Raba   Flores

Mataram   Hu'u

10   11   12   Sumba

Réunion inset:

Indian
Ocean

St Denis

Ste Suzanne

Le Port   La Brûlé

St Paul   St Benoît

RÉUNION

1   St Leu   Cilaos   Ste Rose

St Pierre   Tremblet

St Joseph

15 km
15 miles

Mauritius inset:

N

15 km
15 miles

Indian
Ocean

Grande
Baie   Goodlands

Port Louis

MAURITIUS

Medine

Quatre Bornes

2   Tamarin

Manébourg

Bel Ombre   l'Escalier

Souillac

Bali/Java inset:

N

25 km
25 miles

Bali
Sea

Situbondo

Banyuwangi

JAVA

Singaraja

Lumajang   Bali
           Strait   Negara   BALI   Bangli

Jember

Lombok
Strait

Denpasar

Indian
Ocean

Blambangan
Peninsula   8   Jimbaran

7

9   Bukit
    Peninsula   Penida

Grey clouds roll across the sky as you check the windblown line-up. The tide is too high, you can see this even through the rain-spattered window. No need to even turn off the engine, which rumbles away in the background. On to check the next spot; back on the road, more driving. Bright headlights flash across the windscreen causing you to squint. You open your eyes. The sun is streaming through the porthole, the thrum of the diesel engine seems to back off and the splash of the anchor hitting the water signals a new spot has been reached. Through the porthole the lefts of Macaronis are reeling towards the boat as it sits in the channel. It had all been a nightmare. No rushing between breaks in the cold and rain of home. During the night you've been delivered to yet another primo Mentawais spot. This is the new Indo dream. The best waves delivered to your doorstep complete with air-con, cool beers and satellite TV so you don't even miss the games back home. It's oh so different from how it all began.

Looking at the coastline of Indo on the map it looks custom-built for surfers. It sits at tropical latitudes to ensure that those pesky wetsuits can be left at home. The arcing curve of the coastline lines up perfectly to catch those endless swells that zero in from the southern reaches and the Roaring Forties. The fringes are peppered with islands, points and bays, allowing the constant swells to find a range of platforms on which to break, and the trade winds are favourable for the peak seasons. Add to this a rich culture and stunning scenery and there is no wonder that Indo has become probably the number one surfing destination for travelling surfers.

To the northwest, the breaks of Sri Lanka and the atolls of the Maldives see more visitors than ever arriving year on year to sample their less extreme offerings. Réunion and Mauritius are volcanic peaks sticking their heads above the surface of this pleasantly warm ocean. This is where reeling barrels fire along shallow points and reef passes, where sharks cruise the busy line-ups and the beautiful people sun themselves on the sand. The Indian Ocean offers some of the most luxurious surf camps and charter boat exploration on the planet, but it is still a region where you can push out, get back to basics and where unridden perfection could be waiting to be discovered just around the next bend in the coastline.

Surfing Indian Ocean

The Cape of Good Hope, at the southern tip of South Africa, was named by ancient sailors with a degree of irony that belied the fact that this was a place where huge South Atlantic storms often turned ships into matchsticks. However, once through these troubled and turbulent waters, the huge azure expanse of the Indian Ocean opened out, offering a whole world of trading possibilities. Silks from China, spices from Zanzibar, tea from Ceylon – the Indian Ocean was a veritable motorway of schooners, frigates and galleons, driving the fledgling wheels of international commerce. For many it was also the passage to a new life in the colonies of India, Australia or New Zealand.

Pros & cons

Indonesia

Pros

Dry season coincides with offshore trades and favourable localized winds for key spots.

Consistent swell catcher.

Away from camps and charters, the cost of living is very low.

Warm weather and water year round.

Awesome reef breaks.

The land of the left… as well as some world-class rights.

Still huge potential to explore quieter regions.

Culturally rich.

Cons

Pockets of political instability and outbreaks of terrorism.

Busy around most well-known surf breaks.

Recently hit by a spate of natural disasters.

Transport infrastructure is basic.

Malaria and dengue fever in some areas.

Pros & cons

Western Indian Ocean

Pros

Long optimum swell season.

Warm waters and great climate.

Home to some world-class reef breaks.

Beautiful, volcanic landscapes.

Cons

Réunion is pretty pricey.

Real shark threat.

Incidences of localism.

Limited number of breaks.

The mosquito-borne Chikungunya virus.

Opposite page: Still feeling indo-cisive about making the trip?

Surfing moved through these waters like a creeping vine, colonizing the fringes, jumping from spot to spot with amazing speed. Although the sport was first practiced at Kuta in the late 1930s, it was in the late sixties, according to legend, when whispers of quality waves in Bali first filtered back to Australia via a surfing flight-crew member. The early expeditions soon struck gold and with a beachhead established at Kuta, they immediately pushed south onto the Bukit Peninsula. Those pioneers enjoyed days filled by the empty waves of Uluwatu and nights of nasi goreng washed down with Bintang and Arak, the air heavy with the scent of kreteks (clove cigarettes). Others soon followed and the push was on to strike out to the islands of the east and the northwest. At the same time surfers had discovered the 'Forgotten Island' of Mauritius, off the coast of Madagascar. The long lefts of Tamarin Bay became the stuff of legend and a pincer movement saw surfers pushing up the western sides of the Indian Ocean, through Réunion, the Seychelles and the Maldives, while on the eastern fringe adventurers were already making inroads through Sumatra and into Sri Lanka. The spirit of adventure and exploration was a hard habit to kick and this region just seemed to offer more and more. Each glance at the map lured those pioneers a little further on down the road – which was probably little more than a rutted, potholed track (if they were lucky).

Contest surfing arrived with the OM Pro of 1980, the first professional event held in Indonesia, which took place on the hallowed waves of Uluwatu. Since Terry Fitzgerald lifted that title there have been other events including the Quiksilver G-land Pro, hailed as one of the greatest surf contests of all time. Though the event was short-lived, due to political instability in the region, it did help to reshape the contest venues and was a step on the road to establishing the 'dream tour' that we see today.

When it comes to homegrown world-class surfers, the Balinese enjoy a slight head start with the influx of international stars who regularly drop in on their waves – literally. Pioneers such as Ketut Menda can now see the likes of Made Kasim, Made Switra and Rizal Tandjung making an impact at world level. In Réunion the WQS regular Fred Robin has helped raise awareness of the excellent surf they have on offer and young Jeremy Florez has already become one of surfing's most promising prospects.

Today, Kuta is a bustling resort town where speeding 'bemos' race the tarmac streets and surf shops sell the latest surf gear. St Leu on Réunion is known around the world as a 'surfer's village' and hosts an annual international surf contest. The once unknown Mentawai Islands, off the coastline of Sumatra, now hum with charter boats and the sound of surf camps being hastily erected. But there is still a whole lot of coastline out there for those who like the chance to explore. "Despite the increasing number of boats and crowds at the well-known breaks, it's amazing how many new spots keep being 'discovered' each year," says Peter Neely, author of *Indo Surf & Lingo*. "There are still plenty of solo sessions out there, and they are definitely the best waves on the planet."

Position

The Indian Ocean is the third largest of the Earth's oceans, after the Pacific and the Atlantic. It covers an area five and a half times the size of the USA with 68.5 million sq km lying between the coast of Africa in the west, India to the north, Indonesia to the northeast and Australia to the east. Indonesia is by far the most populous of the countries featured here, with over 245 million inhabitants, while Mauritius has a population of 1.24 million and Réunion 787,000.

Culture

The Indian Ocean basin is a rich melting pot of cultures. This open mass of blue waters, with its complex blends of oceanic currents and trade winds, has been the trading corridor between continents for centuries. African, Arabian, Asian and European merchants have navigated these routes, each bringing precious cargos to trade and many settling on these distant shores, helping to add to the mix of diverse ethnic populations. Réunion offers a blend of French, African and Asian influences on a truly unique tropical island. The food, language and music are influenced by all aspects of the island's rich heritage. Food is spicy and the language is Creole, a fusion of French and other regional dialects.

As one of the largest archipelagos in the world, diversity is the name of the game in Indonesia's culturally rich society. While the majority of Indonesia embraces Islam, making it the most populous Muslim

nation in the world, the main religion on the island of Bali is Hindu. Indonesia is a smiling nation that prizes manners highly, so dressing respectfully is important, especially when visiting temples or villages off the beaten track. And while pointing is rude, eating or shaking hands with your left hand is seen as downright disgusting – this hand is for bathroom business only!

Climates and seasons

The equator runs through the centre of Sumatra, with the island of Nias in the northern hemisphere and the Mentawais in the southern. In this part of the world daylight lasts around 12 hours and Indonesia has a tropical monsoon climate meaning there are only two main seasons: April-September is the dry season; October-March the wet. However, heavy showers can still be frequent even in the dry season. During the dry season the predominantly southeasterly trade winds bring dry air off the Australian continent and favourable winds to the westerly facing breaks such as Uluwatu and G-Land. During the wet season, the predominantly west to northwesterly winds bring moist air off the Indian Ocean. During this period easterly facing breaks turn on. For a few weeks during the changeover months of April and October, the doldrum belt, or inter-tropical convergence, moving north or south across the islands, results in lighter, more variable winds. The Mentawai Islands are less affected by the trade winds but fall prey to more localized wind patterns.

Sumatra and its surrounding islands have high humidity year round and although temperatures vary little throughout the year, November tends to be one of the wettest months with average rainfall around 520 mm, while in May it drops to 315 mm. Further south, Bali tends to have more defined wet and dry seasons with January experiencing an average 345 mm of rainfall, while June gets only around 60 mm.

Réunion and Mauritius are both in the southern hemisphere and their wet season runs from November to April, while they both enjoy drier weather from May to October. During the wet season on Réunion, warm, moisture-saturated air blowing in from the east hits the high peaks of the island bringing heavy rains to the western side. December to March marks the cyclone season with disruptive and sometimes destructive weather patterns and associated high rainfall. In the cooler dry season, the air blowing in from the east is less loaded

Below: It's clear the reefs here mean business.
Opposite page: Cheyne Cottrel proving that Indo waves aren't just about barrels.

CORY SCOTT

◉ WAVEWATCH	Dec-Feb Summer	Mar-May Autumn	Jun-Aug Winter	Sep-Nov Spring
INDIAN OCEAN				
Wave size/direction	SW 2-4'	SW 3-5'	SSW 6-8'	SSW 6-8'
Wind force/direction	W F2	N F2	SE F2	E F2
Surfable days	10-15	15-20	20-25	20-25
Water/air temp	28/26°C	28/29°C	28/29°C	27/27°C

with moisture. Here the climate variation is more noticeable with highs of around 27°C in January coupled with high humidity levels and around 215 mm rainfall. July sees temperatures dropping back to around 21°C with moderate humidity and rainfall averaging 28 mm.

Wavewatch report by Vic DeJesus

The Indian Ocean provides some of the most consistent year-round surf on the planet. The primary source of quality swell in this ocean comes from intense low-pressure systems travelling eastward in the Roaring Forties. During the southern hemisphere winter months these storms reach maximum intensity, sending large southerly to southwesterly swells averaging well overhead for open areas. This also occurs during other months of the year, although swell sizes are typically smaller. This area attracts surfers primarily in the winter months as the northern Indian Ocean destinations see their most favourable conditions with generally drier weather and southeasterly winds. South Africa and southwestern Australia get impacted with some of the largest swell, but often deal with severe weather and unfavourable winds associated with these storms.

Geography and breaks

The geology of the main surf areas within the Indian Ocean region is volcanic by nature. The region is fringed by tectonic plates and upwellings of lava have formed the main landmasses of western Indonesia and the islands of Tamarin and Réunion. This process continues due to the region's many live volcanoes, but what nature gives, nature also takes away, as demonstrated by two of the biggest explosions ever witnessed – those of Krakatoa west of Java and Tambora in Sumbawa, which created a caldera more than 1100 m deep.

The predominant breaks in this region are therefore lava-based coral reefs and points. The southwesterly facing islands of Indonesia face straight into the predominant swell, so local geography is critical in wave formation. Breaks like Uluwatu, G-Land and Desert Point are long, tapering point breaks made up of a lava base with coral angled perfectly for these swells to peel, producing long, reeling waves. Some of the breaks in the Mentawai Islands, such as Lances Right, rely on swells wrapping around the southern end of the island and onto the reef which sits on the far side. Compared with the number of reefs, there are few beach breaks. Many beaches are fringed by outer reefs that can cut out most of the swell.

Health and safety

Indonesia has suffered periods of political instability and has been subjected to spasmodic acts of terrorism, most notoriously with the Bali bombing of 2002 which saw the Sari Club in Kuta, a spot popular with surfers, razed to the ground and hundreds killed. In 2005, a second bout of suicide bombings again targeted Kuta and a neighbouring village, this time leaving nearly 40 dead. This has to be

JS CALLAHAN/TROPICALPIX

put in context, however, as the terrorist threat is present in many countries around the world. Due to the volcanic nature of its geography, Indonesia has suffered a number of natural disasters: earthquakes, eruptions, rainy season flooding and, most devastatingly, the tsunami of Boxing Day 2004. Other more common problems include the threat from pickpockets as well as the nerve-wracking and sometimes dangerous roads.

The general level of health care in Indo is basic and prevention is always better than cure. Try to avoid being bitten by mosquitoes which, depending on season and location, could be delivering a dose of dengue fever, malaria or even Japanese B encephalitis. Make sure you cover up, use a decent repellent that includes DEET and talk to your GP or clinic before you start your trip about which course of prophylactics to take. The Mentawais, Lombok, east and western Java as well as Sumbawa are all 'at-risk' areas for malaria. The water throughout the region is not safe to drink or even clean your teeth with, so ensure you have a good supply of bottled water. This also extends to avoiding ice in your drinks and peeling fruit and veg before you eat it. If you do succumb to 'Bali Belly' the best thing to do is rest, stay out of the sun and keep fluid levels up to avoid dehydration. If you have diarrhoea for more than three days, pass blood or are in any doubt, seek immediate medical attention.

Aside from the stonefish in Mauritius, the sharks patrolling the Indian Ocean include some of the deadliest species on the planet. One great white was recently recorded leaving South African waters and migrating all the way to Western Australia. Réunion has a particularly bad reputation, with attacks averaging about one per year on the island. Mauritius and Réunion are also badly affected by malaria and dengue fever and have also suffered a recent outbreak of the debilitating Chikungunya virus, which in rare cases can be fatal.

Throughout the Indian Ocean, reefs – some armed with urchins – often lurk close to the surface so packing reef boots and a helmet can be a good health policy. Some surfers at the shallowest reefs even wear full wetsuits for added protection. Ensure all jabs are up to date including Hep A, Typhoid, Tetanus and Polio. For up-to-date health alerts check out the World Health Organization, www.who.int, or www.fitfortravel.co.uk.

Surfing and the environment

The Indonesian archipelago consists of an estimated 17,000 islands stretching over 5000 km from east to west. Some parts remain relatively undiscovered while others have undergone an industrial and tourism boom in the past 30 years, with all the associated waste and water treatment issues. However, this hasn't always translated into environmental awareness and an expansion of sewage treatment facilities. It is not uncommon, in certain areas, to see refuse and sewage in the sea. This puts the coral reefs that fringe the islands under threat as well as putting the health of residents and visitors at risk. Various organizations and projects have been set up in an effort to help tackle these problems. Some aim to help improve water quality through educational and practical projects at both a national and local level whereas others are fighting to improve the environment as a whole. Surfaid (www.surfaidinternational.org) is a non-profit humanitarian aid organization whose aim is to improve the health and well-being of people living in isolated regions such as the Mentawai Islands. This is achieved through direct healthcare programmes and associated environmental action. Surfaid also work with local partners including Yayasan Pantai Peduli Saroke (YPPS) (the Saroke Beach Care Club), an NGO established to clean up and 're-green' Nias following the 2005 earthquake that devastated the region.

Commenting on the recent spate of blows dealt to Indonesia in terms of natural disasters and terrorism, Peter Neely says, "Visiting surfers won't notice any difference in the surf, just fewer tourists on the streets. The beaches near Aceh city in North Sumatra have seen a slow increase in surfers enjoying uncrowded perfection lately, now that the infrastructure has been rebuilt, plus quite a few aid workers are learning to surf. But the west coast is still off the list for the foreseeable future. The earthquake actually improved the wave at Lagundri, it breaks more often, is longer and hollower, but the Nias locals are still suffering from the effects of the earthquakes, so anything visiting surfers can do to help the locals rebuild their lives is particularly appreciated and encouraged."

WILLY URIBE

STEF FOURNET

The Indo regular says, "All over Indonesia times have never been tougher for the locals. More unemployment. More poverty. Higher fuel and food prices. And thanks to misguided terrorists there are fewer tourists. I tell my friends that there's never been a better time to extend our generosity, to tip an extra dollar in cafés or to taxi drivers, or even help sponsor a family."

Surfing resources

In Indonesia, surf culture is expanding. *Magic Wave* (www.magic wave.tv) is a free monthly surf community newspaper in Indonesian, Japanese and English that covers local surf news and interviews as well as travel essentials. You can pick up a copy in Internet cafés and bars in the main surfing hubs of Bali and Java as well as some of the other islands. There is also *Surf Time* (www.surf-time.com), a magazine which mixes local surf and skate news with features. *Indo Surf & Lingo* (www.indosurf.com.au) by Peter Neely is a great tool for the travelling surfer as it combines regularly updated break information, travel essentials and images with a crucial section on language. "Without the lingo you're seen as just another rich tourist," explains Peter. "But with the lingo you're seen as a respectful traveller immersing yourself into their culture and attempting to truly understand the locals' lives." As well as the global surf resources *Wavewatch* and *Surfline*, good local swell prediction resources for Indonesia include www.balisurfreports.com and www.balisurfcams.com.

> ❝❞
> Despite the increasing number of boats and crowds at the well-known breaks, it's amazing how many new spots keep being 'discovered' each year... There are still plenty of solo sessions out there, and they are definitely the best waves on the planet.
>
> Peter Neely, author of *Indo Surf & Lingo*

JS CALLAHAN/TROPICALPIX

Top: The tiny volcanic island of Rodrigues lies off the east coast of Mauritius and is a great place to recapture that 'Morning of the Earth' feeling.
Right: Sunset at Uluwatu's iconic temple.
Opposite page: If this was your home break you'd have been styling as a kid too.

Surfers' tales
SurfAid International

Have you ever felt the desire to give something back and make a difference? As surfer's we are often drawn to this train of thought. Through surf travel and exploration we come across so many different worlds and varieties of life, and as a result, realise what a gift it is to have our health and to enjoy the deep stoke one can find through a great surf session with friends. Humanity starts with that appreciation for what we have and a desire to help and inspire those less fortunate.

In 1999 on a surf trip to the Mentawai islands, Dr. Dave Jenkins discovered indigenous communities suffering and dying from the ravages of malaria and other preventable diseases. Plagued by the discrepancy in lifestyle from his semi-luxury life aboard a private chartered yacht, and the dead and dying only meters away, he dedicated himself to helping the Mentawai people and formed SurfAid International, as surfing's humanitarian vehicle.

The mission of SurfAid International, a non-profit organisation, is to improve the health of the people living in isolated regions connected to us through surfing.

The areas serviced by SurfAid have one of the highest child mortality rates in the world. Staggering statistics show that in the worst affected villages, one quarter of the children will not live past the age of twelve. The problem is wide spread in these remote communities; people are dying from treatable and preventable diseases, despite the fact that solutions to stop them – bed nets, modern medicine, spraying, and simple education – are both known and affordable. Due to isolation,

extreme poverty, and a serious lack of basic healthcare resources, Malaria, Measles, Tuberculosis, Cholera, Dengue Fever, Dysentery, Diarrhoea and Malnutrition are needlessly taking lives. SurfAid's answer was to establish the Malaria Control Programme and the Childhood Health Project on the islands off western Sumatra, specifically located in villages on the Mentawai island chain, the Hinakos and Nias.

Malaria is rampant in the Mentawai. With a population of over 73,000 there is a sustainable base for the malaria parasite to survive. Statistics show that half of all families will lose at least one child. However, there is hope. In SurfAid's two Malaria Control Project pilot villages, initial testing showed an active malaria parasite within thirty-four per cent of the population. After four years of participation with SurfAid's programmes – further testing has shown positive cases of malaria have dropped by ninety per cent.

Using a model based in the Community Development Philosophy, SurfAid's focus is to drive effective partnerships that create a lasting change. A band-aid solution is not good enough. Community development provides an outside impetus for empowerment, enabling communities to solve serious issues by working together. For development to be successful, it has to be sustainable, and community led. By helping people help themselves, SurfAid is ensuring the programme evolves into a lasting legacy. The SurfAid International key programme criteria demands proven impacts that are cost-effective, sustainable and have strong ability to be replicated.

In December of 2004 a massive earthquake in the Indian Ocean generated a tsunami that devasted parts of the region. Due to the geographical layout of the islands, the Mentawai chain was miraculously spared. However, the loss of life to the north in both the Aceh province and the island of Nias were insurmountable. In March of 2005, just three months after the initial tsunami disaster, a magnitude 8.7 earthquake hit Nias killing another 839 people and leveling 13,000 homes.

SurfAid International responded to both these disasters switching into emergency relief mode for more than seven months. SurfAid's knowledge of the region, its people and local agencies as well as relationships with local boat captains became of great value. SurfAid dispatched emergency medical personnel to the Western Islands of Sumatra, including Nias, Simeulue, the Banyaks and the Tellos Islands, all devastated regions within SurfAid's scope of reach. The medical teams set up emergency triage and treatment centers to cope with the sick and wounded as well as mobile vaccination, nutrition and malaria control clinics. After the Nias quake they evacuated by sea and air more than 63 critically injured people. Many lives were saved as a result of this huge effort. In addition, a much feared second wave of disaster, the outbreaks of disease including measles, malaria and dysentery, was averted.

SurfAid vessels also carried vital supplies to these fatally-hit communities. This multi-pronged response was underscored by the rapid actions and regional knowledge of local surf operators and boat captains who helped SurfAid take its mission where it was needed most. As a consequence of the disaster, local roads and bridges became impassable. The use of boats and a helicopter provided to SurfAid by donor NZAID saved many lives that would otherwise have been lost. Early on in SurfAid's relief effort, the teams were also joined by the international health NGO Helen Keller International (HKI) who provided nutritional supplements to those showing signs of malnutrition and anemia while surveying women and children to check their overall health.

UN's head of emergency field office, Morgan Morris had this to say:

"SurfAid was a valuable source of information because of their previous work in the area even before the Tsunami, and it was this information that proved invaluable to the search and rescue operations by being able to help identify landing sites for the helicopters and sites where beach craft could be used. I think it is no exaggeration to say that the SurfAid teams saved many lives that could have been lost with out their prompt action. SurfAid will be remembered and respected by the people of these islands and the many UN and NGO agencies who worked with them, for many years to come."

With the support of government agencies, AusAid, NZAid and The Mentawai Health Department as well as partnering with other NGO's lives are being saved and great change is being put into motion.

Consistent scientific evidence points to another major earthquake occurring in the Mentawai region, most likely within the next five years. It is not a matter of if, but when. Based on studies of previous earthquakes, a Tsunami is still very much a possibility. In the Mentawai's many coastal villages are extremely vulnerable due to isolation and poverty. Preparedness for self-reliant survival is the top priority.

SurfAid's numbers as of August 2005

- Over 157,500 reached
- Over 16,700 children immunized between the ages of 6 months and 12 years of age
- Over 2,900 people treated for emergency medical conditions; 65 people evacuated
- 22,904 impregnated mosquito nets distributed
- 325 tons of food and emergency aid distributed
- Over 10,000 disinfectant soaps distributed
- Over 15,000 vitamin A and micronutrients given to children

Two years ago the global surf community heard our call to action and stepped up to support SurfAid's programmes. Individuals and surf companies from all over the world gave generous donations, helped promote the need, volunteered and lent their brand to give notice to the cause. This support has allowed SurfAid to expand Malaria Control from its beginnings in two villages to more than seventy, and has also allowed SurfAid to expand the Core Health project from one disease and one village to six diseases and fifty three villages.

With the support of the surf industry, the Australian and New Zealand governments, SurfAid has made great progress in the battle to fight disease and increase healthcare & education in the region but the need is still great. SurfAid's current goal is to expand this success throughout more villages and to develop and implement a community disaster preparedness program for the region. We need your support more than ever.

"The need is great…we can stop very preventable diseases from stealing children's lives" - Kelly Slater 7x world champion.

SurfAid hopes that we can look forward to your compassion and support. You can find ways to help by visiting us on our web site. Helping can be expressed in the way of donations, volunteering, individual or group fundraising with your friends and peers. Everyone has a part to play and anyone can contribute. SurfAid International is one of many great causes, but one in which we are united by our common interest, surfing. The problems are great but a solution is possible with your help. You can make a difference, join SurfAid today. www.surfaidinternational.org.

St Leu

Location:	Western coast, Réunion Island
Break type:	Left-hand reef break
Conditions:	All swells
Size:	3-10 ft
Length:	50-100 m
Tide:	All tides
Swell direction:	Southwesterly
Wind:	Southeasterly
Bottom:	Coral reef
Ability level:	Advanced
Best months:	Apr-Oct
Access:	Easy paddle
Hazards:	Crowds, reef, urchins, sharks

THIERRY ORGANOFF

Above: Jake Patterson taking the high line.
Opposite page: St Leu.

"What else does the island have to offer?" Fred Robin ponders for a second, his blonde hair almost white in the midday sun. "Well, the food is amazing. Inside the island it is beautiful – we have some mountains and a volcano. There is the forest and the beach is also amazing." Fred tries to put into a few short sentences the whole complex mix of factors that go into making this island such an exquisite surfing destination. It is one of those rare outposts still under colonial rule. The island was a major asset to France as it lay on the main trade route for ships sailing between Europe and the east. That is until the Suez Canal opened, in 1869. The French still have it and they don't like giving things back.

Off the east coast of Madagascar, Réunion is a truly volcanic island. Part of the Mascarene Archipelago, which also includes neighbouring Mauritius and Rodrigues, these islands were created millions of years ago by a hot-spot volcano. Réunion rises from deep water to a height of 3069 m and has a live volcanic peak, Piton de la Fournaise, which still belches into life at regular intervals. The landscape is angular and fractured, but smothered with lush rainforest. The island has a mere 125 miles of coastline, most of which is pretty unsurfed due to access problems and prevailing wind directions blowing out the entire eastern seaboard. The prime surfing region lies between St Gilles and St Pierre on the western side, where the southeasterlies are offshore and the geology produces some excellent reef formations. The prime spot on the island has to be the fishing village of St Leu. "St Leu is a long left, it's a reef and you can ride for more than 20 seconds on the wave," says local pro surfer Fred Robin. "You can have good tubes on

the inside. It can be 3 ft when you take off on the outside, then on the inside section it can be double the size. Also the wave is not straight, it turns like a bowl. It's amazing to surf there."

St Leu lies on the central west coast of the island. The predominant southwesterly swells hit the outside of the reef and wrap a full 90 degrees, offering fast, walling waves with the opportunity for some barrel sections. During the cooler, drier winter surf season, this is a consistent wave. It may break at 6 ft for more than half the days in any month. But after a flat spell, the crowds will be frothing for a wave, and the tension levels can rise in the water. "There can be maybe 40 people out on a busy day," says Fred, "especially when there is not a lot of swell and everybody is waiting for something – then the locals are stressed and it is busy. But in the winter you can surf St Leu every day. When there is a lot of swell, you can go out after a week, and some days you might surf by yourself. You just have to be relaxed."

There are some visitors to the line-up who are pretty numerous, but a lot less visible and a lot less desirable. The shark risk on Réunion should not be totally dismissed. Currently the number of attacks is averaging about one a year, but these tend not to be fatal. Advice, as always, is to avoid surfing at dawn and dusk, and at cloudy rivermouth breaks.

The classic waves of St Leu have also been a firm favourite and regular contest site for the ASP World Tour. "We always consider the break of St Leu as one of the prime venues in the world," says WCT Tour

Manager Renato Hickel. "In the opinions of many – the judging panel, surfers and media – it is a wave of top quality. On top of that, Réunion is one of the most exotic places in the world. It is a dream location." The island has also produced a young surfer that many consider one of the hottest new talents on the tour – Jeremy Florez. With a tropical climate, consistent world-class waves to surf, and new role models to follow, the future looks bright for the raft of young surfers currently filling the St Leu line-up. "There are some hot surfers there now," says Fred. "You just keep an eye open and you'll soon see."

Locals and legends
Fred Robin, WQS ripper Jeremy Florez, David Grainville, Christophe Allary, groms Damien Chaudoy and Adrien Toyon.

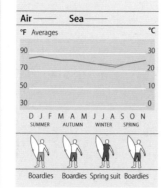

St Leu Board	
6'2" Rawson Hyper Skate	
Shaper: Pat Rawson	
6'2" x 18¼" x 2¼"	
Designed for all around surf in the 2' to 8'+ range.	
Fast and drivey through turns and cutbacks with enough stability to hold in the steep hollow sections.	
Futures FTP1 fins.	
ⓘ Boards by Surftech www.surftech.com info@surftech.com	

Air ——	Sea ——	
°F Averages		°C
90		30
70		20
50		10
30		0

D J F	M A M	J J A	S O N
SUMMER	AUTUMN	WINTER	SPRING
Boardies	Boardies	Spring suit	Boardies

Nearby breaks The west coast has a number of reef breaks that work in southwesterly swells. To the north of St Leu try **Trois Bassins** on small swells as there are a number of spots which pick up heaps of swells. **L'Hermitage Pass** is a reef pass, which has a right and left that are pretty consistent but are best with little wind.

Tamarin Bay

Location:	Tamarin, west coast, Mauritius
Break type:	Left-hand reef break
Conditions:	Medium to big swells
Size:	3-10 ft +
Length:	50-200 m
Tide:	All tides
Swell direction:	Southwesterly
Wind:	Southeasterly to easterly
Bottom:	Coral rock reef
Ability level:	Advanced
Best months:	Apr-Oct
Access:	From bay
Hazards:	Busy, shallow, sharks

The Forgotten Island of Santosha was pure uncut discovery. When Larry Yates' iconic film and associated *Surfer Magazine* article were pumped into the swollen vein of mid-seventies surfing culture, they went straight to the core of the surfing psyche. It was exotic, it was mystical and it was out there somewhere. The unnamed, barrelling left was seen in all its reeling, 8-ft glory, filling the dreams of those already hyped on the new strain of Indian Ocean glass suddenly filtering out of the tropics. Magazines and films fuelled the demand and the surfing airwaves fizzed with the spreading word of mouth. The search for Santosha was on. This 'migration' would lead to the discovery of many new classic surf breaks, many new Santoshas. Surfing spread through the equatorial regions of the Indian Ocean like an unstoppable weather front, ever rolling onwards. The original 'Forgotten Island' and the original wave, Tamarin Bay, were soon uncovered and over the years rumours of dark clouds have filtered out. But what of Santosha today and the waves that did so much to inspire so many? While spots like Nias, G-Land and Ulu's have retained their place as the grand dames of surfing's golden age, and the Mentawais have taken over as the most recent hunting ground, Mauritius seems to have slipped off the surfing radar. It seems *The Forgotten Island of Santosha* turned out to be a pretty prophetic title. Here is a wave that has fuelled so many imaginations and yet has remained so quiet for so long.

The Mauritius of today is a popular tourist destination with white, sandy beaches backed by luxurious hotels. Honeymooning couples walk the beaches at sunset, hand in hand, while holidaying pensioners knock back the cocktails under their all-inclusive beach umbrellas. Resting in the tropics just to the northeast of Réunion, this reef-fringed island is a melting pot of cultures. The Spice Route brought traders from many nations and the island has been under Spanish, French and Portuguese rule over the centuries. Today, it has a harmonious mixture of religions and ethnic groups, as well as a rich and interesting history and culture mixed with enough sun, sea and sand to attract the resort developers. Nowadays, though, the 'blissed-out' vibe is more likely to refer to one of the spas or retreats rather than any remnants of the flower power generation that made its way here looking for nirvana.

This left-hand reef is a world-class spot. As swell lines bend into the bay, they begin to peel along the shallow coral reef that fringes its southern side. The wave walls and grinds along a reef that is pretty much precision perfect, offering both fast vertical sectors, followed by racing barrel sections. The almond-shaped tubes are at their most critical at low tide, when the reef is at its most shallow, but on higher tides the coral is more forgiving. Take the drop, bury the rail and pump out onto the face and T-Bay will reward you with a racing charge through the pristine waters to a safe inside pull-out and gentle paddle back out to the peak. Although Mauritius lies in the path of the swells that roll out of the southern reaches of the Indian Ocean, the band of storms known as the Roaring Forties, the bay itself sits about a third of

Below: Santosha revisited.
Opposite page: Long perfect lefts bend into Tamarin Bay, barely registering as a blip on the surfing radar.

STEF FOURNET

STEF FOURNET

Tamarin Board

6'0" Rusty Piranha

Shaper: Rusty Preisendorfer

6'0" x 20.1" x 2.18"

This hybrid fish catches and attacks a ton of different waves!

The 3-winged, pulled in swallow tail allows you to surf vertically.

Ideal for waves knee to head high.

Futures fins.

ⓘ Boards by **Surftech**
www.surftech.com info@surftech.com

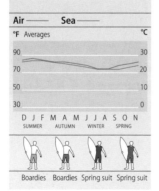

Air ——	Sea ——
°F Averages	°C
90	30
70	20
50	10
30	0

D J F M A M J J A S O N
SUMMER AUTUMN WINTER SPRING

Boardies Boardies Spring suit Spring suit

If you mentioned Tamarin Bay 10 years ago, the first thing that would probably have sprung to mind would be the White Shorts, a group of local, mostly ex-pat, surfers who established a reputation for fierce localism which became part of the wave's folklore. The truth is that, today, with the increase in travel by all surfers, with Mauritians visiting abroad and with over 30 years of visiting surfers at T-Bay, the traveller who surfs respectfully should have no trouble. In an age when surfing is scouring the globe for the 'next big thing', the waves of Santosha seem to have slipped from our memories. It seems that the original 'Forgotten Island' seems to be living up to its name.

Locals and legends

Larry Yates, Joey Cabell, Rick Ely, island champion Stellio Bauda 'Toyo', Cederic Holl, Roger Thevenau, Ricardo Naidoo, Bradley Britter.

the way up the western side of the island with an almost northwesterly orientation. These southwesterly swells must bend into Tamarin Bay before hitting the reef. For this to happen the swell needs to be in the medium to big range, meaning that Tamarin Bay probably breaks, on average, about 10 times per month during the peak season. This combination of a fickle nature, world-class quality and growing local surfing community has led to an unfortunate slide into localism. Suddenly there was trouble in paradise.

Nearby breaks Black Rock is a right-hander on the opposite side of Tamarin Bay. If there is no swell at T-Bay, travel south to Le Morne and check out **One Eyes**, a reef break that has long hollow lefts breaking down the side of a pass. On the other side sits a hollow right-hander. Boat access is required for both.

Lagundri Bay

Location:	Lagundri Bay, Nias, West Sumatra
Break type:	Right reef break
Conditions:	All swells
Size:	3-8 ft +
Length:	25-100 m
Tide:	All tides
Swell direction:	Southerly to southwesterly
Wind:	Light northerlies
Bottom:	Coral reef
Ability level:	Intermediate to advanced
Best months:	May-Oct
Access:	Through the Keyhole
Hazards:	Reef, board breakages, malaria

Nias: an island, a wave and an indelible image. Just the word alone conjures up visions of emerald green barrels reeling along a shallow reef while surfers lounge in hammocks on the upper decks of losmen, the wooden shacks on stilts that line the Sorake seashore. This is one of the world's truly great right-handers, in an archipelago dominated by world-class lefts. From day one 'The Point' at Lagundri Bay, on Nias, was a bit special. The story of its discovery has it all. The spirit of adventure that defined an era: reaching out into the unknown and the joy of discovery ultimately tinged with tragedy. Back in 1975 Nias was a

Below: Lagundri Bay overview.
Opposite page: Another legendary Nias right.

little-known island dozing off the western coast of Sumatra. No surfers had ever set foot on this lush, green oasis. Indo pioneer, Peter Troy, was already an experienced explorer by this point having navigated his way through Ulu's, G-Land and onwards. While travelling the coastline of Sumatra with his girlfriend, his attention was drawn to the island of Nias. At the same time, two young Aussies, 21-year-old Kevin Lovett and 23-year-old John Giesel, were boarding the same ferry. Troy spotted their surfboards and arranged to spend a few days exploring the island with them. On the third day they stumbled across a perfect 6 to 8-ft right reef break in an area known as Lagundri Bay. Little did they realize they had discovered one of the top waves on the planet. During the next few days they enjoyed some of the most perfect surf of their lives before Troy left to continue his journey. Giesel and Lovett however stayed on The Point, building a makeshift camp.

The guys enjoyed epic surf and mingled with the astonished local villagers for six weeks. Unfortunately the area was infested with malaria-carrying mosquitoes and before long both had succumbed to the disease. While they headed off to seek medical attention the jungle moved back in to reclaim their camp. The trip to Nias ended tragically for Giesel who continued on to Iran where he died of a bout of pneumonia brought on by the malaria. Within a year, Lovett was drawn back to The Point and word of this mystical right soon began to leak out. By 1979 Nias was establishing a reputation for both legendary waves and a high risk of disease. Aussie surfers have been renting losmen on the beach ever since and the village has expanded on the back of this surfing influx. Not even the hardcore nature of the Nias experience has put surfers off the trail of this epic, barrelling

PAUL KENNEDY

Lagundri Bay Board
6'8" Brewer Backdoor
Shaper: Dick Brewer

6'8" x 18" x 2¼"

Brewer designed this board with Hawaiian Myles Padaca for big gapping barrels.

Single to double concave for rail to rail, down the line speed and stability in the tube.

Futures fins.

ⓘ Boards by Surftech
www.surftech.com   info@surftech.com

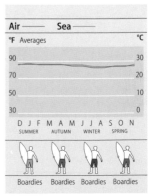

Air —— Sea	
°F Averages	**°C**
90	30
70	20
50	10
30	0

D J F M A M J J A S O N
SUMMER   AUTUMN   WINTER   SPRING

Boardies   Boardies   Boardies   Boardies

Indian Ocean Lagundri Bay

right-hander. Looking at pictures of the palm-fringed, green barrels casting huge rainbows of spray, it's easy to feel yourself been drawn in by the mesmerizing, hollow waves.

The U-shaped bay sits on the southwestern tip of the island. A steady stream of swells come out of the southern reaches of the Indian Ocean, heading north past the Mentawais and into Lagundri Bay. The fabled right-hand reef, known as The Point, sits to the west of the bay and is formed by a shallow lava platform. The waves peak and throw out a long, hollow right-hander that will barrel along giving deep-throated tube rides to the brave. This is not a wave for the faint-hearted – the drops can be vertical and the lip punishing. In a land endowed with world-class lefts, Lagundri Bay is one of the few epic rights and, as such, draws a hungry crowd. The line-up can be busy and the peak a hassle. But the emerald, ruler-topped waves are of such a calibre that many people pitch up on The Point and soon a short trip extends into a longer stay.

Lagundri Bay was largely spared the horrors of the 2004 Boxing Day tsunami but a few months later, on 28 March, a massive earthquake rocked Nias. Over 600 people died and more than 2000 were injured as shockwaves registering 8.7 on the Richter Scale destroyed buildings across the island. Houses around the Sorake Beach area of Lagundri were not spared and the fabled reef bore witness to the sheer power of the forces involved in the upheaval. The platform that the waves break on now sits a couple of feet shallower than before the quake, ironically making the wave even better than it was before. The quake also helped galvanize surfers from around the world into providing aid and support for both the short-term and long-term restructuring of the area. Within weeks, surfers were back on the upper decks of the rebuilt losmen and back in the reformed line-up, helping to make sure that the enduring image of Lagundri Bay was not one of disaster but one of hope and a brighter future.

Locals and legends

Kevin Lovett, Peter Troy, John Giesel plus Kornelius Zagoto, Pilipus Zagoto and Magdalena Wau of the Saroke Beach Care Foundation whose aim is to help improve and clean up the Saroke Beach Area.

Nearby breaks Inside the bay was a wave called **Kiddieland** that worked in small swells and was utilized by local beginners. Since the earthquake, smaller swells now break on The Point producing a smaller version of the pre-earthquake waves. This is good for the majority of surfers but not so good for the beginners of Kiddieland.

Lance's Right

◈ **Location:**	Sipura, Mentawais, West Sumatra
◐ **Break type:**	Right-hand reef
◑ **Conditions:**	Small to medium swells
◉ **Size:**	3-8 ft
◍ **Length:**	50-100 m
◔ **Tide:**	Mid to high
◎ **Swell direction:**	Westerly through to southerly
◑ **Wind:**	Light northwesterlies
◒ **Bottom:**	Lava coral reef
◉ **Ability level:**	Intermediate to advanced
◍ **Best months:**	Apr-Nov
◔ **Access:**	Boat only (or crazy feral)
◉ **Hazards:**	Shallow, malaria

When the Mentawais first hit the headlines, Lance's Right seemed to be the ultimate regular footer's dream wave. We'd seen Ulu's, G-Land and a whole host of other left points come out of the woodwork – or jungle – but here was a wave that seemed to sum up what surf travel was all about. Images of flawless, reeling, head-high barrels peeling ruler-perfect and crystalline in warm tropical waters just made you want to be the silhouetted figure casually tucked into the backlit tube ride of a lifetime. It was almost clinically perfect. It wasn't an intense, Sunset-style, do-or-die meatgrinder; it looked like a wave you could surf. What's more, this perfect wave wasn't discovered by the charter boats that were scouring the coastline looking for perfect waves – it was found by some guy called Lance. Heck, it could have been you. If, that is, you'd have trekked halfway round the world, taken dodgy, leaky boat rides to malaria-infested jungle locations, hundreds of miles from the nearest medical help. But still, in that daydreaming corner of your mind, it could have been you. *Indies Trader* skipper Martin Daly was there from day one. Well, day two actually. "Lance's Right was originally named after Lance Knight who was the first person to surf it in 1991. Ironically, a few friends and I pulled up the very next day and surfed it with Lance in small, offshore, afternoon surf. It was this discovery that fulfilled my lifelong mission to discover a right-hander that was better than Lagundri Bay in Nias."

Lance's Right sits in a sheltered position on the southern tip of the island of Sipura off the coast of Sumatra. Southwesterly swells wrap around the point and into the bay where the easterly facing reef awaits. The bottom here is a coral covered lava slab that slopes gradually into the sea, but its orientation makes it ideal for the light sea breezes that blow through the island chain. The wave has three take-off zones, the most infamous being 'The Office'. The drop here leads into a straight, reeling, barrelling right that is respected by the world's best and can be punishing when the swell tops 6 ft – one of those instances when a day at the office can lead to a nasty beating and a few stitches. It may look gracefully smooth and simple in the videos, but it is shallower and heavier than it appears. "Lance's Right is a fast, perfect, barrelling right-hander," explains Martin Daley, "and 'The Office' serves up the heaviest, scariest, roundest, most mesmerizing barrels in the world."

These days, the Mentawais really are the domain of the charter boat – for ease of access there's really no better way. Along with Macaronis, Lance's has become *the* surfing ace in the Mentawais pack. It draws the boats and the crowds with its sheer quality, beauty and consistency. It is a shoo-in when it comes to Indo's top waves. "Without a doubt, it's the best (make-able) right-hand barrel in Indo," says Dion Ahern. "Justifiably well documented in the surfing media, Lance's is the yardstick of any Mentawais trip. Although fairly short, it's absolute perfection from start to finish." Despite the fact that it has been splashed across magazines and starred in videos for over a decade now, its peeling precision hasn't lost any of its power to inspire. "Lance's has become a photo studio due to the golden afternoon light and throwing barrels," says *Surfline* editor Marcus

JASON CHILDS

Right: A little bit of Sipura magic.
Opposite page: An early session payback for South Africa's Sean Holmes.

JS CALLAHAN/TROPICALPIX

Lance's Right Board

6'1" Byrne Tom Carroll

Shaper: Phil Byrne

6'1" x 18⅜" x 2⅛"

Designed with 2-time world champion Tom Carroll, this highly responsive round pin works well in just about any surf from small to large.

FCS fins.

ⓘ Boards by **Surftech**
www.surftech.com info@surftech.com

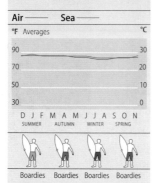

the threatening menace of the skulking shallow reef waiting below for mere mortals to make a mistake. But the wave has also developed a duality in the sense that it has also acquired two names. In the mid-nineties the wave also became known as 'HTs' or 'Hollow Trees' after the shell of a long dead tree rooted out on the reef. The tree is now long gone, but the name Lance's Right has a powerful ability to invoke something still deeply rooted in the surfing psyche. It is a symbol of discovery and surfing adventure. It proves that it is still possible, even in the 21st century, for one person to strike out on that mission to find the perfect wave.

Locals and legends

Lance Knight and every young and old pro who's boarded a boat for the Mentawais.

Sanders. "But it's still one of the best waves in the Mentawai chain. Super-fast, reasonably dangerous but fun as all hell." Hawaiian legend Buzzy Kerbox agrees, "It's the perfect hollow right."

Lance's has the duality of image versus reality. The smooth magazine persona of the world's elite tucked into pure glass versus the reality of

Nearby breaks To the west is the more exposed **Lance's Left**, a rippable left which offers something for everyone with walls and barrels up to 10 ft. **Telescopes** – a fun left without the serious side effects of some of the other more critical waves – is at the northern end of the island. Hop on board your boat and sail south to the next island and **Macaronis** (see page 224), considered by many to be the most complete left on the planet.

Macaronis

⚓ **Location:**	Pagai Utara, Mentawais, West Sumatra
◐ **Break type:**	Left-hand reef break
🌊 **Conditions:**	Small to medium swells
🌐 **Size:**	3-6 ft
⦿ **Length:**	25-100 m
🌊 **Tide:**	Mid
🌀 **Swell direction:**	Westerly to southwesterly
🌬 **Wind:**	Light easterlies
⬚ **Bottom:**	Reef
◉ **Ability level:**	Intermediate
✹ **Best months:**	Mar-Sep
⊙ **Access:**	Boat access only
⊖ **Hazards:**	Crowded, heavy when over 6 ft

The tall, grey, naked tree stands alone in the shallows – watching. It has seen little change here over the past few decades. The occasional fishing boat coming close enough to fringe the reef, but the islands that lie off the western coast of Sumatra have traditionally been a paragon of peace and isolation. The cylindrical waves that wrap and peel into the lagoon have done so for centuries, just as the sun has shone and the sumatras (or storms) have rolled across the islands whipping up the ocean into a confused melee of whitecaps. Today, the sun-bleached beacon looks down on a flotilla of anchored boats, sitting just to the north of the point, their dinghies ferrying surfers to and from the busy line-up. When the Mentawais were pioneered back in the early 1990s, no one would have believed just how quickly this wave would go from being an unnamed picture of perfection in the surf magazines to a must-do surf spot on everyone's round-the-world ticket.

Just ask anyone who's been lucky enough to surf there and you'll get a fairly unanimous answer as to why this wave is so popular. "Macaronis in the Mentawais is possibly the most shreddable wave on the planet. The perfect lip for airs and big hacks and it's there every section, every wave, every minute," says Chris Cote, editor of *Transworld Surf*. Marcus Sanders of *Surfline* agrees. "This is a wave that makes you feel like you surf better than you do. Easy tubes, a lip that begs to be smacked and perfect, full speed carve sections. Everyone else knows it too, though." It has become the destination of 'young guns', 'old guns', 'hired guns' and everyone in between. Captain Martin Daly pioneered the islands of the Mentawais in his groundbreaking boat the *Indies Trader*. 'Macaronis' was first surfed in the 1980s by Australian campers. It was named by my good mate Danny Madre in 1990 during his travels through the islands."

Jumping off the dinghy into the channel the water is warm and clear. Paddling up to the take-off spot you'll see that the first section of the wave is shallow and hollow but that it is not a difficult section to make. Once you exit the barrel it's a machine-like wall that reels along the reef, never sectioning, never closing out, never slowing down. "This wave is the funnest, most mechanical left-hander imaginable," says Dion Ahern. "The sometimes throaty barrel section is followed by a top-to-bottom, beautifully shaped wall of joy. Macca's is responsible for pushing the limits of high performance backhand surfing throughout the nineties and early 2000s." Sitting on the western side of the island of Pagai Utara, Macca's is open to all the long travelled southwesterly swells produced thousands of miles away in the turbulence of the Roaring Forties. By the time they have travelled through the vast Indian Ocean, they are clean, long period groundswells, perfectly suited for this wrapping section of reef. Between the months of April and November, the swells arrive at regular intervals and the winds are at their most favourable. This is prime time for Macaronis, and the boats are on it.

The two adjectives that crop up time and time again when describing the waves at Macca's is 'machine-like' and 'rippable.' While many waves

JS CALLAHAN/TROPICAPIX

Left: Travis Logie showing how lip-smackingly fun this spot can be.
Opposite page: This is the view from your floating apartment, if you can bear it.

in the Mentawais have the words 'shallow' and 'dangerous' attached to them, Macaronis seems to be the place that surfers come away from having had fun. It's not a wave to surf big, it's ideal at 3-6 ft. Any bigger than that and the lip becomes thick and the wave less amiable. "It's like a dream," says French ripper Patrick Bevan. "I woke up in the morning at five am and looked out of the window and I was like 'Wow'. I surfed for five hours and then back to the boat and I was eating and I tried to go

back out but I was just too tired. Perfect, too perfect. Like a machine. Macaronis is really fun." This wave seems to sum up the Mentawais dream. Find the perfect wave, surf it with your friends 'til your arms can paddle no more. Then enjoy a cool beverage, watch the sun set and sleep with your dreams filled with those endless Macca's walls.

Locals and legends
Danny Madre named the break but everyone is a legend here.

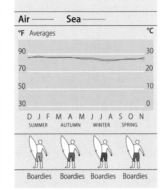

Macaronis Board			
6'1" Stretch Fletcher 4			
Shaper: Stretch			
6'1" x 19.125" x 2.5"			
Designed with world-class aerialist Nathan Fletcher.			
Full nose and tail which straightens out mid-section inducing speed.			
Four fin makes it ride like a tri-fin with more drive and acceleration.			
Ultra responsive and fast!			
FCS GX/M5 fins.			
ⓘ Boards by Surftech www.surftech.com info@surftech.com			

Air ———	Sea ———	
°F Averages		°C
90		30
70		20
50		10
30		0

D J F	M A M	J J A	S O N
SUMMER	AUTUMN	WINTER	SPRING
Boardies	Boardies	Boardies	Boardies

Nearby breaks Heading north to the next island of Sipura, the first wave is the more exposed walls of **Lance's Left**, a very good spot that can hold swells up to 10 ft but is overshadowed by its right-handed sibling, **Lance's Right**. Along with Macca's, this is one of the Mentawais keynote waves. One that has adorned walls around the globe. **Telescopes** is another quality long, hollow left-hand reef that can be up there with the best waves in Indo on its day. To the south lies **Thunders**, a consistent and popular left, despite its shiftiness.

One Palm Point

- ◈ **Location:** Panaitan Island, Ujung Kulon National Park, West Java
- ◉ **Break type:** Left-hand point break
- ◒ **Conditions:** All swells
- ◉ **Size:** 3-8 ft
- ◉ **Length:** 50-200 m
- ◉ **Tide:** All tides
- ◉ **Swell direction:** Southwesterly to southerly
- ◉ **Wind:** Easterly
- ◉ **Bottom:** Coral lava reef
- ◉ **Ability level:** Expert
- ◉ **Best months:** Apr-Sep
- ◉ **Access:** Boat
- ◉ **Hazards:** Super shallow

One Palm Point Board

6'3" Channel Islands K-Model

Shaper: Al Merrick

6'3" x 18⅝" x 2²/₁₆"

Single to slight double concave for lots of drive and lift with extra nose rocker for steep take-offs and under the lip snaps!

FCS K2.1 fins.

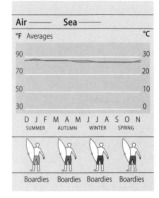

ⓘ Boards by Surftech
www.surftech.com info@surftech.com

Air ⸺	Sea ⸺	
°F Averages		°C
90		30
70		20
50		10
30		0

D J F	M A M	J J A	S O N
SUMMER	AUTUMN	WINTER	SPRING
Boardies	Boardies	Boardies	Boardies

Below: Panaitan perfection.
Opposite page: One guy out at One Palm Point.

JASON CHILDS

The eruption could be heard as far away as Australia. It caused spectacular sunsets across the globe that lasted for years after. When the inspirational expressionist Edvard Munch captured on canvas the vivid, blood-red hues of a fiery Oslo sky as the backdrop to his haunting figure in 'The Scream', he was painting the bigger picture. Light refracting through the dust that originated in a huge explosion just off the western coastline of Java caused panic-stricken New Yorkers to think that an immense fire was burning just beyond the horizon. The eruption of the island of Krakatoa was a classic lesson of how local events can have a global impact. On the afternoon of 26 August 1883, the smouldering conical shape of Krakatau (as it is known locally) was literally vaporized as a great volcanic explosion ripped the heart out of the island. The blast sent a huge tsunami sweeping across the west coast of Java and the eastern seaboard of Sumatra and 36,000 people lost their lives. Today, a new island – Anak Krakatua – is growing out of the waters and this child of Krakatoa is becoming an adolescent with a fiery temper. Just to the south, in the Sunda Strait, the horseshoe-shaped tropical paradise of Panaitan Island is home to one of the last outposts of virgin Javanese rainforest and one of the world's most hotly contested waves – One Palm Point.

The uninhabited Panaitan Island is part of the Ujung Kulon National Park, one of only two World Heritage Sites in Indonesia. The park extends onto the peninsula that makes up the southwestern tip of the mainland and is home to the few remaining Javanese rhino on the planet, as well as many other rare and endangered species of plants and animals. The south coast of the island is a large, crescent-shaped bay that points directly into the Indian Ocean and is home to a series of world-class breaks. Inside the bay's eastern rim sits a coral point along which perfect, machine-like barrels peel with mesmerizing regularity. One Palm Point, named after a single tree that watches, like a sentinel, over the point, has become the epitome of isolated surfing perfection. It is a classic Indo point set-up. Coral covered lava reef angled perfectly to catch the swells from the southern Indian Ocean. The forest fringes the narrow stretch of beach and creates a stunning backdrop. So far One Palm Point has managed to avoid the super crowding that other spots are beginning to suffer from. But there is a good reason for this. Ask Peter Neely, author of *Indo Surf & Lingo*, about the best waves in Indonesia and he'll say "One Palm Point has to be separated into a class of its own. It's such a deadly shallow reef that you couldn't recommend anyone but the most experienced surfers give it a try." At 4-6 ft, One Palm reels off the most inviting-looking barrels, the aquamarine blue tubes wide open and round. What the view from the boat doesn't tell you is that the reef is very shallow and brutal in its punishment of any mistakes made here. "Full rubber and helmets are necessary," says Peter Neely, "but you'll probably still get cut somewhere. But you might get the best 14-second tube ride of your life, before you get sliced on the reef."

Traditionally, the only way to reach this epic set-up was by charter or to buy a permit to visit the national park, and then pay one of the local boat owners to take you. This has recently changed and is threatening the very survival of the fragile habitat of Panaitan Island itself. The aim of a World Heritage Site is the preservation of the ecosystem for the benefit of everyone on the planet. But there have always been those nibbling away at the fringes of this reserve. The National Parks Authority claims that poaching and illegal fishing is taking place and that in the past surfers have illegally camped on the island. During the off season of 2004-05, the whole situation altered when a developer erected a surf camp on the island, clearing large areas of forest and building a jetty so that boats from the mainland could dock. The critical uproar caused by these actions focused the world spotlight on the impact of the camp. Many doubt that a development to house up to 38 surfers, fired by four booming generators and with waste disposal issues, will do anything to enhance this once uninhabited paradise. On top of this, problems have arisen over the subject of access to the waves. The camp claims on its website that it has exclusive access to the waves on Panaitan Island, which raises the possibility that surfers from outside the camp will be turned away.

However, there is more at stake here than simply access issues. It is more about the bigger picture. Could a once pristine uninhabited island, with its own unique wildlife and fragile ecosystem, be irreparably damaged, with the global consequence that yet another species is quietly extinguished from the face of the earth?

Locals and legends
The Javanese rhino.

Nearby breaks The bay on the southern side of Panaitan is open to several classic wave set-ups. There is a fast, hollow right called **Apocalypse**, another experts'-only shallow reef that produces some long, driving barrels. Inside the eastern side of the bay is another classic left reef called **Napalms**, a less intense option with hollow sections.

JASON CHILDS

Indian Ocean One Palm Point

G-Land

🜂 **Location:** G-Land, Java	
🜁 **Break type:** Left-hand reef	
🜄 **Conditions:** All swells	
🜃 **Size:** 3-15 ft	
🜅 **Length:** 50-200 m	
🜆 **Tide:** All tides	
🜇 **Swell direction:** Southwesterly, southerly, southeasterly	
🜈 **Wind:** Southeasterly	
🜉 **Bottom:** Sharp, coral crusted, lava reef	
🜊 **Ability level:** Advanced	
🜋 **Best months:** May-Oct	
🜌 **Access:** Walk then paddle over the reef	
🜍 **Hazards:** Shallow reef, heavy waves, long hold-downs	

Looking down from 200 ft up, past the lush greenness clinging to the rock face over a newly discovered piece of paradise. Late afternoon. Sun-baked, salted skin. A new swell is already wrapping into the Bukit Peninsula and bending around the cliff base. Long, empty lefts unravel along the reef, the line of which is easy to make out through the crystalline waters below. This really is nirvana.

But not for everyone. Surveying this still fresh view of Ulu's, American Bob Laverty feels a sense of rising panic. It's 1972 and he knows the clock's ticking, that word is out and the hordes will soon follow. He

looks to the horizon and a memory is recalled: a view from an aeroplane window onto an as-yet undiscovered piece of paradise, 20,000 ft below – pure potential screaming along an almighty arcing reef at the edge of dense jungle. Jolted by the recollection, he knows this is the time to strike out. He is a man with a plan. Armed with maps, mopeds and a mate – Aussie surfer Bill Boyum – he will set off for Java and an exploration into the unknown.

Charts are checked, boards and provisions are strapped on, roads are driven, waterways are crossed, officials are negotiated and dense jungle is trekked through at nightfall. But this is a journey where effort equals reward. Eyes adjusting to the morning light, Boyum and Laverty awake to the vision of cavernous G-Land pits reeling along a seemingly endless point. Now this is something special.

On the southeastern tip of Java, the quasi-mythical G-Land is hidden away on the edge of the Plengkung National Forest, with its roaming tigers. Pointing south, its back turned on neighbouring Bali, swell lines wrap around the western edge of the Blambangan Peninsula and as they near the wide mouth of Grajagan Bay, a huge, arcing reef transforms the lines into a mile-long racetrack of powerful, hollow lefts and some of the most consistent waves in Indonesia. From May to October the southeasterly trade winds blow offshore every day, kicking in after a civilized breakfast. If Uluwatu is enjoying 2-3 ft, it will be a cranking 4-5 ft here. The platform upon which these pitching barrels break is a classic Indonesian, coral-encrusted lava reef – not something you want to get too familiar with. "I was there when Derek Ho injured himself at G-Land," says former world champion, Lisa Andersen. "I took a little glance at his injury and spooked myself. I didn't go surfing for at least two days. I hit the reef there one year. I was really lucky I had a helmet on."

Below: Kelly Slater – tucking into a cup of Java.
Opposite page: G-whizz Land.

G-Land Board

6'10" Wayne Lynch Free Flight

Shaper: Wayne Lynch

6'10" x 18½" x 2½"

Solid semi-gun for the long deep tubes of G-Land.

Single to double concave for racing down the line, with extra nose and tail rocker to handle the steep elevator drops.

FCS G7 fins.

ⓘ Boards by Surftech
www.surftech.com info@surftech.com

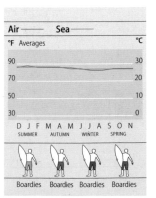

Air ——— Sea ———	
°F Averages	°C
90	30
70	20
50	10
30	0
D J F M A M J J A S O N	
SUMMER AUTUMN WINTER SPRING	
Boardies Boardies Boardies Boardies	

The long, curving point appears to produce an unending wave, continuous and machine-like. "It is actually a consistent freight-training left-hand barrel with multiple sections and multiple personalities," explains NZ surfer Dion Ahern. Each is punctuated by a close-out section and a handy rip. Reaching the line-up means choosing your section and picking carefully over the reef before an extremely well-timed paddle- out. The outside point is Kong's. A more rippable and forgiving wave, it is best ridden on small days when the fun walls may also throw up the occasional nice barrel. This section is the most exposed so picks up the most swell and is rarely flat. Inside Kong's is Moneytrees, one of the most popular sections with long, hollow, almond-shaped barrels and the kind of fantasy waves that draw surfers from around the globe. It can be fairly gnarly at low tide but does offer 200-m of dream tubes that are best at 6-8 ft but can be bigger. After a close-out section, a take-off at the appropriately named Launching Pads leads into Speedies or Speed Reef. Working best in bigger swells at high tide, this can throw up long, fast, gaping tubes that thunder along a 200-m racetrack finish. It is extremely challenging but can result in a 20-second barrel of a lifetime. As American WCT surfer Pat O'Connell explains, "It can be the longest tube ride of your life, or the longest hold down of your life!"

Despite the fact that Java is one of the world's most crowded islands, G-Land remains fairly isolated and as such an idyllic surf spot. The only visitors are those staying in the surf camps – Bobby's Camp or Jungle Surf Camp – and have come to surf. Capacity is about 150 and there is no other accommodation. Although there has been some modernization, it still feels like an adventure. "Every surfer should visit G-Land at least once in their lives," says Hawaiian legend Gerry Lopez. "It is more than a wave – it is a true surfing experience." One of Lopez's G-Land companions in 1973 was Sultan of Speed, Terry Fitzgerald. "In actual fact I had been there a week already with some Rip Curl guys, but we had been cleaned out by Maduran pirates who took clothes, food and water. We were on our way back when we ran into Gerry's boat going over. I jumped ship for the simple fact that our trip, although good, was not epic and with the tides better the next swell was looking awesome. Needless to say it was – long, clean and mean – and without leg ropes! That swell was so awesome, I've never felt the need to go back!" Some waves and some surf trips will leave you wanting more – more adventure, more fun, more cover ups, more isolation. But this is G-Land, this is something special. For most, this is enough.

Locals and legends

Bob Laverty, Bill Boyum, Gerry Lopez, Peter McCabe, Tom Carroll, Rizal Tandjung, Made Kasim, Ketut Menda.

Nearby breaks If G-Land is massive, the appropriately named **Chickens** can provide fun lefts on the inside near the boat channel. **20/20's** is another left 30 minutes' walk north. Other waves are a bit more of a trek including **Tiger Tracks** and **Grajagan Rights** but to be honest, if you've come to this peninsula, you've come to surf G-Land.

Indian Ocean G-Land

JASON CHILDS

Padang Padang

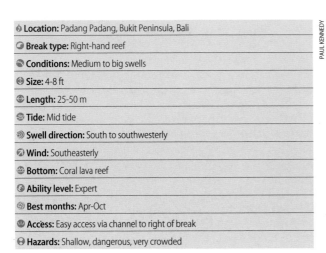

🜂 **Location:**	Padang Padang, Bukit Peninsula, Bali
🜂 **Break type:**	Right-hand reef
🜂 **Conditions:**	Medium to big swells
🜂 **Size:**	4-8 ft
🜂 **Length:**	25-50 m
🜂 **Tide:**	Mid tide
🜂 **Swell direction:**	South to southwesterly
🜂 **Wind:**	Southeasterly
🜂 **Bottom:**	Coral lava reef
🜂 **Ability level:**	Expert
🜂 **Best months:**	Apr-Oct
🜂 **Access:**	Easy access via channel to right of break
🜂 **Hazards:**	Shallow, dangerous, very crowded

PAUL KENNEDY

It's a classic view, looking south from Bingin through Impossibles and along the Bukit Peninsula. Lines seem to march north at an inexorable rate, whitewater framing the base of the vertical cliffs and backlit barrels spinning ever onward. The occasional cluster of huge boulders the size of houses show where the ocean has claimed a slight victory in its timeless battle against the landmass of the Indonesian archipelago, born of fire and eroded by the sea. Padang Padang sits just out from a deep channel, the waves pinwheeling around the shallow reef in a huge arc. A local fisherman sits perched on one of the rocks, watching the line-up, mesmerized.

Waves along the Bukit will always hark back to the seventies and a golden era in surfing. Names like Padang, Uluwatu, Bingin and the evocative Dreamland all stimulate dormant images of that relaxed tube stance, shoulders slightly hunched, single fin pin-tails hooked in the curl. Like a kind of surfing 'muscle memory'. But although Padang Padang is a classic, it's no 'old skool' cruiser's wave; it is still cutting edge. It was originally christened the 'Bali Pipeline' and not much has happened to change that. The tube-riding seen at this shallow, dredging left-hand barrel is still world class as it feels and reels its way along the big slab reef that waits just under the boiling surface, ready for the slightest mistake. Locals brought up on the Padang waves can transfer those skills to any wave on the planet. Rizal Tandjung, raised on a diet of the tube-riding of Indo pioneers such as Gerry Lopez and Peter McCabe, made the finals of the trials for the 2002 Pipeline Masters in Hawaii, beating many of the North Shore's top Pipe chargers.

As the traditional, life-affirming bemo ride comes to an end, the view opens up to take in the fickle lefts of Impossibles reeling away to the north, and the classic Padang Padang set-up just to the south across the channel. It is so simple to access the line-up, the relaxed, dry-hair paddle-out giving no indication of the hair-raising experience that is to follow. The approaching lines hit the edge of the reef, ledging up into an oval barrel on take-off and proceed to thunder around the edge of the reef platform, water draining away off the sharp, highly visible coral. Surfers take a high line in the tube as they race the plunging lip, the wave wrapping and racing almost 90° into the channel. These are the most sought after barrels on the island and

Padang Padang Board
6'1" Minami M-1
Shaper: Glen Minami
6'10" x 18⅜" x 2⅜"
For the tubular perfection of Padang, you'll need the 6'10" Minami to drive you through the mindless barrels.
Extra rocker and a tight round pintail.
FCS fins.

ⓘ Boards by Surftech
www.surftech.com info@surftech.com

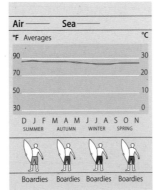

Air —— **Sea** ——

°F Averages   °C

90			30
70			20
50			10
30			0

D J F   M A M   J J A   S O N
SUMMER   AUTUMN   WINTER   SPRING

Boardies   Boardies   Boardies   Boardies

Above: Bukits of barrels are on offer here.
Opposite page: Keeping watch at Padang.

there is a heavy crew all over the small take-off zone (hesitant surfers need not apply). As one charger drops into the barrel, the rest are scattering to get into position for the next wave. Drop-ins are both dangerous and not uncommon as the whole zone takes on an almost gladiatorial feel. A trip over the reef here is something to be avoided. Padang Padang used to be ridden on a mid tide but today it is ridden whenever it breaks, through the full range. As this is one of the most fickle of the Bukit waves, every last barrel is picked over.

"I remember my first trip to Bali, paddling out at Padang Padang," says Shane, an Aussie traveller, sitting in the afternoon sun overlooking the break. "Just being in the line-up was amazing. There was so much going on. I was looking up at the cliffs, there were surfers paddling in every direction and these beautiful barrels were just screaming through one after the other. There were guys getting burnt, shouting,

broken boards – it was chaos, like being back on Legian Street." Indo guide author Peter Neely rates it as one of the island's primo spots. "Padang Padang is a totally awesome wave, but it needs a mega swell to turn on, and these days get ultra crowded." While it is still possible to score those quiet, uncrowded sessions that reflect the days when Bali was still the 'Morning of the Earth', today the bustle and crowds and the speed and beauty of Padang offer a more modern take on the Bali experience. Climb on board and take a ride.

Locals and legends

Gerry Lopez, Peter McCabe, Jim Banks, Made Kasim, Ketut Menda, Rizal Tandjung, Made 'Bol' Adi Putra, Pepen Hendrix, Wayan 'Betet' Merle.

Nearby breaks Just to the north of Padang Padang sits the left-hand reef break of **Impossibles**, a sectioning reef with fast walls that on the right swell can offer up three distinct peaks, but can often end in nasty close-out sections. Next is **Bingin**, another left that is again subject to swell and tide but at shoulder high will throw up some tasty barrels. It gets busy. The wonderfully named **Dreamland** is a peak that has a short right and a longer left that breaks in deep water so is best surfed at low tide. Southeast trade winds are offshore for all these breaks.

Desert Point

⟐ **Location:**	Desert Point, Lombok
◔ **Break type:**	Left-hand point break
◓ **Conditions:**	Big swells
◉ **Size:**	3-8 ft +
⟐ **Length:**	50-200 m +
◒ **Tide:**	Low to mid tide
◈ **Swell direction:**	Southerly to southwesterly
◐ **Wind:**	Southeasterly
◉ **Bottom:**	Coral lava reef
◉ **Ability level:**	Advanced
◉ **Best months:**	May-Oct
⟐ **Access:**	Easy by boat, walk south round point if by foot
⊖ **Hazards:**	Tough conditions, malaria, shallow reef, rips

Desert Point is a true feral endurance test. No satellite television here; no air-con or hot tubs. This is a test for the best. A balancing act of pain versus pleasure, with the added risk of malaria. The hot, dry and dusty days blend into a mind-bending flat spell as this fickle wave refuses to show. Just getting here is tough, via the overland road that bounces out fillings on the final leg into Bangko-Bangko. Then during the night the sounds begin. The percussion of the wave changing from the high register notes to the low frequency bass of an arriving swell. At first light the whole crew is ready. Time for the payback. Time

Below: Hawaiian shaper Gerald D'Sena.
Opposite page: It's days like these that make it all worthwhile.

for some magic. Out in the line-up bob the luxury yachts with their cold beers and surf DVDs. It doesn't matter. There is a reason why this torture has been endured, and that reason is unfolding, peeling relentlessly in front of everyone's wide eyes. Desert Point has awoken.

The Lombok Strait that separates Bali from Lombok is more than just an 18-km stretch of treacherous waters. The deep channel dividing the islands marks the Wallace Line – a delineation noted by 19-century naturalist Sir Alfred Wallace between the two geological regions and biomes of Asia and Australasia. This biogeographical fault line cuts straight through the heart of the Indonesian archipelago. While Bali to the west is lush, green and tropical, Lombok has brown hues in evidence and is a more arid environment and experience. And while Bali has seen the rush of tourists and the over-development of Kuta, Lombok has remained further off the beaten track.

There are differences in the surf spots too. The fabled point at Bangko-Bangko has been described as everything from frustrating to fickle or 'whimsical'. The wave sits on the southwestern corner of Lombok and while the southwestern breaks of Bali, like Uluwatu, are consistent swellcatchers, Desert Point needs just the right swell to angle up the strait and to be of just the right size to bend along the point. It is a more exact science. But then this is a place where the oceans practice their alchemy. Here the Lombok Strait acts as a channel to transfer the warm, low salinity waters of the Pacific into the western reaches of the Indian Ocean; constantly regulating and balancing. Tide is another critical factor here. At high tide the wave can be shy and elusive but as the tide drops back it will build into

PAUL KENNEDY

Desert Point Board
6'4" Webber Afterburner
Shaper: Greg Webber

6'4" x 19⅛" x 2⅜"

Semi-fish, enough width and thickness to increase glide without surfing flat like a standard fish.

Slightly lower rocker gives drive of a high-performance shortboard.

More range than any standard fish.

FCS fins.

ⓘ Boards by Surftech
www.surftech.com info@surftech.com

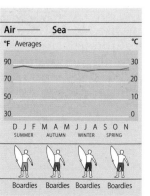

Air ———		Sea ———	
°F Averages			°C
90			30
70			20
50			10
30			0

D J F M A M J J A S O N
SUMMER AUTUMN WINTER SPRING

Boardies Boardies Boardies Boardies

the longest barrel in the whole of this wave-rich archipelago. The wave hits the top of the point and peaks, the left reeling off, getting bigger as it winds down the point, arcing and wrapping in as it speeds down the reef.

Those who have caught Deserts in all its glory will never forget it. "One of my favourite waves has to be Desert Point in Indo," says Damien Hobgood. "It's just so fast and so long." NZ surfer Dion Ahern agrees: "Deserts is seemingly endless perfection. Deserts is a fickle wave that requires precisely the right direction swell and wind conditions for it to fire. When it does, a left-hand barrel grows and throws the more it speeds down the reef. When Deserts is 6 ft and smoking, it's arguably the best wave in the world."

For some people, Deserts is a once-in-a-lifetime pilgrimage; a chance to ride the fabled point to see what all the fuss is about. For others, it becomes a draw that's hard to resist, calling them back time and time again. In a land where there are many more consistent waves, many less crowded waves, and many more waves where the going is easier, Bangko-Bangko just keeps calling them coming back for more. And the thing they come back for is the pure essence of surfing – the wave. In 2001, *Tracks* magazine voted

Desert Point the best wave on the planet: period. Ahead of G-Land, Cloudbreak and Kirra. That's a mighty big call, and one that makes most surfers sit up and wonder what all the fuss is about. "One of my favourite waves would be Deserts in Indo," says Joel Fitzgerald. "Never been, but keeping the dream alive!"

Locals and legends
Hard-core spot mostly manned by travelling Aussies.

Nearby breaks To the north of Desert Point sits a high tide left called **Safari** that is even more fickle than Deserts. It needs a huge swell to roll up the Lombok Strait. On the southern coastline of Lombok lie many breaks, with Kuta (not the Bali Kuta) providing a good base camp.

CORY SCOTT

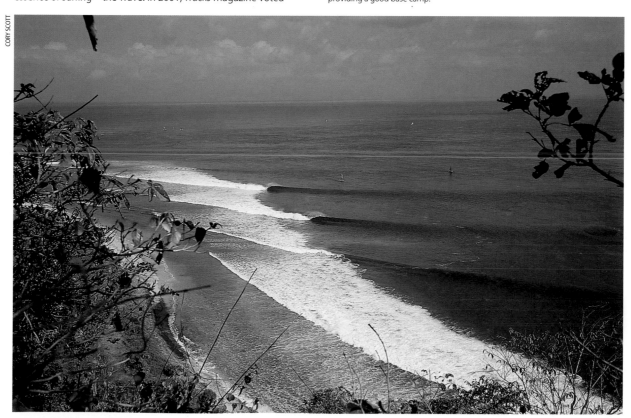

Lakey Peak

- **Location:** Lakey Peak, Hu'u area, Sumbawa
- **Break type:** A-frame peak
- **Conditions:** Small to medium swells
- **Size:** 4-6 ft
- **Length:** 25-75 m
- **Tide:** Mid tide
- **Swell direction:** Southwesterly
- **Wind:** Light northeasterly to southeasterly
- **Bottom:** Flat reef
- **Ability level:** Intermediate to advanced
- **Best months:** Mar-Oct
- **Access:** Long paddle or boat
- **Hazards:** Heavy when bigger, shallow at low tide, crowds

It serves as a useful way of lining up with the peak. Like an old woman paddling in the sea, lifting her skirt to avoid the lapping waters of the lagoon, the judging tower stands there looking down on the wave with a mixture of weathered confusion and worldly contentment. She's saying 'I don't really know what I'm doing here but it's not really a bad place to be'. From the crystal-clear, deep-blue line-up it seems to sail slowly across the surface as you drift in the light current. Lakey offers that wonderful and tantalizing choice that few waves in Indo can match. Paddle slightly to the south and take the right, or stroke slightly north and hook into one of the lefts. Both waves have their own personalities, their own foibles. Each is a world-class option. It is this opportunity, this choice, that brings surfers to the Hu'u area of Sumbawa and to the A-frame that is Lakey Peak.

Right: Troy Hirst goes deep cover at Lakey.
Opposite page: A-frame delights.

CORY SCOTT

As a surf spot, this is as flexible as it gets. Lakey promises a little something for everyone. The peak offers classic rights and lefts, and just off to the south there are the heavier ledges of Lakey Pipe, a wedgier cousin that offers some hollow, thick-lipped lefts when the swell kicks in. To the right there is the long, left-hand point at Nungas, a flexible reeling wave that offers up walls and cover-ups depending on tide and swell. Lakey has accommodation to suit all pockets. Gone are the days of the stark contrast between the basic camp and the relatively palatial Monalisa. Today there's a range of places to stay and a range of surfers who occupy them. And the reputation of the wave certainly packs in the punters. During the peak season at 'the Peak' there can be jostling crowds swarming over the morning glass. But this is also one of the most consistent spots in the country, so there are usually plenty of waves to go round. Unlike the more fickle spots such as Desert Point, there's no need to gorge on barrels before the next wave famine here. It's also possible to catch the place when it's less busy in the early and late season, and the surf can still be classic.

Light, early morning offshores are the order of the day as southwesterly swells roll into the bay. The wave peaks on the triangular, flat reef, which lies a couple of hundred metres offshore in the fringes of the Teluk Cempi inlet. The peak throws out and reels to the right and left, glassy blue walls spinning away. The optimum size is in the 4 to 6-ft range when the left will offer a winding wall with a couple of round barrel sections as it speeds towards the channel. For those who charge there's the chance to backdoor the peak and pull into the hollow right that makes up for its shorter rides with wide open barrels. Once the swell gets into the 6 to 8-ft range, the wave becomes a different proposition – a much gnarlier and heavier beast which will punish mistakes with a board-snapping ferocity.

The wave is situated in the central southern coast of Sumbawa, a dry, arid island lying to the east of Lombok, and just getting to it can be a mission in itself. The cheaper route is the ferry from Bali to Lombok and overland to the eastern port town of Labuhan. From here it's another ferry over the Selat Alas straits to Poto Tano on Sumbawa, followed by (yes, you've guessed it) more overland – about seven hours – to Hu'u. But really, if you're on a two-week break from your nine-to-five, you don't have to do that to yourself. The easiest choice is a flight from Denpasar in Bali to Bima on the northeast of the island. From there it's around a three-hour winding bemo ride to the waiting waves of Lakey. Remember, this spot is all about options and choices. It can be as easy or as difficult as you want to make it.

Locals and legends
Two of the top local surfers are Dedi Gun (Dedi Satriani) and Muhammad Joid 'Joey Barrel'.

Lakey Peak Board

6'6" Bushman Pancho Model

Shaper: Jeff Bushman

6'6" x 19⅜" x 2½"

Built for power!

Single to double concave for down the line speed and power gouges in the pocket.

FCS fins.

(i) Boards by Surftech
www.surftech.com info@surftech.com

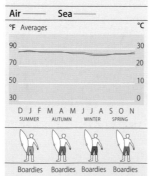

Air ——	Sea ——	
°F	Averages	°C
90		30
70		20
50		10
30		0

D J F M A M J J A S O N
SUMMER AUTUMN WINTER SPRING

Boardies Boardies Boardies Boardies

Nearby breaks Lakey Pipe is for the more advanced surfer, especially when the swell kicks in. Paddle over and you'll see why. Better tackled on a mid to high tide. **Nungas** is the left point and is best when the swell tops 8 ft. Avoid low tide as the wave becomes shallow and more sectiony. **Periscopes** is a fickle right-hander about a mile up the coast that needs a more southerly swell and mid to high tides. Best in the morning or evening when the winds are light offshore.

Periscopes

⬡ **Location:** Periscopes, Hu'u, Sumbawa

◔ **Break type:** Right-hand reef break

◉ **Conditions:** Big swells

⬡ **Size:** 3-6 ft

⬡ **Length:** 50-75 m

◐ **Tide:** Mid to high

◈ **Swell direction:** Southerly is best but also southwesterly

◑ **Wind:** Light northeasterly

☺ **Bottom:** Coral lava reef

◉ **Ability level:** Intermediate to advanced

◉ **Best months:** Apr-Oct

⬡ **Access:** On foot from Lakey, then paddle out through channel

◒ **Hazards:** Shallow so best mid to high

Surf videos: big, bulky, noisy and going the same way as the eight-track and the laser disk. Forced into obsolescence by the DVD that will soon be replaced by simple digital files downloaded from the Internet onto a chip. But it's hard to let go of the things that inspired you as a grom. The posters, the images, the video segments from long deleted stock. It's the early nineties and neon's on its way out. A young grom sits alone in his bedroom, the flickering screen of the TV, the only light. He's been waiting to watch this video, furtively swapped for another during first period maths. It has already been fast forwarded to the right section and now he peers, goggle-eyed and slack-jawed at the action unfurling in front of him. Head turned on one side, he tries for a better angle as he wonders out loud, "How did he manage to get so deep?" Pause. Rewind. A young Aussie drops down a glassy face, grabbing the rail he pulls into the barrel, classic pig-dog stance, hand trailing in the face. "Where is that?" A perfect, round, smooth, glassy head-high barrel that just reels and reels. No sections. No close-outs. Nothing life threatening. The caption flashes up on the screen. 'Neal Purchase Jnr, Periscopes'. His grommet brain has no idea where it is. But he knows he has to go.

Flying over the southern reaches of Sumbawa's undulating coastline, with its sweeping bays and limited road access, offers an insight into a fascinating world of surfing possibilities. While the eyes of the world are focused on the western Mentawais, the islands to the east of Bali are still filled with enough surfing possibilities to make your head spin. The deep, southwesterly facing Teluk Cempi

bay is home to the breaks of the Hu'u area: the consistent A-frame delights of Lakey Peak, the ledgy Lakey Pipe and the fickle right-hand tubes of Periscopes. Hidden further inside the bay, Periscopes has a narrower and more specific swell window. A south swell hits the reef better than a southwesterly.

Walking away from good surf is never considered a wise move. But to sample the reeling barrels of Periscopes, that's exactly what you have to do. Leave behind the early morning glass of Lakey and head north into the bay, passing the long, walling lines of Nungas. Plodding on as temperatures begin to rise, the beach curves round until you come to your destination. Timing is everything. If you've guessed right, made all the right calculations, crossed your fingers and said the right prayers, within 40 minutes you should feel the light morning winds coming down off the mountains to groom the reeling barrels. Offshore should lie one of the best but most fickle right-hand tubes in the whole of this reef-fringed archipelago. "Periscopes. Oh yes, Periscopes, in the morning sun at dead high tide," says Terry Fitzgerald. "That would be my number 10 best wave."

"It's a pretty easy paddle-out here," says Aussie Periscopes veteran CJ. "There's a channel with a helpful rip that takes you about 100 m out. Best time to surf is at high tide, when there's plenty of water on the reef. Catch it good and it's one of the best world-class rights in Indo." Mornings and evenings are prime times as the wind needs to be light and from the north. The take-off hooks into a peeling barrel that bundles along the reef. Pull in and set the rail, aim for the exit that

Below: Periscopes, Sumbawa.
Opposite page: Perfectly primed Periscopes.

CORY SCOTT

opens safely into a channel. It is a regular-footer's paradise. "Periscopes is one of those waves that's not right out there in front of you," says CJ "but the trek and the mission can bring rewards. Just make sure you know your tides and bring some water."

The lone grommet in his bedroom has kept his promise. He's seeing it for real, but first a little digital sequence for posterity. It's a kind of

cheap camera but then you can't really risk anything too flash on long travels. Panning back the wave comes into view. There are a few surfers in the line-up and the head-high waves reel along the reef. There isn't a breath of wind and the temperature is still pleasant in the morning sun. The focus locks on a paddling surfer who pops to his feet, angles right and tucks under the lip. He's gone from view for one second, two seconds, three seconds then suddenly bursts out and onto the shoulder. That's just too much. He puts the camera down and stashes it among his things, grabs his board and dashes for the channel. Now time to secure some real memories.

Locals and legends

Top local surfers from the Lakey area are Dedi Gun (Dedi Satriani) and Muhammad Joid 'Joey Barrel'.

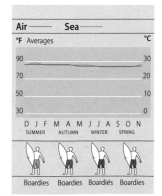

Periscopes Board
6'3" JC SD-3
Shaper: John Carper
6'3" x 18.15" x 2.2"
John Carper designed with Shane Dorian for steep hollow waves.
Round pintail, single to double concave, finely tuned rails.
Fits deep tubes, flies down the line and turns tight in the pocket.
Futures JC1 fins.
ⓘ Boards by Surftech www.surftech.com info@surftech.com

Air ——	Sea	
°F Averages		°C
90		30
70		20
50		10
30		0

D J F	M A M	J J A	S O N
SUMMER	AUTUMN	WINTER	SPRING
Boardies	Boardies	Boardies	Boardies

Nearby breaks **Lakey Pipe** sits back in the Lakey area and is best left to the more advanced surfer. Better tackled on a mid to high tide. **Lakey Peak** is an A-frame that offers quality lefts and rights. Best from 3 to 6 ft. **Nungas** is the left point and is best when the swell tops 8 ft. Avoid low when the wave is shallow and sections more.

ANDREW SHIELD

Australia & New Zealand

Coolie barrel – city backdrop.

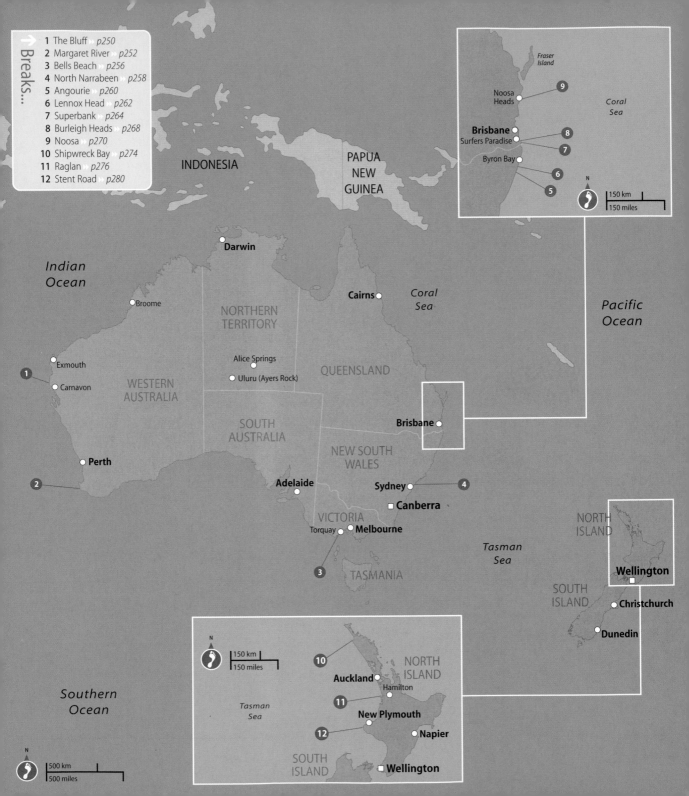

INDONESIA

PAPUA NEW GUINEA

Indian Ocean

Darwin

Cairns

Coral Sea

Pacific Ocean

NORTHERN TERRITORY

Broome

Alice Springs

Uluru (Ayers Rock)

QUEENSLAND

WESTERN AUSTRALIA

Exmouth

1

Carnavon

SOUTH AUSTRALIA

Brisbane

NEW SOUTH WALES

Perth

2

Adelaide

Sydney

4

Canberra

VICTORIA

Torquay Melbourne

3

TASMANIA

Tasman Sea

NORTH ISLAND

Wellington

SOUTH ISLAND

Christchurch

Dunedin

Fraser Island

Noosa Heads

9

Coral Sea

Brisbane

Surfers Paradise

8

7

Byron Bay

6

5

N

150 km
150 miles

Southern Ocean

N

500 km
500 miles

N

150 km
150 miles

Tasman Sea

10

Auckland

Hamilton

NORTH ISLAND

11

New Plymouth

Napier

12

SOUTH ISLAND

Wellington

Australia and surfing was a love affair destined from the start. When legendary Hawaiian surfer Duke Kahanamoku visited just after the First World War, the seeds of surfing fell on fertile ground and have blossomed like nowhere else. The climate, geography, people and lifestyle have combined to produce one of the world's truly great surfing playgrounds. In fact, if it weren't for all the other surfers this place would be ideal. The classic points of Queensland and the beach breaks of Sydney have been a hotbed of talent for decades, with ultra-competitive line-ups fighting for each world-class wave that rolls through. Down south, the cooler water at Bells Beach is so steeped in surfing tradition that it was proclaimed the world's first 'surfing sanctuary'. To the west, the breaks around Margaret River and The Bluff, pounded by constant swells, have become a testing ground for young Aussies bound for the giant waves of Hawaii. The chill waters around Tasmania are home to the skulking shapes of huge White Pointers and wonderful wilderness breaks – not all as warped and fearsome as the terrifying 'Shipstern's Bluff'.

Oz has produced a seemingly endless stream of surfers of the highest calibre: Midget Farrelly, Nat Young, Wayne Lynch, Terry Fitzgerald, Michael Peterson, Mark Richards, Rabbit Bartholomew, Ian Cairns, Cheyne Horan, Tom Carroll, Damien Hardman, Mark Occhilupo and Layne Beachley, and the new crop including Chelsea Georgeson, Taj Burrow, Joel Parkinson and Mick Fanning. Is it any surprise that in recent years around half the WCT has been made up of Aussies?

While Australia and New Zealand are close neighbours, they are, in many ways, worlds apart. While you can drive for days on end in Australia with hardly a change of scenery, New Zealand's topography can morph from lush alpine vista to coastal plain and from deep valley to moorland in the bend of a road. And looming, smouldering snow-capped volcanoes can provide a none-too-shabby backdrop to a surf session. Australia and New Zealand are like surfing's yin and yang – one of the world's quietest surfing destinations next door to one of the world's most crowded and competitive. With few exceptions, NZ line-ups are colder, less sharky and quieter than their Australian counterparts and there are plenty of isolated spots where locals will 'phone a friend' just for some company on an epic, glassy morning session. But where are all the NZ surfers competing on the WCT? They are busy enjoying the perfect, empty points and reefs at home, of course.

Surfing Australia and New Zealand

Australia didn't invent surfing. But when the sport arrived on their wave-rich shores they certainly picked up the board and ran with it. Not only that, they were reluctant to give it back. After all, this is a society that worships sport, lives predominantly by the coast, and has an intense competitive streak woven into the fabric of its genes. As former Aussie WCT surfer Neridah Falconer explains: "The entrenched Australian attitude – unlike that of France, US, Brazil and a number of other surfing nations – is that you are only really good when you have beaten the world's best. Surfing has become an Australian icon and an important part of our lifestyle."

also has a huge effect on the changeable climate. Summers are warm and mild while winters are wet and cool. It is also located slap-bang in the path of the 'Roaring Forties' (see below). As the winds sweep in from the west across the southern oceans they collect enough moisture to ensure heavy rainfall on the green, lush, western coast of New Zealand, concentrated particularly on South Island. New Zealand receives between 630 mm to 1520 mm rain per year. Add to this the frequent southerly winds bringing cold air from the Antarctic to the eastern part of the country, and you soon realize that New Zealand is home to a hardy bunch of surfers.

Wavewatch report by Vic DeJesus

Australia and New Zealand are washed by the Indian and South Pacific oceans and receive their most consistent and largest surf during the southern hemisphere winter months of May to September. During the months of December to March swell continues to come in from large low-pressure systems to the south, although usually not as big. During this period tropical cyclone swells are also common with several wind-swells year round. Most surfers consider the months of March to May as the best time to visit Australia when all the elements seem to be in place.

Cyclones

During the December to March cyclone season tight, powerful depressions can spin offshore in the Coral Sea sending epic northeasterly swells onto the points of Queensland and New South Wales. These cyclones are fed by warm air and can cause massive destruction if they reach land. However, should they remain at sea they can spin in a southerly direction, sending pumping swell out from their centres for up to a week, before the colder waters to the south cause them to weaken and eventually peter out. These tropical cyclones can also generate good swells for the northeast coast of New Zealand. While the winter sees more reliable low pressure swells, summer cyclones can be legendary.

Roaring Forties

The belt between the latitudes 40° and 50° South is known as the 'Roaring Forties' – an area notorious for its constant stream of strong westerly winds and conducive to the formation of spiralling lows which track through the Southern Ocean. The huge seas generated by these perpetual storms have been the stuff of legend and a danger to shipping since the dawn of transoceanic voyages. This almost continuous swell travels out of the Southern Ocean and hits Australia's western and southern coastlines and Tasmania as well as the west coast of New Zealand, with usually the most favourable conditions on the more distant North Island.

Geography and breaks

Australia is not just the smallest continent in the world, it is one of the lowest and flattest and, until some time between 55 and 10 million years ago, it stood adjacent to chilly Antarctica. During the last ice age, sea levels were over 100 m lower than they are today. Rivers eroded and sculpted the land so that when sea levels rose again many valleys were drowned. Some of these channels remain in what is now the ocean floor, helping to funnel swell into those mysteriously consistent breaks while others formed natural harbours at locations such as Sydney.

The majority of Australia is bounded by a broad continental shelf, with the exception of NSW where the shelf is narrow. In northern Queensland the offshore continental shelf is the bed upon which the Great Barrier Reef has built up over the past two million years. It is the largest natural feature on earth, stretching more than 2300 km from north to south and is visible from space. The reef lives up to its name and acts as a barrier to swell, making this region of coastline all but unsurfable. The tropical coastline of the Northern Territory picks up little swell, but the rest of the continent's exposed shoreline

provides a virtually infinite combination of geographical and geological combinations for wave formation. A lot of the Australian coastline is the result of the accumulation of sediment. In some areas there are large accumulation beaches – Fraser Island, off the Queensland coastline, is the largest natural sand island in the world and home to 75 Mile Beach – while others feature a series of rocky headlands separated by beaches, such as at New South Wales's Lennox Head and Broken Head, with 7 Mile Beach in between. Australia and Tasmania are surrounded by thousands of islands, which comprise nearly 40% of the total length of Australia's 59,736-km coastline.

Along with neighbouring Australia, New Zealand was once part of a supercontinent known as Gondwanaland, before breaking away about 80 million years ago. Stretching across the Australian tectonic plate to the north and the Pacific plate to the south, New Zealand is a country of regular seismic activity but though earthquakes are frequent, they are rarely felt. The country is divided into two islands, North Island and South Island, covering an area about the size of California and slightly larger than Great Britain –268,021 sq km. Both

Below: Cyclops – where dreams and nightmares meet.

islands have a spine of mountain ranges running down their length. While the North Island is a hotbed of volcanic activity, with Ruapehu being the most active in recent years, South Island's interior is famed for its excellent snowfields and glaciers with Fiordland National Park – a series of fiords or glacial valleys filled with sea water – covering its southwest coast. With over 15,000 km of coastline, ranging from huge open black sandy beaches in the northwest to the volcanic boulder points of Taranaki and the rugged coastline of the South Island, there is plenty of scope for exploration and discovery.

Health and safety
With no specific immunizations required, Australia and New Zealand are both fairly safe zones in terms of infectious diseases. However, particularly intense UV rays (Australia has the highest skin cancer rate in the world), heat exhaustion, sunburn and heatstroke can pose serious problems. So slip, slap, slop, and drink plenty of water.

To compensate for its lack of deadly diseases, Australia has more than its fair share of dangerous stingers and biters. If the great white (white pointer), tiger, bronze whaler or bull sharks don't get you, maybe the box jellyfish – with up to 3-m-long venomous tentacles and deadly sting – will.

The risk, though, is surprisingly small, so long as you use common sense and heed warnings. According to the Australian Shark Attack File, there have only been around 60 fatal shark attacks recorded in Australia over the past 50 years. A sting from a box jellyfish, or 'sea wasp', can be fatal, however. They are most prevalent in northern Queensland during the October-March wet season and many beaches carry warnings or have netted areas for swimming.

New Zealand has no snakes or dangerous wild animals to speak of except of course the sharks fringing the coastline. But in comparison with neighbouring Australia the risk is relatively low.

Surfing and the environment
Australian settlement patterns have seen the expanding population grow at an exponential rate over the past century, moving outwards along the coastal fringes, where the climate is more pleasant and the living less harsh than the arid interior. Today, over 80% of the population resides in the coastal regions, and although this vast nation is surrounded by a seemingly endless blue ocean, it is not immune from the problems that plague the coastal regions of other industrialized nations. The issues of waste disposal, erosion, sewage, loss of coastal land to development, and breakwater and marina developments are all issues that the Australian surfriding community and environmental groups are confronted with.

In 1992, Surfrider Foundation Australia was established and today has more than 20 active branches nationwide with more than 2000 members. Surfrider Foundation Australia's

core programme revolves around CARE – Conservation, Activism, Research and Education. According to Surfrider, key issues they are tackling include:

Fighting plans for a cruise ship terminal and deepening of the harbour and extension of the break wall that will affect South Stradbroke Island and access to the surf in Queensland.

Stop the sewage outlet at Lennox Head in New South Wales.

Campaign against plans to build a break wall on Bastion Point at Mallacoota in Victoria.

Campaign against plans to build a paper mill and inappropriate ocean outfall in Northern Tasmania.

Campaign against plans to build a break wall in Torquay, Victoria.

Resolve access problems to the surf at Kangaroo Island in South Australia.

Campaign on desalination plants and ocean discharges at Gold Coast, Sydney and Western Australia.

There are many issues that impact upon the environment around the Australian coastline. To find out what you can do or to become a member log on to www.surfrider.org.au.

Surfing resources
Tracks (www.tracksmag.com) magazine is the self-christened 'surfers' bible' and over its 35 years has been edited by some of waveriding's greatest luminaries. *Australia's Surfing Life* (www.surfinglife.net) is the continent's other great surfing institution and rivals *Tracks* in its irreverent and distinctly Australian view on surf lifestyle. Other magazines on the newsstands include *Australian Longboarding*, *Waves* and *Stab*. Good online surf forecasting resources for Australia include www.coastalwatch.com.au, www.swellnet.com.au and www.realsurf.com.

For New Zealand, there's *Kiwi Surf Magazine* and *New Zealand Surfing Magazine* (www.surfingnz.com), plus longboarding mag *Slide* (www.slidemagazine.com).

A couple of good resources are www.surf.co.nz and www.surf2surf.com for forecasting and news.

The Bluff

◈ **Location:**	Between Carnarvon and Exmouth, Western Australia
◔ **Break type:**	Left-hand reef
◕ **Conditions:**	All swells
◉ **Size:**	3-12 ft +
◎ **Length:**	50-100 m
◉ **Tide:**	All tides
◎ **Swell direction:**	South to southwesterly
◉ **Wind:**	Southeasterly through to northeasterly
☺ **Bottom:**	Limestone and coral
◉ **Ability level:**	Advanced
◈ **Best months:**	Apr-Oct
◉ **Access:**	By 4WD
◈ **Hazards:**	Isolated, heavy wave, shallow bottom, urchins, sharks, snakes

Red Bluff, or 'The Bluff', was splashed across the surfing press through the 1980s and has become the epitome of the Oz desert surf experience. Images of the hollow, turquoise left-hander pitching out on the end of the sun-scorched limestone point, its barrels reeling along the reef towards the camera lens, became the iconic image for those wanting to escape the crowds and luminous wetsuits of the surf boom. The fact that it had no amenities, shops, accommodation or even running water seemed only to add to its appeal. Telling people that you'd just been on a trip to 'The Bluff' was like mentioning you'd just returned from a weeks surfing at Cactus – it was a 'real' surf trip, one which was pretty much as back to basics as it gets, but one which could have 'real' consequences if things went wrong.

The present-day campsite at Red Bluff sits above the beach with a perfect view of the point to the south. From April to the end of October, the site bustles with travelling and 'local' surfers, all keen to score some legendary Bluff barrels. The site does provide very basic amenities – a number of 'drop' toilets and swarms of flies – but due to its isolation, everything else needed for the duration of the stay must be brought in: food, water, medical supplies and petrol. The 140-km drive to Red Bluff takes about 1½ hours from Carnarvon, the nearest town and the nearest gas station. When you hit the prophetic 'King Waves Kill' sign, turn left if you want to be blown away by the

blowholes and right for Quobba Station and the Red Bluff. You're only about half way there and this is where the sealed road ends and the corrugated, dust road adventure begins.

The coastline around this section of Western Australia is a diverse region of low limestone cliffs, rocky shores, reef and occasional sandy beaches. The Bluff sits at the southern end of a newly extended Ningaloo Marine Park (NMP), which stretches south from Northwest Cape. The park protects this unique natural environment and Australia's largest fringing coral reef ecosystem. Despite the dry and arid appearance of the land, the sea here is teeming with a large and diverse spectrum of sea life – some of it friendly, some not so friendly.

HILTON DAWE

Right: The Bluff.
Opposite page: Can't bluff your way out of this one.

Surfing The Bluff takes a certain degree of skill and a great deal of bravery. It works best on a mid tide when a 4 to 8-ft swell will pitch onto the reef in a steep take-off zone and then bowl through a fast, hollow barrel section along the shallow reef. The first part of the wave is pretty critical and with the wrong timing, can result in a meeting with the urchin-infested reef. Make it out of the barrel and the wave may line-up into a long wall before backing off into the sadistically-christened 'Shark Pit', an area of clear, deep water designed to put the spooks into the paddling surfer by reminding them that a cruising tiger shark could quite easily be skulking around below. It sure helps to get everyone back into the line-up that little bit quicker. Many people recommend wearing boots and a helmet here as a precaution against the many urchins that wait in the reef for the unsuspecting foot and the shallow sections where the reef waits frighteningly close to the surface. But then, considering all the factors that put The Bluff out there on the edge, this isn't a spot that really attracts the safety conscious.

Locals and legends
Look around the campsite, that's it.

The Bluff Board
6'8" Brewer Backdoor

Shaper: Dick Brewer

6'8" x 18" x 2¼"

Brewer designed this board with Hawaiian Myles Padaca for big gapping barrels.

Single to double concave for rail to rail, down the line speed and stability in the tube.

Future fins.

ⓘ Boards by **Surftech**
www.surftech.com info@surftech.com

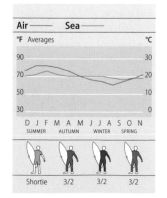

Air —— Sea ——

°F Averages   °C

90   30
70   20
50   10
30   0

D J F M A M J J A S O N
SUMMER AUTUMN WINTER SPRING

Shortie 3/2 3/2 3/2

Nearby breaks To the north of Red Bluff sits the **Gnaraloo** (pronounced *narloo*) sheep station, a vast open region that is home to some epic but remote surf spots like **Tombstones** (**Shipwrecks**), **Centres**, **Midgies**, **Indicators** and **Monuments**. As with The Bluff, accommodation is limited to camping. The closest break to Red Bluff is **Turtles**, lying just to the north, and is worth checking if the swell is not quite hitting The Bluff. This reef break picks up more swell and produces rights or lefts up to 6 ft. It is accessible through sand dunes by 4WD.

Margaret River

Location:	South of Perth, southwest corner of Western Australia
Break type:	Left-hand reef
Conditions:	All swells
Size:	3-15 ft
Length:	50-150 m
Tide:	All – tidal variations are small in this area
Swell direction:	Southwesterly to westerly
Wind:	Southeasterly to northeasterly
Bottom:	Reef
Ability level:	Advanced
Best months:	Year round; more onshores late autumn/winter
Access:	From the beach
Hazards:	Shallow reef, heavy waves, big sharks

Margaret River Board

6'3" JC SD-3

Shaper: John Carper

6'3" x 18" x 2.2"

For advanced surfers who want to drive through the barrels of Margaret River and The Box.

Single to double concave with a narrow outline for high performance surfing in steep critical barrels!

Made for Shane Dorian.

Futures fins.

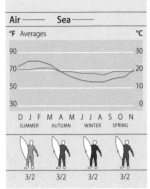

Boards by Surftech
www.surftech.com   info@surftech.com

While the east coast of Australia is home to some true thoroughbred waves, such as Burleigh and Noosa, the west coast is an altogether more hardcore experience. Here the waves are more like prize bulls, and none commands more respect than the left at Margaret River. Just looking at a map of the world, it's easy to see why this part of the west coast is such a beefy experience.

Jutting out on the southwestern tip of this huge country, it sits directly in the path of the energy generated by the 'Roaring Forties'. All the power of Mother Nature is directed at this region, either in the shape of fine groundswells groomed by the huge fetch of the Southern Ocean or powerful storms that batter the limestone coastline. "We'd surf every

JAMIE SCOTTIMAGES.COM

weekend at Margaret River" says top shaper Nev Hyman, "and get either perfect surf or get stuck in northwest storms for the whole weekend and not even be able to get out of the door." As legendary surfer and Margaret River native Ian Cairns says, "There are probably only 10 days of the year when the surf is below waist height and many when the surf is way overhead, so it is the most consistent surf area on the planet." Climate-wise, it sits at a latitude that means it is blessed with Mediterranean conditions year round. However, Margaret River is not just a single break, but a region that stretches the length of the coastline between Cape Naturaliste and Cape Leeuwin. There are many excellent surf spots along this coastline but the left-hand reef that most people know simply as Margaret River is the most famous.

Looking out on the azure blue of the Indian Ocean from the rock-lined sandy shore, the Margaret River main peak, also known as The Point or River Reef, can look deceptively benign. In small swells from the right angle, a short right peels away to the south and a long, walling left reels away towards the north. A broad wedge of flat limestone reef extends out into the Indian Ocean, with deep channels on each side. Swells that have travelled huge distances peak and break on the end of the reef producing what can look like a perfect A-frame. However, it is not always mellow and inviting. In bigger swells, the take-off is steep and critical leading onto the left, which can produce long, wide walls, heavy, grinding barrels or both – depending on its mood. This is a wave that has been likened to a reverse Sunset. With waves rideable at over 15 ft, the reef here can be punishing and humbling, even at half that size. That's without adding the real danger of the local shark community.

The stretch of coastline around Margaret River is Australia's very own version of the North Shore of Oahu. It picks up so much swell and the

Above: Damon Eastaugh at Margaret River.
Opposite page: Chris Ross – thinking inside The Box.

waves break with such brutal power and size that many of the country's best surfers cut their big-wave-riding teeth here. For Ian Cairns, the waves of Margaret River were the perfect training ground for his first trip to Hawaii. "I was 20 when I first surfed Hawaii. It was just like a big day in West Australia where I had been getting bashed by big, powerful reef waves for years, so I just stepped right in. Of course I was really brash and confident – like most Aussies, so that helped, but I had the reef background that gave me a big head start."

However, in the boom of the early 1970s, spots like Kirra and Burleigh on the east coast were the epicentre of the surfing world. It was the place many west coast surfers upped and moved to. Today, many surfers are reversing the trend and heading west, away from the overcrowded Gold Coast. Many come to Margaret's to try to recapture what they see as Australia's lost surfing soul. "When I was in Western Australia back in the seventies everyone dreamt of leaving there," says Nev. "Now everyone dreams of going there! There's so many more waves being surfed there now than when I was there." Western Oz

local, Amber Gourlay agrees, "WA has so many waves to offer I could almost put my whole top 10 here!" Being able to lose the crowds, the bustle, the mayhem and take on this classic reef break means that Margaret River is a constant favourite. "Margaret's is in my top 10 – one of Australia's favourite waves," says Joel Fitzgerald. "The huge mountains of water breaking on the shallow reef, the climate and tropical water conditions all make it a surfer's dream."

Locals and legends

Tony Hardy, Robert Conneely, Ian Cairns, Mitch Thorson, Damon Eastaugh, Josh Palmateer, Taj Burrows, Jake Patterson, Paul Paterson, John Davies, Tom Innes, Melanie Redman-Carr.

Nearby breaks "Margaret River is really a surf area," explains Ian Cairns, "with many breaks in a 30-mile stretch of coast that resembles the North Shore of Hawaii." Across the bay is a shallow, hollow right that, until a few years ago, was not really considered surfable. Now **The Box** has become one of the most photographed waves on the whole coastline, due to the insane square barrels and death-or-glory antics of the surfers who take on this wave. Other spots to check out include **North** and **South points** near Gracetown and the many spots around **Yallingup** to the north. Jimmy O'Keefe says North Point is "an imperfect, sectioning grinder of a wave. Its offshore ribs collapse with violence and beauty", while Damien Hobgood says: "I love North Point as you can get so deep in Barrel."

Surfers' tales
The landlord comes to collect

Man in the Grey Suit. To a Londoner the expression conjures up an image of the daily grind, crammed into a tube carriage next to bland people in bland attire waiting to be released into another rain-laden morning. An American may think of their boss, their bank manager or some guy they met in a Manhattan wine bar. But to an Australian it has a whole different meaning. 'The Man in the Grey Suit' is dangerous. He's always out there. Somewhere. When you enter his territory, you do so on his terms. You never see him until the day he swings by to collect. Sharp, smooth, mean, cold-blooded – like Joe Pesci on steroids. In typically Australian dramatic underplay, the 'Man in the Grey Suit' is the most feared predator on the planet – the man-eating shark.

The inner fear that out there, somewhere, circles the most efficient killing machine ever to evolve on this planet is something that every surfer has to come to terms with in some way. Europeans just put their fingers in their ears and pretend we don't have them, ignoring the fact that the biggest great white ever caught was pulled out of European waters. Americans become experts on the behaviour of these predators and develop a morbid fascination with the Discovery Channel's 'Shark Week'. Australians, however, live in an environment where everything has the potential to kill. Red back spiders, box jellyfish, king snakes, crocodiles, scorpions, they even have a killer octopus. The only thing they don't seem to have a killer version of is butterflies – but that's probably just because it hasn't been discovered yet. To them, sharks are just another environmental inconvenience.

Shane Stops is Tasmanian. Being from 'Tassie' is not the same as being Australian. Tasmanians have traditionally been the butt of the same jokes that the English used to tell about the Irish. But the island they inhabit is lush and green and has retained many of Australia's lost indigenous species. The weather is cooler and wetter, and the environment is more akin to the motherland than the mainland. It's British – but with the killer wildlife. The water is colder, the Antarctic swells are massive and the sharks are bigger still, which roughly translates to, "Tasmanian surfers are as hardcore as it gets". Down here the 'Man in the Grey Suit' is more a case of the 'Sumo wrestler in a large Grey Parka'.

It was early morning when Shane reached the point. Facing south, the bay funnelled in swell generated thousands of miles away in a region of the southern oceans known as the 'Roaring Forties', a place dreaded by sailors for its mountainous seas and raging storms. The waves peeling along the densely wooded headland had reached land after an epic journey, during which the once-turbulent, chaotic swell had become lined and organized. Clean, head-high waves rolled down the point as long, green walls. This looked better than corduroy. This was haute couture: made-to-measure. Scanning the line-up he noticed there were no other surfers in. "Better get in there before the crowds arrive", he thought as he pulled on his wetsuit. He launched into the water and paddled for the line-up. The water was cool and he shivered as he duck dived, opening his eyes in the green-tinged water and surfacing with a shake of the head. "It was beautiful. I couldn't believe there was no one else out," says Shane. "It was so quiet; a perfect morning."

Shane reached the take-off spot and sat up on his board. The early morning line-up had an oily quality in the still air. A set approached and he turned and paddled into the second wave. "Because no one else was out I could just pick whichever wave I wanted," says Shane. He dropped down the face, carved off the bottom and aimed for the shoulder. His board was flying, in that magic spot where friction seems to have been left behind. He gouged a cutback and turned into the pocket, accelerating again out onto the face. The board rose and fell in perfect trim, linked by arcing turns, until he popped over the back of the wave and began to paddle back up the point towards the line-up. "I had a big smile on my face. I turned a couple of times to see if anybody was paddling out but there was still no sign of anyone yet. I got to the take-off point and sat up. It felt great just sitting there, peacefully, catching my breath." A group of seabirds were floating a hundred yards out to sea, like a feathered raft. Shane scanned the approaching waves, looking for the next set.

Suddenly the birds scattered noisily, taking to the air in one squawking mass. "It made me jump and subconsciously the thought of sharks popped into my head. It's one of those signs that people warn you about." Suddenly there was a boil, the shadow of movement under the glassy surface. "I couldn't believe it when I saw something break the surface. It was like a submarine emerging. First it was just a small trail but then a fin slowly began to rise out of the water. I kept waiting for it to stop but the fin just got bigger and bigger. I knew it was a great white and it was now so close I knew there was no way I could out run it to the shore." Every muscle in Shane's body screamed with adrenaline and his mind was racing with options. "Everything I'd ever heard suddenly came rushing back and I knew I had to stay still and try not to panic." Easy enough to say, but hard to put into practice, especially when that huge fin you are watching begins an arching turn towards where you lie, like an hors d'oeuvre on a cracker. "I watched it slip beneath the surface and my brain was still locked in a screaming debate – 'paddle for your life', 'no, don't move a muscle'. It went quiet for a few seconds and then a huge mass erupted beside me." A black, staring eye was momentarily visible before its massive grey flank grated along the length of his board. As it lunged beneath the surface, a huge tail sprayed him with water. It disappeared into the murky depths, which gradually settled down into an eerily tranquil sheen, as though it had all been a terrible dream. Only below its glassy surface, in the dark, lurked a man-eating stealth bomber.

"It went quiet for a second, as though nothing had happened. But I knew it was still down there. I began to consider making a run for it when the fin appeared again, about 30 m away, slowly surfacing. I couldn't believe it." The shark seemed in no rush. It carried on circling, as if weighing up its options. Methodically it turned and Shane watched in horror as the fin made a beeline for him. "I watched it getting closer and closer. I just raised every part of my body that it was possible to out of the water. The huge shark was pushing a bow wake in front of it. I thought that this was it – that I was going to die." Bang, the shark changed direction at the very last second, thumping the board and almost knocking Shane off. It sunk into the depths again. He was still alive. "I was more scared when I couldn't see the thing as it could be anywhere. It could hit me any second. At least when I could see it I knew where it was." He didn't have to wait long. The huge fin reappeared and began to circle again. Great whites don't eat humans as a primary food source. Most shark attacks are a case of mistaken identity. But that's no consolation when you're being circled by something that could bite clean through you and your board just to check out if you would make a good meal.

Slowly the fin sank. "I couldn't believe what was happening. So many things go through your brain at once. I knew by now that ten minutes or so must have passed. I knew it could come back and it might all be over in a second. Then it surfaced and turned to make another pass." As the shark closed in Shane began to feel angry. Why was it doing this? It was like a cat playing with a mouse. This time, at the last minute, it turned and cruised beneath him, its entire length passing under his lifting board. His mind made an instinctive calculation at the length of the silent behemoth. It was at least three times longer than his 6 ft board. This was like psychological torture. He looked at the disappearing fin and his mind-set changed. "I began to lose it. I was really angry. I knew I would probably die. I think the adrenaline was beginning to wear off. I started beating the water and screaming, 'Come on then you bastard! If you're gonna do it, just do it.' I was left looking around, wondering where it was, waiting for it to appear next to me." Then the world was silent. He scanned the water for any sign of movement. The seconds then minutes crept by. "A voice in my head said 'Now. Go. Paddle for your life!' so I just started paddling and I never looked over my shoulder. It seemed to take forever to reach the shore. It was like paddling through gravy. The last few metres were the worst. I thought it was waiting until I was almost safe." Exhausted, Shane caught some whitewater and, beaching his board, collapsed. "I couldn't believe I had survived. Looking out at the sea, it was like it had never happened. There was no sign of the shark. Just a quiet, peaceful line-up. But I knew that it was out there somewhere."

Bells Beach

◈ **Location:**	Three miles southwest of Torquay, Victoria
◌ **Break type:**	Right-hand reef
◌ **Conditions:**	All swells
◉ **Size:**	2-12 ft
◉ **Length:**	50-300 m
◈ **Tide:**	All tides
◉ **Swell direction:**	Southwesterly through to southerly
◉ **Wind:**	Northwest to westerly
◉ **Bottom:**	Flat rock
◉ **Ability level:**	Intermediate-advanced
◉ **Best months:**	Mar-Oct
◉ **Access:**	From the cliff-top car park down onto the beach
◉ **Hazards:**	Busy, especially during holidays and Easter

There is only one road that leads to the spiritual home of Australian surfing and its name is as grand as its function. The Great Ocean Road parallels the roaring Southern Ocean bringing pilgrims past the Twelve (now reduced to 11) Apostles to a place steeped in surf history and arguably the most famous surf spot on the continent. The name 'Bells Beach' is right up there in the recognition stakes with Malibu and Sunset. Okay, so there isn't a Bells Beach Barbie Doll but then this brooding cold-water bruiser isn't that kind of wave. It attracts a whole different type of clientele.

Looking down from the cliff-top car park of the world's first 'Surfing Recreation Reserve' on this piece of surfing history, you are confronted by a fairly small, sandstone-walled crescent. It seems like

an anti-climax, until you realize that it has been blessed with a flat reef – the perfect foil for the swells that roll out of the 'Roaring Forties' to the south. In a classic swell, the long, reeling walls of Bells peel towards you while the fast, feathering lines of Winkipop (see below) fire away from you to the northeast. No fickle, shifting sandbanks to be dealt with here. The water is, however, ice cream-headache cold in the winter.

Bells was originally considered a big wave spot that could also be ridden when the swells were smaller. Today, with the almost daily redefinition of big wave surfing, it has been reclassified as a great performance break. Site of the world's oldest surf contest, the Bells Easter Pro, Bells Beach has become more than just a wave. It is a part of surfing's soul and surfing folklore. "It's more hard core down there, and there's the tradition, and I think that's the key," says surf legend Simon Anderson. "Bells combines all the elements of surfing. You can go down the coast surfing, there's the contest, the partying, cruising in the combi. It's what surfing's all about."

The geography of the area makes Bells a really fun spot to surf. With predominantly westerly winds, the wave peels along a flat, sedimentary rock reef, peaking out to the southwest edge of the bay and forming a right-hander that can wall-up for up to 300 m in the right conditions. Due to the bay's exposure to southern swells, the surf here can be epic and on special days you can ride from Centreside, through Rincon, Outside Bells and the Bowl.

Below: Winki-pop reeling right.
Opposite page: Classic Bells.

Bells Beach Board
6'6" Lynch Round Pin
Shaper: Wayne Lynch
6'6" x 19½" x 2⁹⁄₁₆"

A little extra overall volume and softer plan shape curves creates great paddling qualities plus the ability to run across flat sections and maintain speed.

FCS fins.

ⓘ Boards by **Surftech**
www.surftech.com info@surftech.com

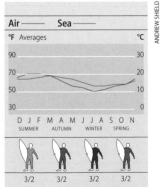

Air —— Sea ——

°F Averages   °C

DJFMAMJJASON
SUMMER AUTUMN WINTER SPRING

| 3/2 | 3/2 | 3/2 | 3/2 |

ANDREW SHIELD

The physical characteristics of this spot means it is especially suited for competition surfing. It has long, fast, walling sections perfect for racing down the line and gathering speed before the wave slows, providing a perfect stage for a manoeuvre to take the surfer back into the pocket. MP's grab rail cutback, Terry Fitzgerald's soul arch, Occy's explosive backhand re-entry and Slater's crisp, fins-out snap – Bells has been the canvas for them all. Even on an onshore day it has occasionally opened up to provide Tom Curren with the most unlikely of barrels. The wall then speeds on its way before again offering up a welcoming lip. For the finale it lunges onto the beach, allowing for one final floater in the shore break. The paddle back to the peak after a set wave is a long but satisfying one.

These attributes combine to make Bells a good wave but were it discovered today, would it make the top waves in the world? One of the factors that allows it an automatic inclusion is that few places in the world can rival the rich surfing heritage and history in which Bells Beach is steeped. Waves have been ridden here since the late 1940s. The 1961 Bells contest signalled the start of an event held every Easter since – one that is still a highlight of the World Championship Tour. Those who have won here and rung the famous 'bell' trophy reads like a Who's Who of surfing – Nat Young, MR, MP, Carroll, Curren, Slater, Fanning. Like a vein of fossil-layered rock recording the passage of time, this event is imprinted with the evolution of waveriding: from hollow, wooden cigar boards to Balsa to foam through single fins to

twinnies. In 1981, Simon Anderson made history by winning the Bells event on a board design that immediately revolutionized surfing. In 15-ft plus surf he broke the mould on a three-finned surfboard – christened the 'thruster' due to the thrust the extra fin generated. Over 25 years later, it is one of surfing's most enduring design decisions.

The region around this bay has also become one of the focal points of the Australian surf industry over the years. Industry giants Quiksilver and Rip Curl were spawned here and grew into two of the first Australian companies to become global players in international trade – not bad for a bunch of surfers. With so much history, with so many memorable contests and with just a few famous drinking sessions, it is no wonder that this stretch of coastline has become known as the 'Surf Coast'.

Locals and legends

Peter Troy, Joe Sweeney, 'China' Gilbert, George 'Ming' Smith, Doug 'Claw' Warbrick, Troy Brooks, Jirah Laws, Amy Stewart.

Nearby breaks Torquay has a beach with a number of sand covered reefs to try and a nearby right-hand point. To the west is the bustling beach break of **Jan Juc**, where shifting sandbanks can produce good quality waves. Between here and Bells lie a number of reef breaks including **Bird Rock**, a steep, hollow right, **Sparrows**, a slightly easier proposition, and **Boobs**, a hollow peak. **Winkipop**, just to the east of Bells, is a high quality right-hand reef that reels off long, walling waves for up to 200 m. It gets very crowded here as it's both a high quality wave and close to Bells. To the west check out **Point Roadknight** in Anglesea, **Fairhaven** and, for the experienced surfer, **Cathedral Rock**.

North Narrabeen

🜨 **Location:**	Narrabeen, Northern Beaches, Sydney, New South Wales
⬤ **Break type:**	Beach break
☁ **Conditions:**	All swells
◉ **Size:**	3-8 ft
⬡ **Length:**	20-150 m
🌀 **Tide:**	All tides
⬙ **Swell direction:**	Northeasterly to southeasterly (best northeasterly to easterly)
⬙ **Wind:**	Northwesterly to westerly (even sheltered on northeasterly)
⬛ **Bottom:**	Sand
◉ **Ability level:**	All
⬢ **Best months:**	Dec-Mar (for cyclone season)
⬤ **Access:**	Beach access is easy
⊖ **Hazards:**	Crowded and competitive locals

The beach break at North Narrabeen is legend in the surfing world. It has a fine tradition for producing world-class surfers who grow up in this hothouse competitive environment, a domain which sees friends, foes and even family fight it out tooth and nail for every wave. Little wonder that this stretch of Sydney sand is credited with producing a constant stream of competition maestros – from the likes of Terry Fitzgerald, Simon Anderson and Mark Warren, to twice world champ Damien Hardman and former WCT surfer Nathan Webster.

North Narrabeen is found in the heart of Sydney's Northern Beaches – a 20-mile sweep of highly charged and consistent surf, which runs from Manly, just half-an-hour north of Sydney, and continues past

SEAN DAVEY

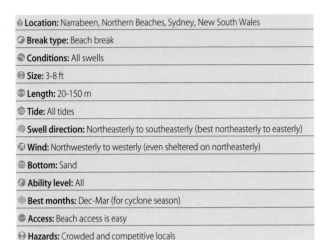

North Narrabeen Board

6'3" M10 The Kid

Shaper: Geoff Rashe

6'3" x 18¾" x 2⅜"

Deep single to double concave with added tail rocker make this board super fast down the line yet it feels loose and accelerates through tigh turns.

It'll bring out the kid in you.

Futures fins.

ⓘ Boards by Surftech
www.surftech.com   info@surftech.com

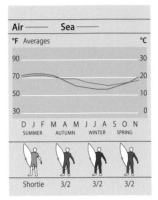

Air ——— Sea ———	
°F Averages	°C

D J F M A M J J A S O N
SUMMER AUTUMN WINTER SPRING

Shortie   3/2   3/2   3/2

famous names such as Dee Why, Newport and Avalon to Palm Beach. Found at the top end of a 3-mile stretch of beach, North Narrabeen is protected by a curving headland. This is an excellent quality beach break formed where the outflow from the Narrabeen Lagoon reaches the sea, the water flow depositing a steady stream of sand that builds up into a quality triangular sandbank. "This is one of the most consistent waves in Australia," say local pro Joel Fitzgerald. "It always packs a punch. The sandbank is formed from a river mouth at the entrance to the lagoon. It's a sick wave for both goofy or natural." The beach is open to swells from all directions, but those from the northeast or east provide the best quality waves. The lines angle into the bay and send reeling lefts along the sandbar. The waves can be fast and walling or grinding barrels with bowling inside sections. In a southerly or southeasterly swell, rights peel towards the mouth of the inlet providing some quality waves that run into the rip, known as the Alley or Shark Alley. Further down the beach, in front of the car park, there is a quality right-hander imaginatively known as Car Park Rights.

Narrabeen is a challenging and changing surf spot. The combination of wind, swell, tide and sand build-up all combine to offer an endlessly morphing surfers' playground. Waves can go from long, walling lefts to short, barrelling rights to an A-frame within a few days. As legendary surfer Terry Fitzgerald says "North Narrabeen has more moods than a harem – perfect one day, unsurfable the next. But you can ride waves there more than 80% of the time and it can go no longer than two or three days without changing. And that's what keeps it interesting." It is this constantly shifting environment that is

Left: Narrabeen's famous left.
Opposite page: Moody Narrabeen.

credited with helping the area to produce surfers able to compete at the highest level and in the wide-ranging conditions that confront competition surfers.

Narrabeen has also been on the contest circuit since the '70s, meaning that a constant pool of talent was always coming to the beach with the latest boards and the latest moves. Not that the locals are easily impressed. "Locals at North Narrabeen are nasty!" warns Joel. "Simon Anderson, Terry Fitzgerald, Hardman and Col Smith ruled the line-up. Now you have to battle with the other hundred locals like Hedge, Davo, Cattle, Banno and the Fitzy's Groms – North Narrabeen might intimidate even the seasoned Pro." Former WCT surfer Nathan Hedge definitely feels that the competitive line-up here helped push him to become a better surfer. "Growing up in Narrabeen I got to see heaps of talent out in the water. There was so much depth there, and so much talent, that from an early age I got to watch a lot of really great surfing, which kind of pushed me to surf better and get out there amongst it."

In its heyday, the scene at North Narrabeen was almost as renowned for its drinking, partying and brawling as it was for its surfing. Then

there was the North Narrabeen 'Grommet Pole', a place where, legend has it, troublesome grommets were tied up and subjected to the kind of 'high jinx' that would probably end in a lawsuit had they taken place in the US. Narrabeen is not just the home of world-class waves, or world-class surfers, it's home to a scene that has been bursting with energy and vitality since the 1960s and has been at the cutting edge of surfing for over four decades. Just as the rivermouth feeds sand to reshape the banks, so the next generation of supergroms is always snapping at the heels of the established crew.

Locals and legends

Col Smith, Terry Fitzgerald, Mark Warren, Simon Anderson, Nat Young, Ron Ford, Grant Oliver, Damien Hardman, Mark Bannister, Nathan Webster, Joel Fitzgerald, Nathan Hedge, Chris Davidson, Matt Cattle.

Nearby breaks Out in front of the car park at Narrabeen is **Car Park Rights**, a hollow and powerful right-hander that comes to life in southerly swells. A short drive to the north will bring you to the legendary waves of **Avalon**, home to some excellent rides and some serious crowds. Just north of Newport, **Bilgalo** is a beautiful and flexible beach where less experienced surfers can catch a few waves away from the crowds.

SEAN DAVEY

Angourie

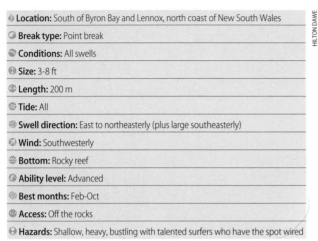

Location:	South of Byron Bay and Lennox, north coast of New South Wales
Break type:	Point break
Conditions:	All swells
Size:	3-8 ft
Length:	200 m
Tide:	All
Swell direction:	East to northeasterly (plus large southeasterly)
Wind:	Southwesterly
Bottom:	Rocky reef
Ability level:	Advanced
Best months:	Feb-Oct
Access:	Off the rocks
Hazards:	Shallow, heavy, bustling with talented surfers who have the spot wired

HILTON DAWE

Angourie has been ridden since the sixties and has helped produce some world-class designs, styles and surfers. In 1964 groundbreaking American surfer Joey Cabell was in Australia to compete for the World Surfing Championships. The outcome of the event – which eventually saw Aussie Midget Farrelly crowned champion – may still be disputed by some but one thing that is agreed by all is that Cabell's barrel-riding during a free-surfing session at Angourie set the wheels in motion for the redefinition of Australian surfing. As with Lennox Head, this was also a place for innovation and refinement. Shapers from McTavish to Luke Short test-drove their latest models here. Early surf movie pioneers were also drawn to the empty waves of this classic right-hand point: Paul Witzig for his 1967 film, *The Hot Generation* and Alby Falzon for his 1972 epoch-making classic, *Morning of the Earth*. The most famous Angourie resident was 1966 world champion Nat Young, who lived there for many years before moving on after the infamous 'Surf Rage' incident which saw him beaten up in the line-up. Top shaper Phil Grace, who used to visit the point before the surf boom, saw the line-up get busy: "Angourie was one of my favourite waves before it got too crowded. It seemed to be like a mini 'Sunset', where it had a nice take-off and you could set yourself up for that inside tube section. You could get a tube, you could cutback, it could be performance or it could be hollow. It had it all."

South of Yamba and the mouth of the Clarence River, Angourie Point juts out into the South Pacific – a lightning rod to any passing swell. The wave steps up on the outside ledge offering up a steep and challenging take-off before the lines spin into the bay, like the spokes of a wheel. But it is more complex than a mere pin-wheeling point and it is here that it starts its magic metamorphosis. The lines begin to bend round into the bay, the wall arcing and racing along the rocky bottom. The waves here are not uniform. They have subtle nuances and moods. "Angourie is a tiny bay with a refracted right bowl, relentlessly curving back on itself like a boomerang," says ex-*ASL* magazine editor Jimmy O'Keefe, who rates this point as one of his top 10 surf spots in the world. The locals have a definite advantage here having put in the time to learn the many changing characteristics of this bowling right-hander. The wave finally wraps through to unload onto the boulders on the inside, allowing a wide paddle back into the line-up.

The area around Angourie has avoided the mass development of regions such as Surfers Paradise. Angourie itself is a small village with basic amenities and anything more than essentials means a trip to Yamba for its residents. There is an unspoilt beauty in this region with many native species of flora and fauna. "It's a beautiful area and it's rural, just as I like it – being a country girl," says former WCT surfer and Scotts Head local, Neridah Falconer. The surrounding Yuraygir National Park is populated by melaleucas (or tea-trees) and the Mara Creek, a freshwater stream stained red from the forest, bleeds into the sea at Angourie Back Beach, to the south of the point.

Above: Rare solo session.
Opposite page: Angourie lighting up.

HILTON DAWE

Although not machine perfect, this has always been considered one of Australia's top 10 waves. It is not particularly easy to master but that is part of what makes it so special to the loyal and competitive locals. Time spent in the line-up is rewarded with a greater understanding of the wave and its quirkiness. The prized bounty is access to those reeling, bowling Angourie set waves.

Locals and legends

Local legends included Chris Brock, Gary Keyes, Nat Young, Baddy Treloar, George Greenough, Bob McTavish. Today's locals include Laurie Towner, Navrin Fox, Neridah Falconer, Jeremy Walters, Dan Ross.

Angourie Board

6'1" Byrne Tom Carrol

Shaper: Phil Byrne

6'1" x 18³/₈" x 2¹/₈"

Ideally suited for the high-performance bending waves at Angourie.

Designed with 2-time world champion Tom Carrol, this highly responsive round pin works well in almost any surf from small to large.

FCS fins.

ⓘ Boards by Surftech
www.surftech.com info@surftech.com

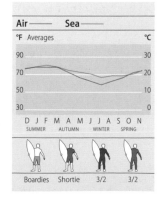

Air ———	Sea ———	
°F Averages		°C
90		30
70		20
50		10
30		0

D J F M A M J J A S O N
SUMMER   AUTUMN   WINTER   SPRING

| Boardies | Shortie | 3/2 | 3/2 |

Nearby breaks Angourie **Back Beach**, on the southern side of the headland, is a quality left worth checking out when the wind is from the northeast to northwest. There are further peaks to the south, all of which pick up any southerly or easterly swell out there. To the north of Angourie sits **Spookies**, a vicious, shallow reef for experts. Further north, **Pippies**, or Pippi Beach, is a good bet for surfers of all abilities.

Lennox Head

◈ **Location:**	South of Byron Bay, north coast of New South Wales
◔ **Break type:**	Right-hand point break
◍ **Conditions:**	Medium to big swells
◔ **Size:**	3-12 ft
◉ **Length:**	50-200 m
◒ **Tide:**	All tides
◎ **Swell direction:**	Southerly to southeasterly
◈ **Wind:**	Southerly to southwesterly
◉ **Bottom:**	Boulder and sand
◔ **Ability level:**	Advanced only
◉ **Best months:**	Mar-Aug
◍ **Access:**	A well-timed jump off the boulders
◔ **Hazards:**	A badly timed jump off the boulders, crowds, shark risk

The lush green pastures that blanket the flanks of Lennox Head form the perfect contrast to the deep-blue, corrugated lines that wrap and filter along this ultimate symbol of Australian pointbreak perfection. Lennox lacks the frenetic atmosphere of Burleigh and the urban bustle of Kirra. As cows casually graze above the ocean, the scene can look relaxed, almost mesmerizing as machine-like curls grind their way along the boulder shore. However, Lennox is not the chilled out wave it appears to be. As the song goes, "It can be heaven or it can be hell".

The wave at Lennox Head is a classic right-hand point. "It's J-Bay with warm water," says Jimmy O'Keefe of one of his top 10 waves.

SEAN DAVEY

Interestingly, Craig Jarvis, ex-editor of South Africa's *Zig Zag*, also rates it as one of his top 10s. It can have long, walling sections and offers some nice barrels as well. It also works in big swells of up to 12-ft plus – and becomes much more challenging. The powerful waves and super-tricky exit make it the domain of a hardcore local crew who have the place wired. On 4 to 6-ft days Lennox will have a bustling and competitive line-up. The crowd here are serious and committed but respectful of proficient visitors who follow the correct etiquette. Just getting into the line-up can be an ordeal and timing is paramount if you don't want to face being dragged over the boulders and losing your fins. "Lennox is a great wave, nice walls and barrel sections but getting in and out is a nightmare," says British surf photographer The Gill. "You have to negotiate boulders that are like soap-covered space hoppers with razorblades on them. You realize why the locals are all wearing boots."

The barrels of Lennox have a special place in the surfing psyche – albeit a somewhat subliminal one. In 1969 pioneering filmmaker and kneeboarder George Greenough took us deep inside the soul of Lennox, filming groundbreaking water footage from inside the barrel, delivering a fresh perspective for his film *Innermost Limits of Pure Fun*. In *Crystal Voyager*, his 1973 collaboration with Alby Falzon and David Elfick, the film again culminated with a mesmerizing surfer's-eye view from inside the Lennox tube. This dramatic climax of 'everything green and submarine' was set to the haunting Pink Floyd track *Echoes*, a song that the band were inspired to write after seeing Greenough's earlier tube's-eye footage on a visit to the legendary artists' hang-out the 'Yellow House'. Elfick made a trade, persuading the band to allow him to use the track as the finale of *Crystal Voyager* in return for permission for Floyd to use the footage as part of their stage show.

This view from within the 'Green Room' inspired a generation of waveriders to say, "I want to do that." At a time when surfboard design was going through a seismic shift, it helped facilitate the move from open face hot-dogging to the search for the perfect barrel. When board shapes were changing surfers looked for new waves to suit the shorter designs – and Lennox had the power and speed to make it the perfect test site. "Lennox was the testing ground in the late 60s early 70s," says shaper Phil Myers. "Nat Young, George Greenough, Bob McTavish, Ted Spencer, Chris Brock, Baddy Treloar and Michael Peterson were regulars at Lennox in those days, so you got to surf

Left: Lennox Lines.
Opposite page: Jay Davies – going for the lip hit.

great waves with great surfers. I was always experimenting with board design at Lennox during the 70s and 80s and worked with the late Col Smith on the channel design here. The first time we surfed Lennox with Col was a classic session, everyone was checking the boards and they were perfectly suited to Lennox as they gave you all the speed you needed to surf with confidence."

Legendary surfer and shaper Bob McTavish became a Lennox local in the 60s and rates it as one of the world's best waves. "I moved there in 1967," says McTavish "because it had warm water and took the big swells needed for the new short board designs. I decided it was a great place to raise a family, so lived there for over 30 years. I still surf it regularly." So Lennox has it all. It has an amazing history that has helped shape the boards we ride and the films we watch, yet it remains as challenging now as it was when it was first ridden. Just don't forget your boots…

Locals and legends

George Greenough, Ron 'Shorty' Connors, Terry Iderdale, Brad Myers, Mark Smith, Chris Brock, Bob McTavish, Brett Maher, Ed Standfield, Phil Myers, Wayne Laidlaw, Garry Timperly, Steve Kearney, Danny Wills, Ty Smith, Adam Melling, Glen Curtis.

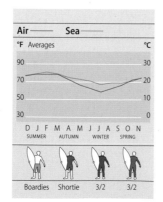

Lennox Head Board

6'3" Lynch Round Pin

Shaper: Wayne Lynch

6'3" x 19¼" x 2½"

Great board for the long lined up walls of Lennox Head.

Double concave and low entry rocker gets you into waves easy with heaps of speed yet manoeverable in the pocket.

FCS Fins.

ⓘ Boards by Surftech
www.surftech.com info@surftech.com

Air ——— Sea

°F Averages   °C

90   30
70   20
50   10
30   0

D J F   M A M   J J A S O N
SUMMER   AUTUMN   WINTER   SPRING

Boardies   Shortie   3/2   3/2

Nearby breaks Lennox sits just south of the popular surfing destination of **Byron Bay**. **The Pass** is an excellent sand-bottomed right point at Byron that draws surfers from across the globe and is always crowded. Between Byron and Lennox is the excellent right-hand pointbreak of **Broken Head**, considered by many to be one of Australia's finest waves. To the south lie the breaks of **Boulder Beach**, **Flatrock** and **Ballina**.

Superbank

- ⚜ **Location:** Between Snapper Rocks and Kirra Point, Gold Coast, Queensland
- ◔ **Break type:** Point break
- ☁ **Conditions:** Medium to big swells
- ◉ **Size:** 2-12 ft
- ⟨ **Length:** 2-km-long point
- ☂ **Tide:** All tides but best at mid
- ⟨⟨ **Swell direction:** Southeasterly through to northeasterly
- ◎ **Wind:** Southwest to westerly
- ☺ **Bottom:** Sand-covered rocks
- ◉ **Ability level:** Intermediate-advanced
- ☷ **Best months:** Jan-May
- ⚓ **Access:** Paddle off the Coolangatta Beach or jump off the Big Groyne
- ⊖ **Hazards:** Packed, and a long walk back from Kirra to Snapper

Australia is a great country – just ask any Australian. It's home to the Great Barrier Reef and the Great Ocean Road, the world's largest sand island (Fraser Island) and the largest monolith (Uluru or Ayers Rock). Little surprise then that this nation has spawned what may just be the greatest wave of the new millennium – the aptly titled, 'Superbank'.

If there's one wave that consistently featured in surfer's favourites, it was the Superbank. Jimmy O'Keefe, former editor of *ASL* magazine simply says: "A set wave here will change your life." However, had we questioned the world's top waveriders 10 years ago, it would be a completely different story – for the simple reason that it did not exist. It is also one of the most controversial waves we discussed, a fine

example of the old proverb, "One man's shit is another man's gold." While guys like top shaper Phil Grace and top Aussie pro Mick Lowe may mourn the death of Kirra and Snapper – previously super waves in their own right – others embrace the notion of 'super-sizing'. "How can you argue with a four-minute ride?" asks *Surfline* editor Marcus Sanders, commenting on Coolie kid, Damon Harvey's 2002 wonder-wave. "Guys are getting the longest sand-bottomed barrels ever recorded here on a solid swell. Plus, the water's warm."

The Superbank is a man-made phenomenon that, through the redistribution of dredged sand, has resulted in one of the world's most incredible breaks and the linking up of Snapper and Kirra. However, no one expected the scheme to produce such an amazing sandbank or to have such a profound effect on the surf. The dredged sand has filled in the bays at Snapper, Rainbow Bay and Greenmount with such efficiency that they form one long, seamless sandbank.

Turning up at the Superbank, there are a number of things that strike you. Even the most jaded surfer has been known to stand and watch in awe before heading for the line-up. On a perfect day, machine-like waves roll along the shallow sandbank in one mesmerizing, unending, unstoppable runaway steam train of a wave. It is like one of the old domino spectaculars, where huge lines topple in one endless swoop of kinetic energy. Only here the energy is poured onto a shallow bank in the form of a mile-long, hollow, peeling wave. There are a number of spots where surfers join the line-up. The push of the ocean sends a strong rip down the point, distributing both the sediment and the

Below: Superview over the Superbank.
Opposite page: Superclear Superbank.

Superbank Board

6'0" Webber Squash

Shaper: Greg Webber

6'0" x 18⅛" x 2⅛"

High-performance shortboard designed for advanced surfers.

Single to double concave makes it fast down the line, yet turns tight in the pocket.

FCS Fins.

ⓘ Boards by **Surftech**
www.surftech.com info@surftech.com

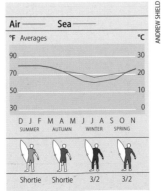

Air		Sea	
°F	Averages		°C
90			30
70			20
50			10
30			0

D J F M A M J J A S O N
SUMMER · AUTUMN · WINTER · SPRING

Shortie	Shortie	3/2	3/2

ANDREW SHIELD

pack of surfers. It's possible to enter at the jumping-off spot at Snapper and snag a few waves down the line, exit and walk back up, or continue all the way down the point to Kirra. Traditionally the point at Kirra has always been a tube-rider's dream. The sudden shallow sandbank causes swell to fall over itself onto the compacted sandbar, producing hollow waves with huge, thick, sand-filled lips. It could be the longest barrel of your life, or a pounding you'll never forget.

The Coolangatta area has been one of the world's premier surf spots since the late 1960s, churning out world-class surfers and grinding pits with equally freakish ferocity and regularity and producing legends such as Michael Peterson (MP), ex-world champions Peter Townend (PT) and Wayne 'Rabbit' Bartholomew, current world tour surfers Mick Fanning and Joel Parkinson, as well as world-class waveriders such as Dean Morrison and Neal Purchase Jnr. The 'Golden Era' of Kirra in the early '70s saw surfers like MP shaping some of the most progressive boards on the planet at the factories like Joe Larking's. When Australian surf movie *Morning of the Earth* hit screens across the world, the footage that captured the synergy of MP at Kirra propelled him onto the international stage and set the scene for the intense, even antagonistic, competition between himself, Rabbit and PT that would become one of the central forces in the birth of professional surfing.

Today, the annual Quiksilver Pro is one of the most popular stops on the professional World Championship Tour and brings with it worldwide media coverage. "They call it the Superbank but it looks beyond that – it's just truly amazing," says X3 World Champion Andy Irons. "To get to surf it with just one or two other guys out during the Quiksilver Pro is the ultimate. Even to get just one good wave from amongst the crowd is as good as 100 waves anywhere else."

The population boom in the Coolangatta region, coupled with the surge in the popularity of surfing, has caused a massive increase in numbers in the water on any good day. The Superbank now has a supersized reputation and everyone wants to sample it.

Locals and legends
Wayne 'Rabbit' Bartholomew, Michael Peterson, Peter Townend, Mick Fanning, Joel Parkinson, Dean Morrison, Neal Purchase Jnr, about 200 other rippers.

Nearby breaks Duranbah or **D'Bah** is a beach break just to the north of the mouth of the Tweed River, inside the rocky breakwater. The swell creates wedgy peaks and is a super consistent spot that sucks in the crowds as it sucks in the swell. Home to some of Australia's most talented surfers, its ultra-competitive line-up is home to some great waves. The sand provides plenty of board-breaking peaks that are keenly fought over.

Surfers' tales
Superbank

ANDREW SHIELD

When word first started to trickle out, it sounded like the surfing equivalent of 'Fisherman's Tales' – one part truth mixed with nine parts exaggeration; Carwyn Williams returning from Oz and talking about riding from Snapper Rocks through to Kirra. Suddenly it was real – with a name: the Superbank. It all sounded too good to be true. A sand-bottomed, point break wave over a mile long. But where had this thing come from? Was it a freak of nature that would soon be gone? A sign of the changing ebb and flow of the planet – something that would be retold to future generations who would look back with an 'Oh, yeah, right gramps' look on their faces? But no, the Superbank was here to stay, and what's more, it was a man-made phenomenon. It was the result of co-operation between civic authorities with a liberal sprinkling of surfers' input. Who would have thought that?

To the south of Coolangatta sits the Tweed River, delineating the end of New South Wales and the start of Queensland. It has always been a treacherous waterway due to the build up of shifting sandbars in the shipping channel. Several man-made attempts were made to make the channel safer for shipping, including the building of the rock breakwaters at the rivermouth in the early sixties ('62-'65). This served to trap and disrupt the natural south to north

sand movement. However, during the late sixties and seventies a series of cyclones stripped sand back from the volcanic rock points just to the north – home of Snapper Rocks, Rainbow Bay, Greenmount and Kirra. These bays could no longer be naturally replenished by longshore drift, as sand flow was now being disrupted by the breakwaters at the mouth of the Tweed. Suddenly local businesses and tourist authorities started to fear for the threatened beaches and the impact their loss could have on the region's tourist industry. In the early nineties a scheme was proposed that would facilitate the removal of sand from the mouth of the Tweed (where it isn't wanted) and its relocation to the sand-deprived northerly points. Ex-world champion and local surf legend, Wayne 'Rabbit' Bartholomew, and Bruce Lee of the Snapper Rocks Surfriders Club were involved with the consultation and the new scheme was completed in 2001. Sand is now pumped from the mouth of the river, underground to spots at Froggies Beach, just to the south of Snapper, as well as Rainbow Bay and Kirra. Natural drift redistributes the sand in a northerly direction along the point. The new system also has the ability to pump sand out at Duranbah if the wave quality is affected by less sand accumulating on the beach.

The Superbank has built up to a point where the sand has now filled in the bays at Snapper, Rainbow Bay and Greenmount with such efficiency as to form one long, seamless sandbank. It is capable of producing rides of 2 km in length and numerous 10-second barrels. But the irony is that it is often so irresistible that there are multiple drop-ins on each wave. One surfer riding the length of the Superbank would make for not many waves being ridden by what is probably the hungriest pack of surfers on the planet. So, for sheer sanity, the set-up is often better when it forms sections, giving more surfers more waves and keeping the competitive line-up moving. It's not all perfection and 10-second barrels. This is not an easy wave to ride. The take-off can be dredging, the tubes can wobble and need to be steered through, and then there are the crowds. The Superbank is located right in the middle of one of the world's biggest and most competitive surf communities. When it breaks, there are hundreds who want the wave you are paddling for. They include super-fit grommets, who will outstroke anyone against the continuous rip that pulls the pack down the point, local legends with the knowledge and guile to gauge just where to sit to pick off the most waves, WQS surfers who'll backdoor the peak and take the wave right from under your nose, and ex-world champs who'll sit so far back in the barrel they are dropped in on by over-excited shoulder hoppers. There are so many drop-ins, it can start to resemble a gladiatorial battle. Recently there have been incidences of surf rage and violent attacks that have left some local politicians threatening the imposition of 'Surf Police' in the line-up.

Some say that the loss of the separate bays with their different waves and unique characteristics has been to the detriment of the area. Others assert that this is a return to the way the headlands were before the original stone breakwaters were built. Whatever the effect on the characteristics of the pre-Superbank waves, few would dispute that the sand has produced a true surfing phenomenon. "There are some longboarders and some of the old guys who think that it's a change for the worse," says Rabbit. "They miss the mellower waves that were there before, but the guys who like tube-riding think it's heaven on Earth." As Joel Fitzgerald says "It is the longest barrelling wave I have ever seen. Sunny, sandy, beautiful! It's the best wave in the world, but can be your worst nightmare if selfish egos get the better of you on the day."

Below: Superbusy Superbank
Opposite page: Looking south.

ANDREW SHIELD

Burleigh Heads

◈ **Location:** Between Kirra Point and Surfers Paradise, Gold Coast, Queensland

◗ **Break type:** Right-hand point break

◓ **Conditions:** Medium to big swells

◉ **Size:** 2-12 ft

◒ **Length:** 50-200-m-long point

◈ **Tide:** All tides

◈ **Swell direction:** Southeasterly through to northeasterly

◉ **Wind:** Southwesterly to westerly

◈ **Bottom:** Sand covered rocks

◈ **Ability level:** Intermediate-advanced

◈ **Best months:** Jan-May

◈ **Access:** Off the rocks

◈ **Hazards:** Very busy, competitive line-up

When it came to handing out names, Gold Coast officials managed to miss the real Surfers Paradise by 13 km. Rather than the high-rise-backed beachie a short drive to the north, the classic Gold Coast point of Burleigh Heads is the epitome of waveriding perfection. Water shots of surfers in the barrel with the signature backdrop of the forest-fringed mid-rise buildings have been inspiring generations of grommets since the 1970s. "I moved up to Queensland because my dream was to surf Burleigh," says legendary shaper Nev Hyman. "I'd see all the photos in *Tracks* magazine of grinding barrels and I got there in time to see Michael Peterson win the Stubbies Pro in 1977. It was just epic. There are probably only a few waves in the world where I've screamed myself hoarse from excitement and this is one of them. I've had absolutely mindlessly perfect waves – so good it's like you're on another planet."

Right: Burleigh lines.
Opposite page: Kovac hooks into a Burleigh barrel.

ANDREW SHIELD

Burleigh Heads sits 16 km to the north of the classic points of Kirra and Snapper Rocks. The wave is nestled on the northern side of the headland formed from the eroded flank of a huge, prehistoric volcano. Sand is deposited at the Tallebudgera rivermouth, pushed north by ocean drift and groomed along the point. Here it forms a long, tapering sandbank that protects the volcanic rock of the headland and produces sublime, hollow waves for the huge number of local devotees. Like other sandy points, wave quality is dependent upon how the sediments have been deposited. After a storm the sand can erode and wave quality may suffer, but when the bank lines up with a perfect southeasterly swell, the hollow waves that peel through can be of epic proportions.

Waves of up to 3 m can break on the outside section known as 'The Cove'. This picks up the most swell and snagging a wave here means beating the crowds, many of whom have the place wired. "In the days before leashes, it took real commitment paddling into a big set wave at The Cove", says Burleigh regular, Rabbit Bartholomew. "It was a long swim in from there. But the rewards if you made it were long, winding barrels through the inside section." There are a number of tube-riding opportunities on the right day as the ruler-topped waves throw out firing barrels. The level of surfing here is extremely high and is still at the cutting edge, with some of the world's best tube-riders locked in on the set waves. As a tourist hotspot and being so close to Brisbane, crowds have always been a factor here and the locals have had to become adept at dealing with them. Weaving through the masses there will be every kind of waveriding vehicle and every level of waverider, all competing for what could be the wave of their lives.

But it hasn't always been this way. "I remember going to the Australian Nationals held in Coolangatta in 1966," says Phil Grace. "I was in the Victoria team with Wayne Lynch and I was riding a 9-ft board. Back then the tallest building on the Gold Coast was three

stories high. We drove up to Burleigh and in those days no one was really surfing there – it was too radical a wave for the equipment we were riding at the time. Then the shortboard revolution came along and it all changed." In the mid '70s, the world of surfing was being forged in the firing points of the Gold Coast. Queensland became the testing ground for a generation who would go on to change surfing forever. The 1977 Stubbies Classic is generally regarded as the first surf contest of the modern professional era. It featured man-on-man heats – where two riders go head to head – a format that survives on the WCT to this day. Local legend Michael Peterson took the crown at Burleigh and made history. He beat the likes of Mark Richards, Peter Townend, Rabbit Bartholomew and Ian Cairns. He was the best surfer of his era and this was his final victory.

Burleigh is a bit like Australia itself. It has been around for millennia, was only recently discovered, but once it was on the map everyone could see that it was a true surfers' paradise.

Locals and legends

Locals include Peter Drouyn, Ken Adler, the Neilsen brothers, Dick Van Straalen, Jay Thompson, Joe Engel, Thornton Fallander, Dwayne and Peter Harris, Ryan Gray, Nick Heath, Brad Jeffries, Kyle Robinson, Jackson Close, Luke Egan, Dave Rastovich.

Burleigh Heads Board

6'1" Byrne HP

Shaper: Phil Byrne

6'1" x 18⅜" x 2⁵⁄₁₆"

High-performance shortboard ideally suited for the long spinning tubes of Burleigh Heads.

Single to double concave.

FCS Fins.

(i) Boards by Surftech
www.surftech.com   info@surftech.com

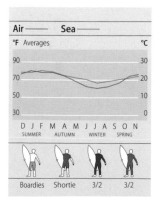

Air —— Sea ——

°F Averages   °C

90   30

70   20

50   10

30   0

D J F   M A M   J J A S   O N
SUMMER AUTUMN WINTER SPRING

Boardies   Shortie   3/2   3/2

Nearby breaks When the swell is small, there may be waves along the stretch of beach running north between Burleigh and **Surfers Paradise**. It closes out when big but in a small, angled swell there can be good waves on offer. Another spot worth checking is **The Alley** at Currumbin. It can be busy but this right point gets good as it peels towards the rivermouth. To the south of Currumbin are the legendary points of **Kirra** and the **Superbank**.

Noosa

- **Location:** Sunshine Coast, QLD – south of Fraser Island, north of Surfers Paradise.
- **Break type:** Point breaks
- **Conditions:** Medium to big swells (cyclone swells)
- **Size:** 3-8 ft
- **Length:** 50-250 m
- **Tide:** All tides
- **Swell direction:** Northeasterly to easterly or big southeasterly
- **Wind:** Southerly or southwesterly
- **Bottom:** Sand and rock
- **Ability level:** Beginner to advanced
- **Best months:** Jan-Jul
- **Access:** Various jump-off spots
- **Hazards:** Urchins and crowds, falling koalas

It sounds like something out of *The Wizard of Oz*: drive north from Bribie Island up the Sunshine Coast and along the Sunshine Motorway, turn off towards Sunshine Beach and once there, get out of your car and follow the 'yellow brick road' onto the headland of Noosa National Park, pass the Devil's Kitchen, Lion Rock, Blowhole and through Hells Gates. Approaching Noosa Heads from the south there are no clues to the plethora of perfect waves that await you. The landscape from here on in is a smorgasbord of right-hand point breaks, from the challenging through to the downright playful. For a regular footer, there's no place like Noosa.

Jutting out into the Coral Sea, this rocky headland has been subtly shaped by Pacific swells for millennia and the lush forest of the National Park area has changed little over this time. With the prime surfing to be found on the sheltered, north-facing side of Noosa Heads, it is no surprise to learn that these surf-shy points are consistently inconsistent and have the reputation as one of the most fickle spots in Australia. But with its prime position on the Sunshine Coast and sub-tropical climate, the locals will forgive the odd flat spell.

While Kirra is a byword for frenetic, death-or-glory barrels, Noosa has become associated with crystal, peeling walls and soul arches. It is home to five point break waves heading out along the headland. Each one peels along a rocky fringe into a sand and rock bay weathered over time by oceanic storms. They can be shallow and rocky, steep and fast, or mellow and rolling and there is always the

odd urchin (or shark) lurking in the shallows. Facing north, these precocious points really come to life during the tropical cyclone season. From December to March, the tight, powerful depressions of spiralling winds form in the warm waters off the northeast coast of Australia and can push regular epic swells down towards the primed Queensland points.

The walk out along the northern bush track to the tip of the headland follows a path first trodden by surfers in the '60s. Leaving the beach, First Point, the site of the annual Noosa Longboard Contest, is the closest spot and as such can attract insane crowds. It's best taken on at low tide and doesn't get above head high unless there's a monster swell running.

Next up is Johnsons, a faster wave and more challenging, but still relatively easy and beginner-friendly. On a good day it can connect through from National Park, the next bay along. National Park sits on the parks boundary and is framed by this stunning backdrop. The main take-off point is a dramatic and compressed area known as the Boiling Pot, where the tussle for waves can be a contrast to the quiet location. However, in a decent swell surfers do become spread through the National Park line-up, picking off waves that peel over the sand- and rock-covered bed at various points along this surfing travelator.

Tea Tree Bay may be a 20-minute walk along the point but don't expect that to have any effect on the number of hungry surfers in the water. When a good swell arrives and the banks are lined up, this is the most challenging of the waves at Noosa. Breaking along sand and urchin-encrusted boulders, the take-off here is critical and there is a lot of competition for every wave. These steep walls make for long, fast rides. "When it's overhead, it has some of the most perfect, mechanically-shaped, rippable walls on the planet," says Aussie surf writer Jimmy O'Keefe. "Great rainforest backdrop as well." Final stop on the bush track is Granite Bay. It may not be the best wave on the headland, but it is more of a swell catcher and the furthest to get to, so crowds can be less of a factor here.

Noosa may try the patience of a saint at times, but when it is on, that saint will be out there for five straight hours making the most of every wave that reels through. There will be generations of surfers young and old, on all variety of boards, from pro's to beginners, all sharing the same pulse in ocean energy. Legendary shaper Bob McTavish rates two of the

Opposite page: Small but perfectly formed Noosa.

Noosa waves as being in his all time top 10. "Ti-tree Bay, Noosa is the best small wave on planet Earth, with rainforest to the water's edge. It was best in the 70's when no-one had a longboard for those waist-high days. My other favourite is National Park. It's a long, long wave with many challenging sections, and a final spin-cycle into zipperland."

The Aboriginal root of the word Noosa means 'shade' and the chic town of Noosa Heads certainly sits in the shadow of the headland at the southern end of Laguna Bay. It consists of a collection of settlements clustered around the National Park in a region that has undergone a boom recently thanks to the huge increase in tourism

and a swathe of new urban developments. "I grew up surfing Noosa," says legendary shaper Chops Lascelles. "There were so few of us back then that we happily surfed Johnsons and National Park for a couple of years before we even knew Tea Trees existed. There wasn't the crowd pressure to push us to explore further up the point. Today it gets so crowded – up to 700 people on the points – that you could virtually run along the heads in the line-up like stepping stones!" Lured by the wonderful climate and countryside, Noosa attracts everyone from young backpackers and surfers to retired couples looking for a piece of paradise. Catch Noosa on a good swell and you just might choose to join them.

Locals and legends

Tom Wegener, Luke Jory, Jackson Close, Darren Magee, Josh Constable, Grant Thomas, Phil Jarratt, Ryan Campbell, Julian Wilson, Chris de Aboitiz, Lauren Ringer.

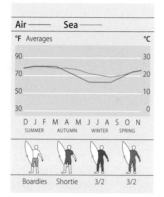

Noosa Board	
9'1" McTavish Razor	
Shaper: Bob McTavish	
9'1" x 22½" x 2⅞"	
Your everyday every-wave longboard.	
Designed by legendary shaper Bob McTavish.	
From 2ft to 10ft, noserides to barrel rides this board does it all.	
2+1 fin set up.	
ⓘ Boards by **Surftech** www.surftech.com info@surftech.com	

Air ——— Sea ———

°F Averages °C

90 — 30
70 — 20
50 — 10
30 — 0

D J F M A M J J A S O N
SUMMER AUTUMN WINTER SPRING

Boardies   Shortie   3/2   3/2

Nearby breaks If the swell and wind aren't favourable for the northern breaks, then the eastern side of the headland is home to the swell-hoovering beach break and nudie spot **Alexandria Bay**, with another stretch of consistent banks at **Sunshine Beach** just to the south.

SEAN DAVEY

Surfers' tales
Sean Davey's Perfect 10

Tasmanian native Sean Davey spent his teens immersed in the Sydney surf scene of the late '70s and early '80s, developing his passion for surfing and photography. From here he began an annual pilgrimage to Hawaii's infamous North Shore where he now lives with his wife Lane. As one of the world's leading surf photographers he has travelled across the world, from Europe to the Pacific Islands via North and Central America, Indonesia as well as closer to his homeland – New Zealand and Australia.

Top 10 perfect surf scenarios

1: Semi secret beach break on King Island, Australia, known affectionately as Martha. Breaks a lot like Kirra, but with no one around. Surf the place with Derek Hynd because he rides a fish there like no one else. Frankie Oberholzer and Joe Curren too. They've both been there and sampled Martha's charms.

2: Marrawah region on the north of the Tasmanian coast early February with a bunch of my mates. Camping out under the stars. Stinking hot by day, but super refreshing in the ocean. Typically 4 to 5-ft beachies and reef breaks with hardly another surfer in sight. Just magic!

3: Malaysian wave pool, just cause it'd be interesting to give it a go.

4: Hanging out at Manoa Drollet's house in Tahiti and cruising with him and Pancho Sullivan on the numerous perfect, and just about always unridden, outer reefs. There's dozens of perfect waves other than Teahupoo.

5: Surfing with a couple of mates on the northeast coast of Tasmania, February to March. Usually a bit of east swell off the odd cyclone and pumping waves everywhere. Downside is that this region isn't exactly a constant wave magnet.

6: Surf trip around the mid New South Wales coast, particularly the area just south of Forster which is as close to a perfect surf town as one can get. Lots of different breaks facing in numerous different directions and quality waves everywhere.

7: Cruising on a luxury yacht anywhere in Indo WITHOUT all the other boats can't be bad.

8: Maldives looks pretty attractive, but again without all the crowds.

9: Galápagos Islands – it'd be just as interesting to see the creatures as much as the surf.

10: New Zealand rocks just for its amazing scenery and diverse array of surf breaks.

Top 10 shots

1: Anything with Slater on it because he really is the man! I'd like to shoot him at Lance's Right – him and Shane Dorian together.

2: Shipsterns Bluff with Dorian, Kieren Perrow and Jamie O'Brien, because it's a heavy wave and they are all up for crazy sheeyat.

3: A 10 to 15-ft Teahupoo with Jamie O'Brein and Kelly Slater because it would be ridiculous, watching those two trade-off there. Even better if shooting from a chopper.

4: A 10 to 15-ft Pipeline from a chopper. Something I've always wanted to do, but kind of too hard basket these days because of all the complaining residents and the odd angry local.

5: The Carolina Islands look real nice. Any surfers would be good to shoot there, I guess.

6: Maldives has always been there in the back of my mind. I like the blue clear lagoons and stuff. I'd have to have a supermodel on hand, to really get some great shots. Doesn't all have to be surfing.

7: Northern California would be awesome, but I'd have to be with crew who knew the area. It's a big, big place.

8: I've always liked the look of the British Virgin Islands.

9: Lord Howe Island (off the east coast of Oz) looks absolutely stunning.

10: Dream trip: Mark Richards, Tom Carroll, Tom Curren and Martin Potter, Bugs on a boat trip somewhere in Indo, far away from all the other boats and particularly far away from all their usual daily pressures these days. They all have incredible style, even today.

273

Below: Kieren Perrow charging through the dark heart of a true Tasmanian devil.
Opposite page: Dan Ross – Marrawah – looking on the bright side of Tassie.

SEAN DAVEY

Raglan

⬦ **Location:**	West of Hamilton, west coast, North Island
⬤ **Break type:**	Three left-hand point breaks
⬤ **Conditions:**	Medium to big swells
⬤ **Size:**	3-12 ft
⬤ **Length:**	100-300 m
⬤ **Tide:**	All tides, more hollow at low
⬤ **Swell direction:**	Southwesterly
⬤ **Wind:**	Southeasterly to easterly (can work in southwesterlies)
⬤ **Bottom:**	Rocky reef
⬤ **Ability level:**	Intermediate +
⬤ **Best months:**	Year-round
⬤ **Access:**	Off the rocks
⬤ **Hazards:**	Crowds, sharks, rocks

If it weren't for the classic 1964 surf film *Endless Summer*, New Zealand might still be a virtually unknown waveriding destination. It may not have had the impact that *Lord of the Rings* did on New Zealand's tourist industry, but it did lift the veil and reveal a potential for world-class waves that might have otherwise remained hidden for decades. Unlike some nations, local surfers don't feel the need to shout about the amazing waves that break every day along their 15,046 km of coastline. As North Island resident Ian Coutanche explains, "There are still days when I turn up at my local point break to find it head high, perfect and empty. I have to ring round to find people to come and surf!"

When Robert August and Mike Hynson stopped off on their '60s surf tour, it was the waves of Raglan that they rode. Despite the numerous world-class waves in New Zealand, it has steadfastly remained the country's most famous surf destination ever since. But don't be fooled by the beach – which can offer up some decent rides – the large headland to the south is the business end of the bay. Rather than consisting of a single wave, Raglan is a goofy footer's nirvana with the three breaks – Indicators, Whale Bay and Manu Bay – creating a trilogy of epic proportions.

Part 1 – The Fellowship. Every time it breaks, Manu Bay throngs with surfers, all keen to pit their wits against a wave that can throw up everything from long, workable walls to dark, cavernous pits. Coming from the beach, Manu is the first in a line of long lefts and is

sometimes referred to simply as 'The Point'. Breaking over a rock and boulder bottom, this is a multi-faceted wave with a critical take-off. Due to its high quality, location and potential for sucking barrels (especially at low tide), it can also be the busiest of the spots. This wave is offshore in an easterly or southeasterly wind and access is a well-timed jump off the rocks, between 'Boneyards' (the outside) and 'The Ledge'; "a deep inside take-off section, which at size can be an ugly, heaving, intimidating barrel," explains NZ surfer Dion Ahern.

Part 2 – The Two Walls. South along the headland from Manu lies Whale Bay. A large, strategically placed rock bisects the line-up here at high tide, carving the wall into two sections but, on lower tides and larger swells, the wave can be ridden in one careful instalment. Whale Bay is the least critical and least hollow of the left-handers. This point break is more of a hot-dog style wave with plenty of time for cutbacks and stylish manoeuvres. Although the most forgiving of the three, entry and exit over the boulders and through the sets can still be a challenge.

Part 3 – Hail to the King. Crowning the headland, Indicators sits the furthest south and furthest outside of the three breaks and can also handle the largest swells. This is a truly regal wave. Although it's the most exposed and therefore most open to adverse wind directions, when it's firing it can be a shallow, hollow challenge of a wave, up there with the best of them. The rides here tend to be fast and walling sprints with barrel sections opening up in the right conditions. Again, Indicators is best in an easterly or southeasterly wind and low tide

Below: Local Daniel Kereopa locks into Manu Bay.
Opposite page: Raglan.

CORY SCOTT

tends to be the most hollow. On the inside tube section, watch for the rocks that can suddenly appear. The outside section, known surprisingly as 'Outsides', has a sucking take-off close to the rocks and can peel all the way through to Whale Bay in the largest swells. "A set-wave from 'Outside Indies' through to 'The Valley' will leave you with jelly-legs and a three-day grin from ear-to-ear," confirms Dion.

Raglan sits on the west coast of the North Island about 48 km from Hamilton. The frequent southwesterly swells that angle up the Tasman Sea from the 'Roaring Forties' reel along the headland of what is universally accepted as one of the most stunning destinations on the planet. "New Zealand rocks just for its amazing scenery and diverse array of surf breaks," says surf photographer Sean Davey.

Locals and legends

Daniel Kereopa, Kelly Clarkeson, Luke Hughes, Leon and Jess Santorik, Zennor Wernham, Morehu Roberts, Luke Cederman, Ruben Noble, Mike Banks, Geoff Hutchison, Larry Fisher.

Raglan Board	
6'2" Byrne Six Channel	
Shaper: Phil Byrne	
6'2" x 18⅜" x 2⅜"	
State of the art performance surfboard.	
Slight concave going into six channels through the tail.	
Designed for long point break waves like Raglan.	
Best in waves from 2ft to 8ft.	
FCS fins	

ⓘ Boards by **Surftech**
www.surftech.com info@surftech.com

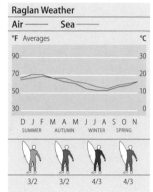

Raglan Weather

Air —— Sea ——

°F Averages		°C
90		30
70		20
50		10
30		0

D J F M A M J J A S O N
SUMMER AUTUMN WINTER SPRING

3/2	3/2	4/3	4/3

Nearby breaks Raglan is a very flexible spot with the left points offering differing degrees of challenge depending on the swell size and direction. If the points are not for you, there are also nearby beach breaks such as **Wainui Beach**, which has excellent access and can produce some quality banks. Best surfed at mid to high tide in smaller swells. **Ruapuke Beach** sits 18 km south of Raglan and is a sandy beach that picks up heaps of swell. There is a right-hander that often works at the northern end of the 8-km beach at low tide and peaks spread along its length.

CORY SCOTT

Australia & New Zealand Raglan

Surfers' tales
New Zealand's Top 10 hot spots Chris Millet, *Kiwi Surf Magazine*

1: Raglan

The first name on any travelling surfer's lips, Raglan is NZ's most iconic break for a reason. As far as point breaks go it's incredibly consistent. While most of the world's points lay dormant for large chunks of the year, only coming alive in exactly the right wind and swell conditions, Raglan has rideable waves over 50% of the time. Consisting of three main breaks, Indicators, Whale Bay and Manu Bay, there's a wave to suit any surfer's skill level. Fancy yourself as a bit of a hot shot? Take on the local rippers at Manu Bay. Rate yourself as a beginner? Go to Raglan Beach, or you could try and take on the slow-moving waves of Whale Bay. More into soul surfing for a bit of solitude? Head for Indicators. When the points are flat there's always the beach breaks of Ruapuke and Bryant Home, a short drive away.

2: Shipwrecks (Kaitaia)

Once a hardly published spot, the advent of Internet surf reporting has made getting Shippies on all too easy. It needs a huge west coast swell to break but, due to the pinpoint accuracy of swell forecasting, it's not uncommon to see hordes of 4WDs trekking north to Kaitaia to pounce just as the waves hit. For a lot of people the mystique of Shipwrecks has been spoilt. The beach and rocks around the point can resemble the Piha car park in the middle of summer. That said, it's still a great wave. There are actually seven different sections/breaks, so head to the one with the least people on it and you'll still enjoy yourself.

3: Stent Road (Taranaki)

Taranaki has many great breaks, and they're all kindly signposted by the 'Surf Highway', a local council initiative to promote the district as a surf destination. They're not exaggerating either – Taranaki pumps. The crown jewel of 'Taradise' would have to be Stent Road, one of the most exposed, so therefore most consistent breaks. A great right-hander, Stent's appeal is its power. Breaking over a sand/rock combo and getting the brunt of the west coast swell, it's a very high-performance wave. Best when the winds are light.

PAUL KENNEDY

4: Wainui Beach (Gisborne)

Ever wondered why Gisborne produced the likes of NZ's top surfer Maz Quinn? Put it down to Wainui Beach. A stretch of sand 2 km long, each undulation in the beachfront makes a different peak. Popping up along Wainui Beach you find the breaks of Whales, Chalet, Pines, Schools, Stockroute and Coopers Street, just to name a few. The beauty of Wainui Beach is that it's open to a variety of swell from the north right around to the south. To surf at a high level you have to be adaptable, and Wainui's ever-changing wave face is the perfect place for aspiring contest surfers to cut their teeth. Normally the best peak will be overrun by hotties, so if it's a mellow surf you're after, head down the beach a bit – there's always plenty of waves.

5: Matakana Island (Mount Maunganui)

A short boat trip or long paddle from Mount Maunganui central, Matakana Island offers up some of most pristine tubes in New Zealand. The island doesn't break as often as some of its east coast counterparts, and scoring the right combination of wind and tide is tricky, but once you've sampled a Matakana tube you'll be wanting more.

6: Whangamata Bar

Back in the day top Aussie surfers used to leave their pumping Gold Coast breaks to get a spot of Whangamata magic. A long, sand-bottomed left-hander, Whanga Bar is one of the North Island east coast's more classic breaks. Best on low tide and with an easy paddle-out through the harbour entrance, its ease of access means there's a lot of 'wave sharing' going on. Patience is a virtue…

7: Murdering Bay

Located on the north side of the Dunedin Peninsula, access is by a steep, slippery, mission of a road. Due to the fact that Murderers needs a big north swell to even think about breaking, which is generally generated by rare-as-hens'-teeth tropical cyclones, the likelihood of seeing this extremely long right-hand point breaking are slim indeed. Those who have surfed it talk of leg-achingly long rides with multiple tube sections, placing it right up there as one of the best waves in New Zealand. Three years ago the National titles lucked into one such swell and competitors gorged themselves as contest organizers mowed through nearly 12 hours of heats in a day. Murderers' epic waves helped make it the best Nationals for waves ever.

8: Papatowai

It's not so much that it's hard to get to or find, more that you need the skill and/or the motor power to take on Papas. The beauty of this spot is the deep-water channel that waves break into. No matter how big it gets, Papatowai will still break properly. The easiest way to take on Papas is to be towed by jet ski. A couple of years back, Aussie big wave chargers Ross Clarke-Jones and Tony Ray followed a massive swell that developed off Tasmania tracking it to Papatowai. Thinking they'd be the only ones on to it, imagine their surprise when they bumped

into several big wave NZ luminaries with the same thoughts in mind. Kiwi madman Doug Young did his best to show them up, using a jet ski for the first time with a makeshift tow rope that had a handle made from a tree branch.

9: Rakatoka Island

As far a surf spots go, this is about as hard a spot to tackle as any. Situated in Foveaux Strait, there are no occupants on the island, just a lighthouse. In fact, it was an ex-lighthouse keeper, Rod Rust, who discovered the wave's potential, although he had to be very careful when surfing it alone. The Quiksilver Rex Von Huben Big Wave Challenge brought Rakatoka Island to the attention of the mainstream press. Competitors have had to brave the freezing conditions, bumpy boat rides and lumpy seas to get a piece of the action. During a warm-up surf one competitor got washed out to sea by the nasty rip and had to be rescued by jet ski, by which stage he feared for his life. Hardly seems worth the effort, ay?

10: Spot X

The irony of this spot is that it's highly visible from land and surf magazines are forbidden from mentioning its true location, but there are only a handful of surfers in NZ crazy or skilled enough to take on this mutant beast of a wave. The dangers are manifold. The island is a seal colony and drops straight into deep water, which triples the likelihood of a shark attack. Making matters worse, the rocks are only inches from the surface in places. Often the wave mutates into weird steps and shockwaves making the chance of a vicious wipe-out way more likely. Hawaiian big wave charger Ross Williams has taken on the world's biggest waves and didn't enjoy his surf at Spot X. "I don't see the point in getting absolutely smashed. What's the fun in that? This is ridiculous," he remarked after only a few waves.

Above: One of New Zealand's top beach breaks – The Pines, Wainui Beach.
Opposite page: Jamie Gordon takes on one of Dunedin's ledges.

Stent Road

Location:	Taranaki, west coast, North Island
Break type:	Right-hand point
Conditions:	All swells
Size:	3-10 ft
Length:	up to 100 m
Tide:	All tides, more hollow at low
Swell direction:	Southwesterly to northwesterly
Wind:	Easterly
Bottom:	Rocky point
Ability level:	Intermediate plus
Best months:	Mar-Nov
Access:	Off the rocks
Hazards:	Crowds, heavy waves, reef

Stent Road Board

6'1" Rusty Pro-ject

Shaper: Rusty Preisendorfer

6'1" x 18.25" x 2.06"

Elliptical curve through tail creates continuity through rail transitions and smooth, pocket-oriented surfing.

Single to double concave for added drive.

Works in slow and fast stuff.

Use it with ease in anything.

Futures fins.

Boards by **Surftech**
www.surftech.com info@surftech.com

Stent Road Weather

Air ——— Sea ———	
°F Averages	°C
90	30
70	20
50	10
30	0

D J F M A M J J A S O N
SUMMER   AUTUMN   WINTER   SPRING

3/2   3/2   4/3   4/3

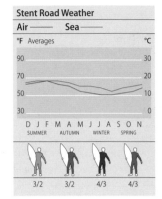

Word is out. Taranaki is on the up. And the more people who visit, the more word is spreading that this region of New Zealand should be up there on every surfer's to-do list. This bulbous protrusion on the west coast of North Island lies in an ideal location to hoover up the regular southwesterly swells that march up the Tasman Sea. The geography of the area provides numerous world-class points and reefs on which the groomed lines can focus. Following Surf Highway 45 around the curved coastal fringe, there are many tracks and roads angling down to the coast, with quality surf breaks waiting at the end. But the real gem lies at the bottom of Stent Road. Pull into the parking lot at the point, park among the small collection of utes and pick-ups and it'll soon be obvious why this wave is so highly prized. That's if you can find the turn-off – the road sign here has an *X-Files*-like tendency of dematerializing.

"The Taranaki locals pride themselves on power surfing and Stent Road is their gold nugget," says surfer Dion Ahern. "This is rural New Zealand at its best." The region is dominated by the dormant volcano that gives it's name to the area. "Situated in the countryside with Mount Taranaki as a backdrop, it's an idyllic setup," says photographer Paul Kennedy. This spectacular volcanic peak, with its dazzling covering of snow, towers over the lush green landscape below. "Stent Road is on the west coast and therefore has great consistency along with the rest of Taranaki," explains Paul. "The wave has great form and power, making it a very desirable and shreddable wave. It is probably the best of many great waves in Taranaki." Stent, a powerful right point that can offer up heavy barrels or open faces, is definitely a wave for the committed. The wave peaks on the end of the point with a ledging, sucky take-off. This leads into a fast section of speeding wall with the occasional cover-up. "Stent Road is the jewel in the crown of the Taranaki Surf Highway, which traverses the semi-circular cape," says surf shop owner Wayne 'Arch' Arthur. "It is not a hollow wave. Any barrel is a well-deserved cover-up more than a barrel. But the spot itself takes the brunt of any swell charging up the Tasman. As such, it is a grunty wave with a performance, shreddable wall." When those big, southwesterly swells unload, Stent can offer up some truly scary waves for those brave enough to take it on. However, the mood of the wave is fundamentally affected by the tide. The break works through

Right: Stent Road.
Opposite page: Luke Kerr powering up in 'Taradise'.

all tides but is hollower and more critical on lower tides. "Stent proper is a heavy, right-hand reef break that can hold waves of quality up to 10 ft," says Dion Ahern. "Taranaki has tidal movements in excess of 6 m, which play a huge role in determining the mood Stent will take. At high tide the waves break a little slower and push right inside the bay, and can be extremely rippable. At mid-tide, Stent can churn perfect spitting barrels, with several sucky bowl sections. And at low tide, it can be a minefield of boils and sharp, submerged, urchin-infested boulders in between dredging waves."

Stent has a long history, having first been surfed nearly four decades ago. "Stent Road was first surfed in the late '60s and named as 'Rovers Point'," explains 'Arch', "due to a different entry by the crew of Doug Hislop and local shaper Robert Walsh in a Land Rover. The easier subsequent entry, by travelling down Stent Road, saw it renamed shortly after." It has been the site for several competitions but still maintains a fairly low profile on the world stage – just the way the many devoted locals like it.

Locals and legends
Robert Walsh, Doug Hislop, Nigel Dwyer, Greg Page, Simon Deken, Jason Lellman, Jarrod Hancox, Nat Day, Jason Zimmerman, Luke Kerr, Jess Terrill, Paige Hareb, Hamish Bowling, Seth Mathews, kneeboarder Hamish Christophers.

Nearby breaks Just to the north and approached via Paora Road are **Rocky Rights** and **Rock Lefts** – two good quality points (right and left respectively) breaking over a boulder bottom on either side of a headland. Accessing Rocky Rights involves crossing farmland, so be respectful. Also accessed via Paora Road, just north of Rocky Lefts, is reef break **Graveyards** which works through the tides offering up quality lefts and rights – just watch out for the rocks.

CORY SCOTT

The Pacific

South Africa's Dave Weare
on Cloud 9

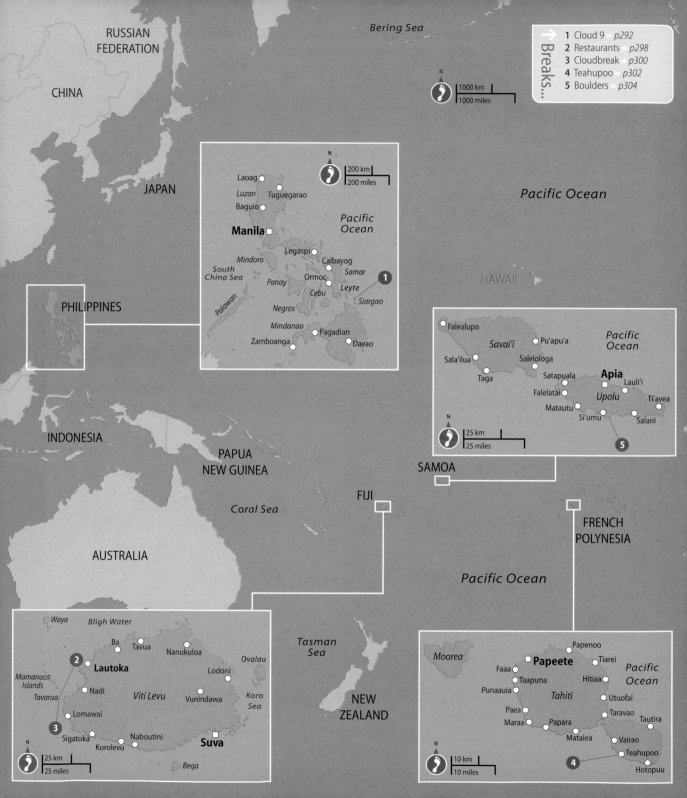

RUSSIAN
FEDERATION

CHINA

Bering Sea

JAPAN

Pacific Ocean

Breaks...
1 Cloud 9 ➔ p292
2 Restaurants ➔ p298
3 Cloudbreak ➔ p300
4 Teahupoo ➔ p302
5 Boulders ➔ p304

N
1000 km
1000 miles

N
200 km
200 miles

Laoag
Luzon
Tuguegarao
Baguio
Manila
Legaspi
Pacific Ocean
Mindoro
Calbayog
South China Sea
Ormoc
Samar
Panay
Cebu
Leyte
PHILIPPINES
Palawan
Negros
Siargao 1
Mindanao
Pagadian
Zamboanga
Davao

HAWAII

Falealupo
Savai'i
Pu'apu'a
Pacific Ocean
Sala'ilua
Salelologa
Taga
Satapuala
Apia
Falelatai
Upolu
Lauli'i
Matautu
Ti'avea
Si'umu
Salani

N
25 km
25 miles
5

INDONESIA

PAPUA
NEW GUINEA

SAMOA

FIJI

FRENCH
POLYNESIA

Coral Sea

AUSTRALIA

Pacific Ocean

Tasman Sea

NEW
ZEALAND

Waya
Bligh Water
Ba
Tavua
Nanukuloa
2 **Lautoka**
Ovalau
Lodoni
Mamanuca Islands
Nadi
Viti Levu
Vunindawa
Koro Sea
Tavarua
3
Lomawai
Sigatoka
Naboutini
Suva
Korolevu
Beqa

N
25 km
25 miles

Moorea
Papenoo
Faaa
Papeete
Tiarei
Taapuna
Hitiaa
Pacific Ocean
Punaauia
Tahiti
Utuofai
Paea
Taravao
Maraa
Papara
Tautira
Mataiea
Vairao
Teahupoo
4
Hotopuu

N
10 km
10 miles

The coarse white sand soon gives way to the fringing reef that thrives in the warm, nutrient-rich shallows skirting this uninhabited Pacific atoll. It is the fabric on which this tiny island was built. You might describe the water as 'clear as glass', but you'd be wrong. Glass takes on a green, heavily distorted cast if it's over a few centimetres thick, whereas this stuff is as clear as the clearest bottled mineral water. Brightly coloured fish dance between the swaying anemones and opaque coral heads.

The landmass sticks its head a mere 2 m above surrounding ocean and yet it is enough to allow a few plants to establish a foothold and literally hold the island together. As luck would have it, the atoll lies at such an angle that when the swells roll out of the southwest the ruler-edged reef catches them on the western corner and a reeling left-hand barrel rolls along the northern edge of the island. Such is the uniformity of the reef that it never sections, never backs off or closes out. The wave gradually diminishes in size until it runs into deeper water at the eastern edge of the flat coral fringe. It is a perfect barrel as long as G-Land, but as flawless as the 530-carat Star of Africa diamond. Its location cannot be revealed yet, because it is yet to be discovered. But it is out there. The statistical probabilities say so. Just look at the huge area the Pacific Ocean occupies, the sheer number of islands out there, and then try to disagree.

One of surfing's great ironies is that the last great final frontier for the true surf adventurer is the place where surfing began so many generations ago. The Pacific covers nearly 30% of the Earth's surface and is littered with islands. Somewhere between twenty and thirty thousand, though no one can be sure because no one has actually counted them. And if they have no idea just how many landmasses are out there in this vast ocean, how can anyone have any idea just how many waves there are waiting to be discovered? How many reverse Sunsets or meaner versions of Teahupoo are still unridden? But where to start looking? One thing you can bet on is that at this very moment there is a yacht moored somewhere out in the great blue Pacific with a surfer looking at a perfect wave reeling along a coral pass and trying to think of an apt name for their new discovery.

SEAN DAVEY

Left: All on its own, somewhere near Tonga, with no one to ride it.
Opposite page: Hawaii's Keala Kennelly is at home in the Pacific whether towing into sub-level Teahupoo or launching an air attack in Fiji.

The Philippines have high year-round temperatures and humidity levels. North and central Philippines have a tropical monsoon climate with a single rainy season coinciding with the southwest monsoon season from July to October. For the southern island of Siargao, lying off the northeast tip of Mindanao and in the direct path of the Pacific trade winds, the wet season kicks in with the northeast (onshore) monsoon. It blows from November to April, bringing with it slightly cooler temperatures and the heaviest rainfall in November to January. December sees temperatures of an average 26°C with 24 wet days delivering around 620 mm of rainfall while in June the temperature rises to around 28°C and a low of 10 wet days with 125 mm of rain. Typhoons are a possibility as the northwest Pacific basin accounts for around a third of all tropical cyclone activity in the world with the threat intensifying between July and November.

Islands are part of the Pacific group, politically they form part of the United States of America. For the purpose of the book, they are featured in the USA and Hawaii chapter.

Culture

The south Pacific islands share a cultural bond where community is paramount. Manners are important here as is dressing respectfully, especially when visiting villages off the beaten track. Each island however has its own nuances. From the name French Polynesia, it comes as little surprise that a trip to Tahiti reveals more than a few Gallic associations. Baguettes, brie and Beaujolais Nouveau are as much part of life here as black pearls, ukuleles and tattoos. No trip to Fiji – the crossroads of the Pacific – is complete without sampling Kava. The pounded root of *piper methysticum* (a plant of the pepper family) is mixed with water to create a muddy-coloured concoction and drunk from the regulation half a coconut shell. It generally makes your tongue tingle and can, allegedly, have the same effect on your mind. Fijians are very hospitable but many do not have a high disposable income so if you are invited to stay with a family, a gift such as groceries goes a long way. Samoa has a culture that emphasizes tradition and respect for elders. Permission to access village beaches needs to be sought when venturing off the beaten track and, as this is a society based on strict sabbatarian principles, Sunday really is a day of rest. That means no surfing. The Philippines has a reputation for political instability and corruption, but travelling here you'll find Filipinos a friendly and welcoming people.

Climates and seasons

The northern Pacific islands (including Marshall Islands, Micronesia, Hawaii and Philippines) follow the same seasons as North America and Europe and run roughly as follows: spring – March to May; summer – June to August; autumn – September to November; winter – December to February. The south Pacific Islands (including French Polynesia, Cook Islands, Samoa, Tonga and Fiji) are south of the equator so follow the opposite seasons.

Fiji, Tahiti and Samoa have typical tropical climates with high humidity throughout the year and high temperatures, with maximum humidity and rainfall occurring from December to April – much of it falling in short, heavy bursts. In January, Fiji sees around 290 mm of rainfall and temperatures of around 26°C. Tahiti is a little warmer and drier – January temperatures hover around 27°C with around 250 mm of rain. Temperatures in Samoa remain around 26-27°C throughout the year with heavy rainfall – 450 mm in January. The easterly/southeasterly trade winds increase from May through October, serving to cool the climates slightly and temper the humidity and precipitation – July sees average Fijian temperatures of 23°C and around 125 mm of rainfall. In Tahiti, temperatures drop to a very reasonable 25°C with just 55 mm of rain and for Samoa around 80 mm of rainfall. Tropical cyclones are less frequent than in the north Pacific but are still a risk to be aware of.

WAVEWATCH	Dec-Feb Summer	Mar-May Autumn	Jun-Aug Winter	Sep-Nov Spring
SOUTH PACIFIC ISLANDS (statistical average centered on Tahiti)				
Wave size/direction	N 3-5'	SW 3-5'	SSW 6-8'	SW 4-6'
Wind force/direction	NE F3	E F2	E F3	E F2
Surfable days	10-15	15-20	20-25	20-25
Water/air temp	27/28°C	26/27°C	25/26°C	27/28°C
NORTHWEST PACIFIC ISLANDS (Philippines, Japan, Guam, Marianas)	(Winter)	(Spring)	(Summer)	(Autumn)
Wave size/direction	ENE 4-6'	E 3-5'	E 3-4'	ENE 4-6'
Wind force/direction	E F3	E F4	W F3	E F3
Surfable days	10-15	10-15	10-15	10-15
Water/air temp	20/18°C	22/24°C	28/28°C	24/25°C

Wavewatch report by Vic DeJesus

South Pacific islands Islands south of the equator have two surf seasons. The winter season lasts from April to October. During this period intense Antarctic lows send large southerly to southwesterly swells northward impacting the shallow reefs that surround these islands and transforming into large, powerful surf. Many of these islands periodically see poor conditions as fronts pass through the area resulting in unfavourable winds. November to March also holds the potential for some incredible surf. North Pacific storms send large swells south, which hit less popular north-facing breaks with solid size and quality. During the warmer months certain areas will also see tropical cyclone swells, mostly for islands positioned west of 170° west. Occasionally many of these islands will bear the full force of the tropical systems, which bring very dangerous and poor conditions.

Northwest Pacific islands The islands in the northwest Pacific Ocean rely on a variety of swell producers. The most popular months to surf these areas are from June to November, which is the peak of the typhoon season. During this time conditions tend to be most favourable and warm as some of the most intense tropical cyclones on the planet take direct paths toward the area incoming from the east-southeast travelling toward the west-northwest. Punchy, raw and powerful surf is the typical result of the intense tropical systems. It is not uncommon to have typhoons as late as December in some years. From December through early spring and into April, there is plenty of swell from trades, cold fronts and the occasional northeasterly groundswell coming off a mid latitude system.

Geography and breaks

The Pacific is immense. It is the largest of the world's five oceans, covering 56 million sq km, or 15 times the area of the USA. The eastern fringe of the Pacific runs into the huge wall of the Americas that continue in one band of coastline from Alaska in the north to Patagonia on the southern tip of Chile. The western edge of the ocean is so far away that it bleeds into the Far East, a huge fractured expanse of jagged coastline peppered with islands running north from New Zealand to Papua New Guinea, the ruptured archipelago of the Philippines, past Taiwan and Japan and onto the Kamchatka Peninsula – Russia's only true surfable coastline.

Between lies a huge blue expanse dotted with the occasional cluster of islands. Collectively this region, including Australia and New Zealand, is known as Oceania. It comprises three groups of islands: Melanesia – the 'Black Islands' – is volcanic in nature and includes PNG, New Caledonia, the Solomon Islands and Fiji; Micronesia is the 'Small Islands' and includes Guam, Marshall Islands, Kiribati and Federal State of Micronesia; New Zealand, Hawaii, Samoa, Tonga, French Polynesia and Easter Island form the group known as Polynesia. Islands within these chains are either high islands, which are volcanic in nature, or low islands or atolls which are reef based. Breaks around the atolls are usually reef passes or

The Pacific Surfing

regions of reef that bend allowing the swell to wrap along the coral. Volcanic islands can also have regions of fringing reefs, as seen in Tahiti but can also have lava-based reefs or boulder breaks as seen on Samoa or on the Hawaiian islands.

Reef passes are formed where the freshwater run-off from a river causes the coral to die back creating a channel through a barrier reef. This space is kept open due to a number of forces including the movement of water into and out of the tidal basin behind the barrier reef. Some reef passes can experience strong and dangerous tidal currents. Although there are sandy beaches on most islands it is very rare to find any quality beach breaks in the Pacific.

Health and safety

Certain areas of the Philippines suffer from political instability and the Mindanao region has traditionally been one of the worst hit. Government agencies actively warn against travel to the central, southern and western parts of the region. There is also a threat of kidnapping in southern coastal destinations and the risk of piracy on inter-island boats, not to mention the risks associated with earthquakes, the active volcano on Luzon, typhoons, and the flooding and landslides they can cause during the July-November wet season.

Below: Chirs Malloy exploring another Philippine dream.
Opposite page: Former world champion CJ Hopgood sets a rail at his favourite stop on the world tour.

Try to avoid being bitten by mosquitoes, which, depending on season, could be delivering a dose of dengue fever, malaria or even Japanese encephalitis. Make sure you cover up, use a decent repellent that includes DEET and talk to your doctor before you start your trip about which course of prophylactics to take. Rabies is also a risk here.

The south Pacific islands of Fiji, Tahiti and Samoa are in a seismic zone so are at risk from earthquakes. They may also fall prey to a passing tropical cyclone, although the threat is fairly low. While there is no risk of malaria, there is the occasional outbreak of dengue fever so mosquito bites should be avoided. Other more common problems include the threat from pickpockets as well as the potentially dangerous roads. On Fiji especially, night driving is not recommended – particularly on the stretch between Nadi and Suva where animals often wander onto the road for a nap or for a game of chicken with a passing tourist.

Tap water throughout the region is not safe to drink, so ensure you have a good supply of bottled water. This also extends to avoiding ice in your drinks and peeling fruit and veg before you eat it. If you do succumb to 'Pacific Rim', stay out of the sun and keep fluid levels up to avoid dehydration. If you have diarrhoea for more than three days, pass blood or are in any doubt, seek immediate medical attention.

This is the Pacific so there are sharks here, including large tiger sharks, which have made the occasional appearance at several popular breaks. Divers rate this part of the planet as the 'shark capital', so while

we may rate reefs around Fiji and Tahiti as excellent surf breaks, divers rate them for the excellent chance of a close encounter with a tiger shark, an experience they willingly pay a lot of money for. Go figure.

Surfing and the environment

Whereas the ocean environment around the industrialized continents such as North America and Europe have many pollution problems that impact directly on surfers, here in the Pacific pollution from factories and large urban areas has traditionally been less of an issue. The small-scale developments and the sheer size of this body of water mean that there may be small pockets near large towns or resorts where sewage run-off is an issue, but the region as a whole generally has some of the cleanest waters on the planet. There are, however, other issues that impact upon the marine environment in certain regions. The postwar era saw nuclear tests carried out by the US, UK and French governments around idyllic atolls, such as the Marshall Islands, Christmas Island in Kiribati and Mururoa in French Polynesia. In the Marshall Islands alone 67 bombs were detonated, and the consequences are still being felt to this day.

The biggest threat to the region comes from actions taken elsewhere in the world. Global warming, caused by emissions of greenhouse gases, is causing higher oceanic temperatures and sea levels to rise. Coral reefs are one of the Pacific nations' most precious resources – not only are they the natural habitat of a vast wealth of aquatic life, they also draw divers, surfers and other tourists. Rising water temperatures threaten the survival of coral polyps and scientists warn that many reefs are now dying back due to the increases in Pacific water temperature. Another consequence of this rise in temperatures is the increase in the number of typhoons the region has been experiencing.

With such a rise in sea levels, lower lying islands are seeing seafronts and beaches eroded at higher tide and a number of isles have already been lost. As the ocean rises, the ingress of saltwater into freshwater reserves contaminates both precious drinking and agricultural land, which can leave whole islands uninhabitable. These problems are predicted to worsen over the next few decades raising the probability of environmental refugees driven from their native lands by actions taken thousands of miles away. Some of the region's governments are considering legal action through western courts to help them with the increasing consequences of global warming.

For more information check out Pacific Regional Environment Programme, www.sprep.org.ws, who are working to protect the future of the Pacific by addressing issues such as waste management, climate change and environmental planning.

Surfing resources

The Pacific surf scene is growing but there is currently no dedicated surf media. Fiji Surfing Association has hooked up with the tourist board and

Whereas in the US, Australia and Europe surfing is a lifestyle to some and a sport to others, here in Polynesia it keeps its status as a cultural activity. The bonds between surfers from islands such as Tahiti and Hawaii are clear to see on the North Shore or in the line-up at Teahupoo.

some good basic information, including shop and camp contact details, can be found at www.fijifvb.gov.fj/web/surf/surf.htm. Check out www.tavarua.com for dream-inducing photo galleries from Tom Servais and Scott Winer's trips to the island plus the camp details. Check out the Fédération Tahitienne de Surf at wwwsurf.pf. For more information about Siargao in the Philippines check out www.surigaoislands.com, which has maps of the island plus practical information such as getting there and accommodation options. For *ASL*'s take on the Samoan surf experience go to www.wavehunters.com/samoa/samoa_swell.asp.

TOSTEE.COM/ASP

The Pacific Surfing

Cloud 9

◈ **Location:** Cloud 9, Philippines

◔ **Break type:** A-frame reef

◔ **Conditions:** Small to medium swells

◔ **Size:** 3-10 ft

◔ **Length:** Up to 75 m

◔ **Tide:** Quarter to high

◔ **Swell direction:** East to northeasterly

◔ **Wind:** Southwesterly

◔ **Bottom:** Reef

◔ **Ability level:** Intermediate to advanced

◔ **Best months:** Jul-Nov

◔ **Access:** Paddle out around peak

◔ **Hazards:** Shallow, heavy when bigger

When you look at a map of the Philippines you have to ask 'why Siargao?' This small island off the east coast of the Philippines certainly has great potential, but then so does much of the eastern fringe of this amazing archipelago. What made the first surfers decide on here? What are the odds of scoring on a blind mission because you look at a spot and think that it has potential? You could be standing on a white sand beach looking out at a flat sea in front of the most amazing reef set up in whole Pacific ocean and have no idea, just because the swell direction is slightly out and passing you by. You'd move on and never know how close you came. You could be surfing an okay left and just around the next headland could be a right-hand G-Land. When do you stop and wait it out and when do you up sticks and move on? It's the great surf travel 'grass is greener' conundrum.

The first wavehunters to rock up on the eastern coast of Siargao in the early eighties were reputed to be a couple of surfers named Steve Jones and Tony Arroza. Towards the end of the decade a guy calling himself Max Walker arrived and set up home at Tuason Point, in front of the reef that would become known as Cloud 9. The story has a tragic turn as Walker passed away after what locals say was an extended cleansing fast and it was not until other surfers appeared that locals discovered that the man who had been living in their midst was really Mike Boyum, the legendary surf traveller who established

the first surf camp at G-Land in the early seventies. "Mike Boyum was in residence on Siargao from December 1988 to April of 1989," says Cloud 9 pioneer John Callahan. "As January to April is the worst time for waves with constant onshore northeasterly winds and heavy rain, and he endured a 44-day fast before his death in April, it is questionable how much surfing he did during his time on Siargao. Tony and Steve told Mike about the island while in Bali, they surfed at Pansukian Reef near General Luna, but never went beyond as far as I know." Callahan headed an expedition in 1992 that including pro surfers Taylor Knox and Evan Slater, who surfed the A-frame reef, giving the wave its now famous moniker. The photographs and article hit the shelves in *Surfer* magazine and a new dream destination was born." I named the break after the local no-melt chocolate bars," says Callahan. "Going into town after lunch for a warm Coke and a Cloud 9 was the highlight of our day."

Cloud 9 sits to the north of the town of General Luna on the Pacific side of Siargao. It produces a beautiful, hollow right-hander with a shorter, but equally hollow left peeling away to the south. "I've travelled around the world and surfed many world-class waves," said Kirby Fukunaga of Japan. "Cloud 9 is probably the most perfect right-hander I've ever surfed. Backdoor Pipeline was my favourite right-hander in the world until I surfed here. The waves I had here were more perfect." It's a shallow reef break that makes surfing at low tide something of a lottery so most sane people stick to mid to high when the wave throws out perfect round barrels. Images of this break aren't easy to forget. "Cloud 9 in the Philippines is the world-class wave that I haven't yet surfed but would love to," says top US surfer Ben Bourgeois. "It's a perfect right barrel and I have seen amazing photos of the place for years."

JS CALLAHAN/TROPICALPIX

Right: Down the line at Cloud 9.
Opposite page: Typhoon swell lights up Siargao Island.

"Cloud 9 is the swell indicator for all other breaks," says Gerry Degan of local surf camp Sagana Resort. "It can be ridden even in small swells but big swells are notoriously inconsistent and coincide with typhoons." The wave is at its best between the months of July and November when small to medium groundswells come through as well as the larger typhoon swells. Luckily this coincides with offshore monsoon winds. While the Philippines may not offer the consistency of Indonesia, and westerners are advised to avoid certain regions of the country, it does still offer a chance to get out and explore fresh surf zones and enjoy quality breaks without the crowd levels found in Indo. "The future looks good for tourism and the local people are benefiting from it," says Gerry. "The locals have really taken to surfing and the young surfers often crowd out the break. But they are good, polite kids who will share. Don't come here if you're aggressive as this only teaches the locals bad manners. The only consequence of this is that the aggro will be returned in the future."

The science of surf discovery is a complex mix of knowledge, motivation and luck. Knowledge and motivation are needed in equal parts and when fate deals you a lucky hand, it may just add up to your own Cloud 9. Knowing when to stay and when to go has less to do with running the numbers and more to do with where you are coming from and where you are going to.

Locals and legends

"Carlito Noguiera and Donisio Espijon are the best current surfers," says Gerry. "Neil Berte and Rudy Figuron are the first locals to surf here." Other stand-outs include Carlito Nogalo and Fernando Alipayo.

Nearby breaks There is a wealth of excellent spots in this area. **Tuason Left** is a nearby left-hand barrelling reef that can be excellent in medium sized swells. **Tuesday Rock** is a picturesque, offshore right-hander that offers up fun, walling rides. Boat access required. **Stimpies** is a world-class thumping left with big hollow barrels.

Cloud 9 Board
6'3" JC SD-3
Shaper: John Carper
6'3" x 18.15" x 2.2"
John Carper designed with Shane Dorian for steep hollow waves.
Round pintail, single to double concave, finely tuned rails.
Fits deep tubes, flies down the line and turns tight in the pocket.
Futures JC1 fins.
(i) Boards by **Surftech** www.surftech.com info@surftech.com

Air ——	Sea ——
°F Averages	°C
90	30
70	20
50	10
30	0

D J F M A M J J A S O N
WINTER   SPRING   SUMMER   AUTUMN

Shortie | Boardies | Boardies | Boardies

Surfers' tales
Finding Cloud 9 JS Callahan

JS CALLAHAN/TROPICALPIX

In September of 1992, I travelled to the Philippines with two surfers, Evan Slater and Taylor Knox. Both were young pros from California, and none of us had ever been to the Philippines before. Other than the name of the island, and the fact that September could be good for typhoon swell and offshore winds, we knew little about where we were going or what we were doing.

After a long journey of planes, cars, trikes and wooden boats, we arrived at the remote island of Siargao in the late afternoon. There was no pier at General Luna then, so we waded ashore through shallow water with our baggage on our heads, like General MacArthur's return 50 years before. We had no idea where to stay, or indeed if there was any accommodation on the island, so Evan and I

made a camp on the beach and played with the kids while Taylor went off to look with several locals. He came back in half an hour or so and said, "Got us a shack on the beach – it's killer." We set up in our 'cottage' and Pilar, the landlady, came by to announce dinner was at seven. She said there were two other people staying there also, surfers from Sydney. "Really?" Evan said, "We can ask them if they found any spots."

We introduced ourselves to Kevin Davidson and Dave Motbey, from Maroubra. They had been here for two days, and had found a good left about an hour away by boat. They invited us to share their boat the next morning, and we all had a great dinner of fish and rice, the first of many. With no electricity on the island at night, we were all asleep by nine.

The next morning, we got in the boat at dawn. A short but very loud ride away on the outer reef was a crunching left-hand reef break, about 6 ft and glassy. Bathtub-warm water, and no one out. The boys had a great session, and everyone was stoked. Perfect hollow barrels. We did the exact same thing for the next three days: wake up at dawn, surf the left with Kevin and Dave for a four-hour session, have a huge late lunch, then relax in the afternoon as heavy tropical thunderstorms pounded the beach and inner lagoon.

On the fourth morning, we surfed the left again. With no other surfers on the island, there was no pressure to go anywhere else. "We should go look for a right," Evan announced. "I'm bored getting barrelled going left." "OK," I said, "I've shot a ton of film on this wave, so when everyone comes in, we'll pull the anchor and look around." Taylor was last, as usual, so his board was on the top of the stack wedged in the front of the long, narrow, hull. Joel the boatman pulled the anchor. "Which way?" Joel asked. No one had any idea, so we turned left, to the north. After 30 minutes of hammering engine noise and close-out waves, we spotted a peak with a nice plume of offshore spray. "Looks OK" I said, then looked at Taylor. After a four-hour session for the fourth straight day, tired and sunburned, Taylor didn't want to leave the shade cover. "Want to paddle over and check it out?" I said. Taylor didn't move, so I pulled his board out

Below: A young Taylor Knox on the original Cloud 9 trip.
Opposite page: Room with a view.

JS CALLAHAN/TROPICALPIX

and handed it to him, "Your board's on top, so you have to do it, dude." I laughed. Taylor jumped in and started paddling.

We all sat in the boat, watching. It was very hot and no one was talking. Joel was watching the current, so we didn't drift into the breaking waves. Taylor reached the line-up, and looked around for any dry reef not visible from the boat. He let a few waves go by. The next set passed under the boat. Taylor took a few strokes and chose a wave, suddenly paddling hard. Evan said, "Here he goes." We all watched as he caught the wave and stood up, dropping into an unknown section. We saw his track through the back of the wave. He was going straight for the channel, very fast. A few seconds later, he appeared in a cloud of spray, flying into the channel, looking back at the boat with his arms over his head, screaming "YEAAAAAAAH!"

Suddenly, the boat was rocking as everyone woke up from their torpor and started moving. "Where's my board? Where's the wax? Where's my housing?" Joel wondered what was going on. "Move the boat out a little bit and drop it" I said, "We're going surfing." We surfed this new hollow right every day for the next week. The swell stayed in the 3 to 6-ft range, and the wind blew offshore about 10-15 knots all day and all night; the typical 'Habagat' southwest monsoon wind of the Philippines. There were no structures on the beach except one broken-down hut, and no other surfers. One day, we asked Joel about the beach hut. He said it was the house of an American, Max Walker, who had died on the island several years before. "Died?" I said. "Of what? Snakebite or something?" "No," Joel replied. "He did not want to live, so he died." Pretty simple. We later learned the hut was the residence of Mike Boyum: surfer, Bali veteran, Maui local, international drug dealer, and, in the mid-eighties, founder of the 'surf camp' concept at G-Land in Java with Gerry Lopez and Peter McCabe. On the run from the law, from fellow drug dealers from whom he had stolen money, and his own destructive personal demons, Boyum came to remote Siargao in late 1988 and died in April 1989. We had no idea who Max Walker really was at the time, if he was a surfer, how he died, and we never looked into the hut.

After 10 straight days of non-stop waves and four to six hours of water-time each day, Evan and Taylor were tired, bug-bitten, sunburned and surfed-out. They didn't care anymore if it was 6-ft empty barrels, so when one afternoon was finally looking sunny without the usual afternoon clouds and thunderstorms, I marched into our hut and said

JS CALLAHAN/TROPICALPIX

© JS Callahan

John Seaton Callahan is one of the most widely published surfing photographers in the world today. He attended UCLA in Los Angeles, compling a BA in design at the College of Fine Arts. His early work took him to every corner of the surfing world: Tahiti, Hawaii, Morocco, Costa Rica, South Africa, Maldives, Réunion, Mauritius, New Zealand, Australia, Japan, Brazil and Indonesia to name a few. His more recent ventures into unexplored waters have made the © JS Callahan/tropicalpix, an internationally acclaimed by-line. Ground-breaking projects over the last decade include Mindanao, Samar and Siargao islands in the Philippines, the Andaman and Nicobar Islands, the Mergui Archipelago and Rahkine coastline of Myanmar, unnamed islands off the Sumatran coast, the Maldives, Andra Pradesh in India, São Tomé and Principé in Central Africa, South Korea, Kenya's Swahili Coast, and the perilous coast of Angola with veteran surf adventurer Randy Rarick.

"Wake up. It's sunny. We should go shoot." I was tired too, after the usual four-hour morning session, but if it was going to be good afternoon sun, we had to be there. As good as the waves had been, there was a problem. The morning sun is behind the wave, giving a backlight look to the photos we were shooting every day. This was a magazine trip after all, and editors demand a variety of angles to make a feature article. No one moved. "Wake up," I said again. Nothing. I saw a broken leg rope on the floor, and used it to beat Evan's legs. "Wake up. It's looking sunny. We're shooting." "Fuck you, Callahan, we're tired," was Evan's response. I explained how it would be good, and we should be out there. Evan slowly got up, and Taylor put on his shorts. The tide was too low to take the boat, so we had to walk the entire way, about an hour in intense afternoon sun. Evan and Taylor were so pissed off they didn't say a word the entire time. When we arrived, it was 6 ft. It was sunny and on the incoming tide every wave was a perfect hollow barrel. After one wave each Evan and Taylor were all smiles in one of the best sessions of their lives.

One of the highlights of our first trip to Siargao Island was taking the short walk into General Luna town after lunch for a warm Coke and a candy bar. One of the brands sold was a local Philippines chocolate bar called 'Cloud 9'. We had many discussions about what to name this fantastic new wave we had found and, while Evan and Taylor never quite agreed, the photographer is the one who captions the material and sends it to the magazine. I took the initiative and named it 'Cloud 9', as the chocolate bars were pretty good, and the wave and the island seemed as close to paradise as any of us had ever been up to that time. The name stuck like glue, and today Cloud 9 is by far the most famous surfing wave in the Philippines, one of Asia's best-known surfing locations, and known by most of the world's six million surfers.

Above: The boardwalk.
Right: The magic no-melt chocolate that inspired the name.
Opposite page: Before his days as editor of *Surfer* magazine, a mini Evan Slater lucks in on a voyage of discovery.

Cloudbreak

- ◊ **Location:** Cloudbreak, Fiji
- **Break type:** Left-hand reef pass
- **Conditions:** All swells
- **Size:** 3-12 ft +
- **Length:** up to 200 m +
- **Tide:** All tides
- **Swell direction:** Southwesterly groundswells to westerly cyclone swells
- **Wind:** Morning glass off
- **Bottom:** Reef
- **Ability level:** Advanced
- **Best months:** Apr-Oct
- **Access:** Limited to camp residents, boat access
- **Hazards:** Great waves but expensive to access

Cloudbreak Board
6'10" Rawson Hyper Skate
Shaper: Pat Rawson
6'10" x 18¾" x 2½"

Designed for all around surf in the 6-8ft + range.

Fast and drivey through turns and cutbacks with enough stability to hold in steep, deep barrels.

Futures FTP1 fins.

ⓘ Boards by **Surftech**
www.surftech.com info@surftech.com

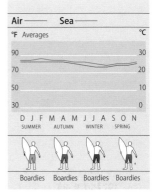

Below: Barrel queen, Rochelle Ballard deep inside Cloudbreak.
Opposite page: Cloudbreak line-up.

KAREN WILSON/ASP

It all started as so many surfers' tales of adventure and discovery do – a message passed on about a perfect wave. A trip undertaken on the strength of a rumour and a discovery made that would become one of the surfing world's true wonders. A pin-up that would adorn walls and feature on the covers of magazines for decades. But this story would have a sting in the tail and the wave would go on to become one of the most controversial surfing destinations on the planet. It is a wave that still rankles many within the greater waveriding community, even in the modern culture of surfing professionalism and entrepreneurism. In the early eighties, American surfer Dave Clark was told of a wave that fitted his definition of perfection. It was enough to send him on a plane to Fiji and the island of Tavarua. By 1984, he had negotiated exclusive surfing rights to the waves of the island and the nearby reef pass of Cloudbreak, establishing a surf camp so that guests could enjoy these world-class waves in a degree of comfort and relaxation. It hadn't been long since explorers were hacking through forests to discover virgin spots in Indo, sleeping under the stars and battling malaria. That surfers would pay good money for the comfort and ease of enjoying quality waves without crowds was a notion ahead of its time, but the issue of access would become a bitter topic of discussion.

Visitors to the Tavarua resort enjoy *exclusive* rights to the waves at Cloudbreak and Restaurants. This is due to an ancient tribal law whereby the fishing rights, and consequently access to a reef and everything associated with it, belong to the local tribal chief. Clark's negotiations mean that the wave is now effectively the exclusive playground of the camp guests. Some other resorts advertise limited access to the break but this only happens on Saturday changeover days with permission from the Tavarua camp. Don't assume you will surf the break unless you are booked into the expensive island resort. This enforced exclusivity is anathema to those whose very lifestyle was built around the notion of free access to the ocean. Some argued that even the most exclusive ski resorts allow you to ride the mountain if you hike to the top. It's the lift pass that you pay money for, not the use of the mountain. Others argue that this is a different culture with different laws. It is a topic that has filled many pages of Internet chat rooms with heated debate. The fire fuelling the debate is of course the sheer quality of the wave.

Tavarua lies in the Mamanucas, a series of islands and passes lying off the western coastline of Viti Levu. The breaks here are consistently bathed in swell from the southwest from lows lying below and in the Tasman Sea, or from cyclone swells generated off the northeastern coastline of Australia. As the waves at Cloudbreak peel along the fringes of an offshore reef pass, they can only be accessed by boat. In photos the wave often looks like a simple, long, peeling barrel, but in reality it is much more complicated. Many liken it to a reverse

KAREN WILSON/ASP

'Sunset'-style wave as it breaks over a huge area of reef and is affected greatly by the swell size and direction. Cloudbreak is broken down into three distinct sections. The outside is known as The Point and it is here that the bigger, but more rippable waves break. This is the section for top to bottom surfing with deep cutbacks, gouging bottom turns and huge roostertails thrown up by slashing off-the-tops. The Middle is next down the line offering waves that wall along the reef and can produce some well-timed barrels. The inside section is the most challenging as the wave speeds up and becomes very shallow and hollow. It is known as 'Shiskabobs' – not a place to get skewered on the reef. In classic swells the three sections will occasionally join to produce one long, incessant wave. Mornings are the best times to surf as this is when there is a good chance of a glass-off, but the waves are still surfable in light trade winds.

Tavarua has been a regular contest venue since 1987 when Tom Curren won the OP ASP event and the tour shake-up saw more prestigious and high quality breaks brought onto the calendar. "Tavarua is just an amazing island paradise with perfect waves," says US pro Ben Bourgeois. "When it comes to my favourite place, there are a lot of good breaks and it's hard to say just one, but I love the Cloudbreak event," says former event winner Damien Hobgood. "The main reason is that it feels more like a surf trip than a contest."

Locals and legends
Discovered by Dave Clark and brought to world's attention by the Kevin Naughton and Craig Peterson *Surfer* magazine article in 1984. Tom Carroll, Jeff Booth, Kelly Slater, Conan Hayes, Andy Irons.

Nearby breaks Tavarua has the world-class **Restaurants** (page 298), a left-hand barrel that speeds along the reef on the north side of the island. Further north of Tavarua sits **Namotu**, another resort island with its exclusive break, **Namotu Lefts**. Further north sits **Wilkes Pass**, a high tide right-hander that peels over a long reef pass.

Teahupoo

⊙ **Location:** Teahupoo, Tahiti	
⊙ **Break type:** Left-hand reef break	
⊙ **Conditions:** All swells	
⊙ **Size:** 3-12 ft +	
⊙ **Length:** 50-100 m	
⊙ **Tide:** All tides	
⊙ **Swell direction:** Westerly to southerly swells	
⊙ **Wind:** North to northeasterly	
⊙ **Bottom:** Live coral reef	
⊙ **Ability level:** Experts only	
⊙ **Best months:** Apr-Oct	
⊙ **Access:** A long paddle or boat ride	
⊙ **Hazards:** Very dangerous	

It all seemed kind of surreal but mesmerizing at the same time. Like seeing a volcano erupt before your very eyes or an avalanche slide down the mountain towards you. When the first footage appeared of this mutant wave it was like watching a slow-motion car crash from which the driver skilfully stepped out unscathed at the last second. The huge barrels, the thick lips exploding onto the jagged reef that seemed to be covered by mere inches of water – it didn't really seem surfable, yet here was the proof. A few obviously crazy chargers scraping through waves where the lip made up half the wave height. Then suddenly there was to be a contest held here. It was like the ultimate dare dangled in front of the best surfers in the world. The gauntlet was thrown down,

an invitation that many would like to have pretended they never received. The event took place in 10-ft plus surf and the contest director, Steve Robertson, repeatedly checked with the surfers to see if they wanted the event to continue given the genuine concerns about serious injury or loss of life. By the end of the final over 30 boards had been snapped and Keala Kennelly had nearly drowned. Freesurfing and Pipe Master Johnny Boy Gomes said, "These are certainly some of the most powerful waves I've surfed." This new wave that people had previously struggled to pronounce, let alone spell, was suddenly a central part of the surfing vernacular. It was the word on everyone's lips.

Tahiti sits in the Pacific Ocean at the heart of the Society Islands in French Polynesia. The Island is a lush, green tropical paradise ringed by a live coral barrier reef. The large seasonal downpours have eroded valleys that channel the abundant rainwater into the sea. This influx of fresh water kills back the coral creating regular reef passes – deep channels where the coral forms angled platforms at the edge – the perfect foil for the regular swells that roll out of the Pacific. On the southern side of the island, at Teahupoo, this translates into what is probably the most breathtakingly cylindrical left yet discovered. The reef is frighteningly shallow where the lip detonates onto the reef, and yet just a few feet away a mass of onlookers float in the safety of the deep channel, staring straight into the eye of the barrel. "Teahupoo is a wave unlike any other in the world," says top female professional Keala Kennelly. "It is the meanest, thickest barrel you will find. It is terrifying and yet one of the most beautiful things you can witness. I still get the butterflies in my stomach when it's over 6 ft there." Keala is a woman who charges at this truly life-threatening wave and is more than aware of the risks here, even on the smallest days. "I almost died there on more than one occasion. I split my head open and had to get seven staples on a small day, so you can never underestimate the power that this wave has."

The spectacle of Teahupoo was like crack cocaine to the surf media. You just couldn't get enough, and every high was bigger than the last. "This is perhaps the best voyeuristic wave on the planet," says *Surfline* editor Marcus Sanders. "More film is burned here than anywhere else except for Pipe. It has a deep channel where you can watch the fear on pros' faces as they airdrop into oblivion and sometimes make it." The dynamics of the wave make mere mortals scratch their heads and

SEAN DAVEY

Left: So much water is drawn off the reef that the wave breaks below sea level.
Opposite page: Staring down the 'meanest, thickest barrel you will ever find'.

wonder just how it is possible to make the drop down the vertical face of a wave that jacks up so quickly, while at the same time drawing water off the reef below. Ex-WCT competitor Russell Winter puts into words what it's like to actually drop into one of these beasts. "The take-off is just so insane, all you can see is reef because the water is so clear. It disorientates you a little bit. You can't even see the wave properly the barrel's chucking out so much, and it's so steep it's amazing what some guys do on it."

Amazing is one of the most understated adjectives used to sum up some of the waves that have since been ridden here. In huge swells and waves up to 20 ft the likes of Laird Hamilton and Shane Dorian have pulled into some of the biggest and most lethal barrels ever ridden. Hamilton's tow-in wave in 2000 made the front page of more surf publications than probably any other wave in surf history. It's hard to imagine these waves being bettered, but then again a few years ago no one would have imagined the kind of surfing taking place at this break. Who knows what the future will bring? Prepare to be amazed.

Locals and legends

Thierry Vernaudon, Vetea 'Poto' David, Raimana Van Bastolaer, Manoa Drollet, Malik Joyeux, Hira Terinatoofa, Laird Hamilton, Cory Lopez, Andy Irons, Shane Dorian.

Nearby breaks Tahiti and the neighbouring island of Moorea have a number of excellent breaks where the barrier reef is broken by passes. The south shore of Tahiti bears the brunt of the peak season swell and during this time slightly less life-threatening waves can be found on the east side of Moorea at **Temae** where right-handers angle along the reef.

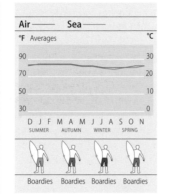

Teahupoo Board

6'10" Wayne Lynch Free Flight

Shaper: Wayne Lynch

6'10" x 18½" x 2½"

Solid semi-gun fits well in the thick, steep, concave pits at Teahupoo.

Single to double concave for racing down the line, extra nose and tail rocker for steep elevator drops.

FCS G7 fins.

ⓘ Boards by **Surftech**
www.surftech.com info@surftech.com

Air ——	Sea ——	
°F	Averages	°C
90		30
70		20
50		10
30		0
D J F	M A M	J J A	S O N
SUMMER	AUTUMN	WINTER	SPRING
Boardies	Boardies	Boardies	Boardies

The Pacific Teahupoo

Boulders

🌀 **Location:**	Boulders, Upolu, Samoa
🌀 **Break type:**	Left point
🌀 **Conditions:**	All swells
🌀 **Size:**	3-12 ft +
🌀 **Length:**	Up to 100 m +
🌀 **Tide:**	All tides, best low to mid
🌀 **Swell direction:**	Southwesterly to southeasterly
🌀 **Wind:**	Northerly
🌀 **Bottom:**	Boulder reef
🌀 **Ability level:**	Intermediate to advanced
🌀 **Best months:**	Mar-Nov
🌀 **Access:**	By boat or from the beach
🌀 **Hazards:**	At high tide the wave breaks close to the cliffs

Imagine being one of the first travelling Aussie surfers to stumble across the point at Aganoa. A world-class point break, sheltered from the trade winds, glassy in the morning, peeling in crystal-blue waters that never dip below a balmy 80°C. Its location couldn't be more perfect: an island paradise where no one surfs and the outside world believes is wave free. Just how did they manage to keep this place a secret? Wouldn't you want to ring your mates and scream down the phone? Somehow Boulders, and the many other waves that Samoa has on offer, managed to stay low, under the radar. Many an Aussie surfer would look at the map and wonder, but questions to a friend of a friend who'd been there usually met with the same answer: "There's no surf in Samoa, mate."

In true western colonial style, the USA, Germany and Britain spent years squabbling over the islands of Samoa before eventually sitting down and working out a deal that split the islands between the USA and Germany. Britain walked away with Tonga and Fiji as a pay-off. German Samoa was formed at the start of the 20th century from the islands of Savai'i and Upolu but at the outbreak of the First World War it was invaded by New Zealand, and German Samoa became Western Samoa. In 1997, after 35 years of independence, the 'Western' part was dropped. Today, three quarters of the population of Samoa resides on Upolu, where the capital Apia is located. This is a place where the climate is tropical, the swells are year-round, the breaks are world class, the people are friendly and have a proud but respectful tradition, and the number of surfers in the line-up is pretty low. This is Samoa in the 21st century.

Boulders is an aptly named break, the point producing long, winding and barrelling left-handers that break over a boulder and coral reef in front of a forest-topped black volcanic stone cliff. Out past the end of the point is the steep take-off into a speeding section. When the swell hits 8-ft plus, this becomes a thick-lipped, barrelling, all-or-nothing section. From here on in the classic point trades off bash-able lips, long walls and barrels – a little something for everyone. It lies on the south coast of Upolu, facing into the swells generated by Southern Ocean low pressures and regularly turns on during the main swell season from March to November. The geography of Boulders helps make it such a consistent spot as it offers a degree of shelter when the predominant southeasterly trade winds, which can blow through May

Below: Patiently lining up.
Opposite page: Aamion Goodwin racing at Samoa's speedway.

Boulders Board

6'6" Channel Islands K-Model

Shaper: Al Merrick

6'6" x 18¾" x 2⅜"

A high-performance board for thick, powerful waves.

Single to double concave for down the line speed with extra nose rocker for steep take-offs and under the lip snaps!

FCS K 2.1 fins.

ⓘ Boards by Surftech
www.surftech.com info@surftech.com

Air —— Sea ——

°F Averages °C

90			30
70			20
50			10
30			0

D J F M A M J J A S O N
SUMMER AUTUMN WINTER SPRING

Boardies Boardies Boardies Boardies

to September, are hammering the more exposed reefs. During this season, morning and evening sessions can offer up some classic glassy conditions. This is a spot that breaks around the 4-ft to 6-ft range during the optimum swell window, and up to well over 12 ft when the cyclone swells kick in. These are the same storms that deliver such epic conditions to Fiji and New Zealand.

There are a number of surf camps that offer access to the waves at Boulders by boat or by road, but the number of surfers is usually pretty low and the line-up chilled. Just as the old adage that there was no surf in Samoa was blatantly untrue, the same goes for the idea that there are no surfers in Samoa. Although there are a number of ex-pats settled on the islands or working at the surf camps, there is also an increasing number of locals. And with the quality of waves they surf, the standard is increasing at an exponential rate. Samoa's Surf Riders Association holds contests and produces a newsletter for local and visiting waveriders. They offer the following advice: "Samoans are a proud group of people, steeped in tradition and culture. Before going surfing at any village sites you must ask the Matai (Chief) or Village Committee. Don't just hit the beach. Always show modesty and keep yourself properly attired, wearing shorts or *lavalava* and a top while in the village grounds. Women should not wear bikinis or revealing swimwear on village beaches. If in doubt, ask. The Samoa Visitors Bureau information *fale* on Beach Road is always a good place to ask

about issues you may not be sure about and they also have a list of things to do when the surf's flat." This is a country where tradition runs deep. For example it is forbidden to surf on a Sunday, a strict day of rest. And yet this is part of what makes this land such a paradise. You have time to sit back and admire just what the island has to offer. Apart from the stunning scenery, world-class surf, warm water and tropical climate, there is virtually no crime, it is religiously tolerant, politically stable and a place where visitors are still welcomed warmly. No wonder those early surf pioneers tried so hard to keep it under their hats.

Locals and legends
Damien Meredith, Gunther Kruse, Charlie Vaal, George Leslie, Neil Lumsden, Jon Long.

Nearby breaks The south shore offers some great breaks including **Coconuts**, a right-hand reef break that can pack a Hawaiian-style punch. **Devils Island** is an offshore break offering a big left-hander with a hollow inside section. There are numerous waves along this stretch of coast including at **Salani** and **A'ufaga**. The north shore of Upolu breaks on the same northerly swells that hit Hawaii in December to February, but are about two thirds the size and arrive three to five days later. **Ti'avea** is a right-hand reef that combines big walls with barrel sections, **Lauli'i** is a good quality right point and **Pudding Rock** is a fun and consistent short right.

GEOFF RAGATZ

Directory

307

Scotland

ZOCO BOARDRIDING

global**TRAVEL**
and**SHELTER**
4**SURFERS**

FUEL YOUR ADDICTION
ZocoTravel.com
ZocoShelter.com

E: info@zocotravel.com
T: (+44) (0)1204 659 394

puro nectar is located in the seaside town of Dunbar with a wide selection of all your surfing needs stockists of john carper (jc) almeric, saltrock, oshea, and nsp boards there is something for every one, also surf hire £20.00 per full day. Wide range of surf wear and accesories.

opening times
mon- wed 10am -5pm
thurs-fri 10am-6pm
sat 10am 5pm
sun12-5pm
or by arrangment by calling
07900617740

puro nectar surf
High Street, Dunbar, East Lothian
EH42 1JJ
tel 01368 869 810
Fax 01368 869 810
web www.puronectarsurf.com

St.Vedas Hotel & Surf Shop
Coldingham Bay
Sales • Hire • Food • Accommodation •
018907 71679
www.stvedas.co.uk
info@stvedas.co.uk

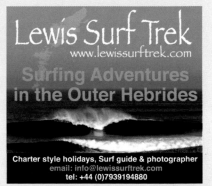

Lewis Surf Trek
www.lewissurftrek.com
Surfing Adventures in the Outer Hebrides
Charter style holidays, Surf guide & photographer
email: info@lewissurftrek.com
tel: +44 (0)7939194880

GREAT ESCAPE

supplers of -
RIP CURL, BILLABONG, ANIMAL, O'SHEA, BIC SURFBOARDS, SOLA, LUSH LONGBOARDS, REEF, DAKINE, CJB'S, VANS, ETNIES, HOWIES, WHITESTUFF, WESTBEACH.

57 high street, north berwick, east lothian, scotland, eh39 4hh
t e l . 0 1 6 2 0 8 9 3 7 9 3
www.greatescapenorthberwick.co.uk

SURFERS WORLD
Surf and Snow Holidays UK and Abroad
www.surfersworld.co.uk
01271 890037
Accommodation and Surf Schools in Devon and Cornwall

Wales

PJ's Surf Shop
LLANGENNITH GOWER
Est. 1979 www.pjsurfshop.co.uk

Llangennith, Gower, Swansea, SA3 1HU
☎(01792) 386669
www.pjsurfshop.co.uk

Open all year round. Stockists of all major brands. Board and wetsuit hire. Surfline 24 hour report ☎ 0901 6031603 (calls cost 60p per minute at all times)

Langland Cove Guest House
4 Rotherslade Road, Langland
Swansea, SA3 4QN, Wales
☎(01792) 366003
gill@eurotelemail.net

We run an up market 5 bedroom (non-smoking) B&B, with two rooms that sleep 3 sharing. Next door is a self catering cottage sleeping up to 4. Situated a minutes walk down the hill from the multiple surf-breaks of Langland Bay. Best time to come for surf is Autumn, Winter and Spring. With 25 years of experience in this area I could send you to the best spots in the region on any given day. Party animals need not apply.

Ireland

Lahinch Surf Shop
Old Promenade, Lahinch, Co. Clare, Eire
☎00 353 65708 1543 Fax 00 353 65708 1684
Surf report on 00 353 (0)818 365 180
Email: bear@iol.ie www.lahinchsurfshop.com

Lahinch Surf Shop was the first surf shop to open in Ireland. It is also closer to the surf than any surf shop anywhere according to visitors who have been in surf shops all over the world. At times it is too close as the storm waves try to come in the door. We are open all year round.

Portugal

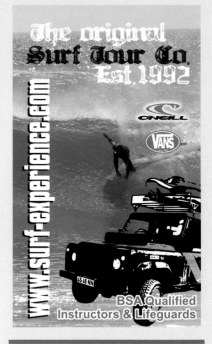
Morocco

I carried the South
American Handbook from
Cape Horn to Cartagena
and consulted it every
night for two and a half
months. I wouldn't do
that for anything else
except my hip flask.

Michael Palin

83rd Edition **83** rd

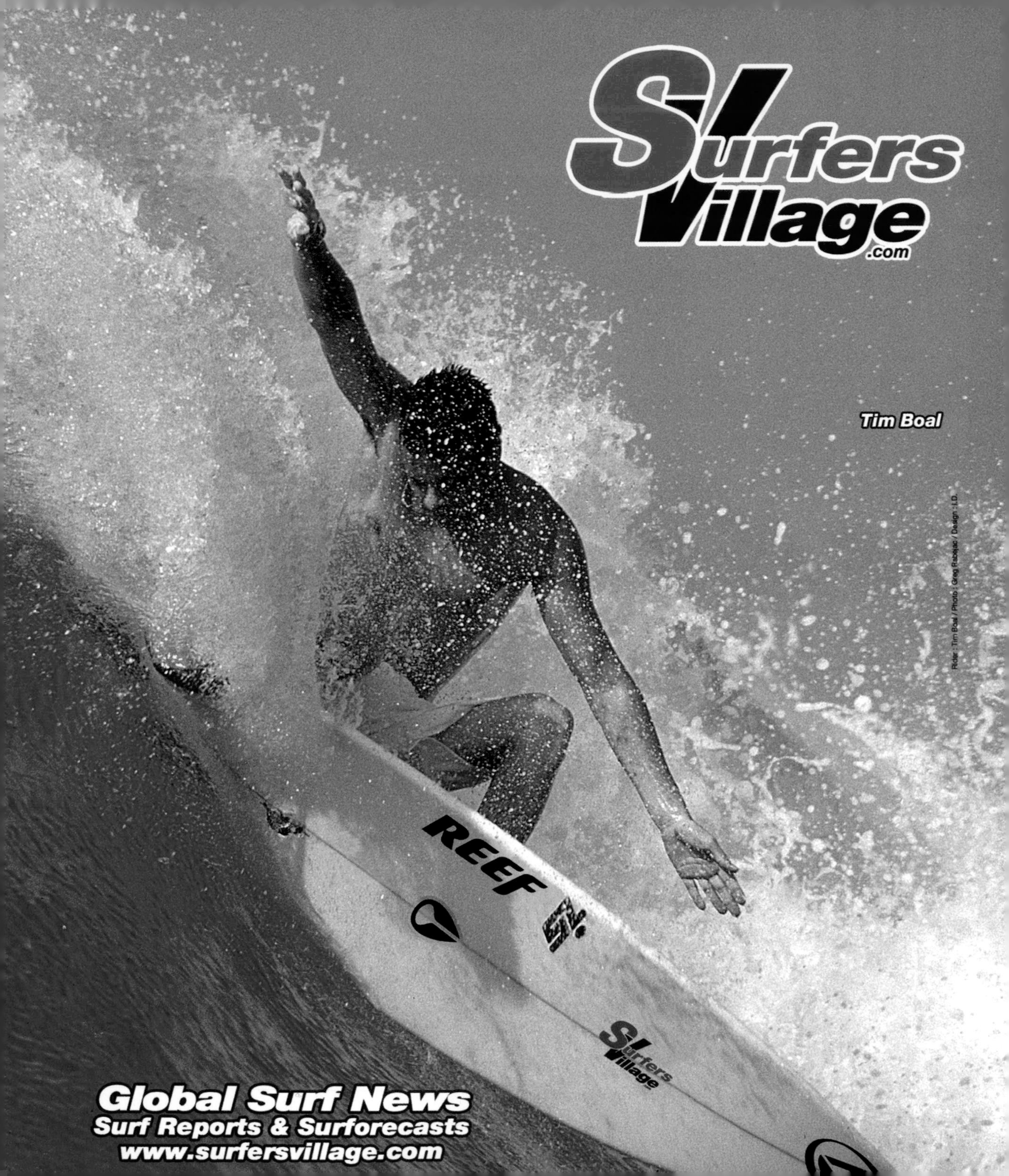

Surfers Village
.com

Tim Boal

Rider: Tim Boal / Photo: Greg Riedisar / Design : I.D.

Global Surf News
Surf Reports & Surforecasts
www.surfersvillage.com

The Great Escape

Little time, sensible budget, **big** adventure

Devised by travel experts, this new full-colour series combines the very best of the region with stunning photos, great maps, top tips and budget-busting ideas.

The guides for intelligent, independently minded souls. Indie Traveller

Footprint credits

Text editor: Alan Murphy
Map editor: Sarah Sorensen
Layout and production: Angus Dawson
Proof reader: Stephanie Lambe
Picture editor: Demi Taylor

Publisher: Patrick Dawson
Editorial: Sophie Blacksell,
Felicity Laughton, Nicola Jones
Cartography: Angus Dawson, Robert Lunn, Kevin Feeney
Design: Mytton Williams
Sales and marketing: Andy Riddle
Advertising: Debbie Wylde
Finance and administration: Elizabeth Taylor,
Daniella Cambouroglou

Photography credits

Title page: David Pu'u (Surfer's Point)
Front cover: Paul Kennedy (Phil Goodrich at Lagundri Bay)
Back cover: Alan Van Gysen/tropicalpix (Japan's Naoto Takanashi in the Northern Atolls, Maldives)
Back cover flap: JS Callahan/tropicalpix

Print

Manufactured in India by Replika Press Pvt Ltd, Delhi
Pulp from sustainable forests

Footprint feedback

We try as hard as we can to make each Footprint guide as up to date as possible but, of course, things always change. If you want to let us know about your experiences – good, bad or ugly – then don't delay, go to www.footprintbooks.com and send in your comments.

Every effort has been made to ensure that the facts in this guidebook are accurate. However, travellers should still obtain advice from consulates, airlines etc about travel and visa requirements before travelling. The authors and publishers cannot accept responsibility for any loss, injury or inconvenience however caused.

Publishing information

Footprint Surfing the World
1st edition
© Footprint Handbooks Ltd
July 2006

ISBN 1 904777 76 7
CIP DATA: A catalogue record for this book is available from the British Library

® Footprint Handbooks and the Footprint mark are a registered trademark of Footprint Handbooks Ltd

Published by Footprint

6 Riverside Court
Lower Bristol Road
Bath BA2 3DZ, UK
T +44 (0)1225 469141
F +44 (0)1225 469461
discover@footprintbooks.com
www.footprintbooks.com

Distributed in the USA by

Publishers Group West

Credits

Publishing stuff Credits